ed by G. Goos, J. Hartmanis, and J. van Leeuwen

rlin
idelberg
w York
rcelona
ng Kong
ndon
lan
ris
gapore
yo

eliable
oftware Technologies
da-Europe 2000

Ada-Europe International Conference
dam, Germany, June 26-30, 2000
ceedings

lume Editors

bert B. Keller
rschungszentrum Karlsruhe, Institut für Angewandte Informatik
rmann-von-Helmholtz-Platz 1, 76344 Eggenstein-Leopoldshafen, Germany
mail: keller@iai.fzk.de

hard Plödereder
iversität Stuttgart, Institut für Informatik
eitwiesenstr. 20-22, 70565 Stuttgart, Germany
mail: ploedere@informatik.uni-stuttgart.de

taloging-in-Publication Data applied for

e Deutsche Bibliothek - CIP-Einheitsaufnahme

liable software technologies Ada Europe 2000 : Potsdam, Germany,
ne 26 - 30, 2000 ; proceedings / Hubert B. Keller ; Erhard Plöderer
l.). - Berlin ; Heidelberg ; New York ; Barcelona ; Hong Kong ;
ndon ; Milan ; Paris ; Singapore ; Tokyo : Springer, 2000
... Ada-Europe international conference ... ; 5)
Lecture notes in computer science ; Vol. 1845)
SBN 3-540-67669-4

Subject Classification (1998): D.2, D.1.2-5, D.3, D.4, C.2.4, C.3, K.6

SN 0302-9743
BN 3-540-67669-4 Springer-Verlag Berlin Heidelberg New York

esetting: Camera-ready by author, data conversion by DA-TeX Gerd Blumenstein
ted on acid-free paper SPIN: 10722060 06/3142 5 4 3 2 1 0

Foreword

The Fifth International Conference on Reliable Software Technologies, Ada-Europe 2000, took place in Potsdam, Germany, June 26–30, 2000. It was organized by Ada Deutschland and sponsored by Ada-Europe, the European federation of national Ada societies, in cooperation with ACM SIGAda and the Gesellschaft für Informatik (GI). We gratefully acknowledge additional sponsorship by the DFG, the German Research Foundation, and by the Forschungszentrum Karlsruhe.

This year's conference marked the 20th anniversary of consecutive annual Ada-Europe conferences and the fifth year of a conference focusing on the general area of software reliability, in which Ada excels as one of the supporting technologies.

The Y2K problem has put the importance of software reliability into the limelight of media and political attention. Luckily, the dire predictions about potentially disastrous failures of critical systems did not prove true at the turn of the year, most likely because an incredible effort was made to update existing software, modernize systems, check-out backup mechanisms, and so on. One cannot but wonder how much more reliable the software could have been if only a percentage of the funds spent on the Y2K problem had gone into enhancements of reliability during the development and maintenance of the software.

We are witnessing a rapid growth of software components in cars, trains, planes, phones, control of biological, chemical, and manufacturing plants, and many other products and processes, where reliability is not just a nice-to-have but a hard requirement. It is not an overstatement to note that our daily life is beginning to literally depend on the reliability of the software embedded in products. Yet such reliability does not come about by accident. It needs to be infused into the software and the processes of the software life cycle by the application of appropriate techniques and technologies.

The conference on Reliable Software Technologies provides the forum for researchers, developers, and users to share their research results, present tools, report on experiences, and discuss requirements that have recently arisen from the ever-changing application domains. As in past years, the conference comprised a three-day technical program, at which the papers contained in these proceedings were presented, along with short presentations on related topics. The technical program was bracketed by two tutorial days, when attendees had an opportunity to catch up on a variety of topics related to the field, at both introductory and advanced levels. Further, the conference was accompanied by an exhibition at which vendors presented their reliability-related products. The notably increased size of the exhibition demonstrates that the market place is beginning to react to the importance of reliability engineering.

This year's conference comprised a truly international program. Authors from Argentina, Australia, Austria, Canada, China, France, Germany, Italy, Japan, Norway, Spain, Sweden, Switzerland, United Kingdom, and the USA presented their results. A total of 23 papers were accepted for the proceedings and eight additional contributions were accepted for presentation at the conference. Two conference sessions were reserved for presentations by vendors of products supporting the development and management of reliable software.

Each conference day was opened by a keynote presentation. The keynote speakers and their themes were:

- Rainer Zimmermann, Head of Unit E2, Directorate General Information Society, European Commission, Brussels, Belgium:
  Support of Technology Development in the Information Society
- Reto Weiss, Kingcat MCAS Project Manager, Paranor AG, Wahlendorf, Switzerland:
  Kingcat MCAS – Monitoring, Control and Alarm System for a Luxury Motor Yacht Implemented in Ada and Java
- Brian Pflug, Chief Engineer, Simulation & Software Engineering, Boeing Commercial Airplanes, Seattle, USA:
  Ada after 10 Years of Usage – Is There a Commercial Future?

We would like to express our sincere gratitude to these distinguished speakers, well known to the community, for sharing their insights and information with the audience.

The tutorial program featured international experts presenting introductory and advanced material on a variety of subjects relevant to software engineers:

- *Java for Ada Programmers*, Ben Brosgol
- *Real-Time POSIX*, Michael González Harbour
- *Ada95 for Beginners and Ada95 for Ada83 Programmers*, David Cook and Les Dupaix
- *Software Metrology Basics – Measurement, Assessment, and Certification of Procedures, Objects, and Agents*, Hans-Ludwig Hausen
- *The HOOD 4 Design Method*, Jean-Pierre Rosen
- *Tree-Based Reliability Models (TBRMs) for Early Reliability Measurement and Improvement*, Jeff Tian
- *Implementing Design Patterns in Ada95*, Matthew Heaney
- *High Integrity Ada Tasking*, John Harbaugh
- *GtkAda, An Ada95 Object-Oriented Graphic Toolkit*, Emmanuel Briot
- *Building Ada Development Tools with ASIS for GNAT*, Sergey Rybin and Vasily Fofanov
- *Windows Development with Ada*, Örjan Leringe
- *Developing Ada Applications for the Java Platform with JGNAT*, Franco Gasperoni

Many people contributed to the success of the conference. The program committee spent part of their Christmas vacation carefully reviewing all the papers and providing detailed evaluations. A subcommittee comprising Lars Asplund, Johann Blieberger, Michael González, Hubert Keller, Erhard Plödereder, and Jürgen Winkler met on a Sunday in January to compose the program based on the reviews. Some committee members shepherded papers to their final versions. We thank the committee for its dedication and hard work. A great help in organizing the paper review were the Start Conference Manager, provided free of charge by Rich Gerber, and Michael Hüdepohl who administered this WWW-based paper submission and review system at the University of Stuttgart.

The organizing committee deserves special mention. Peter Dencker put together an exhibition of unprecedented scope. Theodor Tempelmeier composed the attractive tutorial program. And always helping the organizers was Alfred Strohmeier, Ada-Europe's Conference Liaison.

We also would like to thank Christine Harms, who handled the registration and the local organization at Potsdam.

Foremost, however, we express our appreciation to the authors of the papers submitted to the conference, and to the participants who came to exchange their ideas and results. Without you, there would be no conference. We hope that you were satisfied by the technical program of the conference and enjoyed the social events of this Fifth International Conference on Reliable Software Technologies.

April 2000

Hubert Keller
Erhard Plödereder

Organizing Committee

Conference Chair
Hubert B. Keller, *Forschungszentrum Karlsruhe, Institute of Applied Computer Science, Germany*

Program Co-chairs
Hubert B. Keller, *Forschungszentrum Karlsruhe, Institute of Applied Computer Science, Germany*

Erhard Plödereder, *University of Stuttgart, Institute of Informatics, Germany*

Tutorial Chair
Theodor Tempelmeier, *FH Rosenheim, Dept. of Informatics, Germany*

Exhibition Chair
Peter Dencker, *Aonix GmbH, Germany*

Poster and Publicity Chair
Michael Tonndorf, *CSC Plönzke, Germany*

Ada-Europe Conference Liaison
Alfred Strohmeier, *Swiss Federal Institute of Technology in Lausanne*

Conference Secretariat
Christine Harms,
c/o GMD Forschungszentrum Informationstechnik GmbH, Germany

Program Committee

Ángel Álvarez, Technical University of Madrid
Lars Asplund, Uppsala University
Ted Baker, Florida State University
Stéphane Barbey, Paranor AG
John Barnes, JBI
Johann Blieberger, Technical University Vienna
Jim Briggs, University of Portsmouth
Benjamin Brosgol, Ada Core Technologies, Inc.
Dirk Craeynest, OFFIS nv/sa
Peter Dencker, Aonix GmbH
Marc Gobin, Royal Military Academy, Belgium
Peter Göhner, University of Stuttgart
Gerhard Goos, University of Karlsruhe
Michael González Harbour, Universidad de Cantabria
Günter Hommel, TU Berlin
Yvon Kermarrec, ENST de Bretagne Fabrice Kordon, Université P. & M. Curie
Rudolf Landwehr, CCI
Franco Mazzanti, Istituto di Elaborazione della Informazione, CNR
Paolo Panaroni, Intecs Sistemi
Laurent Pautet, ENST Paris
Jean-Pierre Rosen, Adalog
Edmond Schonberg, New York University & ACT
Alfred Strohmeier, Swiss Federal Institute of Technology, Lausanne
S. Tucker Taft, AverStar, Inc.
Theodor Tempelmeier, FH Rosenheim
Tullio Vardanega, European Space Agency
Debora Weber-Wulff, TFH Berlin
Andy Wellings, University of York
Jürgen Winkler, University of Jena

Table of Contents

Invited Presentations

Real-Time and Safety-Critical Systems

Session: Tools

Session: APIs and Components

Session: ASIS

Session: Risk and Reliability Management

Session: UML

Session: Formal Analysis Methods

Session: Testing

Support of Technology Development in the Information Society

Rainer Zimmermann

European Commission DG INFSO E
Rue de la Loi N O B Brussels Belgium

Abstract

The presentation will cover an overview of the IST Programme under the th Framework of European Research and will then concentrate on the opportunities of the Key Action "Essential Technologies and Infrastructures" The presentation will focus on the framework of the different action types "from research to take up" in particular showing the subjects in the area "Technologies and engineering for software systems and services" The presentation will put emphasis on new developments in the software area showing the importance of embedded systems and open source software Finally the expected time frame and subjects for the next calls will be presented

---

Head of Unit E

H B Keller and E Plödereder Eds Ada Europe LNCS pp

Kingcat MCAS Monitoring Control and Alarm System for a Luxury Motor Yacht Implemented in Ada and Java

Reto Weiss

Paranor AG Juraweg Wahlendorf Switzerland
reto@paranor.ch

Abstract The integrated Monitoring Control and Alarm System MCAS replaces conventional shipboard controls and instruments with a set of touch screens aboard a foot high tech catamaran designed for off shore cruising The Kingcat MCAS Monitoring Control and Alarm System is implemented in Ada and Java

Introduction

The integrated Monitoring Control and Alarm System MCAS replaces conventional shipboard controls and instruments with a set of touch screens aboard a foot high tech catamaran designed for off shore cruising MCAS integrates signals from sources distributed throughout the yacht to provide

- Continuously updated displays of standard navigation data as well as monitoring and control of engines electrical systems and other on board equipment
- Online consolidated alarm tracking for abnormal condition alerts
- Logging of technical data such as system events and sampled values from equipment for analysis and presentation of historical data

The heart of the computer bridge system is a local area network consisting of five workstations environmentally hardened PCs running under Windows NT The captain or crew interact with MCAS primarily via three inch LCD TFT color displays XGA equipped with integrated touch screen panels

Requirements

MCAS had to meet typical soft real time requirements Although response times must be very fast and signal refresh rates may exceed times per second short interruptions or delays if clearly identified and indicated do not result in catastrophic failures such as loss of ship control

Besides high throughput and fast response the most important requirements are robustness and zero maintenance MCAS must provide safe operation even in the case of partial hard or software failures

Kingcat MCAS Project Manager Software Engineer

H B Keller and E Plödereder Eds Ada Europe LNCS pp

The entire system must conform to a full set of Rules for Classification of high speed and light craft as defined by the most rigorous certification agency DNV □ Det Norske Veritas □

□□ Technology Architecture

MCAS is based on the following key technologies□

- Ada □□□ as programming language for all non visual components □ chosen mainly for its robustness and outstanding tasking concept for real time appli□ cations□
- Java for GUI implementation due to its strength for developing state of the art and easily portable graphical user interfaces□
- CORBA for highly reliable communication between distributed heterogeneous objects and because object request brokers □ORBs□ were available for both Ada and Java□

At a very early stage the design team realized the necessity for a generic frame□ work to serve as a foundation to build MCAS on□ This framework which was later named The Anthill Framework was to provide development support and a runtime environment for distributed objects implemented in Ada and Java including system management and monitoring tools□

MCAS consists of a number of rather static distributed objects entirely based on the described frame work□ All objects are inspectable through a specific inspector tool and are continuously monitored by a process manager □life cycle support□ Sig□ nal related components are based on MVC □model–view–controller□ architecture□ communication between objects is implemented as events using a push model□

□□ Conclusions

CORBA kept the promise of interoperability between objects developed with different programming languages and distributed over multiple hosts□ During the entire devel□ opment phase of more than □½ years there was not one single case where communica□ tion was erroneous because of incompatibilities between the two object request bro□ kers □ORBexpress on Ada side and VisiBroker on Java side□

Java proved to have become a mature programming environment especially well suited for graphical user interfaces□ Java □D demonstrated its power for creating nicely polished GUI components□

Ada □□ impressed with its reliability and its outstanding performance together with ORBexpress□ Debugging and testing was fairly easy with the Anthill Framework because it enabled consistent online inspection of all objects through the Object In□ spector implemented in Java□

MCAS was a great experience which clearly showed that even a very demanding application using distributed objects based on the CORBA architecture does work□

Ada after Years of Usage Is There a Commercial Future?

Bryan Pflug

Boeing Commercial Airplanes
Seattle Washington USA

Abstract

Boeing is the leading producer of commercial airplanes throughout the world The company's utilization of Ada throughout our commercial airplane products has been reported extensively as a highly successful application of the language compilers and related technologies on large mission critical systems

During the period Boeing's Commercial Airplanes business unit conducted an extensive review to determine if the then emerging Ada based technologies were suitably mature to support a major new airplane program An industry task force was established with representatives from each of Boeing's major avionics suppliers and was supported by each of the major vendors of Ada technology The decisions that were made by this task force were very important milestones for the commercial application of Ada because Boeing was one of the first firms to voluntarily utilize Ada for such mission critical applications

This presentation will review the findings and conclusions of our task force which led to our original commitment to use Ada The report will also provide an assessment of the changes that have taken place within our industry over the last years and consider the impact of those changes on our continuing commitment to use Ada on future airplane programs Our experiences with using Ada while developing the aircraft will be discussed and recent changes to Boeing's language policy will be described In this regard the role of language selection in the broader context of producing safe systems will be considered

---

Chief Engineer Simulation Software Engineering

H B Keller and E Plödereder Eds Ada Europe LNCS pp

An Open Ravenscar Real-Time Kernel for GNAT*

Juan A. de la Puente[1], José F. Ruiz[1], and Juan Zamorano[2]

[1] Departamento de Ingeniería de Sistemas Telemáticos
Universidad Politécnica de Madrid, E-28040 Madrid, Spain
jpuente@dit.upm.es, jfruiz@dit.upm.es
[2] Departamento de Arquitectura y Tecnología de Sistemas Informáticos
Universidad Politécnica de Madrid, E-28660 Madrid, Spain
jzamora@datsi.fi.upm.es

Abstract. This paper describes the architecture of ORK, an open source real-time kernel that implements the Ravenscar profile for the GNAT compilation system on a bare ERC32 computer. The kernel has a reduced size and complexity, and has been carefully designed in order to make it possible to build reliable software for on-board space applications. The kernel is closely integrated with the GNAT runtime library, and supports Ada tasking in an efficient and compact way.

1 Introduction

The Ravenscar Profile [,] is the best known result of the 8th International Real-Time Ada Workshop (IRTAW8). It defines a subset of the tasking features of Ada which can be implemented using a small, reliable kernel. The expected benefits of this approach are:

- Improved memory and execution time efficiency, by removing features with a high overhead.
- Improved reliability, by removing non-deterministic and non analysable features.
- Improved timing analysis, by removing non-deterministic and non-analysable features.

The tasking model defined by the profile includes tasks and protected types and objects at the library level, a maximum of one protected entry with a simple boolean barrier for synchronization, a real-time clock, absolute delays, preemptive priority scheduling with ceiling locking access to protected objects, and protected procedure interrupt handlers, as well as some other features. Other features, such as dynamic tasks and protected objects, task entries, dynamic priorities, select statements, asynchronous transfer of control, relative delays, or

* This work has been funded by ESA/ESTEC contract no. No.13863/99/NL/MV.

H. B. Keller and E. Plödereder (Eds.): Ada-Europe 2000, LNCS 1845, pp. 5– , 2000.

calendar clock, are forbidden. The profile was slightly revised at the 9th International Real-Time Ada Workshop (IRTAW9) [ ]. An updated full description can be found in [ ].

This paper describes the design of the *Open Ravenscar Real-time Kernel* (ORK), an open-source Ravenscar-compliant real-time kernel for GNAT that runs on bare ERC32-based computers. The kernel is fully integrated with GNAT, and applications built on top of it can be debugged with GDB. The application domain is on-board spacecraft software, which at some time may require a certification process to be applied to the kernel. It is distributed as an open source product, with a GPL license. Its development has been carried out in the framework of the ESA/ESTEC open-source initiative for ERC32-based computers [ ].

The rest of the paper is organised as follows: Section describes how the Ravenscar profile can be implemented in GNAT. Section describes the architecture of ORK. Section compares the design of ORK with other recent real-time kernels. The current status of the work, is described in section . Finally, some conclusions are drawn and plans for the near future are explained in section .

2 The Ravenscar Profile in GNAT

2.1 The Ravenscar Restrictions

The Ada subset defined by the Ravenscar profile can be enforced at compile time by using an appropriate set of restriction identifiers with the pragma Restrictions (ALRM [ ], D.7, H.4). However, not all the Ravenscar restrictions can be enforced by standard identifiers, and thus a number of additional restriction identifiers have been proposed at IRTAW8 [ ] and IRTAW9 [ ] for this purpose. The complete set of Ravenscar restrictions and the proposed restriction identifiers are listed in the profile definition [ ].

The approach adopted in the most recent versions of GNAT is different: an implementation defined pragma (pragma Ravenscar) is used to establish the complete set of restrictions [ ]. However, there are some slight differences between the GNAT Ravenscar pragma and the profile defined by IRTAW [,]. These differences can be overcome by using specific restriction identifiers and, from a practical point of view, it can be said that the "standard" (i.e. IRTAW defined) set of Ravenscar restrictions can indeed be enforced by GNAT. An example configuration file for programs restricted according to the Ravenscar profile is shown in figure .

[1] ERC32 [ ] is a radiation-hardened implementation of the SPARC v7 architecture, which has been adopted by the European Space Agency (ESA) as the current standard processor for computer systems.

```
-- gnat.adc file for Ravenscar programs
pragma Ravenscar;

pragma Restrictions (...);    -- additional restrictions, if any

pragma Task_Dispatching_Policy (FIFO_Within_Priorities);
pragma Locking_Policy (Ceiling_Locking);
```

Fig. 1. Sample configuration file for GNAT

2.2 The GNU Runtime Library

Ada tasking is implemented in GNAT by means of a run-time library called GNARL (GNU Ada Runtime Library)[ ]. The parts of GNARL which are dependent on a particular machine and operating system are known as GNULL (GNU Low-level Library), and its interface to the platform-independent part of the GNARL is called GNULLI (GNULL Interface). Most implementations of GNULL are built on top of an existing set of POSIX thread functions [ ], which in turn may be implemented on top of an operating system (figure).

Ada programs compiled with the pragma Ravenscar use a restricted GNARL that takes advantage of the simplified tasking model of the Ravenscar profile to reduce the size and execution time overhead of the runtime [ ]. This reduced GNARL still uses the same low-level interface (GNULLI) to the underlying operating system.

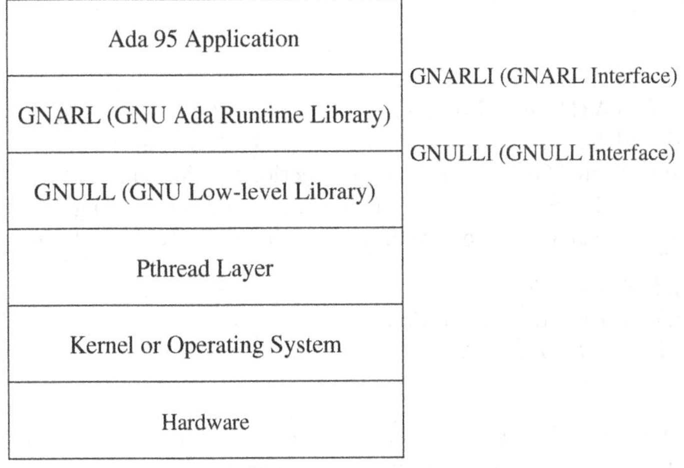

Fig. 2. Architecture of the GNAT run-time system

2.3 Implementing the Ravenscar Profile in GNAT

A specialized real-time kernel The current GNAT approach of building GNARL on top a pthread interface has clear advantages from the portability point of view, but imposes too much overhead on the system, as GNARL already provides most of the functionality which is needed for tasking, and consequently does not use many of the pthread or operating system capabilities. This gives raise to abstraction inversion and, moreover, goes against the Ravenscar purpose to support Ada tasking with a small, reliable runtime.

Our approach is to implement tasking with a small, dedicated kernel, which does not have the unnecessary burden of a full pthreads implementation [ ]. ORK provides an almost direct implementation of GNULLI, with existing GNULL packages acting as a thin glue layer for GNAT (figure).

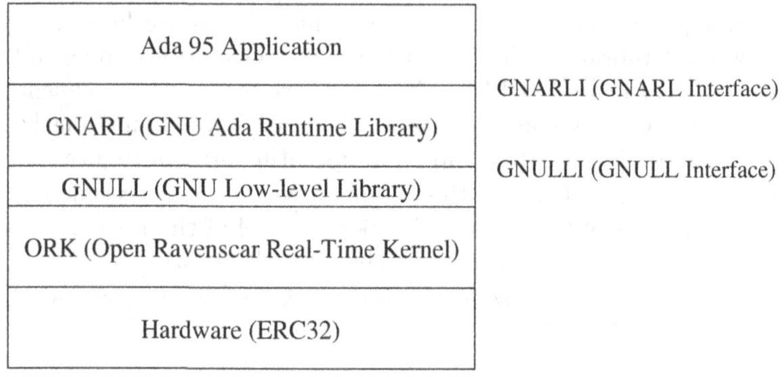

Fig. 3. Architecture of the GNAT run-time system based on ork

Adapting GNARL to the kernel The next step is building a version of GNARL for ORK. In order to do this, the GNULL packages have been re-implemented on the ORK interface (see section). We have kept the specifications compatible with GNULLI, so that only minimum changes to the upper level GNARL packages are required. The modified GNULL packages are:

- System.Task_Primitives
- System.Task_Primitives.Operations
- System.OS_Primitives
- System.OS_Interface

Since ORK provides most of the tasking functionality, the specifications and bodies of these packages contain mostly renames or direct subprogram calls to the ORK interface.

We assume that all programs are compiled with pragma Ravenscar, and therefore only the restricted GNARL is used with the kernel. Of course, this means that full Ada programs cannot run on the specialized version of GNARL, but this limitation is necessary to enable ORK to support only the tasking features required by the Ravenscar profile and thus taking advantage of the possibility of having only a small and reliable kernel.

Under this assumption, only a few parts of the upper level GNARL packages have to be adapted to ORK. The most important ones are:

- System
- System.Interrupts
- Ada.Interrupts.Names

Building GNAT The last step is to build a new version of GNAT with the adapted GNARL for the target platform, i.e. ORK on ERC32. This is straightforward, as the GNAT sources include the necessary configuration tools, which must be slightly modified to include the new target platform.

2.4 Developing Ravenscar Compliant Programs

Once a GNAT version that is targeted to ORK is available, Ada programs can be compiled and linked in the ordinary way, provided the pragma Ravenscar is used. General Ada programs, however, cannot be compiled, as some of the required runtime support is not available with ORK.

3 The Design of the Open Ravenscar Real-Time Kernel

3.1 Overall Architecture

The functionality provided by ORK can be divided into the following sets of services:

- Low level task (thread) management
- Synchronization
- Scheduling
- Storage allocation
- Time-keeping and delays
- Interrupt handling

The kernel is accordingly divided into a set of Ada packages, all of them children of an empty root package called Kernel (figure). This structure is similar to that of the JTK [,] and Top-Layer [ ] kernels.

The main ORK packages are:

- Kernel.Threads. This package provides all the support required for thread creation, scheduling, and synchronization.
- Kernel.Time. This package provides support for the real-time clock and absolute delays.

– Kernel.Interrupts. This package provides support for interrupt identification, and for attaching interrupt handlers to interrupts.
– Kernel.Memory. This package provides limited dynamic storage management.
– Kernel.Parameters. This package defines implementation dependent parameters.
– Kernel.CPU_Primitives. This package contains all the processor dependent elements.
– Kernel.Peripherals. This package provides support for the peripherals available in the target board.

Only the first four of these packages are visible to GNULL. The other three, Kernel.Parameters, Kernel.CPU_Primitives, and Kernel.Peripherals, are used only by other kernel packages, and encapsulate implementation dependent elements in order to make it easier to port the kernel to other hardware environments.

Some of the packages (e.g. Kernel.Threads) have additional children that extend their interfaces so that some of their internal functionality is made visible to other kernel packages.

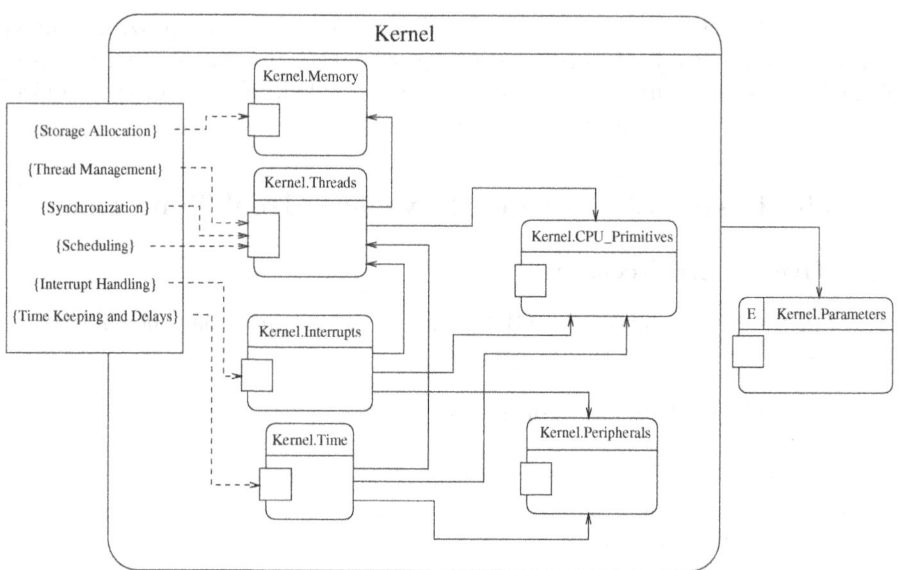

Fig. 4. Architecture of the Open Ravenscar Real-Time Kernel

3.2 Thread Management

Ada tasks are implemented at the lower level by kernel threads. Threads are created at program startup, so that there is no need to dynamically allocate or deallocate resources such as TCBs or stack space.

Threads are scheduled according to the *FIFO within priorities* policy (ALRM [ ], D2). There is a ready queue which is ordered by priority and arrival order. The synchronization primitives directly insert or remove threads from the ready queue.

Two kinds of synchronization elements are provided by the kernel: mutexes and condition variables. These elements are used by GNARL to implement protected objects. Despite the name similarity with POSIX, ORK synchronization primitives are defined in such a way that the related GNULLI elements can be directly implemented, thus enabling a more efficient implementation of protected objects. We have taken advantage of the Ravenscar profile restrictions to implement only one kind of mutual exclusion locks.

Condition variables are also simplified with respect POSIX, in that there are no timed waits and there are no suspended task queues, as the maximum number of tasks that can be waiting on a condition is one. The fact that the Ravenscar profile does not allow select statements, timed wait operations, or ATCs, has also resulted in great simplification.

Locks implement the *Immediate Priority Ceiling Protocol* (IPCP), which is the same as the Ceiling Locking policy defined by the ALRM [ ] (D3).

3.3 Time Management

The package Kernel.Time provides timing support in a very simplified way. A time type is defined that represents both absolute time and time intervals as an integer number of nanoseconds. There is a monotonic clock that gives an absolute time value, measured from system startup.

According to the Ravenscar profile specification, only an absolute delay (delay until) operation is provided. Delayed threads are kept in a delay queue which is ordered by wakeup time. Since a delay cannot be canceled, as there are no abort statements or ATCs, there is no need to keep delayed threads waiting on a condition variable, as current GNARL implementations do.

3.4 Storage Management

Although the Ravenscar profile does not forbid all kinds of dynamic storage management, as the profile does not deal with non tasking features of Ada, it seems reasonable to expect Ravenscar compliant programs not to use dynamic storage pools. Consequently, only a limited form of memory management is provided, in order to allocate TCB and stack space for new threads. Since threads can only be created at system startup, and cannot terminate, this restricted form of storage allocation can be made in a safe way, using a simple linear algorithm.

The task stacks are protected in order to avoid stack overflow or underflow. The hardware segment protection mechanism is used for this purpose.

3.5 Interrupt Handling

An interrupt represents a class of events that are detected by the hardware or the kernel itself. When an interrupt occurs an *Interrupt Service Routine* (ISR) is invoked to make the interrupt available to the kernel. In Ada 95, a high-level handler can be attached to the interrupt so that is is automatically started by the runtime system when the interrupt occurs. The handler may be a parameterless protected procedure or a task entry, although the latter is only included for compatibility with Ada 83.

Current GNARL implementations use interrupt service tasks that are activated when an interrupt occurs, and then call the associated interrupt handler procedure. In this way, priorities and mutual exclusion are handled in the standard way for tasks and protected objects. Interrupt handlers are executed in the context of the interrupt service tasks, which gives a clean execution model compared to other approaches in which the handler is executed in the context of the interrupted task.

ORK follows a different approach. Under the Ravenscar profile restrictions only protected procedure handlers can be defined. Moreover, the only possible locking policy is Ceiling Locking. This means that an interrupt handler can never be blocked waiting for a protected object to become free. Since all interrupts are disabled while updating the kernel internal data (see below), there is no need for complex mutual exclusion mechanisms. Actually, interrupt handlers are executed as if they were directly invoked by the interrupted task, with the difference that the interrupt stack is used instead of the task stack.

The Kernel.Interrupts package provides symbolic interrupt names and operations for attaching and detaching interrupt handlers. The handlers are directly attached to the interrupts, without the burden of using POSIX signals as the current GNARL does.

3.6 Other Design Issues

The kernel interface is a purely procedural one, as there is no need for separate user and supervisor execution modes. All the program runs in supervisor mode, as it is common in embedded systems. Mutual exclusion in the kernel is achieved by means of a monolithic monitor [ ] protected by disabling interrupts, so that interrupt delivery is postponed when a kernel function is executed [,].

Mutex lock operations are implemented by simply raising the locking thread active priority to the ceiling priority of the mutex. This is consistent with the implementation proposed by the Ada Rationale [ ] for protected objects.

4 Related Work

This project builds on some of the results of previous ESA projects which resulted in the development of the current ERC32 GNU Cross Compilation system [ ], which includes an Ada cross-compilation system for the ERC32 computer based on GNAT and RTEMS, an open real-time operating system.

The JTK kernel, which was developed at the Technical University of Madrid, [,], has provided some background for the development of ORK. We have also been inspired by the Top Layer kernel [ ].

Other previous work of interest to the project includes Aonix' *Raven* [ ], and the kernels developed at the Florida State University [,] and the University of York [ ].

5 Status and Availability

The first version of the kernel has been fully implemented, and is available at the ORK project server, . The distribution package includes source patches for the GNAT 3.13 runtime library, and GDB scripts, in addition to the kernel itself.

ORK is free software, and is distributed with the same license as GNAT (a slightly modified GNU Public License). This means that everybody is free to read the ORK source code, modify it, and redistribute it, provided they give others the same freedom.

ORK is currently maintained on a voluntary basis for the general public.

6 Conclusions and Future Work

ORK has been designed to provide an open source implementation of the Ravenscar profile. Although the ORK project is primarily targeted to the on-board space software domain, we expect that it will be useful to the hard real-time systems community at large.

We plan to port ORK to other hardware platforms, starting with the ix86 PC compatible architecture, in the near future. This will enable it to be used in other application domains, and also in real-time systems education.

Acknowledgments

ORK was developed by a team of the Department of Telematics Engineering Technical University of Madrid (DIT/UPM), lead by Juan Antonio de la Puente. The other members of the team were Juan Zamorano, José F. Ruiz, Ramón Fernández, and Rodrigo García. Alejandro Alonso and Ángel Álvarez acted as document and code reviewers, and contributed to the technical discussions with many fruitful comments and suggestions. The same team developed the adapted packages that enable GNAT to work with ORK.

GDB was adapted to ORK by a Jesús González-Barahona, Vicente Matellán, Andrés Arias, and Juan Manuel Dodero. José Centeno and Pedro de las Heras acted as reviewers for this part of the work. All of them work at the King Juan Carlos University of Madrid.

The ORK software was validated by Jesús Borruel and Juan Carlos Morcuende, from Construcciones Aeronáuticas (CASA), Space Division. We also relied very much on Andy Wellings and Alan Burns, of York University, for reviewing and discussions about the Ravenscar profile and its implementation.

ORK was developed under contract with ESA, the European Space Agency. Jorge Amador, Tullio Vardanega and Jean-Loup Terraillon provided many positive criticism and contributed the user's view during the development. The project was carried out from September, 1999 to early June, 2000.

References

1. Ada Core Technologies. *GNAT Reference Manual. Version 3.13a*, March 2000.
2. *Ada 95 Reference Manual: Language and Standard Libraries. International Standard ANSI/ISO/IEC-8652:1995*, 1995. Available from Springer-Verlag, LNCS no. 1246.
3. Lars Asplund, Bob Johnson, and Kristina Lundqvist. Session summary: The Ravenscar profile and implementation issues. *Ada Letters*, XIX(25):12–14, 1999. Proceedings of the 9th International Real-Time Ada Workshop.
4. Ted Baker and Tullio Vardanega. Session summary: Tasking profiles. *Ada Letters*, XVII(5):5–7, 1997. Proceedings of the 8th International Ada Real-Time Workshop.
5. Alan Burns. The Ravenscar profile. Technical report, University of York, 1999. Available at `http://www.cs.york.ac.uk/rts/papers/p.ps`.
6. Alan Burns, Brian Dobbing, and George Romanski. The Ravenscar profile for high integrity real-time programs. In Lars Asplund, editor, *Reliable Software Technologies — Ada-Europe'98*, number 1411 in LNCS. Springer-Verlag, 1998.
7. Juan A. de la Puente, José F. Ruiz, and Jesús M. González-Barahona. Real-time programming with GNAT: Specialised kernels versus POSIX threads. *Ada Letters*, XIX(2):73–77, 1999. Proceedings of the 9th International Real-Time Ada Workshop.
8. Brian Dobbing and George Romanski. The Ravenscar profile: Experience report. *Ada Letters*, XIX(2):28–32, 1999. Proceedings of the 9th International Real-Time Ada Workshop.
9. ESA. *32 Bit Microprocessor and Computer System Development*, 1992. Report 9848/92/NL/FM.
10. Jiri Gaisler. *The ERC32 GNU Cross-Compiler System*. ESA/ESTEC, 1999. Version 2.0.6.
11. E. W. Giering and T. P. Baker. The GNU Ada Runtime Library (GNARL): Design and implementation. In *Proceedings of the Washington Ada Symposium*, 1994.
12. IEEE. *Portable Operating System Interface (POSIX) — Part 1: System Application Program Interface (API) [C Language] (Incorporating IEEE Stds 1003.1-1990, 1003.1b-1993, 1003.1c-1995, and 1003.1i-1995)*, 1990. ISO/IEC 9945-1:1996.
13. Intermetrics. *Ada 95 Rationale: Language and Standard Libraries.*, 1995. Available from Springer-Verlag, LNCS no. 1247.
14. M. Kamrad and B. Spinney. An Ada runtime system implementation of the Ravenscar profile for a high speed application layer data switch. In Michael González-Harbour and Juan A. de la Puente, editors, *Reliable Software Technologies — Ada-Europe'99*, number 1622 in LNCS, pages 26–38. Springer-Verlag, 1999.
15. A. K. Mok. The design of real-time programming systems based on process models. In *IEEE Real-Time Systems Symposium*. IEEE Computer Society Press, 1984.
16. Frank Mueller. A library implementation of POSIX threads under UNIX. In *Proceedings of the USENIX Conference*, pages 29–41, January 1993.

17. José F. Ruiz and Jesús M. González-Barahona. Implementing a new low-level tasking support for the GNAT runtime system. In Michael González-Harbour and Juan A. de la Puente, editors, *Reliable Software Technologies — Ada-Europe'99*, number 1622 in LNCS, pages 298–307. Springer-Verlag, 1999.
18. H. Shen and T. P. Baker. A Linux kernel module implementation of restricted Ada tasking. *Ada Letters*, XIX(2):96–103, 1999. Proceedings of the 9th International Real-Time Ada Workshop.
19. H. Shen, A. Charlet, and T. P. Baker. A 'bare-machine' implementation of Ada multi-tasking beneath the Linux kernel. In Michael González-Harbour and Juan A. de la Puente, editors, *Reliable Software Technologies — Ada-Europe'99*, number 1622 in LNCS, pages 287–297. Springer-Verlag, 1999.
20. W. M. Walker, P. T. Wooley, and A. Burns. An experimental testbed for embedded real time Ada 95. *Ada Letters*, XIX(2):84–89, 1999. Proceedings of the 9th International Real-Time Ada Workshop.

Object-Oriented Programming and Protected Objects in Ada 95*

Andy J. Wellings[1], Bob Johnson[2], Bo Sanden[2], Joerg Kienzle[3], Thomas Wolf[3], and Stephen Michell[4]

[1] Department of Computer Science, University of York, UK
[2] Department of Computer Science, Colorado Technical University, USA
[3] Software Engineering Laboratory
Swiss Federal Institute of Technology in Lausanne, Switzerland
[4] Maurya Software, Ontario, Canada

Abstract. Integrating concurrent and object-oriented programming has been an active research topic since the late 1980s. The majority of approaches have taken a sequential object-oriented language and made it concurrent. A few approaches have taken a concurrent language and made it object-oriented. The most important of this latter class is the Ada 95 language which is an extension to the object-based concurrent programming language Ada 83. Arguably, Ada 95 does not fully integrate its models of concurrency and object-oriented programming. This paper discusses ways in which protected objects can be made more extensible.

Keywords: concurrent object-oriented programming, inheritance anomaly, Ada 95.

1 Introduction

Arguably, Ada 95 does not fully integrate its models of concurrent and object-oriented programming [,]. For example, neither tasks nor protected objects are extensible. When Ada 95 was designed, the extensions to Ada 83 for object-oriented programming were, for the most part, considered separate to extensions to the concurrency model. Some consideration was given to abandoning protected types and instead using Java-like synchronised methods in their place, however, there was no public debate of this issue. Similarly, there was no public debate on the issues associated with allowing protected types or tasks to be extended, although a Language Study Note (LSN-1030) was produced which raised some of the issues discussed in this paper. The purpose of this paper is to discuss ways in which the Ada 95 concurrency model can be better integrated with object-oriented programming.

* This paper extends and unifies the approaches described in [ ] and [ ].

H. B. Keller and E. Plödereder (Eds.): Ada-Europe 2000, LNCS 1845, pp. 16–   , 2000.

2 Concurrent Object-Oriented Programming

Integrating concurrent and object-oriented programming has been an active research topic since the late 1980s. The majority of approaches have taken a sequential object-oriented language and made it concurrent. A few approaches have taken a concurrent language and made it object-oriented. The most important of this latter class is the Ada 95 language which is an extension to the object-based concurrent programming language Ada 83.

In general, there are two main issues for concurrent object-oriented programming:

- the relationship between concurrent activities and objects – here the distinction is often between the concept of an active object, and where concurrent execution is created by the use of asynchronous method calls,
- the way in which concurrent activities communicate and synchronise (and yet avoid the so-called inheritance anomaly [ ]).

3 The Ada 95 Programming Language

The Ada 83 language allowed programs to be constructed from several basic building blocks: packages, subprograms, and tasks. Of these, only tasks were considered to be types and integrated with the typing model of the language. Ada 95 extends the facilities of Ada 83 in areas of the language where weaknesses were perceived. Two of the main innovations were the introduction of data-oriented communication and synchronization through *protected types* and the introduction of object-oriented programming facilities through *tagged types*.

Although task types and protected types are fully integrated into the typing model of Ada 95, it is not possible to create a tagged protected type or a tagged task type. The designers shied away from this possibility partly because they felt that fully integrating object-oriented programming and concurrency was not a well-understood topic and, therefore, not suitable for an ISO standard professional programming language. Also, there were inevitable concerns that the scope of potential language changes being proposed was too large for the Ada community to accept. In spite of this, there is some level of integration between tagged types and tasks and protected objects. Tagged types after all are just part of the typing mechanism and therefore can be used by protected types and tasks types in the same way as other types. Indeed paradigms for their use have been developed (see [ ] chapter 13). However, these approaches cannot get around the basic limitation that protected types and task types cannot be extended.

4 Making Concurrent Programming in Ada 95 more Object-Oriented

There are the following classes of basic types in Ada: scalar types - such as integer types, enumeration types, real types, etc, structured types - such as record types and array types, protected types, task types, and access types. Access types are special as they provide the mechanism by which pointers to the other types can be created. Note that, although access types to subprograms can be created, subprograms are not a basic type of the language.

In providing tagged types, Ada 95 has provided a mechanism whereby a structured type can be extended. It should be stressed, though, that only record types can be extended, not array types. This is understandable as the record is the primary mechanism for grouping together items which will represent the heterogeneous attributes of the objects. Furthermore, variable length array manipulation is already catered for in the language. Similarly, scalar types can already be extended using subtypes and derived types. Allowing records to be extended thus is consistent with allowing variable length arrays, subtypes and derived types.

A protected type is similar to a record in that it groups items together. (In the case of a protected type, these items must be accessed under mutual exclusion.) It would be consistent, then, to allow a protected type to be extended with additional items. The following sections will discuss some of the issues in allowing extensible protected types.

5 Extensible Protected Types

The requirements for extensible protected types are easy to articulate. In particular, extensible (tagged) protected types should allow: new data fields to be added, new functions, procedures and entries to be added, functions, procedures and entries to be overridden, class-wide programming to be performed. These simple requirements raise many complex semantic issues.

5.1 Declaration and Primitive Operations

For consistency with the usage elsewhere in Ada, the word 'tagged' indicates that a protected type is extensible. A protected type encapsulates the operations that can be performed on its protected data. Consequently, the primitive operations of a tagged protected type are, in effect, already defined. They are, of course, similar to primitive operations of other tagged types in spirit but not in syntax, since other primitive operations are defined by being declared in the same package specification as a tagged type. Consider the following example:

```
protected type T is tagged
  procedure W (...);
  function X (...) return ...;
  entry Y (...);
private  -- data attributes of T
end T;

O : T;
```

W, X, and Y can be viewed as primitive operations on T. Interestingly, the call O.X takes a syntactic form similar to that in most object-oriented languages. Indeed, Ada's protected object syntax is in conflict with the language's usual representation of an 'object'.

5.2 Inheritance

This paper proposes that tagged protected types can be extended in the same manner as tagged types:

```
protected type T1 is new T with

  procedure W (...); -- override T.W

  procedure Z (...); -- a new method

private -- new attributes of T1
end T1;
```

The issue of overriding protected entries will be considered in section .

One consideration is whether or not private fields in the parent type (T) can be seen in the child type (T1). In protected types, all data has to be declared as private so that it can not be changed without first obtaining mutual exclusion. There are four possible approaches to this visibility issue:

1. Prevent a child protected object from accessing the parent's data. This would limit the child's power to modify the behaviour of its parent object, it only being allowed to invoke operations in its parent.

2. Allow a child protected object full access to private data declared in its parent. This would be more flexible but has the potential to compromise the parent abstraction.

3. Provide an additional keyword to distinguish between data that is fully private and data that is private but visible to child types. This keyword would be used in a similar way to **private** (much like C++ uses its keyword 'protected' to permit descendent classes direct access to inherited data items).

4. Allow child protected types to access private components of their parent protected type if they are declared in a child of the package in which their parent protected type is declared. This would be slightly inconsistent with the way protected types currently work in Ada because protected types do not rely on using packages to provide encapsulation.

This paper will assume the second method, as it provides the most flexibility, requires no new keywords and is consistent with normal tagged types.

If a procedure in a child protected type calls a procedure or function in its parent, it should not have to wait to obtain the lock on the protected object before entering the parent, otherwise deadlock would occur. There is one lock for each instance of a protected type and this lock is used when the protected object is converted to a parent type. This is consistent with current Ada when one procedure/function calls another in the same protected object.

5.3 Dispatching and Re-dispatching

Given a hierarchy of tagged protected types, it is possible to create class-wide types and accesses to class-wide types; first consider only protected subprograms, for example:

```
type Pt is access protected type T'Class;

P: Pt := new . . .; -- some type in the hierarchy

P.W(...); -- dispatches to the appropriate projected object.
```

Of course from within `P.W`, it should be possible to convert back to the class-wide type and re-dispatch to another primitive operation. Unfortunately, an operation inside a tagged protected type does not have the option of converting the object (on which it was originally dispatched) to a class-wide type because this object is passed implicitly to the operation. There are two possible strategies: make all calls to other operations from within a tagged protected type dispatching, or use some form of syntactic change to make it possible to specify whether to re-dispatch or not. The first strategy is not ideal because it is often useful to be able to call an operation in the same type or a parent type without re-dispatching. In addition, the first strategy is inconsistent with ordinary tagged types where re-dispatching is not automatic. A solution according to the second strategy uses calls of the form `type.operation`, where `type` is the type to which the implicit protected object should be converted. The following is an example of this syntax for a re-dispatch:

```
protected body T is
  ...
  procedure P (...) is
  begin
    . . .
    T'Class.Q (...);
    . . .
  end P;
end T;
```

`T'Class` indicates the type to which the protected object (which is in the hierarchy of type `T'Class` but which is being viewed as type `T`) that was passed implicitly to `P` should be view converted. This allows it to define which `Q` procedure to call. This syntax is also necessary to allow an operation to call an overridden operation in its parent, for example:

```
protected body T1 is -- an extension of T
  ...
  procedure W (...) is -- overrides the W procedure of T
  begin
    . . .
    T.W(...); -- calls the parent operation
```

```
  . . .
  end W;
end T1;
```

This new syntax does not conflict with any other part of the language because it is strictly only a type that precedes the period.

Requeuing can also lead to situations where re-dispatching is desirable. Requeuing to a parent entry would require barrier re-evaluation. Requeues from other protected objects or from accept statements in tasks could also involve dispatching to the correct operation in a similar way.

5.4 Entry Calls

Allowing entries to be primitive operations of extensible protected types raises many inter-related complex issues. These include:

1. Can a child entry call its parent's entry? – This is how reuse is achieved in an object-oriented framework. From the protected object perspective, however, calling an entry is a potentially suspending operation and these are not allowed within the body of a protected operation.

2. What is the relationship, if any, between the parent's barrier and the child's barrier? – There are three possibilities: no relationship, the child can weaken the parent's barrier, or the child can strengthen the parent's barrier.

3. How many queues does an implementation need to maintain for an overridden entry? – If there is no relationship between the parent and the child barrier, it is necessary to maintain a separate entry queue for each overridden entry. If there is more than one queue, the `'Count` attribute should reflect this. Hence `'Count` might give different values when called from the parent or when called from the child. A problem with using separate entry queues with different barriers for overridden and overriding entries is that it is harder to theorise about the order of entries being serviced. Normally entries are serviced in FIFO order but with separate queues, each with a separate barrier, this might not be possible.

4. What happens if a parent entry requeues to another entry? – When an entry call requeues to another entry, control is not returned to the calling entry but to the task which originally made the entry call. This means that when a child entry calls its parent and the parent entry requeues, control is not returned to the child. Given that the code of the parent is invisible to the child, this would effectively prohibit the child entry from undertaking any post-processing.

In order to reduce the number of options for discussion, it is assumed that child entries must strengthen their parent's barrier for the remainder of the paper. The syntax **and when** is used to indicate this. To avoid having the body of a child protected object depend on the body of its parent, it is necessary to move the declaration of the barrier from the body to the specification of the protected type (private part). Consider

```
protected type T is tagged
  entry E ;
```

```
private
  I: Integer := 0;
  entry E when E'Count > 1; -- barrier given in the private part
end T;

protected type T1 is new T with
  entry E ;
private
  entry E and when I > 0;
end T;

A: T1;
```

If a call was made to `A.E`, this would be statically defined as a call to `T1.E` and would be subject to its barrier (`E'Count > 1 and I > 0`). The barrier would be repeated in the entry body.

Even with barrier strengthening, the issue of barrier evaluation must be addressed. Consider the case where a tagged protected object is converted to its parent type (using a view conversion external to the protected type) and then an entry is called on that type. It is not clear which barrier needs to be passed. There are three possible strategies that can be taken:

1. Use the barrier associated with the exact entry which is being called, ignoring any barrier associated with an entry which overrides this exact entry. As the parent type does not know about new data added in the child, it could be argued that allowing an entry in the parent to execute when the child has strengthened the barrier for that entry should be safe. Unfortunately, this is not the case. Consider a bounded buffer which has been extended so that the `Put` and `Get` operations can be locked. Here, if the lockable buffer is viewed converted to a normal buffer and `Get`/`Put` called with only the buffer barriers evaluated, a locked buffer will be accessible even if it is locked. Furthermore, this approach would also mean that there would be separate entry queues for overridden entries.

2. Use the barrier associated with the entry to which dispatching would occur if the object was converted to a class wide type (i.e., the barrier of the entry of the object's actual type). This is the strongest barrier and would allow safe re-dispatching in the entry body. This method results in one entry queue per entry instead of one for each entry and every overridden entry. However, it is perhaps misleading as it is the parent's code which is executed but the child's barrier expression that is evaluated.

3. Allow view conversions from inside the protected object but require that all external calls are dispatching calls. Hence, there is only one entry queue, and all external calls would always invoke the primitive operations of the object's actual type. The problem with this approach is that currently Ada does not dispatch by default. Consequently, this approach would introduce an inconsistency between the way tagged types and extensible protected types are treated.

For the remainder of this paper, it is assumed that external calls to protected objects always dispatch.

Calling the Parent Entry and Parent Requeues So far this section has discussed the various issues associated with overridden entry calls. However, details of how the child entry actually calls its parent have been left unspecified. The main problem is that Ada forbids an entry from explicitly calling another entry. There are two approaches to this problem.

1. Use requeue. – Although Ada forbids nested entry calls, it does allow an entry call to be requeued. Hence, the child can only requeue to the parent. Requeue gives the impression of calling the parent but it is not possible for the child to do any post-processing once the parent entry has executed (as the call returns to the caller of the child entry). As a requeue, the parent's barrier would have to be re-evaluated. Given that the child barrier has strengthened the parent's barrier, the parent's barrier would normally be open. If this is not the case, an exception is raised (to queue the call would require more than one entry queue). Furthermore, if atomicity is to be maintained and the parent requeue is to be part of the same protected action, the parent entry must be serviced before any other entries whose barriers also happen to be open. Hence, this requeue has slightly different semantics from a requeue between unrelated entries.

2. Allow the child entry to call the parent entry and treat that call as a procedure call. – It is clear that calling the parent entry is different from a normal entry call; special syntax has already been introduced to facilitate it (see section). In this approach, the parent call is viewed as a procedure call and therefore not a potentially suspending operation. However, the parent's barrier is still a potential cause for concern. One option is to view the barrier as an assertion and raise an exception if it is not true. The other option is not to test the barrier at all, based on the premise that the barrier was true when the child was called and, therefore, need not be re-evaluated until the whole protected action is completed.

With either of these approaches, there is still the problem that control is not returned to the child if the parent entry requeues requests to other entries for servicing. This, of course, could be made illegal and an exception raised. However, requeue is an essential part of the Ada 95 model and to effectively forbid its use with extensible protected types would be a severe restriction.

The remainder of this paper will assume a model where parent calls are treated as procedure calls (the issue of the assertion is left open) and requeue in the parent is allowed. A consequence of this is that no post-processing is allowed after a parent call.

6 Inheritance Anomaly

The combination of the object-oriented paradigm with mechanisms for concurrent programming may give rise to the so-called "inheritance anomaly" [ ]. An inheritance anomaly exists if the synchronization between operations of a class is not local but may depend on the whole set of operations present for the class.

[1] Special consideration would need to be given to barriers which use the `'Count` attribute in the parent, since these will clearly change when the child begins execution.

When a subclass adds new operations, it may therefore become necessary to change the synchronization defined in the parent class to account for these new operations. This section examines how extensible protected types can deal with this inheritance anomaly.

Synchronization for extensible protected types is done via entry barriers. An entry barrier can be interpreted in two slightly different ways:

- as a precondition (which must become a guard when concurrency is introduced in an object-oriented programming language, as [ ] argues). In this sense, entries are the equivalent of partial operations.
- as a synchronization constraint.

The use of entry barriers (i.e., guards) for synchronization makes extended protected types immune against one of the kinds of inheritance anomalies identified by [ ]: guards are not subject to inheritance anomalies caused by a partitioning of states.

To avoid a major break of encapsulation, it is mandatory for a concurrent object-oriented programming language to have a way to re-use existing synchronization code defined for a parent class and to incrementally modify this inherited synchronization in a child class. In our proposal, this is given by the **and when** clause, which incrementally modifies an inherited entry barrier and hence the inherited synchronization code.

Inheritance anomalies in Ada 95 with extended protected types can still occur, though. As [ ] argue, the root cause of inheritance anomalies lies in a lack of expressive power of concurrent object-oriented programming languages: if not all five criteria identified by [ ] are fulfiled, inheritance anomalies may occur. Ada 95 satisfies only three of these criteria; synchronization based on history information cannot be expressed directly using entry barriers (local state must instead be used to record execution history), and synchronization based on request parameter values also is not possible directly in Ada 95. The example for the resource controller shown in section exhibits both of these inheritance anomalies. Because the barrier of entry `Allocate_N` cannot depend on the parameter `N` itself, an internal requeue to `Wait_For_N` must be used instead. The synchronization constraint for `Wait_For_N` itself is history-sensitive: the operation should be allowed only after a call to `Deallocate` has freed some resources. As a result, `Deallocate` must be overridden to record this history information in local state, although both the synchronization constraints for `Deallocate` itself as well as its functionality remain unchanged.

7 Example – Advanced Resource Control

Resource allocation is a fundamental problem in all aspects of concurrent programming. Its consideration exercises all Bloom's criteria (see section) and forms an appropriate basis for assessing the synchronisation mechanisms of concurrent languages, such as Ada.

Consider the problem of constructing a resource controller that allocates some resource to a group of client agents. There are a bounded number of instances of the resource; contention is possible and must be catered for in the design of the program. [ ] propose the following resource controller problem as a benchmark for concurrent object-oriented programming languages.

Implement a resource controller with 4 operations:

- `Allocate`: to allocate one resource,
- `Deallocate`: to deallocate a resource
- `Hold`: to inhibit allocation until a call to
- `Resume`: which allows allocation again.

There are the following constraints on these operations:

1. `Allocate` is accepted when resources are available and the controller is not held (synchronization on local state and history)
2. `Deallocate` is accepted when resources have been allocated (synchronization on local state)
3. calls to `Hold` must be serviced before calls to `Allocate` (synchronization on type of request)
4. calls to `Resume` are accepted only when the controller is held (synchronization on history information).

As Ada 95 has no deontic logic operators, not all history information can be expressed directly in barriers. However, it is possible to use local state variables to record execution history. The following solution simplifies the presentation by modelling the resources by a counter indicating the number of free resources. Requirement 2 is interpreted as meaning that an exception can be raised if an attempt is made to deallocate resources which have not yet been allocated.

```
package Rsc_Controller is
  Max_Resources_Available  : constant Natural := 100; --  For example
  No_Resources_Allocated  : exception; -- raised by deallocate

  protected type Simple_Resource_Controller is tagged
    entry Allocate;
    procedure Deallocate;
    entry Hold;
    entry Resume;
  private
    Free    : Natural := Max_Resources_Available;
    Taken   : Natural := 0;
    Locked  : Boolean := False;
    entry Allocate    when Free > 0 and not Locked and     --  req. 1
                           Hold'Count = 0;                 --  req. 3
    entry Hold        when not Locked;
    entry Resume      when Locked;                         --  req. 4
  end Simple_Resource_Controller;
end Rsc_Controller;
```

The body of this package simply keeps track of the resources taken and freed, and sets and resets the `Locked` variable.

```
package body Rsc_Controller is

 protected body Simple_Resource_Controller is
    entry Allocate when Free > 0 and not Locked and Hold'Count = 0 is
    begin ... end Allocate;
    procedure Deallocate is begin ... end Deallocate;
    entry Hold when not Locked is begin ... end Hold;
    entry Resume when Locked is begin ... end Resume;
  end Simple_Resource_Controller;
end Rsc_Controller
```

[ ] then extend the problem to consider the impact of inheritance:

> Extend this resource controller to add a method: `Allocate_N` which takes an integer parameter `N` and then allocates `N` resources. The extension is subject to the following additional requirements:
>
> 5. Calls to `Allocate_N` are accepted only when there are at least `N` available resources.
> 6. Calls to `Deallocate` must be serviced before calls to `Allocate` or `Allocate_N`.

Note that this specification is flawed, and the implementation shown in [ ] also exhibits this flaw: if `Deallocate` is called when no resources are allocated, the resource controller will deadlock and not service any calls to `Deallocate`, `Allocate`, or `Allocate_N`. In this implementation, this has been corrected implicitly, because calling `Deallocate` when no resources are allocated is viewed as an error and an exception is raised.

Requirement 5 is implemented by requeuing to `Wait_For_N` if not enough resources are available.

Requirement 6 is implicitly fulfiled because calls to `Deallocate` are never queued since `Deallocate` is implemented as a procedure.

```
with Rsc_Controller; use Rsc_Controller;
package Advanced_Controller is
  protected type Advanced_Resource_Controller is
    new Simple_Resource_Controller with
    entry Allocate_N (N : in Natural);
    procedure Deallocate;
     --  Ada-specific anomaly: because barriers cannot access parameters,
     --  we must also override this method so that we can set 'Changed'.
  private
     entry Allocate_N when Free > 0 and not Locked and      --  req. 1
             Hold'Count = 0;                                 --  req. 3

   Current_Queue : Boolean := False;
     --  Indicates which of the two 'Wait_For_N' entry queues is the one
     --  that currently shall be used. (Two queues are used: one queue
     --  is used when trying to satisfy requests, requests that cannot
     --  be satisfied are requeued to the other. Then, the roles of the
```

```
    --  two queues are swapped. This avoids problems when the calling
    --  tasks have different priorities.)


   Changed        : Boolean := False;
    --  Set whenever something is deallocated. Needed for correct
    --  implementation of 'Allocate_N' and 'Wait_For_N'. Reset each
    --  time outstanding calls to these routines have been serviced.
    --  'Changed' actually encodes the history information "Wait_For_N"
    --   and is only accepted after a call to 'Deallocate'.

   entry Wait_For_N (for Queue in Boolean) (N : in Natural);
   entry Wait_For_N (for Queue in Boolean) when
   not Locked and Hold'Count = 0 and (Queue = Current_Queue) and Changed;
     --  This private entry is used by 'Allocate_N' to requeue to if
     --  less than N resources are currently available.
  end Advanced_Resource_Controller;
end Advanced_Controller;

package body Advanced_Controller

  protected body Advanced_Resource_Controller is
    procedure Deallocate is
      --  Overridden to account for new history information encoding
      --  needed for access to parameter in the barrier of Allocate_N.
    begin ... end Deallocate;

    entry Allocate_N (N : in Natural) when Free > 0 and
              not Locked and Hold'Count = 0 is
    begin ... end Allocate_N;

    entry Wait_For_N (for Queue in Boolean)(N : in Natural) when
               not Locked and Hold'Count = 0 and
              (Queue = Current_Queue) and Changed is
    begin ... end Wait_For_N;
  end Advanced_Resource_Controller;
end Advanced_Controller;
```

8 Conclusions

This paper has argued that Ada 95's model of concurrency is not well integrated with its object-oriented model. It has focussed on the issue of how to make protected types extensible and yet avoid the pitfalls of the inheritance anomaly. The approach adopted has been to introduce the notion of a tagged protected type which has the same underlying philosophy as normal tagged types.

Although the requirements for extensible protected types are easily articulated, there are many potential solutions. The paper has explored the major issues and, where appropriate, has made concrete proposals. Ada is an extremely expressive language with many orthogonal features. The paper has shown that the introduction of extensible protected types does not undermine that orthogonality. The work presented here, however, has not been without its difficulties. The major one is associated with overridden entries.

The paper has considered the basic extensible protected type model. Of course, any proposal for the introduction of such a facility must also consider the full implications of its introduction. It has been beyond the scope of this paper to address these issues - see [ ].

References

1. T. Bloom. Evaluating synchronisation mechanisms. In *Proceedings of the Seventh ACM Symposium on Operating System Principles*, pages 24–32, Pacific Grove, 1979.
2. A. Burns and A. J. Wellings. *Concurrency in Ada.* Cambridge University Press, second edition, 1998.
3. O. P. Kiddle and A. J. Wellings. Extended protected types. In *Proceedings of ACM SIGAda Annual International Conference (SIGAda 98)*, pages 229–239, November 1998.
4. S. Matsuoka and A. Yonezawa. Analysis of inheritance anomaly in object-oriented concurrent programming languages. In *Research Directions in Concurrent Object-Oriented Programming*, pages 107–150. MIT Press, 1993.
5. B. Meyer. *Object-Oriented Software Construction.* Prentice Hall, second edition, 1997.
6. S. Michell and K. Lundqvist. Extendible dispatchable task communication mechanisms. In *Proceedings of IRTAW9, Ada Letters, Vol XIX(2)*, pages 54–59, 1999.
7. S. E. Mitchell and A. J. Wellings. Synchronisation, concurrent object-oriented programming and the inheritance anomaly. *Computer Languages*, 22(1), 1996.
8. A. J. Wellings, S. Mitchell, and A. Burns. Object-oriented programming with protected types in Ada 95. *International Journal of Mini and Micro Computers*, 18(3):130–136, 1996.
9. A. J. Wellings, B. Johnson, B. Sanden, J. Kienzle, T. Wolf, and S. Michell. Integrating object-oriented programming and protected types in Ada 95. YCS 316, Department of Computer Science, University of York, UK, 1999.

Is an Ada Lint Necessary?

Björn Källberg

CelsiusTech Systems AB
S Järfälla Sweden
bjkae@celsiustech.se

Abstract Every month since June has a small C C program been part of an advertisement series for a semantic checker for C C PC lint Each program contains errors which are not detected by a C C compiler but by the company's product Up to December programs have been publicised These C C programs has been analyzed in order to see which of the errors a normal Ada compiler will detect if the programs had been written in Ada The result is that of the errors are detected The remaining errors indicate areas where improvements in Ada compilers are helpful

Background

Ada is a language which is more rigorously defined or has less freedom and less flexibility than the languages C C As a consequence an Ada compiler can do more checks and discover errors that the less checking C C compiler can not detect In order to improve the error checks for C C programs there are semantic checkers which analyze C C programs and give warnings where it is probable that the program author has made a mistake

The first widely spread program of this type was developed for Unix and was called "lint" Since then "lint" has been used as a generic name for these semantic checkers The original meaning of "lint" is the small bits of light fiber which stick to your clothing and you have to use sticky paper to get off The suit is still perfectly useful with the lint on but it looks better if it has been picked clean In the same way a lint program removes the logical lint of a program A difference is that the lint on the suit does not make the suit unusable whereas the lint of a program very often will prevent the program from fulfilling its intended purpose

Ada advocates often claim that these lint checkers are not needed for Ada because the Ada compiler does all these checks anyhow Are these claims true? This paper tries to answer this question by analyzing a set of C C programs The analysis is done by rewriting the test programs in Ada and see if the Ada compiler or runtime will detect the problems In obvious cases the rewriting has only been done mentally e g a program was not written to ensure that the Ada runtime detects attempts to access an array beyond its end

---

PC Lint is a trademark of Gimpel Software

H B Keller and E Plödereder Eds Ada Europe LNCS pp

Test Set

The company Gimpel Software makes a product called PC lint Every month since July a new advertisement with a small C C program has been publicized in trade journals This C C program is a legal C C program which can be compiled linked and executed However it does not produce the result the programmer expected There is an error bug in it By running the program through the company's lint checker at least one warning is produced which indicates the error Fig gives example of a complete program

```
  #include <iostream.h>

  int sum( int a[], int n )
      {
      int i;
      int s = 0;
      for( i = 0, i < n; i++;)
      s += a[i];

      return s;
      }

  int a[10] = { 0, 1, 2, 3, 4, 5, 6,
7, 8, 9 };

  int main()
      {
      cout   <<   "the   sum   is   "   <<
sum(a,10) << "\n";
      return 0;
      }
```

The programmer expected this program to print that the sum is Instead it prints that the sum is How come?

Fig Example program extracted from the advertisement from November

All programs publicized in this series from June through December have been analyzed In total there are programs All programs and the associated warnings are available on the www [ ]

Use of this test set has a number of advantages The programs are printed and distributed and probably read by a large number of people The errors in the programs must also be interesting to the potential buyer of the product If an error is so simple that it can be detected by a glance nobody would be interested to buy a product to detect such an obvious mistake On the other hand the programs and the errors can not be too contrived If so the potential buyer would not be interested either Thus these programs are selected by the advertisers to show common mistakes that an ordinary programmer are likely to make and which are hard to detect

One potential disadvantage with this test set is that errors that are not detected by the company's tool will not be included

Classification

For this study the errors have been classified in four different categories The category name answers the question "Would this error have been detected by an Ada compiler" Table gives a summary of the error categories

Table Classification of errors

Category	Explanation
Yes	The problem will be detected by the Ada compiler during compilation
Yes runtime	The Ada run time checks will detect the problem
Probably	It is possible to write an Ada program which will not detect the problem but such an Ada program will deviate significantly from normal Ada usage Thus in practice the problem will most likely be detected by the Ada compiler
No	The problem will occur also with an Ada program

Below are the different categories explained further An example program belonging to each category is included Also shown are parts of the output from the lint tool together with the reasoning that led to the chosen categorization

Category "Yes"

Errors classified as category "Yes" are the errors that an Ada compiler will detect during the compilation phase

Fig is an example of such a program The output from the PC lint program is

```
for( i = 0, i < n; i++; )
Warning 520: Expected void type, assignment, increment
or decrement
```

The problem is that the programmer has mistakenly written a comma instead of a semicolon Thus the boolean expression becomes part of the init expression the comma being the sequence operator The boolean is evaluated but not used as the exit condition the cond expression Instead the operation i is evaluated as a boolean C C do not have a boolean type but any integer or pointer suffice Thus there is no type conflict The increment operation or loop expression is empty

This error has been classified as being detected by an Ada compiler for multiple reasons First the Ada for statement is simpler but has enough functionality to allow a direct replacement in this case In an Ada for loop statement it is not possible to exchange one character and still have a legal Ada program But even if the C C for loop was translated into an Ada while loop the Ada difference between statements and expressions and the Ada type checking would prevent this program from passing the compiler

Category “Yes runtime ”

Errors classified as category “Yes runtime ” are the errors that an Ada run time system will detect during execution The Ada program will not produce wrong result but an exception will be raised If not handled the exception name will be printed out to the programmer often with a trace back indicating the exact line

```
const int KMAX = 30;
double q[KMAX];

void f( double limit )
          {
          double s = 1;
          int k = 0;
          q[0] = 0;
          while( q[k] <= limit && k < KMAX
              {
              k++;
              s = s * (k+1);
              q[k] = q[k-1] + s;
              }
          }
```

There is a time bomb lurking in this whittled down extraction of a larger program Can you spot it?

Fig Example of a program from Feb where the Ada run time will detect the problem

Fig shows an example of such a program The output from the PC lint program is

```
q[k] = q[k-1] + s;
Warning 661: Possible access of out-of-bounds pointer(1
beyond end of data) by operator '['
```

The problem is that the program will access the array beyond its end The Ada range checking will detect this problem during runtime

Category “Probably”

Some errors are classified as category “Probably” These programs can be translated literally but the resulting program will not use typical Ada patterns If translated literally the problem will be undetected by an Ada compiler However using a translation using normal Ada patterns i e the way an Ada programmer would code the error will not occur

```
#include <stdlib.h>
#include <stdio.h>

void f( int n )
     {
     if( n > 0 )
            {
            int labs, research;

            research = n-1;
            if( research > 15 ) labs = 3;
            else labs = 0;

            if( labs ) labs *= 100;
            }

     if( labs )
     printf( "%d - 1 is greater than 15\n", n );
     }

int main() { f(13); return 0; }
```

This program prints the information that is greater than What's going on and why was no diagnostic produced?

Fig Example of a program from Sep The corresponding Ada program would probably not have this problem

Fig shows an example of such a program The output from the PC lint program is

```
int labs, research;
bug578.cpp(8)  : Warning 578: Declaration of 'labs'
hides 'labs(long)' (line 435, file
C:\msdev5\INCLUDE\stdlib.h)
```

The problem here is that there are two variables named "labs" one hiding the other A declaration in an inner block hides a variable name also in Ada Here the variable is declared in the block of the if clause Fig show a direct translation to Ada

```
with text_io; use Text_io;
with Ada.Integer_text_io; use ada.integer_text_io;
procedure main is
       procedure f(N : integer) is
       begin
            if n>0 then
                declare
                      labs, research : integer;
                begin
                      Research := N-1;
                      if research>15 then
                      labs := 3;
                      else
```

```
                              labs := 0;
                         end if;

                         if labs>0 then labs :=
labs*100; end if;
                    end;
               end if;

               if labs>0 then
                    put(N);
                    put_line("-1 is greater than 15");
               end if;
        end F;

begin
        F(13);
end;
```

Fig Direct translation of program in fig to Ada It is unlikely that an Ada programmer should write the program in this way with an extra block statement

In Ada you do not normally code an if statement with an inner block statement The inherit structure of the Ada if statement if endif makes the use of an inner block statement unnecessary Thus the problem would probably not occur in Ada There are also other factors which make this problem less likely in Ada Very often "use" clauses are avoided preventing this problem The Ada control of name space e g by nesting packaging limits the number of visible identifiers Also the Ada practice of using long explanatory names makes the problem less likely e g using the name "Default_Width" by chance

```
#include "iostream.h"
void f( int i )
    {
    if( i != 4 || i != 5 ) return;
    cout << "hello world\n" ;
    }

int main()
    {
    f( 3 );
    f( 4 );
    f( 5 );
    return 0;
    }
```

The programmer was surprised to receive no output What s going on?

Fig Example of a program from Apr where the problem will occur also in an Ada program

Category "No"

Errors classified as category "No" are the errors will occur also in an Ada program and which the Ada compiler will not detect Fig shows an example of such a program

The output from the PC lint program is

```
if( i != 4 || i != 5 ) return;
Info 774: Boolean within 'if' always evaluates to True
```

The problem is that the logical condition is wrong It is always true The same problem will occur in the Ada code If the fundamental cause of the problem is that the programmer has interpreted "||" as the logical operator "and" instead of "or" then the problem would not occur in the Ada case and the category would be "Yes" instead However in cases like this where the categorization depends on the thoughts of the programmer the choice that is least favorable to Ada has been chosen

Results

Table shows the summary results of the analysis and classification of the programs In table are the classifications for the individual programs given An explanation of the cause of the error is given This explanation is not the text of the warnings that the PC lint program produced but a more specific explanatin It was not always obvious from the warning texts what the problem original problem was

Table Summary of error classification

Category	Count	Percentage
Yes	[illegible]	[illegible]
Yes runtime	[illegible]	[illegible]
Probably	[illegible]	[illegible]
No	[illegible]	[illegible]

Table Error cause in the analyzed programs

Date	Reason	Category
Jun [illegible]	Possibility of passing a null pointer to a library function than can not handle null pointers	Yes runtime
Jul [illegible]	An intended declaration of a class instance with no parameters to the constructor became a function prototype as an empty pair of parentheses were used	Yes
Aug [illegible]	A function is implemented as a macro and has side effects as it evaluates a parameter twice and the parameter has the form p	Yes

Sept □□□□	Declaration of a variable inside a block hides another variable with the same name in an outer scope□ Outside the block the name is used but refers now to an outer variable in the one of the predefined header files□ See Oct □□□□	Probably
Okt □□□□	Possibility of dereferencing a null pointer	Yes □runtime□
Nov □□□□	Programmer wanted to declare a pointer to a □□ character string but created a vector of □□ pointers to a string□ Problem caught by C□□ compiler□	Yes
Dec □□□□	Logical error in program caused a logical expression to always evaluate to false	No
Jan □□□□	Use of uninitialized variable	No
Feb □□□□	Precedence of equality and boolean operator is not what the programmer expected□	Yes
Mar □□□□	Redefinition of delete do not check for null pointers	Yes □runtime□
Apr □□□□	The "default" selector in a switch statement became a label due to misspelling□	Yes
May □□□□	Calls to virtual functions from a constructor will not be dispatching which the programmer intended	Yes
Jun □□□□	Division with unsigned and signed causes surprising results □as the signed value is implicitly converted to unsigned	Yes
Jul □□□□	Calling delete before an object is completely defined causes unpredictable results	Yes
Aug □□□□	Writing a comma instead of a full stop in the comparison □"y<□□□□" As the comma is a sequence operator and the □□ was implicitly converted to float□ no error except wrong result was detected	Yes
Sep □□□□	Programmer did not fully understand how a copy constructor for a base class should be constructed	Probably
Oct □□□□	Same as sep □□□□	Probably
Nov □□□□	Possibility of writing beyond the end of an array	Yes □runtime□
Dec □□□□	Possibility writing beyond the end of an array due to implicit conversion of a signed to an unsigned	Yes
Jan □□□□	Natural way of making an array of subclass instances gives wrong result□ Implicit conversion from pointer to array to pointer of base class□	Yes
Feb □□□□	Access beyond array range	Yes □runtime□
Mar □□□□	Parameter profile of overriding primitive operation is not the same as the original	No
Apr □□□□	Accessing elements of a pointer which is null	Yes □runtime□
May □□□□	Dangling reference by returning address of a variable with a deeper accessability level □i□e□ local variable in subprogram□	Yes
Jun □□□□	Incorrect understanding of order of implicit and explicit type conversions	Yes

Jul	If another default value is used when redefining a primitive operation the default value of the parent operation is used anyhow	No
Aug	Implicit conversions in a comparison between signed and unsigned	Probably
Sep	Precedence of shift operator is not what the programmer expected	Yes
Oct	See Sep	Probably
Nov	An extra pair of parenthesises caused a declaration of a local variable to become an excutable statement type conversion	Yes
Dec	Preprocessor variables do not require a declaration Undeclared variables can be used but are initialized to A misspelling of a variable introduced a new variable	Yes
Jan	Comparing floats for equality	No
Feb	Trying to deallocate a static variable	Yes
Mar	Missing semicolon made following statements part of class c	Yes
Apr	Logical error in program caused a logical expression to always evaluate to false	No
May	Uninitialized variable accessed	No
Jun	Misspelled integer literal a final letter "l" instead of number	Yes
Jul	Uninitalized variable accessed	No
Aug	Implicit conversion to float of the result of a division of integers occurs later than the programmer expected	Yes
Sep	Same as jan	Yes
Oct	Implicit conversion between integer types combined with no range checking	Yes
Nov	Used comma instead of semicolon in a for loop which caused the loop not to be executed	Yes
Dec	Incorrect use of break programmer thought it provided an exit of the enclosing loop instead of the enclosing switch statement Cf the ATT bug	Yes

Analysis

In this chapter some of the more common error causes are discussed Three major classes can be distinguished More than half of all errors are caused by these type of errors

Typographical Mistakes

The syntax of C C is such that just a small change in the program text can cause the text to still be valid but its meaning is completely changed The small change can be due to a typing error This is a fairly common problem apr aug nov dec mar jun nov

Too a much larger extent Ada uses unabbreviated keywords instead of special characters which minimizes this risk The flexibility in C C with no clear distinction between expressions and statements as well as the comma operator increases the risk that an unintended meaning is obtained

It was the intent by the original designers of Ada to avoid all such problems where a small typing error was not detected by the compiler [ ] This design goal has obviously been reached

Implicit Conversions

Sometimes when programming in Ada the strict typing without implicit conversions can be felt as a heavy burden You might long for the implicit conversion between the numeric types that C C has However many of the problems in this survey are caused by the implicit conversions jun aug jun aug jun aug oct

Misunderstanding of Syntax

C C has a terse syntax relying to a large extent on special characters These characters are cleverly used in different syntactic constructs The disadvantage is that the meaning of a construct is not obvious and can be misunderstood A programmer might hesitate between two ways of writing it Combined with the flexibility which might make the wrong alternative also to be a valid syntax this causes many errors jul nov feb apr may jul sep jan nov dec All of these but one are definitely impossible to make in Ada and the remaining is classified as "probably detected by the Ada compiler"

Problems Not Caught

Analysis of the problems that are not caught by an Ada compiler can give hints where Ada compilers could or should be improved Ada compilers do not detect four large classes of problems

Uninitialized Variables

Uninitialized variables are a problem in most programming languages jan dec may jul These can cause errors which are very difficult to detect

Unreachable Statements

A program where parts of the code can never be executed is probably wrong Thus detection of unreachable statements can detect logical errors dec apr as well as making it possible to remove unnecessary statements

Unreferenced Variables

A similar problem as unreachable statements exists with variables that are never accessed In the same way unreferenced variables probably indicate a logical error Such warnings are also helpful to clean up programs after modifications where some variables have become unnecessary

Misspelling an Overriding Operation

Misspelling an overriding operation will cause a new primitive operation to be defined instead of redefining the existing one This new operation will of course not be called by dispatching calls One example in the Ada case with controlled types may be to write Initialise instead of Initialize This is similar to the problem mar where a different parameter profile caused a primitive operation to be a new operation instead of overriding an existing one For Ada this became a practical problem with Ada even if the problem also exists for Ada

Improvements

These four types of problems are difficult in two ways Often they cause errors that can be very difficult for the programmer to detect But it is also difficult to implement the checks in a good way It is generally an unsolvable problem to detect these errors in all cases However there are algorithms that can detect a substantial part of these problems Compiler manufacturers are looking at some of these One example is []

Very few Ada compiler vendors incorporate any of these four types of checks in their compilers The first versions of the Dec Ada compiler did a good job in for unitialized variables and unreachable statement In later versions this had been removed The cases analyzed here have been tested with two of the most popular PC compilers GNAT and Aonix With the normal settinwgs the GNAT compiler has a very simple check for uninitialized variables However a switch exists Wunitialized o which will catch the error Otherwise none of these problems are detected

The Ada language defines what constitutes a legal Ada program but gives no restrictions on the warning messages nor any other messages that the compiler can issue Thus there is no formal reason for not implementing extra checks

Practical reasons for not implementing these checks could be longer compilation times too much complexity in an already complex compiler or simply a lack of resources Of course also for Ada a separate lint program could be used Optional error checks in the compiler itself is probably preferred both for ease of use and for compilation and performance reasons

It is the view of the author that it would be very valuable if Ada compilers could do these checks, perhaps not always, but at least optionally.

[illegible] Conclusion

An Ada compiler detects most of the problems that a lint program does ([illegible] more than [illegible] in this survey). However, there are [illegible] large classes of problems, which are normally not detected by an Ada compiler. They account for approximately [illegible] of all problems. These problems can either be detected by a separate Ada lint program, or by improvement of the Ada compilers.

References

[illegible] Homepage of Gimpel Software, http://www.gimpel.com

[illegible] Ichbiah, Heliard, Roubine, Barnes, Krieg-Brueckner, Wichmann: "Rationale for the Design of the Ada Programming Language", SIGPLAN Notices, vol [illegible], no [illegible], pt B (June [illegible])

[illegible] Bernstein, Duff: "Optimizing Ada on the Fly", Ada letters XIX no [illegible], Sep [illegible]

Using Java™ APIs with Native Ada Compilers

Shayne Flint and Brian Dobbing

Ainslie Software Pty Limited
Suite Marcus Clarke Street Canberra City ACT Australia

shayne@ainslie-software.com

Aonix Europe Limited
Partridge House Newtown Road Henley on Thames Oxon RG EN U K

brian@uk.aonix.com

Abstract Ada is an ISO standard Object Oriented programming language specifically designed to support the cost effective development of robust maintainable software Because of this Ada is widely used in the development of critical systems such as commercial aircraft However despite its advantages and general purpose nature Ada is not often used for the development of main stream applications This is partly because of Ada's poor integration with contemporary technologies such as Graphical User Interfaces Described within this paper is a technique which uses the Java Native Interface to provide Ada programmers with immediate access to any software that has a Java API thus substantially improving the suitability of Ada for the development of a wide range of applications

Introduction

For more than a decade Ada has proved to be a superior language for supporting the development and maintenance of large systems [ ][ ] Its use leads to better productivity reduced costs more reuse much lower error rates especially early on and significantly lower maintenance costs While Ada may be an appropriate language for the development of large long lived systems its wider applicability is somewhat limited by a lack of standardised Application Programmer Interfaces APIs to software such as Graphical User Interfaces GUIs Because of this Ada has been largely restricted to the development of software for critical systems such as aircraft railways and air traffic control Ada has seen very little use in main stream computing

Java on the other hand has become popular for the development of portable main stream applications Its flexibility is due in part to the availability of a wide range of portable APIs If these Java APIs are made available to Ada programmers then Ada can become a more viable language for development of the same kinds of applications

H B Keller and E Plödereder Eds Ada Europe LNCS pp

while maintaining the characteristics required for the cost effective development and maintenance of large systems

This paper contains a description of a system called *AdaJNI* which has been developed to support the use of Java APIs with native Ada compilers A number of issues associated with the mapping of Java classes to Ada along with approaches for dealing with them are also discussed

Background

The integration of Ada with Java APIs can be achieved in a number of ways One approach is that adopted within the AppletMagic™ compiler [ ] developed by Intermetrics Inc This is a special Ada compiler which can generate code to run on the Java Virtual Machine JavaVM and is supplied with Ada bindings to the Java API's This approach provides a good solution for the development of portable software such as applets for the internet

There are however cases in which the use of a native Ada compiler is required or desirable In such cases a different approach to that of AppletMagic is needed to integrate Ada with Java APIs The Java Native Interface JNI which supports the integration of Java and C offers an approach to using Java APIs with native Ada compilers The JNI is a C library supplied with the Sun Java Development Kit JDK [ ] It allows C programmers to make requests on the JavaVM to create Java objects call methods and to read write fields By creating an Ada binding to the JNI Ada applications could be written to create and manipulate Java objects in the same way

While JNI Ada bindings are sufficient to provide Ada with access to Java classes they do not provide an 'Ada like' interface to each Java class To call a Java method using JNI bindings the programmer would ordinarily make a series of calls to the JNI to obtain a class ID and method ID to marshal the required parameters for the call and to request the JavaVM to call the method This does not follow the normal Ada procedure calling mechanism and would be impractical for normal application development Ideally an Ada package corresponding to each Java class in a given Java API should be available to the Ada programmer The specifications of such packages would contain subprograms corresponding to the methods of each class thus providing a simple 'Ada style' interface The Ada package bodies would manage the low level interface to the JNI using the JNI bindings

AdaJNI

AdaJNI **Ada** to **J**ava **N**ative **I**nterface is an implementation of the JNI based integration approach described above The runtime system comprises four major components which interact with an Ada application built with a compilation system such as Aonix ObjectAda™ for Windows [ ] and the Java environment provided by Sun JDK [ ] as depicted in Figure The *Java Native Interface Ada Bindings* are the basis upon which AdaJNI is constructed They provide a low level interface to the Java Virtual Machine using the JNI API The *AdaJNI Runtime Packages* manage the mapping of Java language features such as arrays strings and exceptions to Ada as well as the marshalling of parameters passed to Java methods

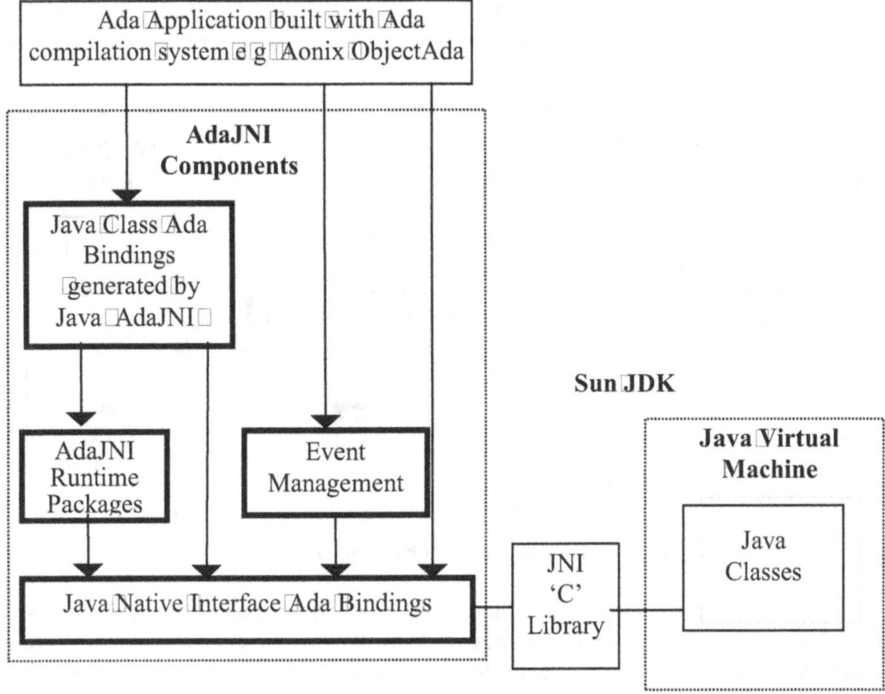

Fig The AdaJNI Architecture

The *Java Class Ada Bindings* provide an interface between the Ada application and Java classes These bindings comprise an Ada package for each Java class required by the application The specifications of such packages provide an Ada Style interface to a specific class including all of the class' constructors methods and fields The binding package bodies contain code which maps the Ada interface to the underlying JavaVM via the *JNI Ada Bindings* and *Runtime Packages*

The *Event Management* component integrates the Java Event Model [ ] with the AdaJNI environment and thus Ada The AdaJNI event management approach is more fully described in section of this paper

Binding Generator Tool

In order to ensure that Ada developers are able to make use of any Java API a tool has been developed to automatically generate the *Java Class Ada Bindings* described above As depicted in Figure *Java AdaJNI* processes Java classes and optionally Java source code to generate Ada source code in the form of Ada packages which provide access to the services of a specified Java class. When a class is processed, *Java AdaJNI* will extract information about the class using the standard *java.lang.reflect* API. This information is used to generate an Ada package specification containing data types and subprograms which correspond to the constructors, methods and fields of the Java class. *Java AdaJNI* also generates a corresponding package body which contains the Ada code required to interface the Java class.

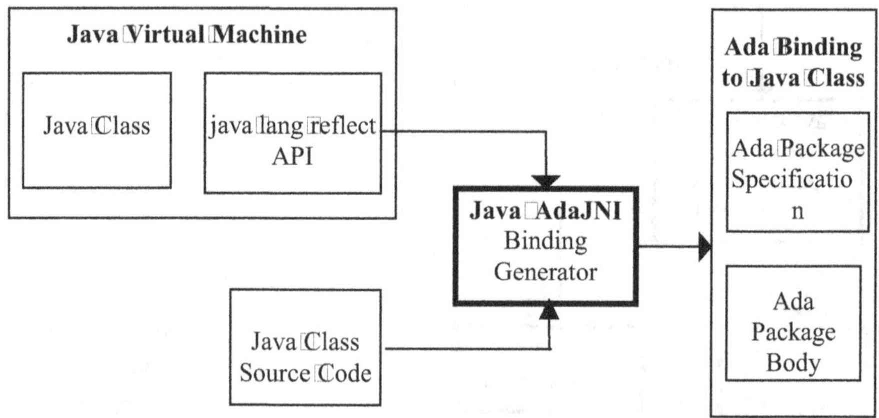

Fig. The Java AdaJNI Binding Generator

While functional bindings can be generated solely from information provided via the *java.lang.reflect* API, such bindings will not have correct parameter names for constructors and methods because the API does not provide parameter name information. In such cases parameters are named P, P, etc.

If, on the other hand, a Java source file is processed, parameter names and *JavaDoc* comments are extracted from the source file. This information is used in conjunction with information extracted via the *java.lang.reflect* API to generate a complete binding which includes the correct parameter names for constructors and methods along with documentation comments.

Java AdaJNI has been used to generate complete bindings to all of the normal Java API's (Awt, lang, net, etc.) [ ] and the Java Foundation Classes [ ] without any manual re-working. The tool can also be used by the Ada programmer to generate bindings to other Java classes. In short, *Java AdaJNI* provides the Ada programmer with immediate access to any software which has a Java API.

Mapping Java Classes to Ada

In general terms, the AdaJNI approach maps each Java class to a separate Ada package. Each package contains a tagged record *Object* type which reflects the corresponding Java class inheritance hierarchy. A *Reference* type is also declared as an access type to the *Object* type. Values of these *Reference* types are initialised by constructors and refer to Java objects managed by the JavaVM. The remainder of each package comprises Ada subprograms corresponding to each constructor and method of the class along with subprograms to manipulate any fields in the Java class.

For a tool such as *Java2AdaJNI* to be effective it must automatically and completely generate these Ada packages so that the Ada programmer can make use of any Java class without delay. In order to achieve this aim a number of issues have been addressed during the development of AdaJNI and are discussed below.

Circularities in Java Classes

Many Java classes contain circularities in dependencies. For example, the *java.lang.String* class depends on *java.lang.StringBuffer* which in turn depends on *java.lang.String* causing a circularity. This is a problem when generating Ada because the language does not allow circularities between Ada package specifications. A strategy which automatically handles circularities in Java classes is therefore adopted by *AdaJNI*.

The strategy involves the use of two package specifications for each Java class. The first (primary) package contains data types for the subject class together with subprograms for each Java class constructor, method and field. A portion of the primary specification for the *java.awt.Button* class is shown below.

```
with Ada_JNI.Bindings.Java_Awt.Component;
package Ada_JNI.Bindings.Java_Awt.Button is
  type Object is new
     Ada_JNI.Bindings.Java_Awt.Component.Object
        with null record;
  type Reference is access all Object'class;
  ... constructors, methods etc.
```

The second (Secondary) package contains similar data types along with array types and associated array handling packages. A portion of the secondary specification for the *java.awt.Button* class is shown below. The major difference between the two packages is in the parent package name. Primary packages are children of the *Ada_JNI.Bindings* package, while secondary packages are children of the *Ada_JNI.Binding_Types* package.

```
with Ada_JNI.Binding_Types.Java_Awt.Component;
package Ada_JNI.Binding_Types.Java_Awt.Button is
  type Object is new
     Ada_JNI.Binding_Types.Java_Awt.Component.Object
        with null record;
  type Reference is access all Object'class;
  type Reference_Array is array ...
  type Reference_Array_2D is array ...
  ... array management packages
```

Note that the secondary specification data types mirror those in the primary specification except that *Object* in the secondary specification descends from *Object* defined in the *secondary* specification for the class *java.awt.Component*. In other words, the type hierarchy in secondary packages is the same as that in the primary packages except that they have a different root.

The primary specification contains the methods and fields of the Java class. It is the parameter data types of these methods that cause the circularities described earlier. By declaring parameters of types declared in secondary packages rather than types defined in primary packages, all circularities can be removed. For example, the following *String* constructor refers to the secondary specification for the *String_Buffer* data type rather than the primary specification. Because the secondary specification contains only the data types and no methods etc., there are no dependencies. There is therefore no chance of circularities.

```
function New_String
  ( Buffer : in  Ada_JNI.Binding_Types
                 .Java_Lang.String_Buffer.Reference
  ) return Reference;
```

Unfortunately, this approach presents a new problem. While all application objects will be of types declared in primary specifications (constructors return data types from primary specifications), all constructor and method parameters are of types declared in secondary specifications. This means that Objects created with constructors cannot be passed as parameters to methods. This problem has been solved in AdaJNI by providing unary "+" operators in each primary specification which convert between primary and secondary data types. Examples of these operators from the *Java_Lang.String* package are shown below.

```
function "+" ( Ref : in Reference )
return Ada_JNI.Binding_Types.Java_Lang.String.Reference

function "+" ( Ref :
      Ada_JNI.Binding_Types.Java_Lang.String.Reference)
return Reference;
```

By using these operators as shown below, the programmer can effectively ignore the presence of the secondary package. In this example, *My_String* is of a primary type, while the *Label* parameter of the *Set_Label* method is a secondary type. The "+" operator is therefore used to convert *My_String*.

```
declare
  My_String :  Ada_JNI.Bindings
              .Java_Lang.String.Reference;
begin
  My_String := New_String("Hello World");
  Ada_JNI.Bindings.Java_Awt.Button.Set_Label
    ( Ref => My_Button, Label => +My_String );
end;
```

This simple imposition requiring use of the "+" operator is the only impact of the strategy to remove all circularities. It is considered to be superior to other techniques which rely on the manual rearrangement of package specifications to resolve circularities.

Mapping Java Names to Ada Names

Java is a case sensitive language which distinguishes between names such as 'Test' and 'test'. Ada, on the other hand, is not case sensitive so that 'Test' and 'test' are considered the same name. Within Java packages and classes it is common to find entities which have the same profile (i.e. methods with the same parameter types or fields with the same data type) and names which only differ in case. Such entities would be considered the same in Ada and therefore illegal.

AdaJNI uses various strategies to resolve such naming conflicts. In general, simple name conflicts such as Test and TEST are resolved by appending integers so that TEST become Test_. Only those name conflicts which are illegal in Ada are resolved and, where possible, the names of methods are changed first, followed by fields, then constructors and finally inner classes. This prioritisation minimises the impact of awkward names with appended numbers.

Within AdaJNI a different approach is applied to the naming of Java packages. There are many cases in the Java API's where Java's case sensitivity is used to distinguish the names of packages and classes. For example there is a package called *java.awt.event* and a class called *java.awt.Event*. These names cannot be distinguished in Ada and adding a number to one of the names would result in awkward class or package names. In order to eliminate this problem, Java hierarchical package names are mapped to a single Ada package name, e.g. *Java.awt* maps to *Java_Awt* and *java.awt.event* maps to *Java_Awt_Event*. Essentially, dots in the Java package name are replaced by underscores in the Ada package name thus avoiding a large class of name conflicts without having to resort to awkward numbering schemes.

Note that the class *java.awt.Event* maps to *Java_Awt.Event* and that if there were two packages named *java.awt.event* and *java.awt.Event*, their names would map to *Java_Awt_Event* and *Java_Awt_Event_*.

Finally, *Java/AdaJNI* converts Java names to Ada style names using a simple well defined algorithm. For example '*clearRect*' becomes '*Clear_Rect*' and '*setXORMode*' becomes '*Set_XOR_Mode*'.

Java Constructors

Java constructors are mapped to Ada functions which take the same parameters as the corresponding Java constructor and return a *Reference* to a new object created in the Java Virtual Machine. This reference is used to refer to the object in subsequent operations. Constructor functions are used as follows:

```
My_Button : Ada_JNI.Bindings.Java_Awt.Button.Reference
  := Ada_JNI.Bindings.Java_Awt.Button.New_Button
       ( Label => +New_String("Press Me") );
```

Abstract Classes and Methods

AdaJNI does not map abstract Java classes and methods to abstract Ada types and subprograms. Instead, AdaJNI maps abstract classes to Ada bindings in a similar way as it does for normal classes That is abstract classes are mapped to Ada packages and tagged types and methods defined in abstract classes including abstract methods are mapped to normal Ada subprograms The only difference between bindings to abstract classes and those to normal classes is that the former do not include any constructors This prevents the Ada programmer from creating instances of abstract classes

This approach is used because Java allows abstract classes to be used as data types for objects returned by methods The *java awt Component getGraphics* method for example returns an object of the *java awt Graphics* abstract class When an Ada programmer calls the Ada binding to this method an object of some unknown class extension of *java awt Graphics* is returned The AdaJNI approach allows the Ada programmer to manipulate such objects using the Ada bindings generated by *Java AdaJNI* for the *java awt Graphics* abstract class Calls to Ada subprograms which map to abstract methods in *java awt Graphics* are passed to the Java Virtual Machine for dispatching to the appropriate concrete methods

Java Interfaces

Java interfaces comprise a set of abstract method specifications which are implemented by one or more classes which claim to implement the interface *Java AdaJNI* processes an interface by generating a normal Ada package specification without any constructors or subprograms corresponding to abstract methods ie all methods declared in an interface

In addition to processing the interfaces themselves *Java AdaJNI* is required to perform additional processing on classes which implement interfaces While a given class can only implement extend a single abstract class it may implement any number of interfaces In addition Java interfaces can be used as types for method and constructor parameters An object of any class which implements an interface can be used as a value of that interface type For example the *java awt GridLayout* class implements the *java awt LayoutManager* interface A *GridLayout* object can therefore be used anywhere a *LayoutManager* object is required Because a class can implement any number of interfaces such classes can be treated as being of more than one type

These are important characteristics of Java interfaces which must be supported in the Ada bindings generated by *Java AdaJNI* When *Java AdaJNI* processes a class that implements one or more interfaces it will generate the bindings in the normal way That is it will generate subprograms for each method in the class including those which implement abstract methods declared in the implemented interfaces *Java AdaJNI* will also generate a special function for each implemented interface which converts objects of the current class to each interface type These functions allow an object of the class to be used wherever one of the implemented interfaces is required

For example the *Ada_JNI Bindings Java_Awt Grid_Layout* package contains the following conversion function because the *GridLayout* class implements the *LayoutManager* interface

```
function To_Layout_Manager
   ( Ref : access Object ) return
     Ada_JNI.Bindings.Java_Awt.Layout_Manager.Reference;
```

This function can be used as shown below Because the *Set_Layout* procedure requires a *Layout_Manager* an interface parameter the "*To_layout_Manager*" function is used to convert "*My_Grid_layout*" an instance of the *GridLayout* class which implements the *LayoutManager* interface to the required type Note the use of the " " operator to convert the parameter to the secondary data type required by Set_Layout

```
Ada_JNI.Bindings.Java_Awt.Container.Set_Layout
   ( Ref => My_Container,
     Mgr => +To_Layout_Manager(My_Grid_Layout) );
```

Java Arrays

Java arrays are either arrays of Java object references or arrays of primitive types int short char etc Java arrays can have multiple dimensions and all indices are natural ranges starting at i e n

Ada array types for primitive Java types are declared within primitive data type packages such as *Ada_JNI Java Boolean* and *Ada_JNI Java Float* Child packages provide subprograms to create Java arrays and to convert between Java and Ada arrays AdaJNI supports one two and three dimension arrays

Object arrays are handled by array management packages generated by *Java AdaJNI* for each Java class These packages provide subprograms to create Java arrays and to convert between Ada and Java arrays The packages support one two and three dimension arrays

From the Ada programmers' point of view all arrays are Ada arrays All parameter and function return array types are defined in bindings as Ada arrays Conversion to and from Java arrays goes on within the bodies of the bindings and need not concern the Ada programmer

String Handling

When *Java AdaJNI* processes the *java lang String* class it generates a number of convenience subprograms in addition to its normal processing Additional constructors are provided to support the creation of Java strings based on the values of Ada strings Functions are also provided to convert between Java and Ada strings

Java Exceptions

When an exception occurs in Java an Exception object derived from the *java lang Throwable* class is created and propagated up the call chain until an appropriate exception handler is found When a call is made to a Java method via the JNI and a Java exception is thrown control is returned to the native code without any indication that an exception was thrown. An exception object is created, but it is not propagated to the native calling function. After each call to the JNI, a native function should call a special JNI function to check if an exception has been thrown on the Java side. If an exception has been thrown the function will return a reference to the exception object.

The *Java2AdaJNI* binding generator handles Java exceptions in a simple and effective manner. When a class ultimately derived from *java.lang.Throwable* is processed by *Java2AdaJNI*, an Ada exception declaration is added to the corresponding Ada package specification. When such a package is elaborated, the exception is registered with the AdaJNI runtime along with a reference to the corresponding Java exception class.

Java2AdaJNI also inserts a call to an exception checking procedure (part of the AdaJNI runtime) after every call to a Java method which may throw an exception. The procedure checks for a Java exception and if one has been thrown by the Java method just called, it will raise the corresponding Ada exception as determined by looking up all exceptions registered with the AdaJNI runtime.

From the Ada programmers' point of view, subprograms in the bindings raise exceptions like any other Ada subprogram.

Inner Classes

Java Inner classes come in various flavours. The only ones that affect the bindings are 'Nested top level classes and interfaces' and 'Member Classes'. Normally these inner classes would be mapped to nested Ada packages declared within the package corresponding to the outer class. Because current releases of the Java Development Kit (JDK 1.1.x and 1.2) do not implement the reflection APIs for inner classes, *Java2AdaJNI* must rely on the fact that Java compilers generate a separate class file for every class and inner class found in a given source file. Each of these class files is processed separately by *Java2AdaJNI* in the normal way. If a class is found to be an inner class, the generated Ada package is declared as a child of the Ada package corresponding to the inner class's enclosing class.

Method and Constructor Parameter Names

The *java.lang.reflect* API (upon which *Java2AdaJNI* relies for class information) does not provide information about constructor and method parameter names. In order to generate bindings with correct parameter names *Java2AdaJNI* is able to process Java source files. When processing a source file *Java2AdaJNI* will use the *java.awt.reflect* API to obtain information about every class declared in the source code. This information, supplemented with parameter names extracted from the source code, is then used to generate Ada bindings.

In order to support the use of parameter names obtained from other places such as class documentation, *Java2AdaJNI* is able to generate a text file, called a Java Class Specification (JCS), which closely resembles the structure of a classes Java source code. These JCS files are accepted by *Java2AdaJNI* as standard Java source code. So, if the original source code is not available for a given class and correct parameter names are required *Java AdaJNI* can be directed to process the class file and to generate a corresponding JCS file The JCS file which contains parameter names such as P P etc can then be edited by hand to add the correct parameter names for methods and constructors *Java AdaJNI* can then be used to process the updated JCS file resulting in the generation of a set of bindings with the correct parameter names

JavaDoc Comments

JavaDoc is a tool delivered as part of the Java Development Kit which generates HTML documentation for any given Java class The documentation is based in part on specially formatted comments in the source code for a class *Java AdaJNI* is able to extract these comments when processing Java source files and to add them to the corresponding Ada package specification

Ada Tasking

When using the JNI a Java environment reference must be passed to all JNI functions This reference is created by the JavaVM and is only valid for a particular thread When a thread wishes to make use of JNI it must first attach itself to the JavaVM This operation returns a new environment reference which must be used in subsequent calls to the JNI from that thread

Because most Ada compilers use threads to implement tasks a strategy is needed to ensure that tasks can safely make calls to the JNI This is achieved in *AdaJNI* by requiring all tasks to make calls to the AdaJNI runtime procedures *Attach_Task* and *Detach_Task* The *Attach_Task* procedure is called at the start of a task It attaches the calling task's thread to the JavaVM and stores the associated Java environment reference using the standard *Ada Task_Attributes* package The *Detach* procedure is called at the end of a task to disassociate the calling tasks thread from the Java VM

Note that the *Attach_Task* and *Detach_Task* procedures are called automatically for the main thread and can therefore be ignored by the programmer of non tasking applications

Event Handling

The *Abstract Windows Toolkit* AWT [ ] and *Java Beans* [ ] share a common event model based on *event listeners* A number of pre defined *event listener interfaces* are provided with Java to model the handling of events associated with things such as mouse use window manipulation and slider control Classes which implement these interfaces are developed by the programmer to provide application specific event processing Instances of these classes are then registered with event source objects such as buttons When an event is generated by a source object it is passed to each registered event listener object for processing

The event management system adopted by AdaJNI integrates the standard Java event model with Ada by providing a set of Java adapter classes and corresponding Ada bindings which implement each of the standard event listener interfaces These adapter classes process events by placing them on a queue to the AdaJNI runtime as depicted in Figure

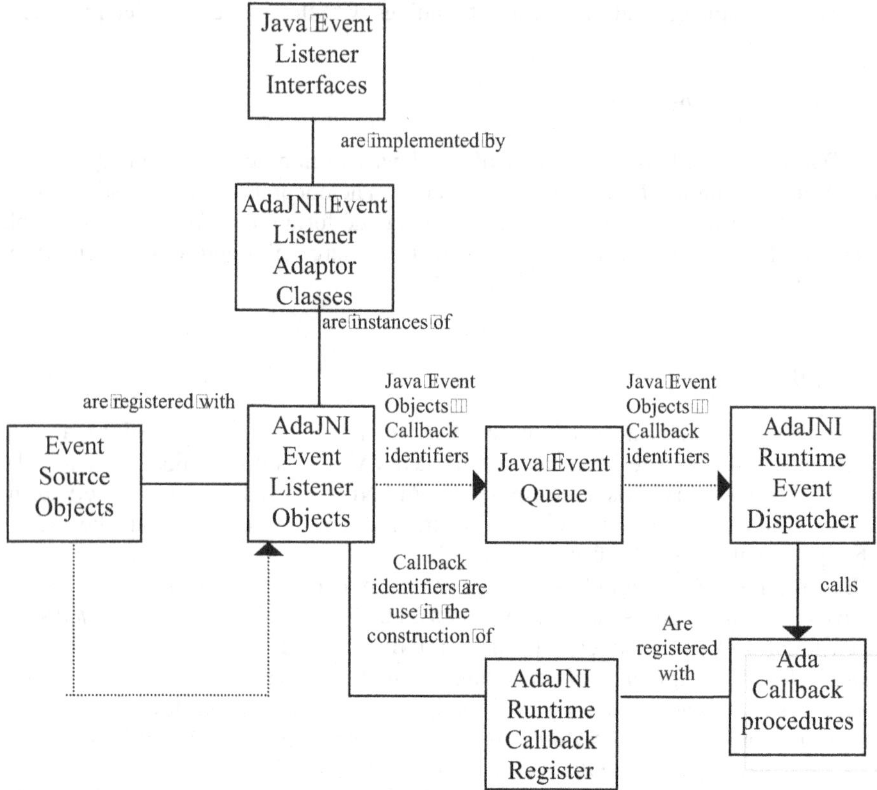

Fig AdaJNI Java Event Management

In order to use the AdaJNI event model an Ada call back procedure is declared for each event of interest Each call back procedure is then registered with the AdaJNI runtime which allocates a call back identifier for each procedure Once a call back procedure is registered its identifier can be used during the construction of an AdaJNI event listener object Once created a listener object is associated with a particular Ada call back procedure

The next step is to register AdaJNI event listener objects with event source objects such as buttons and windows When an event source generates an event it is passed to each registered event listener object These objects then place the events along with the identifiers of associated Ada call back procedures onto a simple queue

Event processing is completed when an Ada application calls an event dispatching procedure in the AdaJNI runtime This procedure will remove an event from the queue and pass it to the associated Ada call back procedure for processing as required by the application

Applications of AdaJNI

AdaJNI supports the use of Ada and Java in a wide variety of software architectures including stand alone applications client server systems and systems distributed over local and or wide area networks Applications can comprise components written in any combination of Ada and Java Ada components can make use of Java APIs and can communicate with components written in Java using the AdaJNI system

In standalone applications Ada programs can make use of Java API s via AdaJNI bindings If such applications are limited to using only the standard Ada packages and Java API s which are supported on a variety of platforms the application code will compile on those platforms without any changes That is the applications are portable at the source level

Applications can also comprise a combination of Ada and Java components AdaJNI can be used to generate Ada bindings to Java components of the application as well as standard Java and third party APIs This architecture allows use of the most appropriate language for each component More importantly it allows the integration of existing legacy Ada and Java code to build new systems

Java provides a comprehensive set of APIs for the development of distributed applications By using AdaJNI Ada programs can make use of the same APIs thus allowing the development of applications comprising Ada and Java components distributed over local and or wide area networks The use of AdaJNI in client server architectures would allow the server component to be developed using robust native Ada compilers The server would use AdaJNI bindings to communicate with clients running in a Java Virtual machine The client software could be written in Java or Ada using one of the Ada byte code compilers

A Small Example

This section shows how AdaJNI can be used to generate an Ada binding to a simple Java class and how that binding can be used to call Java methods from Ada

The Java Class

The following Java class contains a single method which displays the text Hello Ada a number of times as determined by the integer parameter count The remainder of this section shows how this class can be called from Ada

```
public class ExampleClass {
  public void sayHello(int count) {
    int i;
    for ( i=0; i<count ;i++ )
      System.out.println("Hello Ada!");
  }
}
```

The Ada Binding

The *Java AdaJNI* binding generator tools can be used to create an Ada binding to the class described above. The primary specification for such a binding is shown below. In producing this specification, *Java AdaJNI* analyses the Java source file described above along with the associated Java class file produced when the class is compiled using the *javac* Java compiler.

```
package Ada_JNI.Bindings.Example_Class is
  type Object is
    new Ada_JNI.Bindings.Java_Lang.Object.Object
        with null record;
  type Reference is access all Object'class;
  function New_Example_Class (Env :
      Ada_JNI.Java.Java_Env := Ada_JNI.Java.Current_Env
      ) return Reference;
  procedure Say_Hello
     ( Ref   : access Object;
       Count : in Ada_JNI.Java.Int.Java_Int;
       Env   : in Ada_JNI.Java.Java_Env
                     := Ada_JNI.Java.Current_Env );
end Ada_JNI.Bindings.Example_Class;
```

Note that the Java source code is not necessary to generate the above specification. *Java AdaJNI* can generate a complete binding from the class file alone. In such cases, however, *Java AdaJNI* is unable to generate proper parameter names for methods and constructors because they are not stored in Java class file.

Use of the Ada Bindings

The following Ada program makes use of the Ada binding described above. It declares a new object reference called *My_Object*. The body of the procedure creates a Java object by calling the constructor function *New_Example_Class*. Finally the *Say_Hello* method is called for the newly created object.

```
with Ada_JNI.Bindings.Example_Class;
procedure Example is
  My_Object : Ada_JNI.Bindings.Example_Class.Reference
   := Ada_JNI.Bindings.Example_Class.New_Example_Class;
begin
  Ada_JNI.Bindings.Example_Class.Say_Hello
    ( Ref   => My_Object, Count => 10 );
end Example;
```

Conclusion

An approach to using Java APIs with native Ada compilers has been described. The approach, which is based on use of the Java Native Interface, has been implemented in a system called AdaJNI that interfaces to the Aonix ObjectAda™ product [ ] and the Java Native Interface in the Sun Java Development Kit [ ] AdaJNI includes a tool which automatically generates Ada bindings to any given Java class as well as a small runtime to support the operation of such bindings A number of issues associated with the mapping of Java to Ada have been raised and addressed during the development of AdaJNI These issues have been discussed in this paper

Acknowledgements

Brian Dobbing acknowledges Shayne Flint as the principle author of this paper

The authors wish to thank Ed Falis a software engineer at Aonix for using AdaJNI and providing very useful feedback which has led to a number of significant improvements in the technique In addition the authors wish to thank Dr Clive Boughton managing director of Software Improvements Pty Limited for his ongoing encouragement and for his review of this paper

References

Aonix Inc "ObjectAda for Windows" http www aonix com

JavaSoft Sun Microsystems Inc "Java Development Kit" http java sun com products jdk

JavaSoft Sun Microsystems Inc "Introduction to the New AWT Event Model" http java sun com docs books tutorial ui components eventintro html

JavaSoft Sun Microsystems Inc "Java API User's Guide" http java sun com products jdk docs api API_users_guide html

JavaSoft Sun Microsystems Inc "Java Foundation Classes" http java sun com products jfc index html

JavaSoft Sun Microsystems Inc "JavaBeans" http java sun com beans index html

Masters M W "Programming Languages and Life Cycle Costs" Naval Surface Warfare Center March http wuarchive wustl edu languages ada docs advocacy Masters zip

Zeigler S F "Comparing Development Costs of C and Ada" Rational Software Corp'n March http sw eng falls church va us AdaIC docs reports cada cada_art html

Intermetrics Inc "AppletMagic" http www appletmagic com

Static Worst Case Execution Time Analysis of Synchronous Programs

Thomas Ringler

Institute of Industrial Automation and Software Engineering University of Stuttgart
Pfaffenwaldring D Stuttgart Germany
ringler@ias uni stuttgart de

Abstract In this paper a worst case execution time WCET analysis of programs written in synchronous programming languages like ESTEREL is presented Synchronous languages allow the building of deterministic systems and additionally enable formal verification techniques to be applied Executable programs can behave synchronously if they fulfill certain temporal requirements Therefore worst case execution time analysis has to be applied to the programs generated by the synchronous language development environment The paper gives a short overview about existing static worst case execution time approaches and discusses the problems to be addressed by WCET analysis of synchronous programs A concept for static analysis on a high level of abstraction is proposed The concept is evaluated by means of a steer by wire demonstrator

Introduction

The new generation of drive by wire systems currently under development has demanding requirements on the electronic architecture [ ] Functions such as brake by wire or steer by wire require complete deterministic behavior of the whole distributed system In order to satisfy these requirements time triggered technology has been developed by Vienna University of Technology and DaimlerChrysler While the fault tolerant time triggered communication is widely developed and a first silicon implementation of the Time Triggered Protocol TTP C [ ] communication system is available there is still a lack of deterministic application software design approaches in the automotive sector

Synchronous languages like ESTEREL [ ] provide mathematically defined semantics in order to design software on a high level of abstraction and subsequently generate deterministic code based on finite state machines FSM On this foundation it is also possible to apply formal verification techniques [ ] Hence synchronous languages are well suited for the design of safety critical application software The combination of the synchronous application software design approach together with a time triggered communication architecture allows to build completely synchronous and deterministic distributed systems [ ]

To simplify the design process of synchronous application software systems component based techniques have been applied Abstract specifications of software and hardware components and libraries of standard components are provided to construct systems on a very high level and allow the generation of small and efficient platform and application specific code This is the goal of the ViPER **V**isual **P**rogramming **E**nvironment for **E**mbedded **R**eal Time Systems approach [ ]

H B Keller and E Plödereder Eds Ada Europe LNCS pp

Synchronous languages have been developed to simplify the programming of reactive systems They are based on the *synchrony hypothesis* [ ] which makes the following abstractions

- The computer is infinitely fast
- Each reaction is instantaneous and atomic dividing time into a sequence of discrete instants Different reactions cannot interfere with one another
- A system's reaction to an input appears at the same instant as the input

The synchrony hypothesis is a generalization of the synchronous model used for digital circuits where each reaction must be finished during one clock cycle A real system can behave synchronously if it finishes its computations before new events arrive from it's environment see Figure This requires knowing both the minimum inter arrival time MINT of the event as well as the worst case execution time WCET of the program In conjunction with the time triggered protocol the MINT is pre defined and guaranteed However the worst case execution time of the program has to be calculated

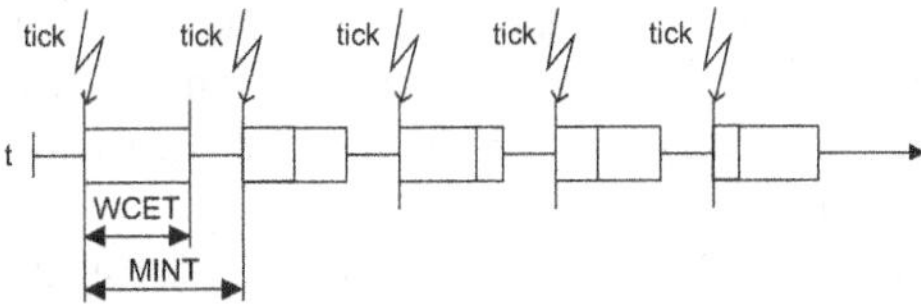

Figure Fulfillment of the synchrony hypothesis The synchrony hypothesis is fulfilled if the WCET is always smaller than the MINT

Existing worst case execution time analysis techniques are not well suited for the C source code generated by the ESTEREL development environment The structure of the generated code is difficult to analyze In contrast to handwritten code the generated code's control structure is not explicitly given by programming languages' control statements like *for* *while* *if* statements but implicitly in data structures respectively by boolean equations Therefore standard techniques cannot be applied for control flow analysis On the other hand control flow analysis is much easier because control flow information is explicitly given by the finite state machine representation

This paper focuses on the worst case execution time analysis of synchronous programs on the example of ESTEREL programs It is organized as follows First the overview about the problems of static worst case execution time analysis is given The following section describes the basics of the synchronous programming language ESTEREL Subsequently the concepts concerning worst case execution time analysis of synchronous languages are discussed Experimental results are presented in the succeeding section Conclusions and an overview of future work appear in the final section

Introduction to Static WCET Analysis

The knowledge of the worst case execution time of real time programs is an important issue in real time engineering since real time programs have to interact with their physical environment at precise times Predicted worst case execution times have to fulfill two requirements they have to be an upper bound of the actual worst case and they have to be tight [ ]

Two generally different approaches exist in determining the execution time of a program Measurements and static analysis by modeling and simulation Measurements can never give a worst case guarantee and are therefore unsuitable for safe determination The worst case execution time of a real time program can be statically computed if all possible paths of a program can be determined and the execution time of the instructions are known [ ] In this case the worst case path can be determined The overall problem WCET analysis can be separated into two sub problems program path analysis and hardware level analysis

Program Path Analysis

The program path analysis deals with the mathematical description of all possible execution paths in an effective way In the approach of Park [ ] all possible execution paths are listed explicitly With increasing code sizes the path information becomes quickly unmanageable Later approaches like [ ] and [ ] only list the execution count of basic blocks and formulate a linear programming problem which has to be maximized A basic block is defined as the maximum sequence of assembly instructions where the only entry point is at the first instruction and the only exit point is at the last instruction [ ]

For simple hardware architectures without caches a linear programming problem can be formulated as shown below Complex hardware can be treated in a similar way with some extensions as shown in [ ] The total execution time T of a program consisting of N basic blocks is given as

$$T = \sum_{i=}^{N} c_i \, x_i$$

The non negative integer variable x_i is the execution count of a basic block B_i and the constant c_i is the execution time of B_i The execution time of a basic block is determined at the hardware level analysis see below For the execution count variables x_i constraints have to be found These constraints can be distinguished into structural and functional constraints The structure of the program can be extracted on assembly code level But it is very difficult to extract path information like functional properties as loop counts and mutual exclusive branches Programs simply do not contain enough information for program path analysis Many researches give the programmer the responsibility to supply this necessary path information At Mok's work [ ] code annotations are done at assembly code level while Puschner and Koza [ ] have introduced new language constructs These constructs allow programmers to put more information about the behavior of the algorithms implemented into their programs The programmer can define maximum execution counts of statements loops etc However this information given by the programmer can be error prone [ ]

There is a chance of getting the necessary path information from a higher level of abstraction than the source code level namely abstract software specification languages used by software development tools In chapter the first step into this direction will be presented. The extraction of the path information out of the finite state machine representation.

Hardware Level Analysis

The aim of hardware level analysis is the determination of the worst case time that is needed to execute an instruction in its context for a given hardware. The execution time of an instruction is the time needed to load the instruction, decode it, load possible operands, execute the instruction, write back the results and possibly additional time needed to synchronize instructions on different pipeline stages. The effort to determine the execution time significantly depends on the hardware architecture. The problem can be distinguished into three cases.

In the case of hardware platforms without pipelines and caches, the execution time of an instruction is independent from other instructions. Hardware need not be to modeled. The execution time of a basic block is simply the sum of all execution times of its instructions.

In the case of hardware platforms with pipelines, the execution time of an instruction depends on instructions that are executed in parallel by the processor at a point in time. Since this is a local problem the execution time of a basic block can be determined by simulating the sequence of instructions of a basic block. Overlapping of different basic blocks must be considered. Therefore the pipeline is assumed to be empty at the beginning of the simulation of a basic block. Afterwards all possible preceding basic blocks are analyzed in order to find the case of smallest overlapping.

In the case of the existence of caches the execution time of an instruction also depends on the instructions and data being accessed before. This is a global problem, since the instructions and data accessed before possibly originate from other functions and modules. While instruction caches can be handled by defining a cache conflict graph for all cache lines for example [ ], data cache analysis is much more difficult since data addresses are much harder to determine than instruction addresses. To model data caches accurately, for every data reference the set of data addresses that may be accessed and the sequence how these addresses are accessed have to be determined. Suitable approaches only exist for some special cases. There is no general solution for this problem [ ].

Before going into details of the WCET analysis of ESTEREL programs, a brief introduction to the synchronous programming language ESTEREL is given. For further readings see [ ].

The Synchronous Language ESTEREL

Programming Model

The programming model of ESTEREL is a specification of modules which are assumed to be executed in parallel. The modules communicate with each other and with their environment by signals. The signals are broadcasted and can be received from each module. A signal has a state and can optionally have a value of an arbitrary type in each instant of time. Sending and receiving signals is performed instantaneously according to the synchrony hypothesis. An ESTEREL program can be compiled to a deterministic finite state machine. Figure shows a small example of an ESTEREL program and the corresponding finite state machine The output O is emitted as soon as both inputs A and B have been received The behavior is reset whenever the input R is received

```
module ABRO:
  input A, B, R;
  output O;
  loop
    [await A || await B];
    emit O;
  each R;
end module
```

Figure ESTEREL program and corresponding finite state machine

ESTEREL only supports some basic data types boolean integer float double and string and operations For other data types data handling functions have to be provided in a host language for example C

The finite state machine is given by a set of states and transitions During a transition input signal presence tests or data tests are taken and their result leads to data action activation [ ] Figure illustrates a state transition in a finite state machine It starts at a previous state root of a tree and ends at a new state leaf of a tree During the transition unary nodes represent data actions and binary nodes represent tests When the leaf is reached execution of the finite state machine of the current activation is finished The execution will be continued in this state during the next activation The execution model is strictly sequential No two finite state machines will execute in parallel

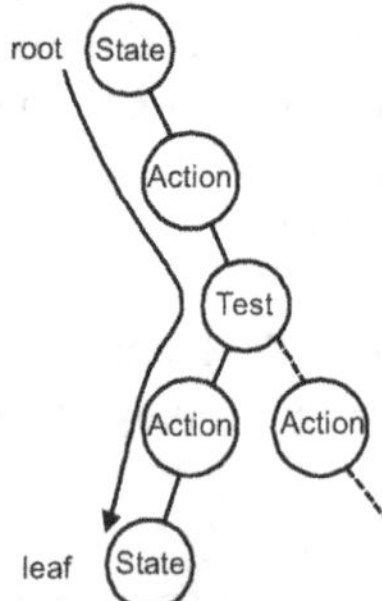

Figure State transition sequence of the finite state machine

Implementation of ESTEREL Programs

The finite state machine can be implemented in many different ways with different consumption of execution time and memory space There are two general possibilities Either the finite state machine is stored explicitly which leads to huge consumption of memory space Or the state machine is implemented implicitly by boolean equations This method leads to slower execution times since the equations have to be solved during run time

Generation Process

Figure illustrates the generation process of an ESTEREL program to an executable object code The ESTEREL compiler performs several transformations to intermediate formats which are used as internal representations of programs written in synchronous languages [ ] The imperative code IC is a high level parallel structured format dedicated to the representation of imperative synchronous programs while the object code OC is a sequential unstructured low level format representing programs as interpreted finite state machines to be used as a target code for compilers The Sorted Circuit Code SSC is also a format used as a target code for compilers representing programs as sorted boolean equations A platform specific target compiler compiles and links the code either OC or SSC together with external data handling functions written in C

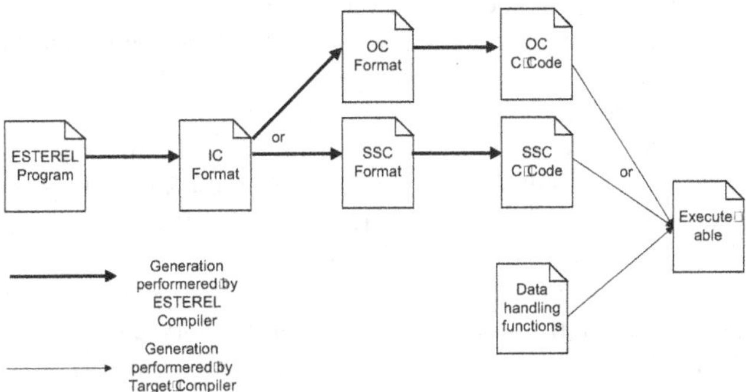

Figure Process of generating object code from an ESTEREL program

WCET Analysis for Synchronous Programs

Problems in WCET Analysis for Synchronous Programs

Validity of the Synchrony Hypothesis For fulfillment of the synchrony hypothesis the finite state machine has to finish the computations before the next activation is initiated for a particular hardware platform for each possible input and internal state In a TTP system the activation is only initiated by the progression of time controlled by the TTP communication system Hence the MINT of the activation is known The difficulty lies in adjusting the inter arrival time as tight as possible to reduce the waste of calculation time Therefore the WCET of the finite state machine has to be calculated as tight as possible

In imperative languages such as ESTEREL the distinction between control flow and data handling is direct at source code level The source code consists of two separate parts data handling actions and a deterministic control finite state machine which "schedules" these data handling actions The finite state machine itself as well

In this approach we have restricted ourselves to the synchronous language ESTEREL But the WCET analysis is also applicable for other synchronous languages since they can be translated into the same intermediate formats as the data handling functions have to be analyzed for each possible state transition□ As already mentioned□ the data handling functions are implemented in the programming language C□ For the WCET analysis conventional methods as described above can be applied□ In the following particular attention will be paid to the analysis of the finite state machine code□ which requires new analysis approaches□

Explicit Automata Representation□ The C code representation of the explicit automata code is stored in data structures□ which are read by a simple while loop □see Table □□left column□□ The program's control structure only consists of one loop□ the real control flow is set in the data structure□ According to the contents of the data structure□ tests and actions are executed during state transitions□ Approaches like [□]□ [□]□[□] are designed for handwritten□ human readable code and therefore not applicable for this kind of code□ since they expect the control structure given explicitly by programming language control statements□

The solution to this is the analysis of the structure of the finite state machine□ in terms of the actions which are executed during the state transitions and the number of read cycles which are executed on the data structure during the state transitions□

Since the code size grows exponential with the states of the state machine the explicit representation is not suitable for real control applications□ This is the reason why attention is paid to the analysis of the sorted circuit code representation□

Sorted Circuit Representation□ The sorted circuit C code representation of the finite state machine has significantly less consumption of memory and can be applied in common microcontrollers [□]□ The generated C code consists mainly of a sequential arrangement of sets of equations and actions which are executed if the result of a set of equations is true □see Table □ right column□□ The previous state is stored in non□ transient registers□ The signals from the environment are passed on by updating the input vector□ The previous state and the signals are the inputs for the sets of boolean equations□

Table □□ Generated C source code by the ESTEREL Compiler from the SSC format □left column□ and the OC format □right column□

SSC C source representation

```
/*data structures */
static __ABRO_indextype __ABRO_sct1 []
= {0,2};
static __ABRO_indextype __ABRO_sct2 []
= {6,3,0,2,4,8,5,4,7,0,3,0,4,5,3,0,5,0,2};
...

/*while loop */
static int __ABRO_engine ()
{
   register __ABRO_indextype x;
   while (x = *(__ABRO_cp++))
   {
      __ACT(x);
   }
   return *__ABRO_cp;
}
```

OC C source representation

```
int ABRO () {
static __SSC_BIT_TYPE E[8];
/*boolean Equations */
E[0] = __ABRO_R[1]||__ABRO_R[2]);
E[1] = (__ABRO_R[3]||E[0]);
...
E[5] = (__ABRO_R[2]&&E[2]);
E[6] = (E[5]&&(__ABRO_A2));
...
/* Action */
if (E[6]) {__ABRO_A4;}
....
/*save state in registers */
__ABRO_R[1] = (E[1]||((((E[3]
                 &&!((__ABRO_A1))))
                 &&__ABRO_R[1])));
...
}
```

The problem of applying known WCET analysis approaches lies in the path analysis by finding the longest path which is executable A closer look to Figure shows that it is easy to find the path with the longest execution time namely the path which passes all actions Figure a But this path is never executable since all existing data processing functions would be executed during one run WCET on basis of this path is highly overestimated and therefore unusable In the example the sequence of actions i j k in Figure a is not executable since no state transition exists in the finite state machine Figure c which passes the actions i j and k However the path that passes the actions i and j is executable Figure b

For determining the paths at the C source code level the sets of boolean equations would have to be solved This is not necessary since the structure of the program is explicitly given on the level of intermediate formats In the next section this concept is presented

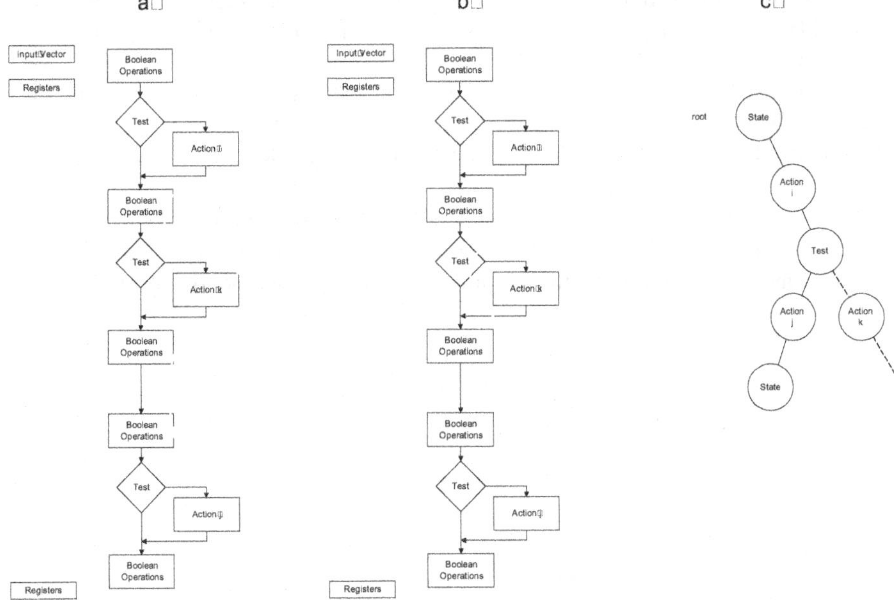

Figure Feasible paths of the program generated out of the SSC format The path at a is not executable since there exists no state transition in the finite state machine at c the path at b is executable

A Concept for WCET Analysis of Synchronous Programs

Our concept is shown in Figure In the ViPER approach the software is graphically composed at the design level out of parallel synchronous software components and data handling functions Afterwards the ESTEREL compiler generates one finite state machine represented as sorted circuit code SSC and as explicit automaton OC as well

Executable code is generated from the sorted circuit code SSC representation On assembly code level the structure is analyzed and a control flow graph CFG is generated Its elements are conditions and two types of basic blocks representing sets of boolean equations and data handling functions On this level each data handling function is seen as one basic block Its worst case execution time can be determined once for a specific hardware platform and stored in the component library So the interaction between functions which could further improve the tightness of the results is not considered in this approach

The basic block WCETs of the boolean equations have to be analyzed after each change of the software at the design level Therefore the assembly code is passed to a hardware analysis tool which simulates the execution of the sequence of instructions and returns the worst case execution times of the basic blocks In the prototype a simulation tool for the Siemens C microcontroller is used which has a stage pipeline

The WCETs of the basic blocks are inserted into the control flow graph During a second step the CFG is traced in order to find the longest executable path Therefore all possible state transitions of the finite state machine OC format are examined in order to extract all sets of actions which are executed during the same state transition This information is used to search for the longest path in the CFG which is executable beginning with the longest worst case execution time Finally the results are visualized at the design level The user is provided with the following information

- The worst case execution time of the whole synchronous program
- The execution times for combinations of input vectors and internal data
- The time consumption of the automaton in comparison to the data handling functions

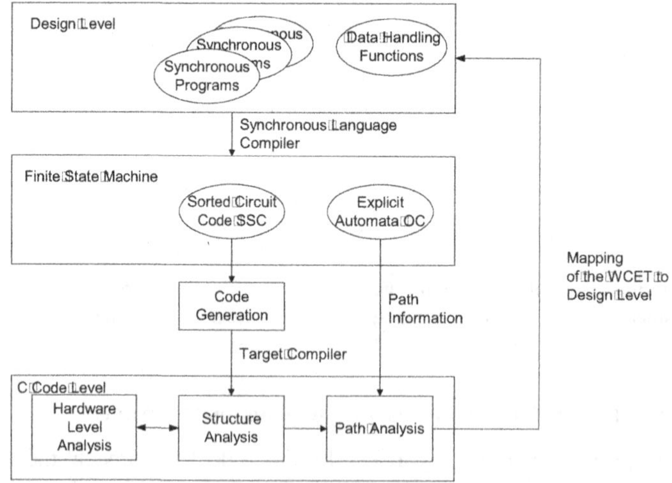

Figure The concept for WCET analysis of synchronous programs

Assembly Code Generation In addition the attempt to directly generate assembly code has been made in order to get simple code structures which have predictable temporal behavior and which are easy to analyze

Compiler optimization techniques change the code's structure significantly therefore linear C code need not result in linear assembly code branches and loops can be added by the compiler The off the shelf compiler used e g is not configurable in the way needed The solution found is direct generation of assembly code out of the ESTEREL intermediate format SSC All information needed to generate linear assembly code can be extracted from the tables of the SSC format In the left column of Table one entry of the equation table SSC format is shown The result of the wire is the disjunction of the registers R and R In the other two columns the assembly code generated by an off the shelf target compiler are opposed to the assembly code generated by our generator The target compiler uses load compare and conditional branch instructions to implement boolean equations This implementation can be faster in some cases If a result is already clear the rest of the equation has not to be taken into account For example R or R with R = is always R has not to be regarded However for worst case examinations a quicker case is not of interest at all

In opposite to the off the shelf compiler we implement the boolean equations as boolean assembly instructions Consequently linear control structure is generated at assembly code level which is always executed completely This method simplifies path analysis since the worst case path is already known for this code segment

Table Comparison of the assembly code generated by the an off the shelf target compiler and sequential assembly code generated by our generator

Equation Table of SSC Format	Assembly code generated by a off the shelf target compiler	Sequential assembly code

`0: wire: or: (31,32)`
 	
`//31 = Register R1`
`//32 = Register R2`
	`MOVB RL1,(_R1)`
	`JMPR cc_NZ,_5`
	`_8:`
	`MOVB RL1,(_R2)`
	`JMPR cc_Z,_6`
	`_5:`
	`MOVB RL1,#01h`
	`JMPR cc_UC,_7`
	`_6:`
	`MOVB RL1,#00h`
	`_7:`
	`MOVB _3,RL1`
		`MOVB RL1,(_R1)`
		`ORB RL1,(_R2)`
		`MOVB _4,RL1`

Experimental Results

Currently the concepts are evaluated by means of a steer by wire demonstrator The application consists of electronic control units Siemens C microcontrollers connected with the TTP C communication system The application software has been graphically designed with our ViPER prototype as presented in [ ]

In the following the code will be discussed which has been generated for the electronic control unit This code is responsible for reading the steering wheel angel and sending it via the TTP communication system The FSM is implemented by boolean equations non transient registers and external data handling functions The generated assembly code for the FSM has approximately lines of assembly code

Figure [illegible] shows the static analysis for all possible paths of the program. White lines represent non executable paths, while black lines represent executable paths. Paths with the identical execution time are merged into one line. The lowest line represents the best case execution time with T_{BECT}= [illegible] ms and the supreme line the worst case execution time with T_{WCET}= [illegible] ms which is not executable. The longest executable path has a WCET of $T_{WCET\,ex}$= [illegible] ms. Assuming the T_{WCET} as worst case leads to about [illegible] overestimation in this example. For applications with longer execution times of data handling functions this becomes even worse. The real WCET of the example has been determined by measurements as T_{wm}= [illegible] ms. So the calculated worst case execution times are tight and safe.

The execution times of the code shown in Table [illegible] have been determined for the used hardware. The execution time of the code generated by the off the shelf target compiler varies between [illegible] µs and [illegible] µs dependent on the values of the registers R[illegible] and R[illegible]. Whereas the generated linear code always takes [illegible] µs for execution. In this simple example the worst case of the linear code is even faster than the best case of the other.

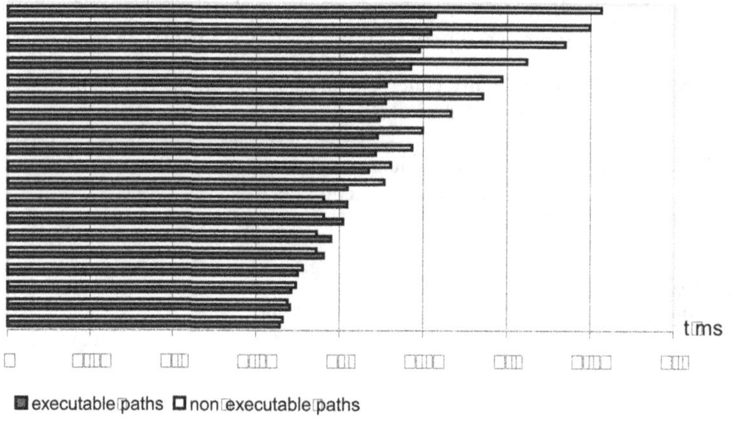

Figure [illegible] Statically analyzed paths of the program

Conclusions and Outlook

A worst case execution time analysis approach for programs written in the synchronous language ESTEREL has been presented. In the main the concept consists of two parts: Mapping of path information from an abstract software design level to the WCET analysis and generation of easily analyzable code structures.

In the presented prototype tool the generation of easily analyzable code structures bypasses the off the shelf compiler. For commercial use however this method has to be integrated into the compiler. Moreover, for time triggered, highly dependable systems, a new generation of compiler optimization techniques are required, which generate analyzable code structures and optimize with respect to the worst case execution time and not with respect to average performance as existing optimization techniques do.

In this approach hardware architectures with an instruction pipeline without caches Siemens C microcontroller has been assumed Cache analysis is still a great challenge however code generation gives the advantage of mapping the static variables in an efficient way This is a necessary condition for every cache analysis approach

Path information is extracted from a finite state machine representation of the synchronous program Although the approach has been presented by means of the programming language ESTEREL it is also applicable for other imperative languages which can be translated into the OC and SSC format like ARGOS [ ]

Synchronous languages are well suited for building deterministic reactive systems In contrast to that data handling functions are commonly designed with modeling and simulation tools like MATLAB Simulink or MATRIXx The code generated by these tools also requires worst case execution time analysis We see a chance in gathering path information especially maximum loop iterations from abstract software specification used by these tools

References

Th Ringler J Steiner R Belschner and B Hedenetz Increasing System Safety for by wire Applications in Vehicles by using a Time Triggered Architecture Safecomp Heidelberg

H Kopetz et al A Prototype Implementation of a TTP C Controller SAE Technical Paper Series February

G Berry and G Gonthier The ESTEREL Synchronous Programming Language Design Semantics Implementation Science of Computer Programming November

M Gunzert Building Safety Critical Real Time Systems with Synchronous Software Components IFAC Workshop on Real Time Programming WRTP Schloß Dagstuhl Germany

M Gunzert Th Ringler ViPER – A Component Based Approach for Designing Real Time Systems Proc ISA TEC INTERKAMA ' Düsseldorf

P Puschner Timing Analysis for Real Time Programs Ph D Thesis Institut für Technische Informatik Vienna University of Technology

Y Li S Malik Performance Analysis of Real Time embedded Software Kluwer Academic Publishers Bosten Dordrecht London

C Y Park Predicting Deterministic Execution Times of Real Time Programs Ph D Thesis University of Washington Seattle August

Alfred V Aho Ravi Sethi Jeffry D Ullman Compilers Principles Techniques and Tools Addison Wesley ISBN

A K Mok et al Evaluating Tight Execution Time Bounds of Programs by Annotations Proceedings of the th IEEE Workshop on Real Time Operating Systems and Software pages May

P Puschner C Koza Calculating the Maximum Execution Time of Real Time Programs Journal of Real Time Systems Volume Number p Sep Reprint in IEEE Tutorial Advances in Real Time Systems p IEEE Computer Society Press

P Puschner R Nossal Testing the Results of Static Worst Case Execution Time Analysis IEEE Real Time Systems Symposium Madrid Spain

G Berry The Foundations of Ersterel Proof Language and Interaction Essays in Honour of Robin Milner G Plotkin C Stirling and M Tofte editors MIT Press

The Common Format of Synchronous Languages The Declarative Code DC Version Ecole des Mines de Paris and INRIA Route des Lucioles Sophia Antipolis CDX

A Supporting Tool for Development of Self-Measurement Ada Programs

Yusuke Nonaka[1], Jingde Cheng[2], and Kazuo Ushijima[1]

[1] Department of Computer Science and Communication Engeneering, Kyushu University
6-10-1 Hakozaki, Fukuoka, 812-8581, Japan,
TEL : +81-92-642-3867, FAX : +81-92-632-5204
{yusuke,ushijima}@csce.kyushu-u.ac.jp

[2] Department of Information and Computer Sciences, Saitama University
255 Shimo-Okubo, Urawa, 338-8570, Japan.
cheng@ics.saitama-u.ac.jp

Abstract. Large-scale and highly reliable concurrent systems are more and more required and it is indispensable for them to keep on measuring and monitoring in order to ensure their reliability. The most intrinsic behavioral characteristic of a concurrent system is its wholeness. According to it, we propose the measurement specifications for systematic development of self-measurement Ada programs. The measurement specifications can designate what kind of events to measure, which part of the program to measure, which variables to measure in a concurrent system. We present the architecture of our tool based on the measurement specifications to support development of self-measurement Ada programs. It can automatically construct a self-measurement concurrent system from the functional part, the measurement part, and the measurement specifications of the system.

1 Introduction

In recent years, there are more demands for large-scale concurrent systems, i.e., parallel and/or distributed computing systems. Most of the reliable functioning of infrastructures for modern society depend on concurrent systems. However, since many concurrent systems currently used are not so reliable, we can't regard the infrastructures which depend on them as reliable. How to design, develop, and maintain highly reliable concurrent systems has become a very important issue.

The most intrinsic behavioral characteristic of a concurrent system is its wholeness, i.e., the behavior of a concurrent system is not simply the mechanical putting together of its parts that act concurrently but a whole such that one cannot find some way to resolve it into parts mechanically and then simply composes the sum of its parts as the same as its original behavior[ ].

As a result of wholeness, there is "the uncertainty principle" in measuring and monitoring the behavior of a concurrent system, i.e., the behavior of an observer such as a run-time monitor cannot be separate from what is being observing.

H. B. Keller and E. Plödereder (Eds.): Ada-Europe 2000, LNCS 1845, pp. 69– , 2000.

Almost all existing concurrent systems are designed, developed, and maintained in a function-oriented and/or separate-measurement methodology, i.e., the systems are usually constructed only by some function components and there are no measurement components as permanent components of the systems. As a result, when we want to measure and monitor the behavior of a concurrent system, we have to use a separate measuring and/or monitoring tool that is independent of the target system. However, it is even impossible to grasp the "true" behavior of the target system in this way. The most serious problem resulting from the function-oriented and/or separate-measurement methodology is that the reliable functioning of a concurrent system, which is designed, developed, and maintained according to the methodology, cannot be fully guaranteed in its working stage even though the system was tested and debugged in its development and/or maintenance stage.

Consequently, if the measurement of the concurrent system would be done only sometime during development and after that the measurement part would be removed when the system would be made in operation, the behavior of the system on working might be different from the one under development, so the reliability which was ensured during development would be lost.

The self-measurement principle[ ] requires that a large-scale, long-lived, and highly reliable concurrent system should be constructed by some function components and some (maybe only one) permanent self-measurement components that act concurrently with the function components, measure and monitor the system itself according to some requirements, and pass run-time information about the system's behavior to the outside world of the system.

It is important to make the measurement part reusable. One of the reasons is that the measurement part must be highly reliable and it must be very effective for ensuring reliability to reuse highly reliable existing component. On the other hand, two different systems which have different functional parts may demand a common measurement part. Possibly, a generic measurement and monitoring component may be effective for constructing almost all systems, for example, a deadlock detector.

We suppose that some systematic solution to develop and maintain self-measurement concurrent systems is needed. In this paper, we present an architecture and a prototype implementation of our supporting tool for development of self-measurement concurrent systems with Ada 95 programs[ ][ ]. The programming language Ada is one of the most suitable languages for development of highly reliable concurrent systems.

2 Architecture of the Supporting Tool with Measurement Specifications

In this section, we present the architecture of our supporting tool for development of self-measurement Ada programs.

Fig. shows the architecture of the supporting tool with measurement specifications. The functional part is the part of the software system which is expected

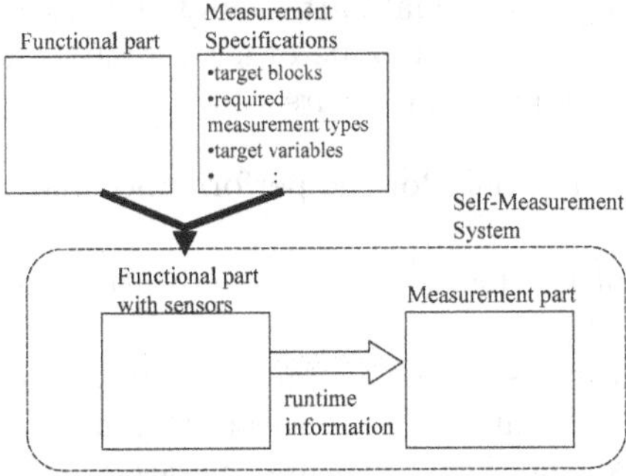

Fig. 1. The architecture of the supporting tool with measurement specifications

to perform the original role of the system, and the measurement part is another important part of the same software system which is expected to measure and monitor the behavior of the functional part. Each measurement part has corresponding measurement specifications, which represent what kind of run-time information the measurement part requires during execution of the functional part measured by it. Sensors are statements for sending run-time information to out of the functional part. We can generate the functional part with sensors from the functional part and the measurement specifications for it. The functional part with sensors and the measurement part can compose a self-measurement system.

If the functional part has statements to send information of itself to the measurement part, the measurement part can get information of run-time status for the system. However, since there would be no explicit distinction between statements for original functions and statements for measurement, this approach would reduce readability of the program. We hope that statements for measurement could be described to be distinguished from statements for original functions, like exception handlers of Ada, but Ada has no facility for it. By the programming languages which have reflective facilities, we suppose that we could put this approach into practice to describe statements for measurement in some meta-object[ ][ ], but the excess programmability of these languages causes the lowering of performance and several studies have been kept on doing about this problem still now.

To cope with the above problem, we introduce the notion of measurement specification. What are described in the measurement specifications are:

- what kinds of tasking events the measurement part should measure,
- which scope it should measure for each kind of tasking events,
- which subprograms it should measure the subprogram calls to,

– which entries it should measure the entry calls to,
– which variables it should measure when they are assigned and referred,
– what information the functional part should give, for example, a task ID of the provider of information, a value of a variable, a scope name by dotted notation where a tasking event occurs.

Of course, it is effective not only for the performance and the memory problem, but also reuse problem.

For the language of the measurement specifications, we adopt the package specifications of Ada.

Subprogram declarations in the package specification as the measurement specifications represent what kinds of tasking events the measurement part should measure. We call those subprograms queries. Each kind of tasking events corresponds to a subprogram name, and if a subprogram declaration corresponding to the kind of tasking events is in the package specification, the kind of tasking events is needed for the measurement. For example, if a subprogram named as RENDEZVOUS_START is declared in the package specification, the functional part of the target system must send some information when some rendezvous is starting.

Table 1. Some of queries for the measurement specifications

function BLOCK_ELABORATION_START	starting of block elaboration
function BLOCK_ELABORATION_COMPLETION	completion of block elaboration
procedure BLOCK_EXECUTION_START	starting of block execution
procedure BLOCK_EXECUTION_COMPLETION	completion of block execution
procedure SIMPLE_ENTRY_CALL	just before simple entry calls
procedure PROTECTED_ENTRY_CALL	just before protected entry calls
function TASK_ACTIVATION_START	starting of task activation
procedure ACCEPT_START	just before accept statements
procedure RENDEZVOUS_START	starting of rendezvous
procedure RENDEZVOUS_END	completion of rendezvous
procedure FUNCTION_CALL	just before function calls

Table shows the list of some of such queries. There are 38 kinds of queries, too many to show all of them here.

Parameters of those subprogram declarations represent what information the functional part should give. Each kind of information which can be sent by the functional part corresponds to a certain name of a formal parameter of subprogram declarations, and if the formal parameter corresponding to the kind of information is included by a subprogram declaration, the functional part must send the information to the measurement part when the tasking event corresponding to the subprogram occurs.

Pragmas which are defined for only the measurement specifications (and are not standard ones) represent:

- which scope the measurement part should measure for each kind of tasking events,
- which subprograms it should measure the subprogram calls to,
- which entries it should measure the entry calls to,
- which variables it should measure when they are assigned and/or referred.

These pragmas are used with subprogram declarations as the queries. For example, the pragma Designated_Subject designates a specified scope to measure, and if it is described with the subprogram declaration named as RENDEZVOUS_START, rendezvous in scopes only specified by the pragma can be measured.

As a concrete example, in case we would want to measure occurrence of an entry call from scopes contained in "main" to the entry "task1.get" and task IDs of the callers, we must describe the following declarations in the measurement specifications:

```
pragma Designate_Entry("task1.get");
pragma Designate_Subject("main*");
procedure Simple_Entry_Call
    (Callee_Task : in Task_ID);
```

Table shows the list of such pragmas. The available range for a certain pragma is from a declaration as a query immediately after the pragma to one just before the same kind of the pragma. In each parameter, the scope of the target should be designated with dotted notation. More than two targets can be designated with more than two parameters and/or regular expression.

The supporting tool must be able to analyze the measurement specifications and make the executable program of the whole system with the measurement part by some method.

The measurement part of the target system can be implemented as the package body corresponding to the package specification which is used as the measurement specification, and, if needed, the additional packages which are used in the package body.

3 Design and Implementation of the Supporting Tool

Based on the architecture presented in the previous section, we implemented a prototype of the supporting tool for development of self-measurement Ada programs. Fig. shows the system structure of the tool.

Table 2. Pragmas for the measurement specifications

Designate_Subject(Scope_Name1, ...)	This makes the target scopes of measurement handlers scopes identified by Scope_Name.
Designate_Entry(Entry_Name1, ...)	This limits target entries of measurement handlers for entry calls to Entry_Name.
Designate_Subprogram(Subprogram_Name1, ...)	This limits target entries of measurement handlers for subprogram calls to Subprogram_Name.
Variable_Refer(Variable_Name, [Scope_Name1, ...])	This makes the subprogram declared immediately after this pragma the measurement handler which will be called when the value of the variable designated by Variable_Name will be refered.
Variable_Assign(Variable_Name, [Scope_Name1, ...])	This makes the subprogram declared immediately after this pragma the measurement handler which will be called when the value of the variable designated by Variable_Name will be assigned.

We adopted source code transformation approach for the tool. After the tool analyzes measurement specifications for a concurrent system, the source program for the functional part of the system is converted by using the analyzed information into such one as with sensors to send information designated by the measurement specifications and required by the measurement part. One of the advantages of this approach compared with the run-time environment supporting is performance because all measurement targets are determined statically. If a system is measured on some run-time environment and the measurement targets are determined dynamically, overheads for preparation to measure all targets cannot be ignored. Another advantage is that it is easy to implement the prototype of the tool. Conversely, one of the disadvantages is there are limits of the power of the expression in the target language. Moreover, overlapped information existing in both the run-time environment and the measurement part is often needed in spite of intrinsic unnecessity. One of the examples is information which represents intertask dependences and is used for synchronization of task termination. Ada tasks cannot get such information from run-time environment, so the measurement part must manage the same information by itself.

The tool uses ASIS to get requirements for conversion of functional parts from their measurement specifications[ ][ ]. A package which is in charge of this function is Spec_Reader. This package gets the name of the compilation unit used as the measurement specifications, traverses the measurement specifications

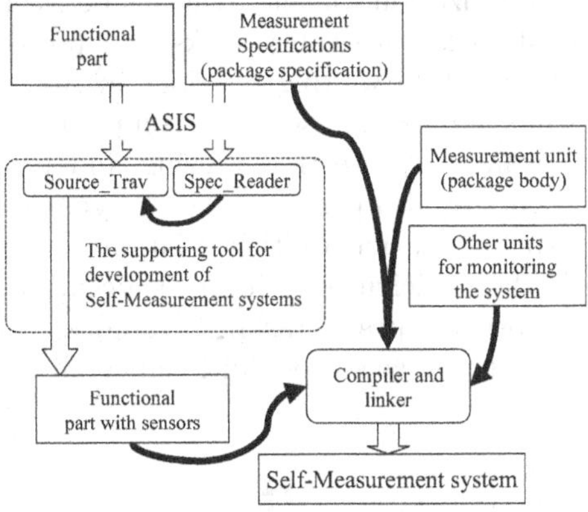

Fig. 2. The supporting tool for development of self-measurement systems

corresponding to the name by using ASIS, and maintains the requirements for the measurement in the package as the implementation-defined data structure.

The tool also uses ASIS to convert source programs for functional parts of target concurrent systems to those with sensors to send information. A package which is in charge of this function is Source_Trav. This package gets the name of the compilation unit used as the functional part, traverses the functional part by using ASIS, and outputs converted source code while it uses the information which Spec_Reader has. This package is based on one of the packages constructing "display source" as an example of ASIS-for-GNAT[ ]. Since the compilation unit which is an output of this package depends on another compilation unit whose specification is used as the measurement specifications, when we build the whole system, the executable file is constructed by both the functional part and the measurement part in the system.

When above conversion is done, each variable which is measured when it is updated and/or referred should be converted to one whose type is protected in order to avoid the whole system might suffer from race conditions.

The implementation environment for the tool to use for testing is gnat 3.11p[ ] and ASIS-for-GNAT 3.11p[ ].

4 A Tasking Deadlock Detector as an Example

For an example of measurement specifications and a measurement part of self-measurement concurrent systems, we present an implementation of a dynamic tasking deadlock detector for concurrent Ada programs which can detect all types of tasking deadlocks at run-time of target programs.

The deadlock detector can detect tasking deadlocks based on the Task-Wait-For Graph(TWFG for short)[ ][ ]. A TWFG is an arc-classified digraph whose vertices denote tasking objects in a run-time state of the target program and whose arcs denote synchronization waiting relations between tasking objects.

Tasking objects contain subprograms, tasks and protected objects in the target program. Synchronization waiting relations in Ada are classified into 7 types: activation waiting, finalization waiting, completion waiting, acceptance waiting, entry-calling waiting, protection waiting and protected-entry-calling waiting. Arcs in TWFGs are also classified into 7 types corresponding to the classification of the synchronization waiting relations. And the existence of a cycle in the TWFG is the sufficient condition for occurrence of some types of tasking deadlocks. The other types of tasking deadlocks, which include acceptance waiting relations, must have some additional conditions to occur.

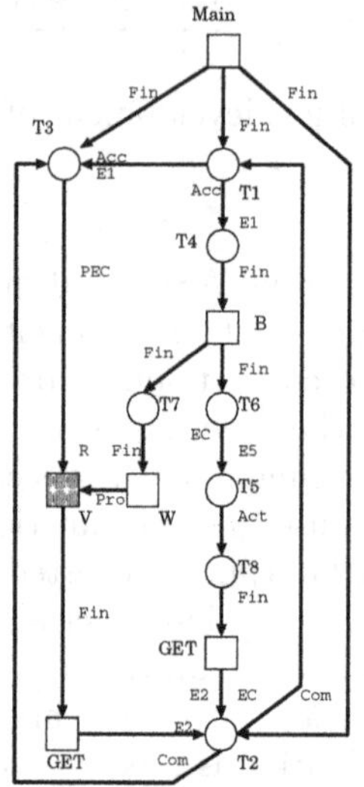

Fig. 3. An example of the Task-Wait-For Graph

Fig. shows an example of the TWFG. For example, the arc from T1 to T4 represents that T1 is "acceptance waiting" for T4, i.e., the task T4 could call the entry T1.E1 and the task T1 is on an accept statement for the entry E1.

Having TWFGs as a formal representation for the waiting state of task synchronization in an execution of an Ada program, a run-time detector for tasking deadlocks can work by monitoring the tasking behavior of the program, managing a TWFG for the program, detecting cycles in the TWFG, and reporting detected tasking deadlocks.

In the package specification of Dd_Spec(Deadlock Detector Specification), which is the measurement specification for the deadlock detector and can be used for any concurrent systems, requirements of information about occurrences of tasking events needed for managing the TWFG are described.

The package body of Dd_Spec is just for the bridge between the deadlock detector and the functional part. When it receives information of a tasking event from the functional part, it invokes a protected operation of TIC, which is presented below.

The package Tasking_Deadlock_Detector is the core part of the deadlock detector. It contains two protected objects, TIC(Task Information Collector) and TWFGM(Task-Wait-For Graph Manager). TIC has protected operations and each operation corresponds to a specific tasking event. Mutual exclusion of TIC preserves partial order of tasking events occurring[ ]. TWFGM has a TWFG as a protected data of the protected object itself and manages the TWFG by information from TIC, and when deadlocks occur, it reports those deadlocks.

This algorithm only depends on partial order of tasking events, so the order of two events which don't depend on each other does not have to be protected from race conditions.

This deadlock detector is an example of generic measurement components. But we have such a problem that the deadlock detector needs static analysis of the target program. The Communication-Dependent Task Set(CDT for short) represents sets of tasks, corresponding to each entry in the target program, where it is possible for the tasks to call the entry. Of course, it is needed to be done static analysis of the target program before executing the program to let the deadlock detector be able to get the CDT of the program at run-time.

But the architecture of our supporting tool for self-measurement systems only allows the measurement specifications to describe requirements for measurement targets of the run-time status. To enable the deadlock detector to be implemented as a measurement component of self-measurement systems, we added two new kinds of queries, "Get_CDT" and "Get_CDT_For_TT" to the specification of measurement specifications. If at least one of these queries is put into measurement specifications, the CDT of each task is sent to the measurement part when the task is elaborated. The CDT of the functional part of the target program are computed by the supporting tool while the functional part is statically analyzed and put into the self-measurement system.

Though the deadlock detector has been enabled to be implemented as a measurement component for the present, if the other measurement components would require static analysis of the target program like the case of the CDT, we must revise the architecture and the implementation of the supporting tool. To ensure the generality of the supporting tool, some methods to describe requirements of static analysis are needed.

We have another problem that performance of systems with the deadlock detector becomes very lower, which we cannot ignore for some applications. Though we mentioned that this deadlock detector was an example of generic measurement components, we must customize the measurement specification for the deadlock detector. To put it concretely, some blocks should be excluded from the measurement. Criteria to decide the exclusion are static assurance that tasking deadlocks must not occur, levels of critical parts in the system, and so on.

5 Another Example and Performance

In this section, we present a simple example of a functional part, a measurement part and measurement specifications for the supporting tool. As an example, we take up a parallel quicksort program. Fig. shows the source program, some parts of which are omitted. The tasks take their shares of the partial array of the target array. After one task divides a sub-array into two arrays, a left sub-array whose elements are less than the pivot and a right sub-array whose elements are greater than the pivot, another task is elaborated and the task takes its share of the right sub-array. The left sub-array is taken its share of by the original task. But the number of the tasks can be limited. If the number of the current tasks has reached the upper limit of the number of the tasks, new task is not elaborated and two sub-arrays are sorted sequentially. The number of elements for this example is 300,000 and the upper limit of the number of the tasks is 100.

```
with Ada.Text_IO; use Ada.Text_IO; with Ada.Numerics.Discrete_Random;
procedure Qsort is
   Max_Elements : constant Integer := 300000;
   Max_Tasks : constant Integer := 100;
   Samples : array(Integer range 1..Max_Elements) of Sample_Int;
   -- A protected object to limit the number of tasks.
   protected Limit_Task is
      procedure Increment(Result : out Boolean);
      procedure Decrement;
      private Count : Integer := 0;
   end Limit_Task;
   protected body Limit_Task is ... end Limit_Task;
   -- A procedure to make an array which has random elements
   procedure Generate_Sample is ...  end Generate_Sample;
   task type Qsort_Iter is
      entry Get_Range(Rfirst, Rlast : in Integer);
   end Qsort_Iter;
   procedure Qsort_Exec(Rfirst_T, Rlast_T : in Integer) is
      :
   begin
      if Rfirst_T < Rlast_T then
   -- To devide elements if greater or less than a certain pivot.
       :
 Limit_Task.Increment(Result);
      -- Result represents if a new task can be elaborated.
 if Result then
    declare Right : Qsort_Iter; begin
       Right.Get_Range(I, Rlast_T);  Qsort_Exec(Rfirst_T, J); end;
 else
    Qsort_Exec(Rfirst_T, J);  Qsort_Exec(I, Rlast_T);
 end if;
      end if;
   end Qsort_Exec;
   task body Qsort_Iter is
      Rfirst_T, Rlast_T : Integer;
   begin
      accept Get_Range (Rfirst, Rlast : in Integer) do
 Rfirst_T := Rfirst;  Rlast_T := Rlast;
      end Get_Range;
      Qsort_Exec(Rfirst_T, Rlast_T); Limit_Task.Decrement;
   end Qsort_Iter;
   Result : Boolean;
begin
   Generate_Sample;  Limit_Task.Increment(Result);
   if Result then
      declare Top : Qsort_Iter;
      begin Top.Get_Range(1, Max_Elements); end;
   else raise Tasking_Error; end if;
end Qsort;
```

Fig. 4. An example of a functional part in a concurrent system

```
-- In the package Global_Types, the type-- Unit_Class is defined
-- and it is used for sending information from the functional
-- part to the measurement part.
with Global_Types; use Global_Types;
package Qsort_Monitor is
   -- To set the measurement target as all of the program.
   pragma Designate_Subject("all");
   -- When an activation of a new task starts,
   -- this function is called.
   function Task_Activation_Start return Boolean;
   -- To limit the measurement target to two
   -- blocks named as "qsort" and "qsort.qsort_iter".
   pragma Designate_Subject("qsort", "qsort.qsort_iter");
   procedure Block_Execution_Completion (This_Unit_Class : Unit_Class);
   -- To limit the measurement target of callees of subprogram calls
   -- to a subprogram names as "qsort.generate_sample".
   pragma Designate_Subprogram("qsort.generate_sample");
   -- After subprogram calls to the designated subprogram are over,
   -- this procedure is called.
   procedure Procedure_Call_Completion;
end Qsort_Monitor;
```

Fig. 5. An example of measurement specifications

Fig.   shows the measurement specifications to measure and monitor the program shown in Fig. . The purposes of the measurement part in this example are

1. counting the total tasks elaborated in the run-time of the target.
2. computing the average number of the tasks per time which exist in the run-time.

To attain these purposes,

1. start and end of the sorting
2. elaboration and completion of each task

must be measured. The measurement specifications in Fig.   represent these requirements.

If you implements subprograms in the measurement specifications in Fig. , the result can be the measurement part of the system. In the body of the Task_Activation_Start, a counter for the number of tasks must be incremented. In the body of the Block_Execution_Completion, if a caller of the subprogram is a task, the counter must be decremented. If not, the result must be displayed. Each time must be recorded when the value of the counter is changed.

How about the lowering of the performance while the system including the measurement part is working? Table   shows the execution times of the two executables of the example, which are programs with the measurement part and without the measurement part. Their environment was Sun Ultra1 (Ultra SPARC 200MHz 1 processor, memory 128MB), Solaris 2.6, gnat 3.09.

Since some concurrent systems are working uncertainly because of the uncertainty principle of concurrent systems[ ], we measured the execution of each program for 10 times and we took up the average of 10 times for each program. We can find that the execution of the self-measurement systems took about 1.04 times as much as the execution time of the non-measurement systems.

Table 3. The execution time of two examples, which are self-measuring one and non-measuring one

	user(s)	system(s)	total CPU time(s)
self-measuring system	13.65	6.59	20.24
non-measuring system	13.07	6.39	19.47

measuring/non-measuring ratio
1.04

We can understand that the lowering of the self-measurement is not too much for such a simple example from Table . However, to ensure enough reliability for each concurrent system, measurement which needs much more loads is possible to have to be done. We should investigate the relation between reliability of concurrent systems and the performance.

6 Concluding Remarks

We have presented an architecture of a supporting tool for development of self-measurement systems with measurement specifications. Concurrent systems have been developed as separated-measurement systems, or each system has been developed while the functional part and the measurement part are confused and the measurement part of each system has been developed individually up to now. Our proposal enables self-measurement systems to be developed systematically. And we have also presented the design and implementation of our tool. We suppose that it should be expected to be a basis of a system to reuse measurement components, and as a result it must contribute improvement of reliability of concurrent systems. Finally, we have presented two examples of measurement components. One is a very generic component. The other is an application-specified component.

As a future work, the capability of the expressions by the measurement specifications must be improved. Since the current architecture only allows descriptions of basic requirements by the measurement components, information which they can get and what they can do for the system are limited.

And we must cope with the problem on race conditions. For example, which of two entry calls to the different two entries has executed earlier can't be detected by our current tool. How to measure tasking events with reserving order of them by source code transformation approach is unsolved problem.

And we formulate a plan about "Measurement Patterns." If there is generic measurement component for each design pattern[ ], measurement of softwares with design patterns become very easy by reuse of measurement components. We will try to design measurement components for design patterns, including patterns for concurrent, parallel and/or distributed systems[ ].

References

1. Barnes, J. : Programming in Ada 95, Addison-Wesley (1995)
2. Cheng, J., Ushijima, K. : Partial Order Transparency as a Tool to Reduce Interference in Monitoring Concurrent Systems, in Ohno, Y. (ed.), "Distributed Environments", Springer-Verlag (1991) 156-171
3. Cheng, J., Ushijima, K. : Tasking Deadlocks in Ada 95 Programs and Their Detection, in A. Strohmeier (Ed.), "Reliable Software Technologies - Ada-Europe '96," Lecture Notes in Computer Science, Vol. 1088, Springer-Verlag (1996) 135-146
4. Cheng, J. : The Self-Measurement Principle: A Design Principle for Large-scale, Long-lived, and Highly Reliable Concurrent Systems, Proc. 1998 IEEE-SMC Annual Int. Conf. on Systems, Man, and Cybernetics, vol.4 (1998) 4010–4015
5. Cheng, J. : The Wholeness Principle of Concurrent Systems and the Uncertainty Principle in Measuring Concurrent Systems, Proc. Int. Sympo. on Future Software Technology '98 (1998) 311–314 ,
6. Colket, C. et al. : Architecture of ASIS: A tool to Support Code Analysis of Complex Systems, ACM Ada Letters, Volume XVII, No. 1 (1997) 35–40
7. Cooper, C. D. : ASIS-Based Code Analysis Automation, ACM Ada Letters, Volume XVII, No. 6 (1997) 65–69
8. Gamma, E., Helm, R., Johnson, R., Vissides, J : Design Patterns: Elements of Reusable Object-Oriented Software, Addison-Wesley (1995)
9. International Organization for Standardization : Information Technology - Programming Language - Ada, ISO/IEC 8652:1995(E) (1995)
10. Maes, P. : Issues in Computational Reflection, Meta-Level Architecture and Reflection(Maes, P. and Nardi, D., eds.), Elsevier Science, North-Holland (1988) 21–35
11. Nonaka, Y., Cheng, J., Ushijima, K. : A Tasking Deadlock Detector for Ada 95 Programs, Ada User Journal, Vol. 20, No. 1 (1999) 79–92
12. Rybin, S., Strohmeier, A., Zueff, E. : ASIS for GNAT: Goals, Problems, and Implementation Strategy. ACM Ada Letters, Volume XVI, No. 2 (1996) 39–49
13. Schmidt, D. C. : Applying Patterns to Meet the Challenges of Concurrent Software, IEEE Concurrency, Special Edition on Software Engineering for Parallel Distributed Systems, Vol. 5, No. 3 (1997)
14. Schonberg, E., Banner, B. : The GNAT Project: A GNU-Ada 9X Compiler, Ada Europe News, No. 20 (1995) 10–19
15. Smith, B. C. : Reflection and Semantics in Lisp, Proc. ACM Sympo. on Principles of Programming Languages (1984) 23–35

On Persistent and Reliable Streaming in Ada

Jörg Kienzle

Software Engineering Laboratory
Swiss Federal Institute of Technology
CH - 1015 Lausanne Ecublens
Switzerland

email: Joerg.Kienzle@epfl.ch

Alexander Romanovsky

Department of Computing Science
University of Newcastle
NE1 7RU, Newcastle upon Tyne
United Kingdom

email: Alexander.Romanovsky@newcastle.ac.uk

Abstract. Saving internal program data for further use is one of the most useful ideas in programming. Developing general features to provide such data saving/ restoring is a very active research area. There are two application areas for such features we believe to be crucial: system fault tolerance and data persistence. Our analysis shows that the features used in these areas have a lot in common: they are to flatten data of different types and save them in a store which can be used later on. The recent revision of the Ada language standard, Ada 95, introduces a new mechanism called streams that allows structured data to be flattened. Streams are sequences of elements comprising values from possibly different types. Ada 95 allows programmers to develop their streams following the standard abstract class interface. In this paper we show how to use the stream concept for developing new features to provide internal program data saving suitable for fault tolerance and persistence. A hierarchy of different storage types, useful in different application domains, is introduced. The standard stream interface is extended, making it possible for programmers to have a better control of the way streams work by separating storage medium control from the actual stream type using the design patterns. The convenience of this new interface is demonstrated by developing a generic package allowing any non-limited object to be written into a storage device. It can be used for providing data persistence and as a state restoration feature in schemes used for tolerating software design faults.

Keywords. Streams, Persistence, Stable Storage, Design Patterns, Ada 95, Object-Oriented Programming, Fault Tolerance.

1 Introduction

Data are often kept in a secondary memory medium to be used in further program execution. It is not difficult to see that many modern services rely on saving data. Starting with databases and sequential files programmers have been trying to develop useful and general concepts in this area. How data are saved, what sort of API is provided, what assumptions are made (e.g. fault assumptions), etc., depends on the characteristics of the feature and on the application. In this paper we will concentrate on features which are used for saving and restoring values of internal program data. There are two main areas which require such features: developing fault tolerant systems and persistent systems.

Two general types of recovery are used in building fault tolerant systems [1]: forward and backward error recovery. When backward error recovery is used, the internal program data are saved in a memory which will not be affected by the faults assumed.

H. B. Keller and E. Plödereder (Eds.): Ada-Europe 2000, LNCS 1845, pp. 82-95, 2000.

Later on, should an error be detected, the program is returned into a previous correct state by restoring its internal data. Depending on the fault assumptions and on the recovery scheme used, the program can be either re-started (if we are dealing with hardware crashes) or a diversely-designed program (alternate) can be tried (if a recovery block scheme [2] is used to tolerate software design faults). The former approach is often referred to as checkpointing. The features which are used for data saving and restoring in the latter are often called state restoration features.

Data persistence [3, 4] relies on saving values of data from a program execution space so that they can be used in a later execution: that is the values "persist" from one execution to another. There are many possible schemes for supporting persistence; for a complete survey, the reader is referred to [5].

In our opinion fault tolerance and persistence are quite distinct program properties and there are important differences in the way data saving is used in these two areas. Persistence relies on saving data values to allow them to be used in a later execution. In fault-tolerant systems the state of the whole program at some moments of time is saved and stored in such a way that the same program can continue execution from one of these states. This means in particular that these states must be consistent. Although very often the designers of the persistence services cannot help extending them to allow some simplified forms of error recovery, in our opinion it is important not to mix them and separate them properly while building, for example, persistence services for fault tolerant systems.

While implementing a persistence service, designers do not take into consideration fault assumptions as this is not relevant. But when we save data for fault tolerance, we should make sure that they will survive all assumed faults; this means for example that for the recovery block scheme we can use main memory for data saving if we assume only design faults. While developing error recovery features one should often take into account that errors can be detected at any time: depending on the failure assumptions, it may be the case that the program crashes and that it is not possible to do any data saving after an error has been detected. Sometimes it should be possible to tolerate media failures as well. When developing a persistence service one can basically assume that the program works/finishes correctly and it can perform all actions required for persistence any time it wants.

The definition of persistence is not specific about how the program finishes. This is why several persistence services have been extended to provide some forms of fault tolerance. Although, this is a reasonable approach for many practical reasons (e.g. performance), generally speaking, these two services can be provided separately and we believe that it is important to view them as such.

The remainder of this paper is organized as follows: the next section explains briefly how Ada 95 streams work. Section 3 discusses our reasons for choosing them to implement persistence and fault tolerance. In the following section a flexible, stream-based approach which implements these properties is described. It allows, in particular, the designers of stable storage to introduce new types of storage for keeping data. Section 5 shows by an example how the persistent and reliable streams are to be employed by the users. Section 6 looks at shared passive packages and the last section outlines our plans for future research.

2 Streams in Ada 95

Ada 95 [6], the recent revision of the Ada standard, does not have elaborate features for backward error recovery or data persistence. This is why many attempts have been made to extend the language, for example, a recovery block scheme in [7], and two approaches for persistent Ada [8, 9]. We believe that extending the language is for many reasons not practical; in this paper we rely on standard Ada 95 only.

Among many other new features, Ada 95 introduces a new concept called streams. A stream is a sequence of elements comprising values from possibly different types. The values stored in a stream can only be accessed sequentially. Ada streams can be seen as one of the first incarnations of the *Serializer* design pattern described in [10]. The CORBA *externalization* service [11] and the Java *Serialization* package [12] are other examples that implement the *Serializer* pattern.

This pattern allows programmers to efficiently stream objects into data structures of their choice, as well as create objects from such data structures. The pattern can be used whenever objects are written to or read from flat files, relational database tables, network transport buffers, etc. The participants of the pattern are: *Reader*/*Writer* and *ConcreteReader*/*ConcreteWriter*, the *Serializable* interface, *ConcreteElement* and *Backend*.

The *Reader* and *Writer* part declare protocols for reading and writing objects. These protocols consist of read respectively write operations for every value type, including composite types, array types and object references. The *Reader* and *Writer* hide the *Backend* and the external representation format from the serializable objects. *ConcreteReader* and *ConcreteWriter* implement the *Reader* and *Writer* protocols for a particular backend and external representation format. The *Serializable* interface defines operations that accept a *Reader* for reading and a *Writer* for writing. It also should provide a `Create` operation that takes a class identifier as an argument and creates an instance of the denoted class. *ConcreteElement* is an object implementing the *Serializable* interface, which allows it to read and write its attributes. The *Backend* is a particular backend, such as a storage device, a relational database front-end or a network buffer. A *ConcreteReader*/*ConcreteWriter* reads from/writes to its backend using a backend specific interface.

The structure of the *Serializer* pattern is shown in the following UML class diagram:

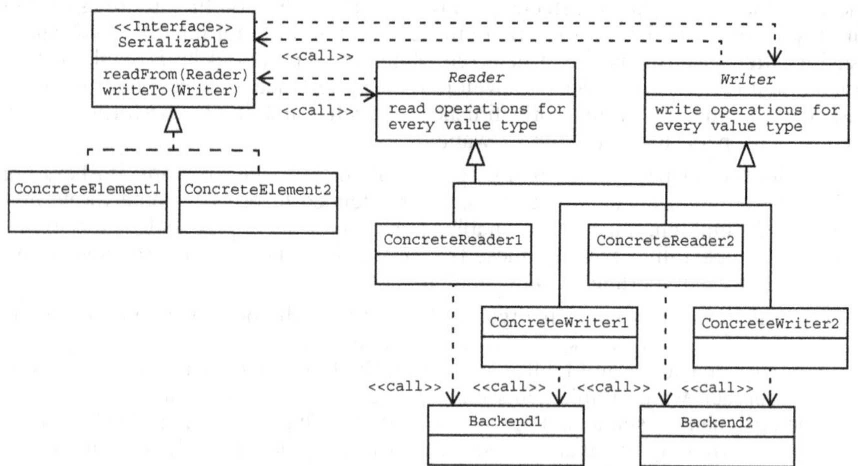

Figure 1: The *Serializer* Pattern Structure

When invoked by a client, a *Reader*/*Writer* hands itself over to the serializable object. The serializable object makes use of its protocol to read/write its attributes by calling the read/write operations provided by the *Reader*/*Writer*. This results in a recursive back-and-forth interplay between the two parties.

We will now show how Ada 95 streams implement the *Serializer* pattern. The standard package `Ada.Streams` defines the interface for streams in Ada 95 [6, 13.13.1]. It declares an abstract type `Root_Stream_Type`, from which all other stream types must derive.

Every concrete stream type must override the Read and Write operations, and may optionally define additional primitive subprograms according to the functionality of the particular stream. Obviously, the root stream type plays the *Reader/Writer* role in the *Serializer* pattern. Derivations of the root stream type incarnate the *Concrete-Reader/ConcreteWriter* and the backend interface.

In Ada 95, the pre-defined attributes 'Write and 'Output are used to write values to a stream, thus converting them into a flat sequence of stream elements. Reconstructing the values from a stream is done with the pre-defined attributes 'Read and 'Input. They make dispatching calls on the Read and Write procedures of the Root_Stream_Type. When using 'Write and 'Read, neither array bounds nor tags of tagged types are written to or read from the stream. 'Output and 'Input must be used for that purpose.

All non-limited types have default implementations of the stream attributes, hence all non-limited types implement the *Serializable* interface and are therefore *Concrete Element*. It is possible to replace the default implementation of the stream attributes for any type via an attribute definition clause. In order to write a value of a limited type to a stream, such an attribute definition clause is even mandatory. Any procedure having one of the predefined signature shown in [6, 13.13.2] can replace the default implementation. The following example shows how to replace the predefined implementation of 'Write for an integer type:

```
type My_Integer is new Integer;
procedure My_Write  (Stream   : access Ada.Streams.Root_Stream_Type'Class;
                     Item     : My_Integer);
for My_Integer'Write use My_Write;
```

The only concrete stream implementation that is defined in the language standard is Stream_IO [6, A.12], a child package of Ada.Streams. It provides stream-based access to files. Stream_IO offers also file manipulation operations such as Create, Open, Close, Delete, etc. The following example shows how to write values of elementary types, array types and tagged types to a stream and how to reconstruct them again:

```
with Ada.Streams.Stream_IO; use
Ada.Streams.Stream_IO;
-- writing
declare
  My_File: File_Type;
  S : Stream_Access;
  I : Integer;
  My_String : String := "Hello";
  T : A_Tagged_Type'Class := ... ;
begin
  Create (My_File "file_name");
  S := Stream (My_File);
  -- do some work
  Integer'Write (S, I);
  String'Output (S, My_String);
  A_Tagged_Type'Class'Output (S, T);
  Close (My_File);
end;
```

```
-- reading
declare
  My_File : File_Type;
  S : Stream_Access;
  I : Integer;
begin
  Open (My_File, "file_name");
  S := Stream (My_File);
  Integer'Read (S, I);
  declare
    My_String: String :=
      String'Input (S);
    T : A_Tagged_Type :=
      A_Tagged_Type'Class'Input (S);
  begin
    -- do some work
  end;
  Close (My_File);
end;
```

3 Our Intentions

Ada streams are a very powerful and universal object-oriented mechanism; our intention is to use them for developing fault tolerance and persistence features. This fits exactly the underlying idea behind Ada streams, which is that programmers can develop their own stream subclasses by inheriting from the given abstract class. These streams can be suitable for different purposes, media, data, applications, assumptions, etc. To the best of our knowledge there has been no research reported along this line.

This approach has many advantages. It allows us to stay within the standard Ada language, which makes our approach useful for any settings and platforms which have standard Ada compilers and run-times. Although proposals discussing various Ada extensions are of great importance for the future language standards, there are useless from the point of view of practitioners designing systems now.

We perfectly realize that the features we intend to develop do not meet all requirements of the *orthogonal persistence* [4], but paper [9] clearly demonstrates that it is impossible to develop it within standard Ada 95. Our intention is to stay within the standard and develop data saving mechanisms as elaborate as Ada allows.

Although, as we have explained before, we treat backward error recovery and persistence as different properties, our analysis shows that a general approach suitable for both areas can be developed, as they share common demands. Our approach will incorporate a class hierarchy of different streams which are intended for saving data so that it can be used for both purposes.

Streams only develop their full potential in the context of different streaming backends such as flat files, relational database tables or network transport buffers. We have found that in spite of the fact that Ada streams are a very general and powerful concept, the `Ada.Streams` package does not well separate different forms of streams, e.g. buffered streams, from different streaming backends. This separation and the provision of additional backend control are vital for applying streams for developing backward error recovery and persistence features in Ada.

In the following part of the paper we will discuss a general extensible object-oriented data saving mechanism suitable for developing reliable and persistent systems. This mechanism will be flexible enough to allow transparent changes of the media and will rely on standard Ada features only.

4 Ada Streams Revisited

This section presents a flexible approach to streaming which can be used for developing both backward error recovery and persistence features.

First we introduce a separation of buffered and non-buffered streams. We believe that these are essentially different and that it is important to introduce this difference on an abstract level. The two main reasons for this decision are:

- the stream control is different for buffered/non-buffered streams
- very often programmers can make performance optimizations because they know the peculiarities of the application with respect to buffering, size of data, phases of the program execution, characteristics of the media which stores the data, etc.

In the first subsection, an extended stream interface is proposed to allow an additional control related to buffered streaming. Secondly, we develop a type hierarchy which includes different storage types: *volatile*, *non-volatile*, *stable* and *non-stable*.

4.1 Buffered Streams

The Ada Reference Manual states that streams can be implemented in various ways, providing access to external sequential files, internal buffers or even network channels [6, 13.13]. The language manual provides an interface for streams by defining an abstract root type in the package `Ada.Streams` from which concrete implementations must derive. The only concrete implementation that is defined in the language standard is the stream type that provides sequential file access mentioned in the previous section. We have seen already that in addition to the operations defined for all stream types, the streams in the package `Stream_IO` provide file manipulation operations such as `Create`, `Open`, `Close`, `Delete`, and stream-related operations such as `Flush`. Calling `Flush` will actually write the data that has been previously written to the stream out to the file. `Flush` is an operation that takes a `File` as a parameter, but from our point of view, `Flush` should be an operation of the stream itself. Whenever streams are used to access storage devices, it is not always a good idea to write the data to the device on every call to `'Write` or `'Output`. At what time the data should be written to the device is largely device dependent. Disk devices for example are usually accessed in fixed-sized chunks of data called blocks. In this case, too many individual write accesses can result in considerable performance loss. It is much more efficient to buffer the data.

We have therefore defined a package `Streams` that provides two stream types, `Stream_Type` and `Buffered_Stream_Type`, both descendants of `Ada.Streams.Root_Stream_Type`.

```
with Ada.Streams; use Ada.Streams;
with Buffer_Types; use Buffer_Types;
package Streams is
   type Stream_Type (Storage : access Storage_Type'Class)
      is new Ada.Streams.Root_Stream_Type with private;
   procedure Read   (Stream   : in out Stream_Type;
                     Item     : out Stream_Element_Array;
                     Last     : out Stream_Element_Offset);
   procedure Write  (Stream   : in out Stream_Type;
                     Item     : in Stream_Element_Array);
   type Buffered_Stream_Type (Buffer : access Buffer_Type'Class)
      is new Ada.Streams.Root_Stream_Type with private;
   procedure Read   (Stream   : in out Buffered_Stream_Type;
                     Item     : out Stream_Element_Array;
                     Last     : out Stream_Element_Offset);
   procedure Write  (Stream   : in out Buffered_Stream_Type;
                     Item     : in Stream_Element_Array);
   procedure Flush  (Stream   : in out Buffered_Stream_Type);
end Streams;
```

This allows the user to choose between a normal stream (one that writes the data to the storage medium on every `'Write`) and a buffered stream (one that buffers the data until the user calls `Flush`). The type of storage that will be used for the stream must be chosen at instantiation time through an access discriminant (see section 4.2). This technique is described in [13] as the *Strategy* pattern.

The participants of the *Strategy* pattern are the *Strategy*, the *ConcreteStrategy* and the *Context*. The pattern defines a family of algorithms, encapsulates each one, and makes them interchangeable. It lets the algorithm vary independently from clients that use it. The most important participant is the *Strategy*, which declares an interface common to all supported algorithms (in our case the storage devices). *ConcreteStrategy* implements a concrete algorithm using the *Strategy* interface. Finally, *Context* is configured with a *ConcreteStrategy* object, and uses the interface defined by *Strategy* to call the algorithm.

An application programmer can instantiate a stream by passing the desired storage type as a parameter:

```
S : Stream_Ref := new Stream_Type (Instance_Of_Storage_Type);
```

4.2 The Storage Hierarchy

As shown in the previous subsection, a user starts by creating an instance of a storage type in order to instantiate a stream. The UML class diagram shown in figure 2 illustrates the hierarchy of storage types and the role they play in the *Strategy* pattern.

We split the storage hierarchy into *volatile* storage and *non-volatile* storage. Data stored in the volatile storage do not survive program termination, hardware crashes or transient errors. A volatile storage can for example be implemented using conventional computer memory. Once an application terminates or crashes, its memory is usually freed by the operating system, and therefore all internal program data are lost. On the other hand, data stored in non-volatile storage remain intact even when the program terminates. Databases or disk storage are commonly used for implementing non-volatile storage. Among the different types of non-volatile storage, we distinguish *stable* and *non-stable* ones. Data written into non-stable storage may get corrupted when the system fails (for instance, during the write operation). Stable storage ensures that the data that has been written on it will never be corrupted, even in the presence of application crashes and other failures [14]. If a crash occurs during the write operation, the previously valid state can still be retrieved. Features of this type are used in atomic transactions [15] to guarantee the durability of the database systems.

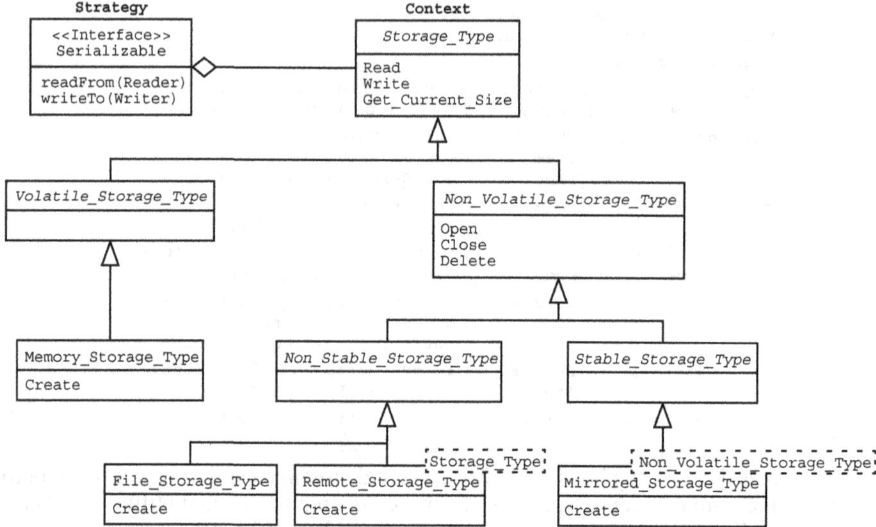

Figure 2: The Storage Type Hierarchy and the *Strategy* Pattern

The only two concrete storage types currently implemented are volatile memory and non-volatile, non-stable disk storage. The generic class `Remote_Storage_Type` allows any storage to be called remotely using the Ada Distributed Systems Annex, thus transforming the storage into a non-volatile storage. There are also two generic classes that allow to create stable storage based on non-stable storage, `Mirrored_Storage_Type` and `Replicated_Storage_Type` (not shown in the figure due to space reasons).

The interface of the top-level `Storage_Type` is given below:

```
with Ada.Streams; use Ada.Streams;
with Ada.Finalization; use Ada.Finalization;
package Storage_Types is
   type Storage_Type (<>) is abstract tagged limited private;
   type Storage_Ref is access all Storage_Type'Class;
   procedure Read   (Storage  : in out Storage_Type;
                     Item     : out Stream_Element_Array;
                     Last     : out Stream_Element_Offset) is abstract;
   procedure Write  (Storage  : in out Storage_Type;
                     Item     : in Stream_Element_Array) is abstract;
```

```
      function Get_Current_Size (Storage : in Storage_Type)
         return Stream_Element_Count is abstract;
   private
      type Storage_Type is new Limited_Controlled with null record;
   end Storage_Types;
```

Storage_Type is privately derived from Limited_Controlled in order to allow concrete storage implementations to perform automatic initialization and finalization, if necessary. Disk files for instance should always be closed, network ports should be freed, etc. Storage_Type is limited, so it can store, if necessary, other limited data, such as for example file descriptors. Finally, the public view of Storage_Type has unknown discriminants. That way the user of a storage type is forced to call one of the constructor functions of a concrete storage type; he can not just declare an instance of the type and thereby bypass correct initialization.

The operations provided by Storage_Type are Read, Write and Get_Current_Size. The Read and Write procedures are equivalent to the ones required for the stream type. Actually, the Read and Write procedures of the stream type are just call-though procedures to the associated storage device. The Get_Current_Size function returns the current length of the data associated with the storage in stream elements. This function has been introduced to simplify buffer management.

4.3 The Buffer Hierarchy

It is not difficult to see that to declare an instance of a buffered stream the user of the new Streams package (section 4.1) must first instantiate a buffer. Buffers here come in two flavors, unbounded and bounded.

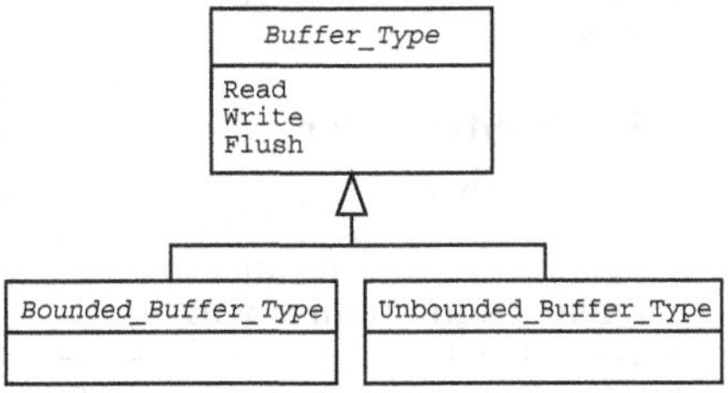

The package describing the abstract buffer type is shown below:

```
   with Ada.Streams; use Ada.Streams;
   with Ada.Finalization;
   use Ada.Finalization;
   with Storage_Types; use Storage_Types;
   package Buffer_Types is
      type Buffer_Type (Storage : access Storage_Type'Class)
         is abstract new Limited_Controlled with private;
      type Buffer_Ref is access all Buffer_Type'Class;
      procedure Read   (Buffer    : in out Buffer_Type;
                        Item      : out Stream_Element_Array;
                        Last      : out Stream_Element_Offset) is abstract;
      procedure Write  (Buffer    : in out Buffer_Type;
                        Item      : in Stream_Element_Array) is abstract;
      procedure Flush (Buffer : in out Buffer_Type) is abstract;
   private
      type Buffer_Type (Storage : access Storage_Type'Class)
         is abstract new Limited_Controlled with null record;
      procedure Finalize (Buffer : in out Buffer_Type);
   end Buffer_Types;
```


Figure 3: The Buffer Type Hierarchy

When using buffered streams, the user must first decide what kind of buffer he wants to use, instantiate it and pass the reference to the buffered stream. When instantiating a buffer, a storage device must be passed as a discriminant.

The buffer type is derived from Limited_Controlled in order to perform proper finalization of the associated storage device. The Read and Write operations of the buffered stream will call the Read and Write operations of the buffer type. In the Write procedure, the data is first written into a memory buffer, and only when Flush is called, the data is written out to the corresponding storage. Read does the inverse, that is it will try and read all the data or as much data as fits from the storage device into the buffer upon the first call to read. Subsequent calls can then be served without accessing the storage.

When implementing the unbounded buffer class, it was possible to use an instance of the volatile memory storage type to buffer the data. This illustrates the increased possibilities of reuse.

4.4 Non-Volatile Storage

Compared to volatile storage, data stored in non-volatile storage will survive program termination. It is therefore necessary to provide housekeeping operations similar to the ones provided by Ada.Streams.Stream_IO for files. These include above all operations for creation and destruction of such non-volatile data. The non-volatile storage type provides three new operations for this purpose:

```
procedure Open (Storage : in out Non_Volatile_Storage_Type) is abstract;
procedure Close (Storage : in out Non_Volatile_Storage_Type) is abstract;
procedure Delete (Storage : in out Non_Volatile_Storage_Type) is abstract;
```

Open allows the user to establish a connection between already existing data on the device and the storage type. This is for instance needed for files, but also for network sockets or databases. The Close operation severs the association again, leaving the data on the device. Delete is used to definitively remove the data from the storage device.

4.5 Identifying Non-Volatile Data

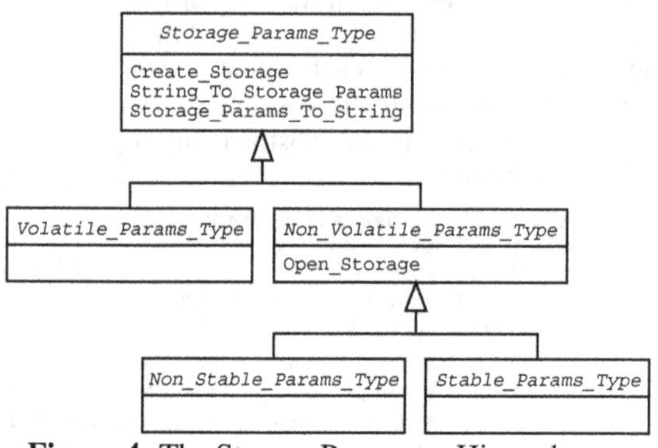

Figure 4: The Storage Parameter Hierarchy

Since the actual data stored on non-volatile storage will survive the lifetime of the object instance that represents it during program execution, there must be some means to uniquely identify the data in order to be able to manipulate the data again on subsequent runs of the application. Files usually have file names associated with them, but other storage types may use different identification techniques. Data stored in persistent memory for instance can be identified using addresses. In order to provide correct identification for each storage type, a hierarchy of storage parameter objects has been introduced. The class diagram in figure 4 shows the structure of the storage parameter hierarchy. It is identical to the one for storage types.

The first function, Create_Storage, allows a user to create an instance of the storage type that corresponds to the supplied storage parameters. This technique is known as the *Factory Method* pattern. A concrete Create_Storage will call the appropriate Create function of the storage type[1]. The second function, String_To_Storage

1. Remember that the storage type has unknown disciminants, and therefore the user can not declare an instance of the type without using this constructor function.

_Params, is provided to ease the creation of storage parameters. Strings can provide a common way to identify data, regardless on what actual type of storage device the data is stored on. Using the String_to_Storage_Params function and its inverse function Storage_Params_To_String it is also possible to identify data that moves from one storage device to another one using the same string.

For the same reasons as the non-volatile storage type, non-volatile storage parameters offer a new function Open_Storage that looks for already existing data on the storage device, creates an instance of the corresponding storage type and establishes a connection between the device and the instance.

5 Example

In this section we demonstrate how the new stream interface proposed in section 4 can be used for developing a generic package which can be used to make any non-limited tagged type persistent. The specification of this package is as follows:

```
with Ada.Streams; use Ada.Streams;
with Ada.Finalization; use Ada.Finalization;
with Streams; use Streams;
with Storage_Types.Non_Volatile; use Storage_Types.Non_Volatile;
with Storage_Params.Non_Volatile; use Storage_Params.Non_Volatile;
generic
   type Base_Type is tagged private;
package Persistent_Object_G is
   type Persistent_Type (<>) is new Base_Type with private;
   type Persistent_Ref is access all Persistent_Type'Class;
   function Create (Storage_Params : in Non_Volatile_Params_Type'Class)
      return Persistent_Ref;
   function Restore (Storage_Params : in Non_Volatile_Params_Type'Class)
      return Persistent_Ref;
   procedure Save (Object : in out Persistent_Type'Class);
private
   type Persistent_Data_Type is new Controlled with record
      Storage_Stream : Stream_Ref;
   end record;
   procedure Finalize (S : in out Persistent_Data_Type);
   procedure My_Write  (Stream   : access Ada.Streams.Root_Stream_Type'Class;
                        Item     : in Persistent_Data_Type);
   for Persistent_Data_Type'Write use My_Write;
   procedure My_Read   (Stream   : access Ada.Streams.Root_Stream_Type'Class;
                        Item     : out Persistent_Data_Type);
   for Persistent_Data_Type'Read use My_Read;
   type Persistent_Type is new Base_Type with record
      Data : Persistent_Data_Type;
   end record;
end Persistent_Object_G;
```

As you can see, mix-in inheritance is used to add three new operations to the base type: Create, Restore and Save. Since the persistent object type has unknown discriminants, Create and Restore must be used to declare an instance of a persistent object. Create will create a new instance from scratch, whereas Restore will try and read the contents of the instance from the storage device identified by the storage parameters, assuming that the object has been previously saved to the device. Save is the operation that must be called to store the contents of the object onto the associated storage.

To create persistent objects, the generic package must be instantiated:

```
with My_Types;
with Persistent_Object_G;
```

```
package Persistent_Integer is
   new Persistent_Object_G (My_Types.My_Integer_Type);
```

The following lines of code illustrate how an instance of such a persistent integer type can be saved to a file on disk:

```
with Storage_Params.Non_Volatile.Non_Stable.File_Storage_Params;
use Storage_Params.Non_Volatile.Non_Stable.File_Storage_Params;
declare
   S : Persistent_Integer.Persistent_Ref;
   P : File_Storage_Params_Type := String_To_Storage_Params ("filename");
begin
   S := Persistent_Integer.Create (P);
   S.I := ...;
   Save (S.all);
end;
```

Let's take a look at the implementation of this generic package. `Persistent_Type` adds a controlled component called `Persistent_Data_Type` to `Base_Type`. This `Persistent_Data_Type` contains a reference to a stream. The following lines of code show how this stream is allocated during a call to `Create`:

```
function Create (Storage_Params : in Non_Volatile_Params_Type'Class)
   return Persistent_Ref is
   Result : Persistent_Ref := new Persistent_Type;
begin
   Result.Data.Storage_Stream := new
   Stream_Type (Non_Volatile_Storage_Ref (Create_Storage (Storage_Params)));
   return Result;
end Create;
```

To create a stream, we need a storage object. To instantiate the storage we call the factory method `Create_Storage`, passing as an argument the given storage parameters.

Now we also understand why the persistent data type must be controlled. It is important to free the memory associated with the stream and release the storage device once the object no longer exists. The implementation of `Save` is also quite straightforward:

```
procedure Save (Object : in out Persistent_Type'Class) is
begin
   Persistent_Type'Class'Output (Object.Data.Storage_Stream, Object);
end Save;
```

The contents of the object are output to the stream using the `'Class'Output` attribute. The `Restore` function can then read the object back in using `'Class'Input`.

6 Shared Passive Partitions and Data Saving

Besides Ada streams, there is another standard Ada API that could be used for providing data persistence. The Distributed Systems Annex (Annex E) of the Ada 95 Reference Manual [6] defines so called *shared passive partitions* intended for providing access to global data shared between different partitions in a distributed system. During the configuration of a distributed Ada program, passive partitions are mapped to *processing nodes* or *storage nodes*. Any access of an active partition to a variable declared in a shared passive partition will then automatically be translated into an access to the designated processing node or storage node. A typical example of a shared passive partition is shared memory in a multiprocessor environment.

The Ada standard does not address the questions of whether the data kept in a shared passive partition survive program termination. If a shared passive partition is mapped to a non-volatile storage, such as files for example, the data stored in it may do so. The

Ada standard does not require this as it does not impose any links between persistence or fault tolerance, on the one hand, and distribution in general, on the other.

Starting with version 3.12, the GNAT compiler [16] has allowed non-distributed Ada programs to use shared passive partitions. The compiler maps each variable declared in a shared passive partition to a file named after the expanded variable name. In subsequent application runs, the contents of these variables are automatically initialized with the contents stored in the files.

Although shared passive partitions providing automatic data persistence are easier for the application programmer to use, we have decided against using them for many reasons:

- Although shared passive partitions are defined in the Ada standard, they are part of the Distributed Systems Annex, and therefore a standard Ada compiler is not required to support them. Even if shared passive partitions are supported, no guarantees can be given regarding data persistence, since the Ada Reference Manual does not address persistence at all.
- Which kind of storage is to be used for a particular object is decided at configuration time, and is therefore compiler-dependent. It is also less flexible as it is not possible to change the storage of an object during run-time.
- Using shared passive partitions makes adding support of new storage media difficult as the interface becomes compiler-dependent.
- Storage control is less explicit because data saving will occur automatically during every assignment to a variable that has been declared in a shared passive partition.
- Using shared passive partitions can cause a decrease in performance when fault tolerance features are implemented on top of persistence because, to provide fault tolerance, only state that is considered to be *consistent* should be saved to storage. For example, in *transactions* data stored in transactional objects are written to stable storage only when a transaction commits.

Nevertheless, we have contacted the authors of GLADE [17], the implementation of the Distributed Systems Annex of the GNAT compiler, to evaluate the possibility of using shared passive partitions as an interface to our storage hierarchy. A standard interface between the compiler and the storage hierarchy must be defined and the configuration language will have to be extended in order to allow programmers to choose the desired storage.

7 Conclusions and Future Work

In this paper we propose a general approach to developing flexible features for reliable and persistence streaming in Ada. Fault tolerance (via backward error recovery) and persistence supports can be developed using this approach. Our approach uses standard Ada features only and can therefore be used with any standard Ada compiler and runtime system. The approach heavily relies on the peculiarities of object-oriented programming: we propose a class hierarchy of the storages of different types suitable for achieving fault tolerance and data persistence; the resulting approach promotes re-use and object-oriented programming. Our approach uses basic ideas of Ada streams for flattening data of different types and adds the ability to keep the flattened data on different storage devices depending on the application requirements.

We have found that the standard Ada 95 stream interface does not separate sufficiently the different streaming backends from the actual streams. For this reason, a new interface for streams based on the *Strategy* pattern has been designed and implemented. The example of a generic package providing object persistence demonstrates the usefulness of this new interface.

In the future, we intend to gain more experience by implementing different kinds of storages, e.g. interfaces to databases, and by using complex realistic case studies. We will use the new stream interface to add persistence to our shared recoverable objects described in [18], and provide an automatic restore capability after crash failures. Our plans are then to implement some kind of concurrent transactional service built upon these abstractions. Another promising directions of the research is to implement state restoration features which can be used in the Ada recovery block scheme (the challenging task here is to facilitate state restoration and make it transparent for the users as much as possible).

8 Acknowledgements

Alexander Romanovsky has been partially supported by EPSRC/UK DISCS ("Diversity in Safety Critical Software") Project.

9 References

[1] Lee, P. A.; Anderson, T.: “Fault Tolerance - Principles and Practice”. In *Dependable Computing and Fault-Tolerant Systems*, volume 3, Springer Verlag, 2nd ed., 1990.

[2] Randell, B.: “System structure for software fault tolerance”. *IEEE Transactions on Software Engineering* ***1****(2)*, pp. 220 – 232, 1975.

[3] Atkinson, M. P.; Buneman, O. P.: “Types and Persistence in Database Programming Languages”. *ACM Computing Surveys* ***19****(2)*, pp. 105 – 190, June 1987.

[4] Atkinson, M. P.; Bailey, P. J.; Chisholm, K. J.; Cockshott, W. P.; Morrison, R.: “An Approach to Persistent Programming”. *Computer Journal* ***26****(4)*, pp. 360 – 365, 1983.

[5] Atkinson, M. P.; Morrison, R.: “Orthogonally Persistent Object Systems”. *VLDB Journal* ***4****(3)*, pp. 319 – 401, 1995.

[6] ISO: *International Standard ISO/IEC 8652:1995(E): Ada Reference Manual*, Lecture Notes in Computer Science **1246**, Springer Verlag, 1997; ISO, 1995.

[7] Kermarrec, Y.; Nana, L.; Pautet, L.: “Providing fault-tolerant services to distributed Ada 95 applications”. In *TRI-Ada’96 conference*, pp. 39 – 47, ACM Press, December 1996.

[8] Crawley, S.; Oudshoorn, M.: “Orthogonal Persistence and Ada”. In *Proceedings of TRI-Ada’94, Baltimore, Maryland, USA, November 1994*, pp. 298 – 308, ACM Press, 1994.

[9] Oudshoorn, M. J.; Crawley, S. C.: “Beyond Ada 95: The Addition of Persistence and its Consequences”. In *Reliable Software Technologies - Ada-Europe’96*, volume 1088 of *Lecture Notes in Computer Science*, pp. 342 – 356, Springer Verlag, 1996.

[10] Riehle, D.; Siberski, W.; Bäumer, D.; Megert, D.; Züllighoven, H.: “Serializer”. In *Pattern Languages of Program Design 3*, pp. 293 – 312, Addison Wesley, 1998.

[11] Object Management Group, Inc.: *Externalization Service Specification*, December 1998.

[12] Sun Microsystems: *Java Object Serialization Specification*, November 1998.

[13] Gamma, E.; Helm, R.; Johnson, R.; Vlissides, J.: *Design Patterns*. Addison Wesley, Reading, MA, 1995.

[14] Lampson, B. W.; Sturgis, H. E.: "Crash Recovery in a Distributed Data Storage System". *Technical report*, XEROX Research, Palo Alto, June 1979.

[15] Gray, J.; Reuter, A.: *Transaction Processing: Concepts and Techniques*. Morgan Kaufmann Publishers, San Mateo, California, 1993.

[16] Banner, B.; Schonberg, E.: "The Structure of the GNAT Compiler". In *Proceedings of TRI-Ada'94, Baltimore, Maryland, USA, November 1994*, pp. 48 – 57, ACM Press, 1994.

[17] Pautet, L.; Tardieu, S.: "Inside the Distributed Systems Annex". In *Reliable Software Technologies - Ada-Europe'98*, volume 1411 of *Lecture Notes in Computer Science*, pp. 65 – 77, 1998.

[18] Kienzle, J.; Strohmeier, A.: "Shared Recoverable Objects". In Harbour, M. G.; de la Puente, J. A. (Eds.), *International Conference on Reliable Software Technologies - Ada-Europe'99, Santander, Spain, June 7-11 1999*, volume 1622 of *Lecture Notes in Computer Science*, pp. 397 – 411, 1999.

Reengineering the Booch Component Library*

Jordi Marco and Xavier Franch

Dept. Llenguatges i Sistemes Informàtics, Universitat Politècnica de Catalunya
c/ Jordi Girona 1-3 (Campus Nord, C6) E-08034 Barcelona, (Catalunya, Spain)
{jmarco,franch}@lsi.upc.es

Abstract. Component-based software development heavily relies on the ability of reusing components from a library with as little effort as possible. Among others, valuable features for reusing from a component library are: adaptability to many contexts, extensibility, abstraction and high level of robustness with respect to changes in some of their components. In this paper we study one of the most widely used component library for Ada 95, the *Grady Booch's* one, mainly in relation to these features. Our study focuses on the *Container-classes* family, which present some drawbacks mainly due to the fact that some parent-classes depend on the concrete form of their children-classes. We propose a solution centred on changing the *Containers* base class. This new version of the *Containers* class offers a new concept, namely shortcut, that allows not only to avoid the dependencies between parent-classes and their children classes, but also offers some additional advantages, remarkably improving the efficiency of components.

1 Introduction

Component-based software development [,] heavily relies on the ability of reusing components from a library with as little effort as possible. Reusing from a library can only take place when the library fulfils some nice properties. To name a few:

- It should be versatile, offering a wide range of components with different functionalities, and also with the same functionality but different implementation strategies (each one suited for particular efficiency requirements).
- It should be open, in the sense that its users should be able to add easily other components to adapt the library to their own context.
- It should be stable, to avoid new future releases forcing changes on existing software.
- It should be abstract enough, to allow easy use.
- And of course, it should be correct and properly documented.

* This work has been partially supported by the Spanish research programme CICYT under contract TIC97-1158.

H. B. Keller and E. Plödereder (Eds.): Ada-Europe 2000, LNCS 1845, pp. 96– , 2000.

One of the best well-known component libraries for Ada 95 [ ] is the Grady Booch's one. This library was originally created for Ada 83 [ ] and reengineered first for C++ [ ] and later on for Ada 95 [ ]. This library fulfills many of the properties listed above, and it has proven to be very useful in the development of component-based software. However, it also presents some drawbacks that makes it not as powerful as it could be with respect to the following criteria:

- **Versatility.** It offers a wide range of components, but it is not as versatile as one could expect, because all its components have just a single implementation.
- **Efficiency.** Not only does the lack of many implementations provoke a loss of efficiency in some contexts, but some of these implementations are not efficient enough, because component interfaces do not allow direct access to certain parts of the implementation.
- **Openess.** New components and implementations for components could be added, but implementations for already existing components should look very similar to the existing ones, due to the internal structure of the library.
- **Stability.** Some feasible changes on implementations can damage existing programs, because component definitions make use in some places of features that are inherent of proper implementations.
- **Usage.** The mixture of specification and implementation characteristics in component definitions interferes with the easy understanding and use of the components therein.

The purpose of this paper is to make reengineering on the Booch library to solve these problems. The proposal is based mainly on changing a particular base class, *Containers*, in such a way that all the dependencies on a concrete implementation disappear. This new class allows easy integration in the library of new components and also of new arbitrary implementations for every component, even the already existing ones. Moreover, the new *Containers* class offers an enlargement in its interface that make its derived classes more efficient in a wider range of contexts. All the changes in the library do not affect existing programs which are using it; it only needs a recompilation step. However, existing programs could be improved with this new version of *Containers* to make them more efficient.

The rest of the paper is organised as follows. First, in Sect. 2, we analyse the Booch component library for Ada 95 describing the advantages and drawbacks that it presents. Then, in Sect. 3, we introduce the main features of a new *Containers* class that allows solving the problems that the *Booch* library presents. Section 4 explains the implementation details of the new *Containers* class. Next, in Sect. 5, we show the necessary modifications of the *Containers* children-classes and an example. Finally, in Sect. 6, we give the conclusions and future work.

2 Analysing the Booch Component Library for ADA 95

The Booch component library is one of the best-known component libraries for Ada 95 [ ]. This library was originally created for Ada 83 [ ] and reengineered first for C++ [ ] and later on for Ada 95 [ ]. The Ada 95 version of the Booch components is organised into three main super-classes: *Containers*, *Support* and *Graphs*, which have a common parent-class *BC*. The base class *BC* has no functionality at all, it only provides the definition of the common exceptions. The *Containers* category of classes provides a wide range of structural abstractions (lists, bags, sets, collections, etc.) using many widespread implementation techniques (chaining, hashing, search trees and so on). Figure shows the main hierarchy of these components; their code is available at [ ].

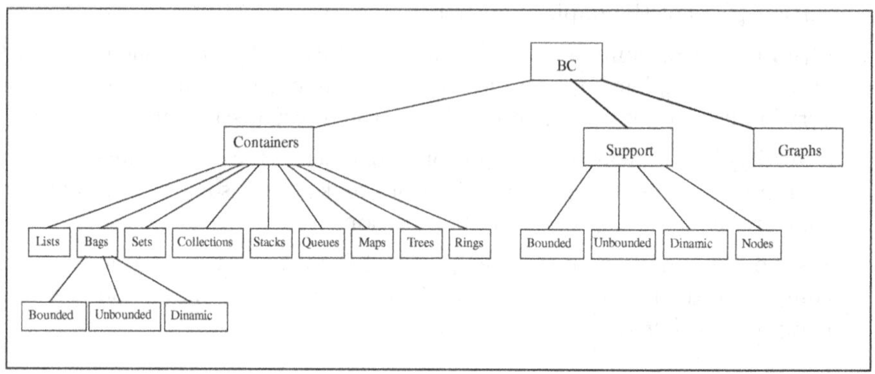

Fig. 1. Hierarchy of the Booch component classes (excerpt)

Our study is centred on the *Container* family of classes, which presents some drawbacks that decrease the potential of reusability of this component library. Most of the problems arise because some parent-classes depend on the concrete implementation of their children-classes. To make it clearer, Fig. shows a typical situation in this library, in which the *BC.Containers.Bags* class depends on the concrete form of its children classes *Bounded*, *Unbounded* and *Dynamic*, which are hashing tables. Notice that the type definition of *Bag_Iterator* forces all the *Bags* children to be implemented by means of a hashing table. This restriction interferes with the possibility of extending the class hierarchy or changing the concrete form of one of its children. All these dependencies exist because iterators are strongly dependent on the concrete container implementation. Similar

1 An iterator is a separate abstract data type, found in most of the existing comercial libraries, that allows iterating through all the items in a structure. Its existence and good behaviour is critical for a library being competitive, and this is why all of the most important component libraries offer them in one way or another.

dependencies can be also found between the classes *Maps*, *Sets*, *Queues*, etc., and their respective children. Therefore, to solve the problems we clearly need to make iterators independent of the specific container.

```
generic
package BC.Containers.Bags is
...
private
type Bag is abstract new Container with null record;
...
type Bag_Iterator (B : access Bag'Class)
is new Actual_Iterator (B) with record
  Bucket_Index : Natural := 0;
  Index : Natural := 0;
end record;
...
end BC.Containers.Bag;
```

Fig. 2. Extract of the generic package *BC.Containers.Bags*

To sum up, the main problems in this library are:

- The hierarchy is not robust enough with respect to changes in some of their components: changes in a component require the modification of other components. This is due to the implementation dependency mentioned above. For instance, changing the current hashing implementation of the *BC.Containers.Bags.Bounded* by an implementation (bounded) with a binary search tree (for instance, because elements must be obtained in some order), requires changing the implementation of the type *Bag_Iterator* (defined in the *BC.Containers.Bags* class) and the implementation of its operations as well.
- Moreover, this hierarchy restricts to a single set of possible implementations for some of the different structure abstractions. This is a serious drawback because some of the implementations provided therein can be inefficient in some contexts (we have already mentioned ordered traversal of *Bags*). For instance, it is not possible to have different implementations of the class *BC.Containers.Bags.Bounded*, because it is not implementation-independent, and hence it forces a concrete implementation strategy (hashing). This problem could be solved adding another level in the hierarchy, making the class abstract and defining their concrete children. This is not possible without changing other parts of the hierarchy, because of the implementation dependency again.
- Low level of abstraction makes the usage of the implementation harder. This happens when dealing with iterators. The iterator type and its operations are strongly dependent on the concrete implementation of the underlying structure. As a consequence, for every concrete implementation of a children-class a new *Actual_Iterator* type must be defined and its operations must

be overridden. This approach, which is different from many other libraries, prevents the easy usage of the iterator facility.
- It is not only the lack of multiple implementations for components that damages efficiency, but also some of the iterator operations have lineal cost in the worst case with respect to a certain parameter (although their amortised cost is constant). For instance, as shown in Fig. , the *Reset* operation could have linear cost with respect to the *Number_of_Buckets.* A similar problem occurs in the *Next* operation.

```
procedure Reset (It : in out Bag_Iterator) is
  begin
    It.Index := 0;
    if Cardinality (It.B.all) = 0 then
      It.Bucket_Index := 0;
    else
      It.Bucket_Index := 1;
      while It.Bucket_Index <= Number_Of_Buckets (It.B.all) loop
        if Length (It.B.all, It.Bucket_Index) > 0 then
          It.Index := 1;
          exit;
        end if;
        It.Bucket_Index := It.Bucket_Index + 1;
      end loop;
    end if;
end Reset;
```

Fig. 3. Reset operation's code of the generic package *BC.Containers.Bags*

- In many contexts in which components often encapsulate data structures, reusability can be damaged due to efficiency requirements: even if a component fulfils a required functionality, the time complexity of its operations may be inadequate given the context in which it should be integrated (either considering them individually or when combining them to build more complex components). The access by means of the operations offered by a component may be costly if the logical layout of the data structure is used; if fast access is required, it becomes necessary to look up the item using directly a reference to it.

It can be argued that these disadvantages are strong enough to reject the use of the Booch library. However, this is not the case; this library offers several advantages that make it very useful, mainly:

- A large amount of robust and well-designed components with appropriate algorithms and data structures.
- It is a well-known library supported by documentation and books.
- It is freeware.
- It has several and complete testing packages for its components.

Given the above advantages we think it is worth improving this library by solving the above mentioned problems, instead of discarding it and looking for building a brand new one.

3 A New *Containers Class*

The goal of this paper is to improve the containers-class family of Booch components library to avoid the problems shown in the previous section. Our approach consists on changing the base class *Containers* in such a way that the items will be stored in a generic container. Then iterators are implemented in this generic container and so they are independent of the concrete implementation of the children-classes. This generic container will offer efficient access paths to the items therein, which we call *shortcuts.* The *Containers* children-classes must store the shortcuts (that allow access to items) instead of the items themselves. In addition, the users can obtain an alternative, efficient and abstract way to access to the items stored in the structure.

The children classes of the new *Containers* class inherit from it the shortcuts and the operations. Therefore, the items stored therein can be accessed not only by using the operations given in the former specification, but also by means of other new ones that use the efficient paths. This results very useful whenever the operations are considered too expensive; on the other hand, since the addition of shortcuts does not affect the former behaviour of the existing operations, they can be used in the other cases as well.

Shortcuts solve the problems mentioned in the previous section:

- The items in the container can be accessed without knowing how they are stored in the container and, therefore, without knowing the underlying representation of the container (with arrays, pointers, linked, in tree-form, ...). Therefore, many implementations can exist together for the same type of container.
- The access to the items in a container by means of a shortcut is achieved in constant time, making it possible to reuse containers even with high efficiency constraints.
- The addition of shortcuts to a container does not modify its functional behaviour. This is assured by incorporating the concept of shortcut into the formal specification of the container (see [ ] for more details). Preservation of behaviour makes possible the substitution of old components by new ones.

Shortcuts are created and destroyed dynamically as items are inserted to and removed from a container; every item is bound to one (and only one) item. The shortcut bound to an item remains the same while it is inside the container, even if the underlying representation requires rearrangements. The access to the items by means of shortcuts is safe because meaningless access to them is avoided: our approach avoids dangling shortcuts or out-of-date ones.

4 Implementing the New *Containers* Class with Shortcuts

The essential point consists in implementing the generic container with a mapping from shortcuts to items. At the same time, items in the children components must be substituted by the shortcut that identifies them. The mapping from shortcuts may be implemented both using dynamic storage or an array; shortcuts are implemented then as pointers or cursors (i.e., array positions), respectively. Fields to obtain (in constant time) the shortcuts to the last item stored and to the *first* and the *last* item in the iterator order are necessary too; the field *first* to reset an iterator and the field *last* to add an item after the previous last item in the iterator order (which is not the same that the last item stored because it can have been added anywhere).

Released shortcuts must be available somehow to allow further reassignment, provided that there are not extra copies of it. When an item is removed from the container, it is marked as deleted. The corresponding shortcut can only be reused when there are no references to it. Therefore, memory management should be incorporated in the implementation. In this paper, shortcuts are implemented by pointers reusing a particular memory manager offered by the Booch's library itself.

To assure efficient and independent iterators we need to create a double-linked list of shortcuts, which means that we need $2 * N * space(\text{pointer}) + N * space(\text{shortcut})$ extra space (where N is the number of items in the container). Then, the iterators are implemented as shortcuts. The waste of this extra space offers a lot of benefits: the iterators are independent of the concrete form of the container, the efficiency of all the iterator operations is constant even in the worst case, and even this waste of space will generate a later saving, when shortcuts substitute identifiers (generally strings, which require more space than pointers or integers) in outer references from programs or other data structures.

Let's now establish formally the equation that assures the saving of space. Let N be the total number of items in the container and R the total number of external references. Since generally,

$$space(\text{item}) \geq space(\text{pointer})$$

then $\exists k \geq 1$ s.t. $space(\text{item}) \geq k * space(\text{pointer})$,
and since $space(\text{shortcut}) = 2 * space(\text{pointer})$ (see below) space is really saved when the relationship

$$R * space(\text{item}) \geq 4 * N * space(\text{pointer})$$

holds, which is satisfied when the following relationship holds:

$$R * k \geq 4 * N \ .$$

Figure shows the implementation of the types of the new class *BC.Containers*. The *Shortcut* type is implemented with a record with two fields: the first one is an access to the *Container* to which the shortcut is associated and the last one is a pointer (reused from *BC.Smart*) to the node where the item is stored. The *Node* type is a record with four fields: the first one is the item itself, the second and the third ones are pointers to maintain doubled-linked list of items and the last one is a boolean to mark the item as deleted when it has been logically removed but there are still some shortcuts that refer to it. The *Container* type is a record that maintains the corresponding fields for the last, first and last added items, and an additional field to obtain the number of items therein in constant time.

```
with BC.Smart;
generic
  type Item is private;
  with function "=" (L, R : Item) return Boolean is <>;
package BC.Containers is
  type Container is new Ada.Finalization.Controlled with private;
  type Shortcut is private;
  type Iterator is private;
  function "=" (L, R : Shortcut) return Boolean;
...
private
  type Node;
  type Access_Node is access Node'Class;
  type Access_Node_P is access Access_Node;
  package SP is new BC.Smart (T => Access_Node, P => Access_Node_P);
  type Shortcut_Pointer is new SP.Pointer;
  function Create_Node(C : Container) return Access_Node;
  type Access_Container is access all Container;
  type Shortcut is record
      Position: Shortcut_Pointer;
      For_The_Container: Access_Container := null;
    end record;
  type Node is tagged record
      Elem: Item;
      Next: Shortcut_Pointer;
      Previous: Shortcut_Pointer;
      Deleted: Boolean := FALSE;
    end record;
  type Iterator is new Shortcut;
  type Container is new Ada.Finalization.Controlled with record
      Cardinality: Natural := 0;
      First_Item: Shortcut_Pointer;      -- For access to the first and
      Last_Item: Shortcut_Pointer;       -- the last items by shortcuts.
      Last_Item_Added: Shortcut_Pointer; -- To obtain the shortcut bound
    end record;                          -- to the last item added.
...
end BC.Containers;
```

Fig. 4. New *BC.Containers* class

This scheme also works, without further considerations, in the case of the linear containers, such as stacks, lists, and so on. Figure , on the left, shows this situation with stacks. Now, the stack contains just shortcuts, and the objects are stored in a generic container, directly accessible by means of the shortcut. In the case of types accessed by some kind of key, like bags, maps, etc., we need to define the functions required for the concrete implementation over the shortcuts (for instance, the equality function and, in case of a hashing table, the hash function). These new functions will consist in applying the original function to the item associated to the shortcut. The scheme is shown in Fig. , on the right, and the Ada 95 code can be found in [ ].

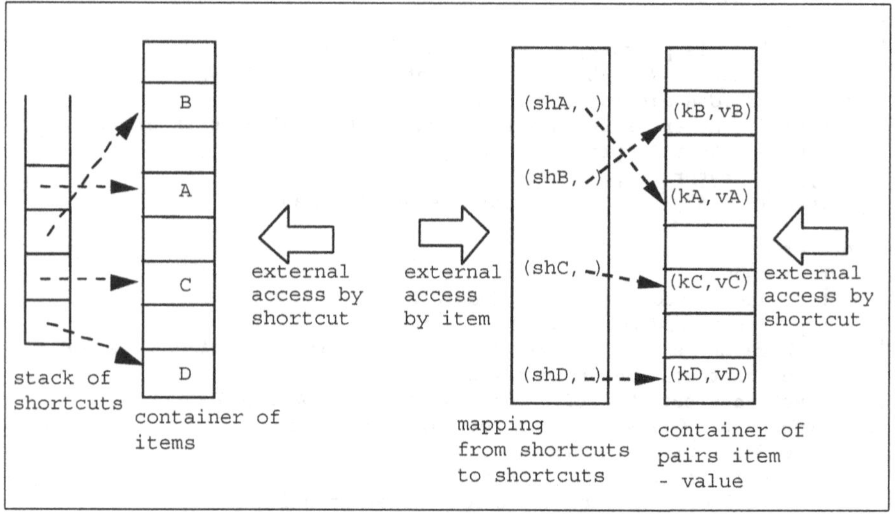

Fig. 5. Adding shortcuts to linear structures (left) and to mappings (right)

The new *Containers* class includes, in addition to the operations offered by the old one, seven new ones shown below. The first three ones are public while the others are private and, as a consequence, can only be used by the children classes (Fig. shows the signature of these operations; see [ ] for a complete implementation). Their behaviour is as follows:

- *Add* adds the given item into the container in the last position (with respect to the iterator order). To be used in concrete containers implementations that do not require a special traversing order.
- *Add_After* adds the given item after the one bound to the given shortcut (with respect to the iterator order). If the shortcut is undefined, an exception arises. To use in concrete containers implementations that require a special traversing order.
- *Shortcut_To_The_Last_Item_Added* returns the shortcut that allows accessing to the last item added (using *Add* or *Add_After*) into the container. If there

are no items in the container, it returns an undefined shortcut. This operation is required to obtain the shortcuts from the data structure; once obtained, it can be stored in other data structures and then coupling of structures without duplication of items is possible.
- *Item_Of* returns the item bound to the given shortcut. If the shortcut is undefined, an exception arises.
- *Defined* returns true if there is an item associated to the given shortcut, otherwise returns false.
- *Remove* removes from the container the item associated to the given shortcut. If the shortcut is undefined, an exception arises.
- *Node_Of* returns an access to the node where the item associated to the given shortcut is stored. If the shortcut is undefined, an exception arises. This operation is required in order to access to the values that have been stored together with the item, if it is the case. In the children classes, public efficient operations to access to these values by shortcuts can be defined. To allow this, the *Node* type is tagged and the children classes can define a new *Node* type with the necessary extra fields; in this case, the *Create_Node* function (see Fig.) has to be overridden.

```
...
generic
...
package BC.Containers is
...
  function Shortcut_To_The_Last_Item_Added
                      (In_The_Container : Container) return Shortcut;
  function Item_Of (The_Shortcut : Shortcut) return Item;
  function Defined (The_Shortcut: Shortcut) return Boolean;
...
private
...
  procedure Add (In_The_Container:in out Container'Class; Elem:Item);
  procedure Add_After (The_Shortcut: Shortcut;
                       In_The_Container : in out Container;
                       Elem: Item);
  procedure Remove (The_Shortcut : Shortcut);
  function Node_Of(S : Shortcut) return Access_Node;
...
end BC.Containers;
```

Fig. 6. Signature of the new operations of the *BC.Containers* class

We remark that the cost of all these operations as well as all the iterator operations is constant even in the worst case. Another important feature is that the operations *Shortcut_To_The_Last_Item_Added*, *Item_Of* and *Defined* are public and they are inherited by the children-classes of Containers. In consequence, all the children classes offer shortcuts and their users can take profit of them to improve the efficiency of their programs.The complete implementation can be found not only in [ ] but also in `ftp://ftp.lsi.upc.es/pub/users/jmarco/`.

5 Using the New *Containers* Class

In this section, we explain the steps required to modify the *Containers* children-classes to adapt them to the new *Containers* class. First, we explain the general changes required and then we applied the required changes to a concrete example, the class *BC.Containers.Bags.Bounded* and its ancestors.

In the general case, the changes required in the *Containers* children-classes are:

- Remove the specification and the implementation of the concrete iterators (i.e., the new *Actual_Iterator*).
- Modify the operations that take into account features that are tied to the concrete implementation of the new *Actual_Iterator.*
- In the class where the container is implemented we must:
  - Replace the items by shortcuts.
  - If there are elements to store together with the item (as in the example below), then define a new *Node* type and override the function *Create_Node* to initialise these elements.
  - If the existing implementation needs some specific functions (e.g., a hash function in the case of a container implemented by hashing), then redefine them working on shortcuts instead of items.
  - For every operation that works with items, add the indirection required to work with shortcuts instead of items.

We present below an example of the (few) changes to be done in the *Containers* children-classes. More precisely, we explain the required changes in the class *BC.Containers.Bags* and *BC.Containers.Bags.Bounded*, respectively. Similar changes should be done to the rest of children-classes.

The only required change in the package specification *BC.Containers.Bags* is to remove the iterators therein, i.e. the new *Actual_Iterator* type as well as its corresponding operations (Fig. shows the part of the specification that must be removed).

The changes required in the package body are: removing the body of all the iterator operations and modifying the *Intersection* operation, because this operation takes into account that the elements in the hashing table can change their position when removals take place. Therefore the iterator to the next element remains the same. Figure presents the new *Intersection* operation (the changes are marked with a comment IS NEW).

The required changes of the *Containers.Bags.Bounded* are to create the hash table with shortcuts as items and as values (see Fig.) and to remove the specification of the functions *Item_At* and *Value_At* and of the type *Bounded_Bag_Iterator* in the specification package. Notice that we need to store the number of copies of an item (because a bag actually owns only one copy of each item and it counts the duplicates). We must then define a new *Node* type to store the number of occurrences together with the item. In consequence, the function *Create_Node* (introduced in Sect. 5) must be overridden. We must also define the function

```
...
generic
...
package BC.Containers.Bags is
...
private
...
  type Bag_Iterator (B : access Bag'Class)
  is new Actual_Iterator (B) with record
    Bucket_Index : Natural := 0;
    Index : Natural := 0;
  end record;
  procedure Initialize (It : in out Bag_Iterator);
  -- Overriding primitive supbrograms of the concrete actual Iterator.
  procedure Reset (It : in out Bag_Iterator);
  procedure Next (It : in out Bag_Iterator);
  function Is_Done (It : Bag_Iterator) return Boolean;
  function Current_Item (It : Bag_Iterator) return Item;
  function Current_Item (It : Bag_Iterator) return Item_Ptr;
end BC.Containers.Bags;
```

Fig. 7. Types and operations of the *BC.Containers.Bags* class that must be removed

```
procedure Intersection (B : in out Bag'Class; O : Bag'Class) is
...
        if not Exists (O, This_Item) then
            Aux := It;                      -- IS NEW
            Next(Aux);                      -- IS NEW
            Detach (B, This_Item);
            It := Aux;                      -- IS NEW
        else
...
  end Intersection;
```

Fig. 8. New version of *Intersection* operation of the *BC.Containers.Bag*

"=" and the function *New_Hash* to take into account the necessary indirection provoked by storing the shortcuts instead of the items.

In the package body, we must add for every operation the corresponding indirection to access to the item besides of the corresponding implementation of *Create_Node*, "=" and *New_Hash*. Figure shows the implementation of these three functions and, as an example of how indirections are added, the implementation of the operation *Add*. In [ ], we present the whole new *Containers* class and the classes *Containers.Bags* and *Containers.Bags.Bounded* with all the required modifications.

In the operation *Add*, we associate first a shortcut to the item, and then we ask if it is already bound to some item in the hash table. If it is already bound, we must increment the number of occurrences using the previous shortcut associated to the item and remove the temporal one.

```
...
generic
...
package BC.Containers.Bags.Bounded is
...
private
  function "=" (L, R : Shortcut) return Boolean;
  type Shortcut_Ptr is access all Shortcut;
  package IC is new BC.Support.Bounded (Item => Shortcut,
                                        Item_Ptr => Shortcut_Ptr,
                                        Maximum_Size => Size);
  use IC;
  package VC is new BC.Support.Bounded (Item => Shortcut,
                                        Item_Ptr => Shortcut_Ptr,
                                        Maximum_Size => Size);
  use VC;
  type Node_Bag is new Node with
    record
      Value : Positive;
    end record;
  function Create_Node(B: Bounded_Bag) return Access_Node;
  function New_Hash(S : Shortcut) return Positive;
  package Tables is new BC.Support.Hash_Tables
     (Item => Shortcut,
      Hash => New_Hash,
      Value => Shortcut,
      Value_Ptr => Shortcut_Ptr,
      Buckets => Buckets,
      Item_Container => IC.Bnd_Node,
      Item_Container_Ptr => IC.Bnd_Node_Ref,
      Value_Container => VC.Bnd_Node,
      Value_Container_Ptr => VC.Bnd_Node_Ref);
  type Bounded_Bag is new Bag with record
    Rep : Tables.Table;
  end record;
...
end BC.Containers.Bags.Bounded;
```

Fig. 9. Changes in the package specification *BC.Containers.Bags.Bounded*

6 Conclusions

Component libraries play currently a crucial role on software development. The existence of a wide variety of such libraries, both general-purpose and also field-specific, is becoming essential and its importance will increase in the future. However, nowadays a twofold phenomena occurs. On the one hand, most of the existing libraries present some features that can be improved, concerning quality factors as efficiency, usability, functionality, etc. On the other hand, potential

```
...
package body BC.Containers.Bags.Bounded is
...
function Create_Node(B : Bounded_Bag) return Access_Node is
  A : Access_Node;
  begin
    A := new Node_Bag;
    Node_Bag(A.all).Value := 1;
    return A;
  end Create_Node;
function "=" (L, R : Shortcut) return Boolean is
begin
  return Item_Of(L) = Item_Of(R);
end "=";
function New_Hash (S : Shortcut) return Positive is
begin
  return Hash(Item_Of(S));
end New_Hash;
...
procedure Add (B:in out Bounded_Bag; I:Item; Added:out Boolean) is
  sh : Shortcut;
  A : Access_Node;
  begin
    Containers.Add(B,I);
    sh := Shortcut_To_The_Last_Item_Added(B);
    if Tables.Is_Bound(B.Rep,sh) then
      sh := Tables.Value_Of (B.Rep, sh);
      A := Node_Of(sh);
      Node_Bag(A.all).Value := Node_Bag(A.all).Value + 1;
      Added := False;
      Remove(Shortcut_To_The_Last_Item_Added(B));
      B.Last_Item_Added := sh.Position;
    else
      Tables.Bind (B.Rep, sh, sh);
      Added := True;
    end if;
  end Add;
...
end BC.Containers.Bags.Bounded;
```

Fig. 10. Implementation of the functions *Create_Node*, =, *New_Hash* and of the operation *Add* of *BC.Containers.Bags.Bounded*

clients of the library tend to simply discard it if it does not fit completely into their context. Our point of view is that both phenomena will be corrected little by little, when maturity in the field will be reached.

Our paper tries to be a contribution to this madurity process. We have presented here a case study of reengineering a good library, the Booch one, that presents a few drawbacks. First, we have enumerated the advantages and disadvantages it presents and then we have proposed a solution to all the drawbacks. The solution is based on designing a new *Containers* base class that avoids the problems and also offers a new type that implement the concept of *shortcut*, as an alternative access path to items in the container. Shortcuts are interesting because, besides of assuring fast access time to items in the container, they are abstract (independent of the implementation of the component), persistent (movements inside the data structure do not affect them), secure (meaningless accesses are not possible) and they preserve behaviour (the new component behaves as the old one). Therefore, both existing and new software can benefit from the nice properties that present the concept of shortcut. We have also shown the few necessary changes in the *Containers* children-classes to use the new *Containers* base class. The paper focuses in the technical details to show the feasibility of the reengineering process and to make explicit the cost of this process.

The library with the modifications presented in this paper can be found in `ftp://ftp.lsi.upc.es/pub/users/jmarco/`.

We would like to point out the benefits of our approach:

- The Booch library is improved from many points of view: versatility, persistence, openess, efficiency and ease of use.
- This improvement has been made in a very comfortable way; with only few changes needed. The core data structures and algorithms are the same without any modification at all.
- The concept of shortcut is general enough to be exported to other libraries. In fact, most of the main existing component libraries offer it in many different ways [,]. The advantage of our proposal is that it provides a systematic way of adding shortcuts to existing libraries, instead of putting them in the library from the very beginning.
- The reengineering process does not interfere with the previous behaviour of the library (both for functionality and for efficiency) and, in consequence, existing software that use this library does not need to be modified; only recompilation is needed.
- But existing software could be modified in a methodical way (basically, changing the way of accessing to the structure) to take profit of the new version of the library. New software, of course, will be built in general using the new layout of the structure, making intensive use of shortcuts.
- The new library has been tested using the *bag_test* provided by the original Booch library without any modification.

References

Ada95. S. Tucker Taft and R.A. Duff (Eds.). *Ada 95 Reference Manual.* Lecture Notes in Computer Science 1246, Springer–Verlag, 1995. ,

Boo87. G. Booch. *Software Components with Ada.* The Benjamin/Cummings Publishing Company, 2nd edition, 1987. ,

BV90. G. Booch and M. Vilot. The Design of the C++ Booch Components. In *Proceedings of Conference on Object Oriented–Programming: Systems, Languages and Applications (OOPSLA)*, volume 25 of *SIGPLAN Notices*, pages 1–11. ACM, 1990. ,

BWW99. G. Booch, D.G. Weller and S. Wright. The Booch Library for Ada 95 (version 1999). Available at http://www.pogner.demon.co.uk/components/bc.

FM00. X. Franch and J. Marco. Adding Alternative Access Paths to Abstract Data Types. To appear in *Proceedings of 2000 Information Resources Management Association International Conference (IRMA)*. To celebrate in May 2000.

Jaz95. M. Jazayeri. Component Programming – a fresh look at software components. In *Proceedings of 5th European Software Engineering Conference (ESEC)*, volume 989 of *LNCS*, pages 457–478. Springer–Verlag, 1995.

MF99. J. Marco and X. Franch. Reengineering the Booch Component Library (extended version). Technical Report 1999–46–R, Departament de Llenguatges i Sistemes Informàtics. Universitat Politècnica de Catalunya, 1999.

MN99. K. Mehlhorn and S. Näher. *The LEDA Platform of Combinatorial and Geometric Computing*. Cambridge University Press, 1999.

MS96. D.R. Musser and A. Saini. *STL Tutorial and Reference Guide*. Addison–Wesley, 1996.

Sit+94. M. Sitaraman (coordinator). Special Feature: Component–Based Software Using RESOLVE. *ACM Software Engineering Notes*, 19(4):21–67, October 1994.

GtkAda: Design and Implementation of a High Level Binding in Ada

Emmanuel Briot[1], Joël Brobecker[2], and Arnaud Charlet[1]

[1] ACT Europe, 8 rue de Milan, 75009 Paris, France
[2] 218-1741 West 10th avenue, V6J 2A5 Vancouver B.C., Canada

Abstract. The purpose of this paper is to describe the design and implementation choices that were made during the development of an Ada binding to the popular Gtk+ graphical toolkit. We concentrate on the methods used to interface between C and Ada, but many topics described in this paper are not tied to Ada and can be applied to other high level languages that need to interface with existing libraries. We also describe the various mechanisms developed to provide a powerful GUI builder with GtkAda.
This paper emphasizes the added value that Ada brings to the task of writing a high level binding over an existing library.

1 Introduction to Gtk+

Gtk+ is a powerful graphical toolkit originally developed as part of the GIMP [ ] (the *GNU Image Manipulation Program*). Since Gtk+ had been designed to be cleanly separated from the rest of the GIMP code, and given the success of the toolkit, it became eventually obvious that the Gtk+ library should be made a stand-alone capability so that other applications could take advantage of it.

Thanks to its elegant Object-Oriented design, its efficiency, and its portability, this toolkit has become very popular and is being used in many applications. In particular, the GNOME [ ] project (the *GNU Network Object Model Environment*) which intends to build both a complete, easy-to-use desktop environment for the user, and a powerful application framework for the software developer, has chosen Gtk+ as its graphical library.

Another important advantage of Gtk+ is that it was designed to make it easy to create bindings to it for various languages. Any construct that could make the binding task more complex, such as procedures with variable arguments for example, were mostly avoided. This explains why there are currently more than twenty different listed bindings based on Gtk+.

Gtk+ has thus become the graphical toolkit of choice. Along with its associated tools, such as code generators like GtkGlade [ ], it offers a complete suite to develop graphical user interfaces in a portable way, and with a common look-and-feel.

H. B. Keller and E. Plödereder (Eds.): Ada-Europe 2000, LNCS 1845, pp. 112– , 2000.

2 The GtkAda Project

The GtkAda project started with the observation that there was no complete high level graphical library freely available for Ada. From this simple idea, we had to decide which library our toolkit would be based on. The obvious choices were Motif and Gtk+. Motif because it was a widely used and known standard; Gtk+ because of its free software status, its modern design, and its open architecture, which makes it easy to interface to it from other languages. The main drawbacks of Motif are the requirement to have an X server to run it, and its "old" interface that suffers some disadvantages that Gtk+ avoids, for example the absence of built-in support for multi-threaded applications.

2.1 Thin and Thick Bindings

A *thin binding* is a simple line-for-line translation that is usually done automatically or semi-automatically, to transform a foreign language interface into Ada specifications. Little attempt, if any, is made to introduce additional type safety and "real" Ada types, such as strings instead of null terminated character pointers, high level constructs such as tagged types, controlled types, etc.

The term *thick binding* usually relates to a library interface that goes beyond – sometimes far beyond – the simple task of mapping the foreign language types and routines, providing an API that is closer to what a similar library written directly in Ada would provide. Ideally, a good *thick binding* should "hide" the fact that it is using an external library internally, turning this into an "implementation detail".

This is where the term *thick binding* seems inadequate, because by providing a language-friendly interface and by adding extra functionalities, we are really making available a complete toolkit on its own. Because of this we like to refer to GtkAda as an *Ada Graphical Toolkit.*

3 How to Add Safety to a C Library

The first level of safety is brought by the Ada language itself. As opposed to C, Ada provides type safety via a strong typing policy which prevents the user from mixing inadvertently 2 different types. *Enumerated types* are also used to our advantage to replace C enums. In contrast to C, where it is possible to use an out-of-range value, Ada enforces at compile-time the usage of valid enumerations values only.

A central difficulty in binding to Gtk+ is the systematic usage of *C strings* (*char∗*), which leads to memory management problems, such as memory leaks, dangling pointers, etc. Instead, GtkAda uses the more natural type String, which allows the user to avoid all these problems. Converting an Ada String to C is achieved by simply appending ASCII.Nul to the Ada strings. Converting a C string to Ada presents additional problems. Although the conversion itself is straightforward with the services provided in Interfaces.C.Strings, the memory management part has to be handled by GtkAda to avoid memory leaks.

A similar problem arises for arrays. Whereas passing an Ada array to a C function in a portable fashion is easy (give the address of the first element), getting an array back is trickier. For instance, it is in general not possible to ask the user to allocate an array, and pass it as an "out" parameter, because this would require knowledge of the size of the returned array. Likewise, unless one knows the internals of the implementation of arrays and their bounds in Ada, i.e. the way the structures are laid out, it is not possible to recreate a complete Ada array without copying the data element by element, which of course is inefficient.

The solution we have used is to provide "flat arrays", that have no real bounds (effectively they have the maximum possible bounds), as seen in figure . With the declarations given therein, a function that interfaces to the C library should return a System.Address, that can then be safely converted into a valid Ada array. Of course, the bounds information has to be read from elsewhere, generally as an out parameter of a C function, since it is not available within the new array. A `Points_Array` structure is created to closely associate the flat array with its real bounds.

```
type Gdouble_Array is array (Natural) of Gdouble;
type Gdouble_Array_Access is access all Gdouble_Array;
type Points_Array is record
   Points     : Gdouble_Array_Access;
   Num_Points : Gint := 0;
end record;

function To_Double_Array is new Unchecked_Conversion
     (System.Address, Gdouble_Array_Access);
```

Fig. 1. Converting from C arrays to Ada arrays

Tagged types provide another level of type safety, in the widget hierarchy of GtkAda. Fig. shows the pattern followed for the declaration of each widget: each widget is declared as an access to a class-wide type. Most of the operations associated with each widget are primitive, thus making them dispatching operations. As a result, the library provides the user with all the advantages of class-wide programming.

Although Gtk+ follows a design that is fully Object-Oriented, the C language imposed some limitations on the implementation itself. Only type inheritance is provided, and the "methods" are not inherited. Therefore, there is no real polymorphism. As a consequence, the user is forced into the frequent use of *type-casts*, as shown in Fig. (a) where a `Gtk_Window` is converted into a `Gtk_Container` by calling the `GTK_CONTAINER()` macro. Experience shows that these type-casts are ubiquitous, increasing development costs and impairing the readability of

```
with Gtk.Object; use Gtk.Object;
package Gtk.Widget is
  type Gtk_Widget_Record is new Gtk_Object_Record with private
  type Gtk_Widget is access all Gtk_Widget_Record'Class;
  --  Followed by all the widget associated operations...
end Gtk.Widget;
```

Fig. 2. All widget declarations follow the same pattern

the resulting software. Moreover, as type-casting is a potentially unsafe operation, programming errors are likely to occur and lead to obscure software faults, which explains the introduction of these casting macros: besides doing a type cast, they also perform a run time type check.

On the other hand, Ada has been designed to provide such type safety in a totally transparent way: these problems were naturally solved in GtkAda with the usage of tagged types. Figure , where the same program is successively written in C and Ada, shows that using tagged types makes the GtkAda toolkit lighter to use and easier to read. The complexity of developing and maintaining the Ada program is therefore decreased.

```
window = gtk_window_new (GTK_WINDOW_TOPLEVEL);
gtk_window_set_title (GTK_WINDOW (window), "reparent");
gtk_container_set_border_width (GTK_CONTAINER (window), 0);
```

(a) C implementation

```
Gtk_New (Window => Window, The_Type => Window_Toplevel);
Set_Title (Window => Window, Title => "reparent");
Set_Border_Width (Container => Window, Border_Width => 0);
```

(b) Equivalent Ada implementation

Fig. 3. The same code extract written both in C and Ada

Furthermore, through a careful use of generics, GtkAda provides at compile-time a type safety which was only available as run-time checks in the C library. As all other GUI toolkits do, GtkAda provides an callback mechanism (functions called whenever an event happens). But this mechanism is much more powerful than most, since its callbacks can have any number of arguments and can optionally return a value, depending on the type of event.

This multipurpose *callback mechanism*, which gives access to functions with variable argument lists, was probably the area where the type safety issue was the most critical. In Ada, this callback mechanism has been translated in a set of collaborating *generic packages* defined in Gtk.Handlers. The user needs to instantiate at least one of these packages for each of the possible profiles of the callbacks, and then use the subprograms provided to connect the widget and the callback.

The idea behind these packages is that by default the argument list is transformed into an array, and passed as a single argument to the callback. However, for convenience, another set of packages, called marshallers, is provided to break this array into its components and then call the user handler.

Figure shows how these generic packages can be used to connect a handler to an event generated when the user tries to close the window using the window decorations. The function `To_Marshaller` creates the marshaller transparently, as explained above, so that the user callback is a standard Ada function.

```
function My_Cb (Widget : access Gtk_Widget_Record'Class;
                Event  : Gdk.Event.Gdk_Event)
                return Gint;
--  The function that needs to be called back

package Return_Widget_Cb is new Gtk.Handlers.Return_Callback
  (Widget_Type => Gtk.Widget.Gtk_Widget_Record,
   Return_Type => Gint);
--  Instantiation of a generic callback package

Return_Widget_Cb.Connect
  (Widget => W,
   Name => "delete_event",
   Marsh => Return_Widget_Cb.To_Marshaller (My_Cb'Access));
--  The compiler checks that My_Cb has the right signature
```

Fig. 4. How to use the generic packages provided by Gtk.Handlers

In combination with generics, *access to subprogram* types are also used systematically to provide additional strong typing. This feature is used, for example, to allow the user to pass in a simple way a self-defined action routine to an active iterator in Gtk.Ctree, as demonstrated in Fig. .

4 Benefits of the Object Oriented Features of Ada

As seen in the previous section, GtkAda is based on a tagged type hierarchy, as are most modern graphical libraries. This has a number of advantages, which will be explained in this section. We also show how this hierarchy is implemented over a non-object oriented C library.

```
with Gtk.Ctree;
with Gtk.Style; use Gtk.Style;

package Access_To_Subprogram_Example is
   package Style_Row_Data is new Gtk.Ctree.Row_Data (Gtk_Style);

   procedure Set_Background
     (Ctree : access Gtk.Ctree.Gtk_Ctree_Record'Class;
      Node : in Gtk.Ctree.Gtk_Ctree_Node;
      Dummy : in Style_Row_Data.Data_Type_Access) is ... ;
   --  The procedure that will be passed to the active iterator

   procedure Run is
   begin
      Style_Row_Data.Pre_Recursive
        (Ctree => Ctree,
         Node  => Gtk.Ctree.Null_Ctree_Node,
         Func  => Set_Background'Access,
         Data  => null);
      --  Changes the background of all nodes of Ctree
   end Run;
end Access_To_Subprogram_Example;
```

Fig. 5. An access to subprogram used with an active iterator

4.1 Why Objects are a Natural Way of Representing GUI Components

This section is not specific to GtkAda, but rather tries to explain briefly why having an object oriented design helps the user to better understand and use a library. The arguments below are language-independent and domain-independent, although we have tried to explain their specific use in the case of GtkAda.

Tight Integration between an Object and Its Operations. The concept of object-oriented programming is to provide both a structure that contains data, and some subprograms to manipulate that structure (called its primitive subprograms in Ada). Such a structure inherits its ancestors' attributes automatically, which makes it easier for the user to locate (and if necessary modify) the relevant subprograms.

For instance, a `Gtk_Button` is a special kind of widget that reacts to mouse clicks. Its parent is a `Gtk_Container`, which has the property of being able to have one child, and thus a button can also have one child which is displayed in the button (like a label, a pixmap, ...). It inherits all the behavior from a container, including the capability to add or remove a child, etc. But a `Gtk_Container` is also a `Gtk_Widget`, that can be displayed on the screen. Thus a `Gtk_Button` also inherits that capability.

Avoiding Type Casting. Since the Ada runtime always knows what exact type an object has, there is no need to dynamically test it in explicit code. The appropriate subprogram is automatically called (this is called dynamic dispatching, or polymorphism).

For instance, this is useful when a widget is returned by one of the functions in GtkAda (for example when you extract a child from a container). You do not need to test what type the child has, since the runtime will automatically know what subprograms apply to it.

In the few cases where an explicit cast (view conversion) is required, Ada checks at run-time that the conversion is valid.

Easy Extension and Creation of New Widgets. The main advantage of object oriented programming is that you can use any type derived from a parent type wherever the library expects the parent type. This makes it almost trivial to extend existing widgets, either by adding your own internal data to them, or by modifying their behavior.

The whole GtkAda library is based on this principle: for instance, a toggle button is a simple button with two possible states: (active/inactive). Instead of rewriting everything to create a toggle button, we just specialize a few subprograms, and inherit the general behavior of a button.

Likewise, it is easy for the user to create his own widgets, either from scratch, or more simply by modifying an existing one. Instead of handling all the low-level details, the user just has to concentrate on the high level differences between the new widget and its parent.

4.2 Providing a Tagged Type Hierarchy over a C Library

Designing the Hierarchy. We have seen all the advantages that an object-oriented design provides. However, it is not always possible to create such a hierarchy over every C library. Fortunately for us, the design of Gtk+, the C library on which GtkAda is based, was already object-oriented, even if not programmed in a strict object-oriented language. This of course made the choice of objects and the design of the hierarchy much easier to do, whereas it is generally one of the hard things when designing from scratch. We will not discuss in this paper the different approaches (UML, HOOD, etc.) available for this task.

A well-designed binding must be easy to maintain and be kept up-to-date vis-a-vis of the underlying C library. It was thus very important for GtkAda to be as independent as possible from the C structures. We did not want to make visible the internals of these structures in the GtkAda interface.

All our objects contain a single private field that is a pointer to the C object (System.Address), and everything is done through that pointer. A couple of subprograms (Set and Get) must be provided for all the public fields of the C interface, and it is in fact sometimes a difficult task to guess whether a given field should be public or private. At this level, the Ada interface is thus much cleaner than the C one, in that the user does not have to read the source to understand whether he is allowed to use a field or not.

This method also makes the interface highly stable: if one field of the C structure is renamed, or removed in a future version of Gtk+, it is still possible to keep the same interface at the Ada level, but change the body of the subprograms.

As we said, accessing the fields is done through a functional interface. This requires an additional small C layer. Using that layer means that we do not have to map all the C structures to Ada records, thus solving the big portability issue of representation clauses.

Links between C and Ada Objects. One implementation problem is worth noticing. It is closely related to memory management (see the next section of this paper). Although it is easy to get the matching C structure given an Ada tagged object (just use the appropriate field of the record), it is sometimes more difficult to convert from a C object to the matching Ada record. This feature is required every time a subprogram (implemented in C in the underlying library) needs to return a widget.

Simply creating a new Ada structure is not possible, since we have to create it with the appropriate type (a C `GtkButton` is mapped to a `Gtk_Button`, not to the more general `Gtk_Widget`), and because the user might in fact have created his own tagged object by inheritance, we need to restore the exact value of the new fields.

This problem can not be solved in a general way for all the C libraries. Fortunately, this is made quite easy with Gtk+, since it is possible to associate some user data with every widget, through a keyword, like a hash-table. Thus, every time an object is created at the Ada level, we also create the C object at the same time, and set some user data to point back to the Ada object.

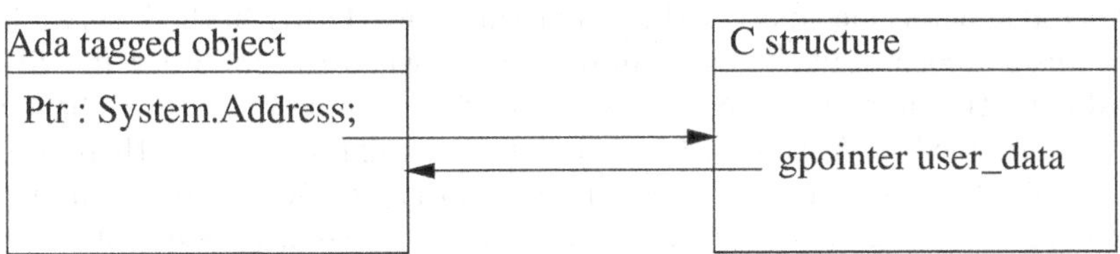

Of course, some widgets are not created by the user, but directly in some C code. For these widgets the user data is absent. In such cases, we simply invoke a more elaborate procedure that tests the C type against all its possible values, and creates the corresponding Ada type. This procedure is time-consuming, but is only executed rarely, since once we have created the new Ada object, it is permanently associated with the C widget.

This mechanism is made easy with Gtk+. In fact, it can easily be done for other foreign languages bindings through a global hash table that the Ada code would maintain.

5 Avoiding Memory Leaks

Library designers are always confronted to the problem of memory management: should the memory allocation and deallocation be done automatically, or should it be left to the user ? Although the first solution is obviously more user-friendly, it generally has some speed tradeoffs, and is not always possible to implement.

Ada offers a very powerful memory management mechanism : controlled types. Initialization and cleanup functions can be called automatically on objects of a controlled type. Although very comprehensive and fine-grained, this mechanism is heavy, and imposes a substantial overhead of function calls.

With GtkAda, leaving the memory management to the user is not an option. This is a difficult issue for GUIs, since it is not always obvious when a widget is still needed and when it can be destroyed. Moreover, when a container is destroyed, all its children must be destroyed as well.

Of course, the same problem appears in Gtk+. The authors of Gtk+ have thus implemented a reference counting mechanism, close to a garbage collector, that takes care of all memory management. This is implemented in the ancestor of all widgets, so that creating new widgets does not require special care.

Whenever a C widget is destroyed, it also frees the memory occupied by all its user data (as seen in the section). Since we can register our own destruction callbacks, this also allows us to free the memory allocated at the Ada level. Thus, GtkAda does not add any overhead over Gtk+.

This system of hooks or callbacks (functions called whenever specific actions are performed by a library) is extremely useful, both for the users of the library and for the people who want to adapt the library to their needs.

In a few cases it wasn't possible to use this mechanism. This is most notably the case for the low-level part of the library, which is very close to the X11 or Win32 protocols. These specific parts are carefully documented, since GtkAda does not provide any memory management for them. Using controlled types is not possible here, since most of these structures have to live in the X server itself, and thus cannot always be freed automatically when the subprogram exits. To avoid potential hidden memory leaks, some of the simplest structures have been directly mapped to Ada record (like points, rectangles,etc.) But there are still a few cases (pixmaps and graphic contexts most notably) where the user must take care of freeing the structure when done with them. Convenient functions are always provided for that usage.

6 Integrating GtkAda with a GUI Builder

GUI builders are one of the most desirable and popular applications built on top of graphical libraries. They are popular because they can automatically generate a major part of a user interface, simply by mouse interactions, or by describing at a high level the desired widget hierarchy. GUI builders obviate the need to write long, repetitious and stereotyped code.

6.1 Finding a Suitable GUI Builder

Up to now, outside of the Windows world, GUI builders were rare and expensive, forcing many people to develop GUIs by hand. With the availability of a popular and open toolkit like Gtk+, many projects can develop GUI builders of their own. The most popular of these projects, called GtkGlade, had reached a sufficient level of functionality when we started to look at a GUI builder solution for GtkAda that we could consider adopting it for Ada needs.

6.2 Generation of Ada Code

Following the design philosophy of Gtk+, GtkGlade had been designed to easily support code generation for any language, by saving the widget hierarchy and properties in an easy-to-read and easy-to-parse XML file. Therefore, we decided to write an *XML-to-Ada* translator, specifically tailored for GtkGlade and GtkAda. During the design of this translator (called *Gate*), we had two choices: either write a completely independent code generator that would contain all the information and properties required for each widget, or enhance our existing GtkAda library by giving each widget the ability to generate the Ada code associated with it.

The second solution looked much more promising for several reasons. First, we had complete control over GtkAda anyway, so making changes in the library itself was not an issue. Second, it would take advantage of the already existing widget hierarchy, thus avoiding the need to recreate many of the needed structures. Finally, giving each widget the capability to generate the code related to its own properties is very natural and fits the object oriented model well. It also makes it easy to add support for new widgets. For example, suppose the user needs to add support for an extended implementation of `Gtk_Drawing_Area` (for instance a double buffer area), instead of having to write a complete support for all the data and properties of the ancestors of this new widget, he only needs to add code generation for the extended features, which is usually a simple task.

6.3 Clear and Easy to Read Output

One common defect that we wanted to avoid in our translator, was the generation of Ada code that no human being could read and understand.

In order to output a clean code that would be easy to examine, we decided to generate a “composite widget” for each top level widget of the interface. A composite widget is an object that extends an existing type (typically a top level window) by adding a set of other widgets to it. This approach makes it very easy to see the group of widgets created, and offers a simple way to access all the fields.

Compared to other possible approaches, this one shows many advantages. If you consider for example the C code generated by GtkGlade, which generates local variables that are then stored in a hash table, this makes the generated code heavier and the user's code more complex.

Figures and provide a typical example of code generated by Gate and GtkGlade.

```
type About_Dialog_Record is new Gtk_Dialog_Record with record
   Dialog_Vbox : Gtk_Vbox;
   Button : Gtk_Button;
end record;

type About_Dialog_Access is access all About_Dialog_Record'Class;

procedure Initialize (About_Dialog : access About_Dialog_Record'Class) is
begin
   Gtk.Dialog.Initialize (About_Dialog);
   Set_Title (About_Dialog, "About The Editor");
   Set_Policy (About_Dialog, True, True, False);
   Set_Position (About_Dialog, Win_Pos_Mouse);
   About_Dialog.Dialog_Vbox := Get_Vbox (About_Dialog);
   Set_Border_Width (About_Dialog.Dialog_Vbox, 2);
...
end Initialize;
```

Fig. 6. Sample Ada code generated by Gate

This example gives a good overview of the advantages that GtkAda brings to Gtk+:

- In order to ensure a clean memory deallocation, the C code duplicates for each subwidget the code to reference a widget (`gtk_widget_ref`) and registers a cleanup function (`gtk_object_set_data_full`). This is done automatically by GtkAda when doing a `Gtk_New`, as explained in section .
- With GtkAda, there is no need to associate artificially the widget children to their parent (using `gtk_object_set_data_full`), since this is done in a natural way by the type extension.
- There is no need to cast the widgets (see section).
- The widgets are typed instead of being anonymous pointers (`Gtk_Button` instead of `GtkWidget *`).
- The *use clauses* even if not mandatory, provide output that is lighter and easier-to-read.

6.4 Merging User's Changes

The ability to go back and forth between the user interface and the generated code is a powerful feature that simplifies greatly the development of user interfaces.

Usually GUI builders approach this need by generating "read only" files and skeleton files that are automatically generated at first and subsequently modified

```
GtkWidget*
create_about_dialog ()
{
  GtkWidget *about_dialog;
  GtkWidget *dialog_vbox;
  GtkWidget *button;

  about_dialog = gtk_dialog_new ();
  gtk_widget_ref (about_dialog);
  gtk_object_set_data_full (GTK_OBJECT (about_dialog), "about_dialog",
                            about_dialog, (GtkDestroyNotify) gtk_widget_unref);
  gtk_window_set_title (GTK_WINDOW (about_dialog), _("About The Editor"));
  gtk_window_set_position (GTK_WINDOW (about_dialog), GTK_WIN_POS_MOUSE);
  gtk_window_set_policy (GTK_WINDOW (about_dialog), TRUE, TRUE, FALSE);

  dialog_vbox = GTK_DIALOG (about_dialog)->vbox;
  gtk_widget_ref (dialog_vbox);
  gtk_object_set_data_full (GTK_OBJECT (about_dialog), "dialog_vbox",
                            dialog_vbox,(GtkDestroyNotify) gtk_widget_unref);
  gtk_widget_show (dialog_vbox);
  gtk_container_set_border_width (GTK_CONTAINER (dialog_vbox), 2);
...
  return about_dialog;
}
```

Fig. 7. Sample C code generated by GtkGlade

manually. The read-only files contain code to build the widgets themselves, taking into account all their properties, while the skeleton files serve as templates where the user implements his callback subprograms. It is occasionally useful to modify some of the generated files themselves. This capability is usually not provided by GUI builders.

With Gate, we decided to implement both. The former because it seemed cleaner to separate the automatically generated construction code from the user's code. The latter because we want to provide the maximum flexibility.

In order to implement this capability, we decided to take a very simple but still powerful approach, based on a shell script and the "patch" and "diff" tools.

Here are the details of the operations performed by our script, to wrap our translator transparently for the user:

- Create the working directory: a different directory is created for each project file. This operation is usually done once.
- Compute a diff between the previously generated files (if any) and the current files (possibly modified).
- Generate the raw Ada files: this is a call to the real translator that does not have to worry about merging code and overriding files.
- Save the raw files as being the "previous files"
- Apply the diff to a copy of the raw Ada files.

Another possibility would have been to use *ASIS* during code generation, to be able to find the right procedures to modify, remove or add. But this would have required much more work than the simple-minded but powerful script described above. Furthermore, this approach would not work when the modified files do not compile properly, which can often be the case when the application is in the development phase.

7 Conclusion

As we explained, many of the choices we made can be applied to the construction of similar bindings for another language. However, it is clear that thanks to the use of some of the more powerful features of Ada (genericity, tagged types and access to subprograms), we have managed to build a high level binding to the Gtk+ library that provides compile-time checks, code readability, reusability and robustness.

Moreover, by integrating the various components of a graphical user interface, GtkAda now offers a complete solution for end-user applications written in Ada.

References

1. GIMP home page. http://www.gimp.org/.
2. GNOME home page. http://www.gnome.org/.
3. GLADE home page. http://glade.pn.org/.
4. GtkAda home page. http://gtkada.eu.org/.
5. GtkAda User's Guide. http://gtkada.eu.org/gtkada_ug.html.
6. GtkAda Reference Manual. http://gtkada.eu.org/gtkada_rm_toc.html.
7. Gtk+ home page. http://www.gtk.org/.
8. Havoc Pennington. *GTK+/Gnome application development.* New Riders, 1999.
9. Eric Harlow. *Developing Linux Applications with GTK+ and GDK.* New Riders, 1999.
10. David Odin. *Programmation Linux avec Gtk+.* Eyrolles, 1999.
11. ACT-Europe home page. http://www.act-europe.fr/.

ASIS-for-GNAT: A Report of Practical Experiences

Sergey Rybin[1], Alfred Strohmeier[2], Vasiliy Fofanov[1], Alexei Kuchumov[1]

[1]*Scientific Research Computer Center*
Moscow State University, Vorob'evi Gori
Moscow 119899, Russia
e-mail: rybin@alex.srcc.msu.su

[2]*Swiss Federal Institute of Technology in Lausanne*
Department of Computer Science
1015 Lausanne EPFL, Switzerland
email: alfred.strohmeier@epfl.ch

Abstract: What are the main difficulties met when implementing ASIS, what are the problems when using ASIS, are there any missing features in ASIS, e.g. when it comes to object-oriented programming, these are some of the topics dealt with in this experience report.

Keywords: ASIS, Ada, Programming Language, Programming Tool, Programming Environment.

1 Introduction

The Ada Semantic Interface Specification (ASIS) [1] [9] is an interface between an Ada environment [7] [20] and any tool or application requiring statically-determinable information from this environment. ASIS defines types: Context represents an Ada environment [17], Compilation_Unit represents an Ada compilation unit, and Element models a syntactic construct, e.g. a declaration, a statement, an expression, etc. Operations on these types and the results of their calls are called "queries" in ASIS terminology.

The authors of the paper have been involved in ASIS activities for more than five years. Most of the time was spent in developing and maintaining the ASIS implementation for the GNAT Ada 95 compilation system, called ASIS-for-GNAT [2], but we also took part in developing the ASIS ISO standard, teaching ASIS, providing technical support to ASIS-for-GNAT users and developing our own ASIS-based tools. We feel that this is a good moment for reporting our ASIS experience, hoping it will be useful to other people working with ASIS and will help further developments of the ASIS technology.

2 History

2.1. ASIS

The first version of ASIS was developed in the mid-eighties by Rational Software Corporation in response to the need for developing tools for supporting the various life cycle phases of an Ada program. Soon after, ASIS was implemented for other Ada 83 compilers, and the ACM SIGAda ASIS Working Group [3] was formed. ASIS version 1.1.1 is the de facto standard for Ada 83, and usually called ASIS 83.

H. B. Keller and E. Plödereder (Eds.): Ada-Europe 2000, LNCS 1845, pp. 125-137, 2000.

The ASIS WG started adapting ASIS 83 to the revised definition of Ada some time before it became the new ISO Ada standard in 1995. The first version of the ASIS definition for Ada 95, called now ASIS 95, was presented in 1994, and several ASIS implementation projects, including ASIS-for-GNAT, were started. The ISO standard for ASIS 95 was adopted at the end of 1998 and officially published in the beginning of 1999.

At the time of writing, there are three ASIS 95 implementations respectively by Ada Core Technologies, Aonix and Rational Software Corporation, and a number of ASIS-based tools have been announced on the net and presented at Ada conferences [10] [11] [14]. In other words, ASIS is now a reality and an important part of the Ada 95 technology.

2.2. ASIS-for-GNAT

ASIS-for-GNAT was started at the end of 1994 as a joint research project of the Swiss Federal Institute of Technology in Lausanne and the Computer Center of the Moscow State University. In the middle of 1996, the development of ASIS-for-GNAT was handed over to Ada Core Technologies, the company providing support for the GNAT Ada 95 technology [4]. Soon after, ASIS-for-GNAT was announced as a fully supported product. Currently ASIS-for-GNAT is developed and maintained by ACT-Europe [5], the European GNAT company.

The general design decisions of ASIS-for-GNAT were described in [15] [16].

By now, a number of ASIS-based tools are available for ASIS-for-GNAT. Some of them are included in the GNAT tool kit.

3 Inside an ASIS implementation

3.1. Main implementation techniques and common implementation problems

ASIS is able to retrieve the complete statically-determinable syntax and semantics from an Ada environment for a tool requiring such information. The only way to achieve this without implementing an almost complete Ada syntax and semantics analyzer is to reuse the front-end of some Ada compiler. Therefore all the existing ASIS implementations are implemented as interfaces to existing Ada compilers, and not as stand-alone products.

The straightforward approach to implement ASIS is to use some intermediate representation, usually an abstract syntax tree, of an Ada program generated by the compiler. Such an intermediate representation contains the results of syntax and semantic analysis performed by the compiler. Conceptually, the implementation of objects of the ASIS types Compilation_Unit and Element are then just references to the component of the compiler's data structure representing the corresponding Ada compilation unit or syntax construct. The fact that the ASIS implementation actually extracts information from the compiler's internal data structure is at the origin of most implementation problems, which, we believe, are common to all ASIS implementations.

The main goals of the compiler are to check the legality of the Ada units being compiled and to generate object code, or to create some data structure from which the object code can be easily generated. Therefore, the compiler may (and most probably every compiler does) transform the original program source in order to simplify syntax and semantic checks, and make code generation easier. Some obvious examples are:

- computing static expressions;
- creating internal implicit types to represent anonymous subtypes with constraints, used e.g. as record or array component definitions;
- replacing some language constructs, such as select statements, with calls to run-time library routines.

As a consequence, the main job of an ASIS implementation is to convert the model used by the compiler to represent the compiled code into what is required by the ASIS definition. How difficult or easy this task is depends on how close the two models are.

The main GNAT internal data structure, the Abstract Syntax Tree (AST) [19], was designed with ASIS in mind. But dozens of small details and many more difficult issues had to be dealt with when the AST is used by the ASIS implementation. Most of the implementation problems arose in the following areas:

- implicit Elements;
- the predefined package Standard;
- accessing the contents of generic instantiations, called expanded generic code in ASIS;
- the Enclosing_Element query.

The difficulty of implementing Enclosing_Element results from the fact that when the compiler rewrites a node in a subtree and redirects the references in its successor nodes to this new node, the references to the original ancestor node are lost.

3.2. ASIS and the source-based compilation model

GNAT is an example of a source-based compiler. This means that GNAT does not create (and then reuse) any centralized library information, and when compiling a unit, it does not use the results of previous compilations of other units upon which the given unit depends. Instead, GNAT processes directly the source code of the given unit and all its supporters. As a result, in a source-based compilation system, we do not have any centralized data structure representing the whole Ada environment (or the whole partition), but we have independent data structures, each of which representing the semantics of some compilation unit, including all its supporting units. The task of the ASIS implementation is therefore to assemble these independent pieces to represent the whole Ada environment.

As already said, GNAT uses an Abstract Syntax Tree (AST) for intermediate code representation. When called with a special option, GNAT can output the AST into a file, called a tree file. ASIS-for-GNAT uses these tree files, and therefore gets access to the very same AST as used by GNAT for every successful compilation. However, whereas the compiler deals only with a single compilation unit, i.e. the root unit of the compilation, ASIS-for-GNAT deals with an ASIS Context, i.e. a set of compilation units. As a consequence, ASIS-for-GNAT must access information in several tree files. A problem arises if the same compilation unit is present in several trees.

An example might help the reader understand the problem (Fig. 1).

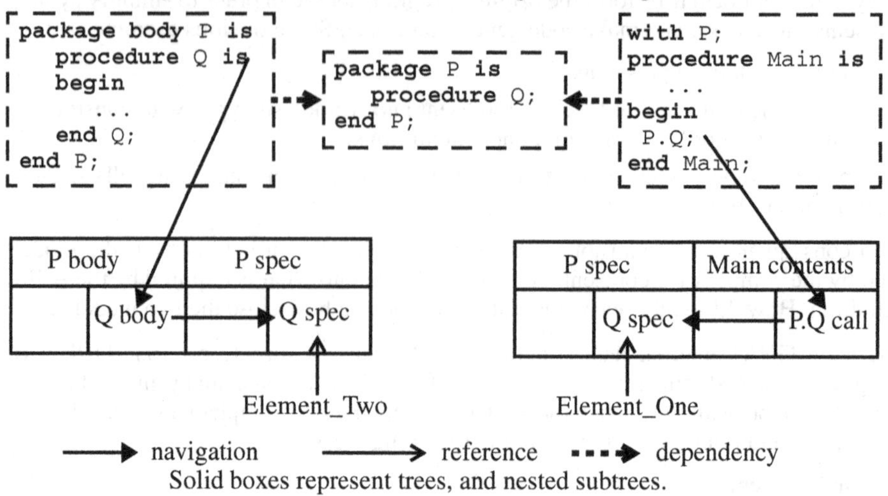

Fig. 1 Example ASTs containing a duplicated subtree

Let's suppose the ASIS Context contains the following compilation units: the procedure Main, and the specification and body of package P. ASIS-for-GNAT will use two trees, one for Main, and another for the body of P. Both these trees contain the specification of the package P. As a consequence, all information related to the package specification P is duplicated. However, ASIS defines features for deciding if two elements, i.e. Ada syntax constructs, are the same or not, and the ASIS implementation must therefore be able to make this decision. On the example, an ASIS-based tool might analyze the source of Main, find the call to P.Q, and from there navigate to the specification of the called unit, i.e. the declaration of Q in P, and name the result Element_One. The same tool might access the body of P, traverse all enclosed declarations, and navigate from the body of the procedure Q to its specification, naming the latter one Element_Two. Even though Element_One and Element_Two are not physically the same, they represent logically the same element, and the result of the call Is_Equal (Element_One, Element_Two) must therefore yield True. Otherwise stated, the implementation of ASIS has to deal with this identification problem, e.g. by using properties of the elements (syntax constructs) not varying with the tree.

An other problem arises if from Element_One, one of the two representations of the specification of procedure Q, we want to find the corresponding body. Indeed, the body is not part of the enclosing tree, and we have to switch in some way to the other tree. Note that getting the body related to Element_Two is straightforward.

The whole issue of dealing with elements (syntactic constructs) having multiple representations in multiple trees becomes even more complicated when it comes to library-level instantiations.

4 Testing an ASIS implementation

Testing is never an easy task, and testing an ASIS implementation is no exception. Moreover, there are several specific problems in the case of ASIS:

- ASIS is not a program but a library containing about 350 queries. To test an ASIS query, the corresponding test driver (or test ASIS application) needs to be written, and the input for an ASIS application is itself an Ada program. This requires additional efforts when preparing and running ASIS tests. But first of all, one has to write a test driver and test it, which by the very nature of ASIS is not a trivial task. Later on, when analyzing the test results, one has to be aware of the fact that a test may fail, either because there is a bug in the ASIS implementation, or in the test driver;
- The main ASIS abstractions (Context, Compilation_Unit, Element) are private types. This makes it difficult and very often impossible to create directly test data and to directly observe and analyze results for the query under test, and the only way to do it is to use other ASIS queries;
- The overall complexity of testing ASIS is of the same magnitude as testing an Ada compiler. Recall that ASIS deals with all the syntax and static semantics of the language, and a coverage criteria is therefore directly related to covering all these aspects of the Ada programming language.

Our approach for testing ASIS implementations, called Quality-for-ASIS [18], is based on two main components:

- The first component is a set of universal ASIS test drivers, corresponding oracles (analyzers of test results), and test set adequacy analyzers. The drivers perform extensive ASIS-based processing of Ada code, and the oracles use different approaches for indirect, and in some situations partial observation of the test results. For example, one of the drivers recreates the source of the Ada unit processed by ASIS by using only ASIS structural queries, and the corresponding oracle tests that the original and recreated sources are semantically the same. Even though such tests are "indirect" and "partial", their use has proved to be effective in practice. Altogether, these drivers provide a completely automated, portable test suite for about 2/3 of the ASIS queries, representing the most important part of ASIS, including structural and semantic queries, source text representation queries, traversal of source code and some other features.
- The second component is Asistant, an interactive interpreter of ASIS queries with log and script capabilities. Asistant itself is an ASIS application. It creates its own environment for evaluating sequences of ASIS queries, e.g. when developing an ASIS application, without having to write and compile the corresponding ASIS application as an Ada program. An early version of Asistant was described in [12]. Asistant is also useful for learning ASIS, e.g. when you are not quite sure about the effect of a sequence of queries, or for debugging "small" pieces of ASIS-based Ada code - you know that there is an error, but you are unable to locate it.

As an input test set for Quality-for-ASIS, we have chosen the ACVC test suite (without the illegal programs called B-tests, which clearly cannot be processed by ASIS). This is quite a natural choice, because ACVC provides a good coverage of the Ada syntax and semantics. We also use the ACVC test set on a daily basis to detect possible regressions in ASIS-for-GNAT.

5 The ASIS ISO Standard - a great success with some small flaws

Authors of this paper participated in the development of the ASIS definition for Ada 95 and in preparing the ISO ASIS standard. Now, that we have some real experience in providing technical support for ASIS users and in developing our own ASIS tools, it is possible to give an overview of what we consider to be shortcomings in the current definition of ASIS.

5.1. Element classification hierarchy versus flat Element classification

ASIS classifies Elements by repeating practically one-to-one the Ada syntax as defined in the RM 95. ASIS defines this classification as a hierarchy: at the top level we have basic notions such as A_Declaration, A_Statement, An_Expression, then we have more detailed classifications for these basic constructs, e.g. An_Ordinary_Type_Declaration, An_Assignment_Statement, and An_Attribute_-Reference, and so on, some positions in this classification requiring still another subordinate classification. Each level in this hierarchy is defined by an enumeration type, and ASIS has a classification query corresponding to each of these levels, e.g. Element_Kind at the very top, then Statement_Kind, Expression_Kind, etc. As a result, in order to know in the application code the exact kind of the element - which is a very common need, because most of the ASIS queries are element kind specific - several classification queries and nested if or case statements are needed.

We have found this classification scheme to be really cumbersome, including when implementing ASIS, because almost all ASIS queries have to detect the kind of the Element which passed as an actual. As a consequence, already at the very beginning of the ASIS-for-GNAT project, we introduced a flat ASIS Element classification scheme; roughly speaking, this classification is implemented by a single enumeration type which combines all the literals from all the classification types from the original ASIS classification hierarchy. Although this idea was thought to be an ad hoc implementation solution, very quickly we found it to be convenient when writing any ASIS-based code, because only one classification query was needed to detect the exact nature of an element, and a single case statement was enough to process an Element of an "unknown" kind. As a result, we provide now this flat classification scheme as an ASIS extension to ASIS-for-GNAT users.

5.2. Name collisions

The better is often the enemy of the good. The ASIS name space is heavily overloaded by synonyms for the Element type, like "subtype Declaration is Element". There are 58 such synonyms. They were thought to provide good mnemonics for the parameter profiles of ASIS queries. But the real consequence is, that if an ASIS application includes a use clause for the top-level ASIS package named Asis (where the main ASIS types are defined), it is impossible to declare names such as "Clause", "Declaration", "Definition", "Name", "Statement", etc.

While this is but a nuisance, the situation with the ASIS-defined name Subtype_Mark is bluntly dangerous. Subtype_Mark is defined as a subtype of Element in the package Asis, and there is a query Subtype_Mark declared in Asis.Definitions, with a single argument of the type Element, returning a result of the type Element.

To show the problem, let's consider the following code:

```
E1, E2: Asis.Element;

...

E1 := Subtype_Mark (E2);
```

In this piece of code, Subtype_Mark (E2) is either a type conversion (from the type Element to the subtype Subtype_Mark) or a call to the Asis.Definitions.-Subtype_Mark query, depending on the use clauses in effect! One of the authors had a very hard time finding an error due to this problem.

There are some other problems with naming.

The package Asis.Compilation_Units declares a query named Compilation_Units. It is therefore impossible to call this query by its simple name.

The set of subtypes of the type Element defined in the package Asis contains a subtype named Record_Component. At the same time, Record_Component is the name of the type implementing one of the main abstractions of the Asis.Data_Decomposition package. In the same program, it is therefore impossible to have use clauses for both Asis and Asis.Data_Decomposition (because type declarations are not overloadable), and the use of simple names is therefore quite restricted.

5.3. Duplicated and missing functionality

One of the primary goals when revising ASIS 83 for Ada 95 was to get rid of redundant queries, i.e. of queries which can be implemented as trivial combinations of other queries.

Many redundant queries were removed from ASIS, but at least one still exists: Asis.Expressions.Corresponding_Name_Declaration is a trivial combination of Elements.Enclosing_Element and Expressions.Corresponding_Name_Definition.

With regard to missing functionality, we would like to point out two things.

In Ada, there can be several occurrences of the same defining name corresponding to the same entity, e.g. the name of a subprogram in its specification and body, the name of formal parameters appearing both in the specification and body of the subprogram, etc. The ASIS definition allows the Corresponding_Name_Definition query to return a reference to any of the defining occurrences, and does not provide any selection mechanism. It is therefore difficult to implement an ASIS-based application maintaining name tables.

Another problem is the impossibility to go from a protected entry declaration to the corresponding entry body declaration, and vice versa; the ASIS standard states that the ASIS queries Corresponding_Declaration and Corresponding_Body are not supposed to work for protected entries. The underlying difficulty is that an entry declaration might be completed by a entry body when part of a protected type or might correspond to one or several accept statements when belonging to a task.

5.4. Do we have upward compatibility of ASIS 83 tools with ASIS 95?

Upward compatibility of ASIS 83 tools with ASIS 95 was one of the primary goals of the ASIS revision. In our opinion, this goal was not reached, and it cannot be. First, there are too many differences between Ada 83 and Ada 95, and as a result too many new positions in the Element and Compilation_Unit classifications, which actually affect most of the ASIS queries. Second, this goal is in direct contradiction with two other important stated goals: removing redundant queries and reducing the number of queries by aggregating related queries into one single query, whenever possible.

[21] gives a detailed report of porting a set of ASIS 83 applications to ASIS-for-GNAT, and shows that porting ASIS 83 code to ASIS 95 is a major undertaking.

5.5. ASIS and object-oriented features of Ada

ASIS' view of a program, or a set of program units, is essentially based on its textual or syntactical structure (Fig. 2). Properties orthogonal to this structure are almost completely neglected. Even in Ada 83, it would have been interesting to get the primitive operations (as they are called now) of a type, or the list of all subprograms called in a sequence of statements.

When it comes to object-oriented programming, the ability to adopt another viewpoint than the textual one becomes essential. In an object-oriented mindset, the world and the program are viewed as a set of interacting objects and a hierarchy of classes. To the contrary of other object-oriented programming languages, like C++ or Java, where the class is the basic syntax and module construct, this view is not "wired" in the syntax of Ada. Tools able to provide such a view, e.g. a class browser, are therefore even more important.

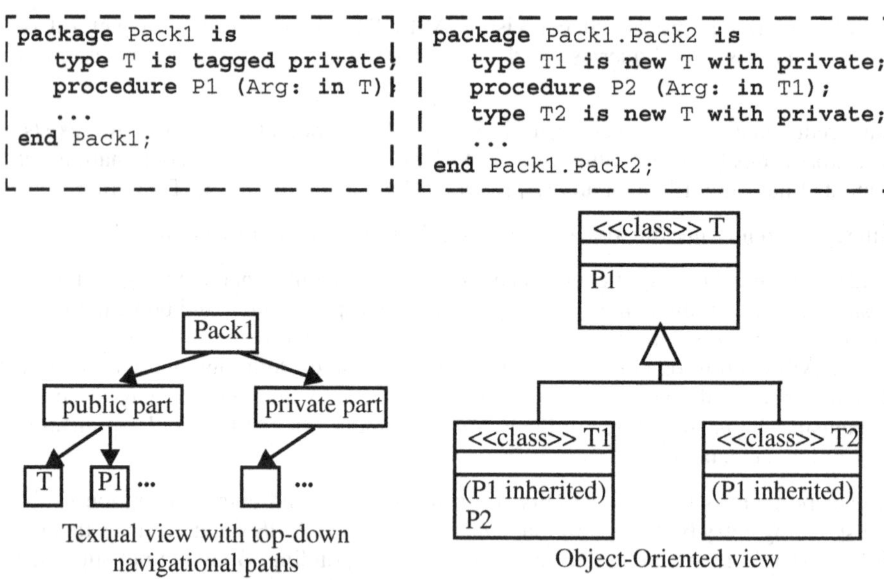

Fig. 2 Textual and object-oriented views of a program

Possible extensions to ASIS providing an object-oriented view are: find a derivation class, find the primitive operations of a tagged type, decide if a primitive operation is overridden, and for a dispatching call, find the list of possible implementations, etc. In section 8.2., we will present OASIS, a research prototype implementing such queries.

To conclude this section, and even though there might be some omissions in ASIS, we want to stress that the most important is that ASIS exists here and now, as a standard and implemented as additions to several compilers, and that it provides an excellent foundation for developing portable tools. A useful standard on time is better than a perfect standard too late, and problems described in this section could hardly be found before ASIS was intensively used.

6 Assisting ASIS users

In our ASIS tutorials one of the main statements is "ASIS is easy-to-start-with and easy-to-use". This is true and not true at the same time. We do believe that a half-day tutorial is enough to get an overview of ASIS and to learn how to write simple ASIS-based programs.

But using ASIS in a real project, i.e. developing a real tool which itself is supposed to process real Ada code, is another story. The main reason making the ASIS learning curve longer than one would expect is the large size of both Ada and ASIS.

ASIS contains 349 different queries, and 157 of them are structural and semantic queries working on more than 370 different kinds of ASIS Elements. Really, ASIS cannot be small and simple, because Ada itself is not a small and simple language. Therefore, typical questions of ASIS newcomers are: "What query should I use to go from an element of kind X to its component Y?"; "What are the kinds of the components of an element having the kind Z?"; "Can I get this semantic property of that element directly, or do I have to compute it myself? And if I have to, how to do it?". Most of these questions are very easy to answer for anybody who has several months of ASIS experience; even a newcomer can find the answers by browsing the ASIS standard. But such an approach takes time, and when there are too many of such questions, and when wrong guesses lead to compilation or run-time errors, then developing an ASIS-based application becomes tedious.

According to our experience in providing technical support for ASIS-for-GNAT during the last few years, quick answers for queries like the previous ones are really helpful for users during their first steps with ASIS.

The Asistant tool mentioned in section 4 can also be used when learning ASIS and as a quick interactive ASIS reference when working on an ASIS-based tool. In Asistant, you can "browse" the structure of Ada code without thinking about which query should be used to go from some element to its components, and while "browsing", you can ask for the kind of each visited element and get a list of applicable queries. In many situations, Asistant gives quick answers to questions like: "How to use ASIS in this situation for that element?".

Another starting help is to provide beginners with a set of easily extendable templates for ASIS-based tools. One example is the style checker program described in [13], which implements part of the Ada style guide [6].

7 Development of ASIS-based tools

We gained our experience as ASIS users by developing several ASIS-based tools: some are tools for testing ASIS implementations, or debugging them, i.e. Asistant, then there is a tool kit for pretty-printing Ada source code, an Ada-to-HTML converter, but also two tools included in the GNAT tool kit, i.e gnatstub which creates compilable body "stubs" for specifications of library packages, and gnatelim which detects unused subprograms.

Even though our experience is limited to about a dozen ASIS-based tools, we think that we can already summarize the first lessons learned from using ASIS.

The first observation is that many ASIS-based programs have a very similar general structure which actually maps quite well to the required sequence of calls to ASIS queries described in the ASIS standard:

(1) Defining the ASIS Context to be processed;

(2) Opening the Context and retrieving the compilation units to be processed;

(3) Iterating through this set of compilation units, and selecting some of them for further processing;

(4) Going into the internal structure of a compilation unit;

(5) Traversing the code of the compilation unit, usually performed by an appropriate instantiation of the generic procedure Asis.Iterator.Traverse_Element.

During this approach, the following points should be kept in mind:

- **Portability of ASIS tools**: One of the main ideas of ASIS is to provide portability of tools. At the same time, ASIS tools can not be fully portable, because the way an ASIS implementation interacts with the underlying Ada environment is implementation-specific, and as a result, defining and processing an ASIS Context is also implementation-specific. The best way to improve portability of ASIS tools is to separate the implementation-specific actions needed for defining and opening a Context from the detailed analysis of Ada code, which is implementation-independent. Coming back to the general structure of an ASIS tool given above, we may say that the result of step (1) is never portable, that there might be some implementation dependencies for the steps (2) and (3), and that the last two steps lead very often to completely portable code.
- **Code templates for ASIS tools**: The code implementing the steps (1) to (4) is very similar in many ASIS-based tools, and what is really different is the code of actual parameters used to instantiate Traverse_Element. The obvious idea is therefore to provide a set of reusable code templates. To build a new tool, a programmer then has only to write the code which is really specific to the tool. The latest version of ASIS-for-GNAT contains a set of such templates.

Another important observation is that in a very early stage of an ASIS-based tool project, a programmer is induced to design a set of so-called secondary ASIS queries. A secondary query is by definition implemented by combining basic ASIS queries and satisfies specific needs of a tool. A tool is indeed often built on top of ASIS and some secondary ASIS libraries. Of course, such a secondary library is mostly tool-specific, but some of the secondary queries may be of general interest. This leads to the idea of developing and standardizing general-purpose ASIS secondary libraries.

8 Extending the functionality of ASIS

8.1. Extending ASIS-for-GNAT

Currently, ASIS-for-GNAT provides about 30 queries extending the basic ASIS functionality. Some of them came from implementation needs, some are generalizations of secondary queries developed as parts of our ASIS tools, some resulted from customer requests.

There are different kinds of such queries, with regard to both their functionality and their implementation.

Some queries supplement the basic ASIS functionality, like the Is_Primitive_Operation and Is_Static boolean functions. It is impossible to implement these queries by combining primary queries, and they are therefore extensions, according to ASIS terminology. Other queries could be considered as secondary queries, but their implementation by combining primary queries is either difficult, or leads to an inefficient implementation, or both of them. Examples of this kind are the boolean queries Acts_As_Spec, Is_Renaming_As_Body, and Is_Completed, but also the query Components which returns the complete list of all the components of an Element, whatever its kind. Finally, some additional queries are GNAT-specific, like Is_Obsolete and Compilation_Dependencies, which work on compilation units and return GNAT-specific information about the validity of a compilation unit, respectively return dependencies between compilation units and source files.

We expect that the set of queries extending standard ASIS will grow. We also believe that every ASIS implementation will have its own set of such queries. It would be important to put this process under control, otherwise the portability of ASIS tools can no longer be guaranteed.

8.2. OASIS

OASIS, an acronym of Object-Oriented ASIS, is a research project aimed at developing an ASIS secondary library. The project is based on the public version of the ASIS-for-GNAT technology. The primary idea of OASIS is to provide a set of abstractions closely corresponding to the object-oriented model. The latest version of OASIS defines the following abstractions, partly illustrated in Fig. 2:

- A Derivation Class corresponds to the hierarchy of the types derived from some root tagged type;
- A Derivation Item corresponds to a node in the Derivation Class.
- A Component corresponds to a component of a tagged type or a type extension, either part of its declaration, or inherited from an ancestor;
- A Primitive corresponds to the notion of a primitive operation in Ada, be it inherited or not;
- A Class-Wide Operation reflects the Ada notion of a class-wide operation;
- A Dispatching Call reflects the Ada notion of a dispatching call.

A first set of queries in OASIS provides an object-oriented view of an ASIS context: it is for instance possible to retrieve all the roots of all the derivation classes in a given context. Then there is a set of queries for navigating in a derivation class: e.g find the ancestor class, find the derived classes, and traverse a whole derivation class. Finally, there are queries to find the components, inherited or not, of a Derivation Item, its inherited and genuine primitive operations, and to decide if an operation is overridden.

8.3. Towards a unified set of ASIS-based libraries

Some time ago, the ACM SIGAda ASIS WG started discussions aimed at unifying the ASIS libraries extending the basic ASIS functionality. The main result of these discussions are the guidelines for developing such libraries provided by Steve Blake [8]. The main points of these guidelines are:

- ASIS secondary queries should be separated from ASIS extensions. ASIS secondary queries are implemented entirely on top of ASIS. Therefore, an ASIS secondary library can be ported from one ASIS implementation to another one. On the contrary, the implementation of an ASIS extension is based on internal compiler mechanisms, and therefore cannot be ported from one ASIS implementation to another without extending the ASIS implementation.
- A simple naming convention should be used to avoid name collisions between ASIS extensions and secondary queries provided by different implementations.

It seems ASIS will evolve like the Ada language itself: the ASIS Standard will be structured in a "core" part, and a set of secondary libraries and extension libraries defined in Special Needs Annexes.

9 Conclusions

At the time of writing, it is already evident that ASIS has become an important part of today's Ada technology. We expect that its use will grow, and that we will see more and more ASIS tools in a very near future. We hope that reporting our experience in working with ASIS might be useful to future users of ASIS, and become a valuable input to the next ASIS revision.

References

[1] Ada Semantic Interface Specification (ASIS); International Standard ISO/IEC 15291 1999 (E).

[2] ASIS-for-GNAT is available electronically as a part of the public version of the GNAT technology from http://www.gnat.com

[3] ASIS home page of SIGAda, the Special Interest Group on Ada of the Association of Computing Machinery (ACM): http://www.acm.org/sigada/WG/asiswg/

[4] Home page of ACT, Ada Core Technologies, http://www.gnat.com.

[5] Home page of ACT Europe, the European branch of Ada Core Technologies, http://www.act-europe.fr.

[6] Christine Ausnit-Hood, Kent A. Johnson, Robert G. Pettit, IV, Steven B. Opdahl (Eds.); Ada 95 Quality and Style: Guidelines for Professional Programmers; Lecture Notes in Computer Science, vol 1344; Springer-Verlag, 1995; ISBN 3-540-63823-7.

[7] John Barnes (Ed.); Ada 95 Rationale: The Language, The Standard Libraries; Lecture Notes in Computer Science, vol 1247; Springer-Verlag, 1997; ISBN 3-540-63143-7.

[8] Steve Blake; Message sent to the ASIS WG technical forum.

[9] Currie Colket et alii; Architecture of ASIS: A Tool to Support Code Analysis of Complex Systems; ACM Ada Letters, January 1997, vol. XVII, no. 1, 1997, pp. 35-40.

[10] Currie Colket; Code Analysis of Safety-Critical and Real-Time Software Using ASIS; Proceedings of the ACM SIGAda Annual International Conference (SIGAda'99), 17-21 October 1999, Redondo Beach, CA, USA, pp. 67-76.

[11] C. Daniel Cooper; ASIS-Based Code Analysis Automation; ACM Ada Letters, November/December 1997, Volume XVII, No.6, pp. 65-69.

[12] Vasiliy Fofanov, Sergey Rybin, Alfred Strohmeier; ASIStint: An Interactive ASIS Interpreter; Proceedings of TRI-Ada'97, St. Louis, MO, USA, November 11-13 1997, Susan Carlson (Ed.), ACM Press, 1997, pp. 205-209.

[13] Vitali Kaufman; The ASIS rule checking program of Vitali Kaufman is available from http://www.kolumbus.fi/vitali.kaufman/gch and as a link from http://www.acm.org/sigada/wg/asiswg.

[14] W. Pritchett, IV, J. Riley; An ASIS-Based Static Analysis Tool for High-Integrity Systems; Proceedings of the ACM SIGAda Annual International Conference (SIGAda'98), 8-12 November 1998, Washington D.C., USA, pp.12-17.

[15] Sergey Rybin, Alfred Strohmeier, Eugene Zueff; ASIS for GNAT: Goals, Problems and Implementation Strategy; Proceedings of Ada-Europe'95, Toussaint (Ed.), LNCS (Lecture Notes in Computer Science) 1031, Springer, Frankfurt, Germany, October 2-6 1995, pp. 139-151.

[16] Sergey Rybin, Alfred Strohmeier, Alexei Kuchumov, Vasiliy Fofanov; ASIS for GNAT: From the Prototype to the Full Implementation; Reliable Software Technologies - Ada-Europe'96: Proceedings, Alfred Strohmeier (Ed.), LNCS (Lecture Notes in Computer Science), vol. 1088, Springer, Ada-Europe International Conference on Reliable Software Technologies Montreux, Switzerland, June 10-14, 1996, pp. 298-311.

[17] Sergey Rybin, Alfred Strohmeier; Ada and ASIS: Justification of Differences in Terminology and Mechanisms; Proceedings of TRI-Ada'96, Philadelphia, USA, December 3 - 7, 1996, pp. 249-254.

[18] Alfred Strohmeier, Vasiliy Fofanov, Sergey Rybin, Stéphane Barbey; Quality-for-ASIS: A Portable Testing Facility for ASIS; International Conference on Reliable Software Technologies - Ada-Europe'98, Uppsala, Sweden, June 2-8 1998, Lars Asplund (Ed.), LNCS (Lecture Notes in Computer Science), Springer-Verlag, 1998, pp. 163-175.

[19] E. Schonberg, B. Banner; The GNAT Project: A GNU-Ada 9X Compiler; TRI-Ada'94 Proceedings, ACM Press, 1994; pp. 48-57.

[20] S. Tucker Taft, Robert A. Duff (Eds.); Ada 95 Reference Manual: Language and Standard Libraries, International Standard ISO/IEC 8652:1995(E); Lecture Notes in Computer Science, vol 1246; Springer-Verlag, 1997; ISBN 3-540-63144-5.

[21] Joseph Wisniewski; Transitioning an ASIS Application; Proceedings of the ACM SIGAda Annual International Conference (SIGAda'99), 17-21 October 1999, Redondo Beach, CA, USA, pp. 53-65.

Generation of Interface Design Description Documents Using ASIS

Steven V. Hovater[1], William Marksteiner[2], and Allen Butturini[2]

[1] Rational Software
Lexington, Massachusetts, USA
svh@rational.com
[2] Raytheon Electronic Systems
Bedford, Massachusetts, USA
William_K_Marksteiner@res.raytheon.com
Allen_Butturini@res.raytheon.com

Abstract. Creation and recreation of Interface Design Description documentation can be automated by using representation clauses and annotations for key record types, and through the use of ASIS-based tools to extract this information from the source code. ...

1 Inception

The Interface Design Description Extraction Tool (IDDET) was conceived out of the need for a defined and controlled way of assuring that the documentation regarding interfaces on the THAAD (Theater High Altitude Area Defense) radar program was consistent with the as-built interfaces in the software.

Past programs have had serious issues with the consistency between documentation and design. Particularly in the area of interfaces, such consistency is important, because it is typical that entity A which interfaces to entity B does not have access to (or, perhaps more importantly, care to have access to) entity B's actual design or code materials. They thus rely on the interface documentation for information which influences their own design. If this interface documentation does not coincide with the actual interface, problems arise later in the integration phase of the program.

The Department of Defense (DOD) dictates via the J-016-1995 standard that interfaces be documented in a particular way, namely the Interface Design Description document, or IDD. Particular content is prescribed, down to the detail of attributes like size, data type, and precision. In addition, the IDD prescribes that not only element level data be included in the document, but also message level formatting information.

The Interface Requirements Specification (or IRS) precedes the IDD ina normal DOD development cycle. The IRS specifies, usually at a high level, what the interfaces must transfer. Those specifications are then met by the software

[1] The THAAD Radar is an air defense radar which is being developed for the U.S. Army by Raytheon Company.

H. B. Keller and E. Plödereder (Eds.): Ada-Europe 2000, LNCS 1845, pp. 138– , 2000.

design, and the software design is then documented in the IDD, usually by laborious means.

2 Elaboration

2.1 Theory

The Ada Semantic Interface Specification (ASIS) is a programmatic interface which enables tools to be written that can navigate the compiler-generated semantic network (DIANA) representative of the Ada source code.

The Ada programming language provides the record type as a means of aggregating disparately-typed components within a single structure. There are no requirements in the Ada Language Reference Manual that compiler vendors ensure their product provides identical memory layout of components within record types between compiler versions.

The Ada language also provides the record representation clause, a means for the programmer to specify the memory layout for objects declared of the record type. Thus programmers can ensure the components within their records conform to a predictable, defined memory layout. The representation clause can also ensure data portability between different hardware architectures.

Raytheon's goal was to create an application that would combine these concepts to generate Interface Design Description documentation. For record types or record components that require additional documentation beyond what is obtainable via programmatic examination of the compiler-generated semantic information, the application will extract (optional) annotations associated with those components or record types.

2.2 Practice

The initial work began by examining the information produced by running the Ada Analyzer report "Display Expanded Type Structure". There we observed that the Ada Analyzer could navigate through the type structure, and collect information such as the base type, size, and sub-components.

The next step began with the creation of a very crude stand-alone prototype in Ada83 using the ASIS interface provided by Rational's Apex product.

The prototype took a record type declaration and decomposed it into the record component names. Our next iteration extended the prototype to also display the record component type names. Per our requirements, the application would be recursive in the sense that when we encountered a record type in the component list, the application would display the component record type component's components, and so forth, so that all record types were fully decomposed into scalar (e.g. non-record) types. Furthermore, each scalar type would be reduced (if appropriate) to its base type and constraints.

[2] Recently approved as an ISO standard, ISO/IEC 15291:1999.

[3] Descriptive Intermediate Attributed Notation for Ada.

[4] Ada Analyzer is a trademark of LittleTree Consulting.

From a documentation viewpoint, the top-level record should be at a section level, and any record types found during the navigation of the top-level record component should be represented in subsections following the description of the top-level record component. This represented a design challenge - the most straightforward coding of the ASIS record decomposition routine would produce a nested table of record components, not a series of individual tables related by parent-child relationships.

The solution to this challenge was to create an intermediate memory-based structure which had entries corresponding to the top-level components. For components whose type was also a record type, a link for that component would be created to a new instance of the intermediate structure, the child record type components recorded, and ultimately, execution would return to the top level record component navigation. Thus, the recursive ASIS program could be written, but the results would be stored in the appropriate area in the intermediate representation, allowing complete tables to be constructed, with the nesting represented by the links.

With proof that we could indeed extract the information we needed, we then considered whether we should build a stand-alone tool, or create a new customization to the Ada Analyzer. We opted for the quickest route - that of using the framework already provided by LittleTree's product, which would allow us to use the wealth of utilities that support the Ada Analyzer.

The prototype was then frozen, and for our next iteration, we began implementation of the IDDET tool as an Ada Analyzer extension.

3 Construction

3.1 Structure

Since at the top-level we are concerned with only record structures, the application was designed to accept only record structures at the initial point of the ASIS navigation code. There are two flavors of record types that we considered (in ASIS terms):

1. A_Record_Type_Definition
2. A_Derived_With_Record_Type_Definition

Furthermore, there was the requirement that the tool be able to handle discriminated record types. For components of discriminated record types, the constraint upon the discriminated record type (required by Ada for the declaration of a component with a discriminated record type) is used as the default value for the discriminated record decomposition. However, top-level discriminated record types offered a challenge.

Since the intention of the tool is that it run in a batch mode, the most practical way to handle top-level discriminated record types was to impose the restriction that any top-level discriminated record types have default values for their discriminants. Hence, if the tool encounters a discriminated record type at the top level, it assumes the default values for the discriminated record type. Top-level record types with no default discriminants are reported to the user as an error condition.

Another restriction placed on tool usage is that if the users wanted to get a bitmap of the structure table for a record type, the type must have a representation specification.

The Ada language has a rich support for representation clauses, with the interesting complications for our implementation efforts:

1. Not all components of a record need be rep spec'd to have valid code.
2. The order of the declarations in a representation clause may differ from the order of the declaration of the components in the record clause.
3. Ada does not require that the entries in the representation clause be listed in address/bit order.

Our way of working through this, is to first compare the number of record components (including any discriminants) to the number of the entries in the representation clause. If the two counts are different, we flag the type as "not-bitmap-able". If, however, the two counts are identical, we take the next step, which is to sort the representation clause entries into address/bit order. Finally, we sort the internal representation table of record components into the same order as the (reordered) representation clause entries.

For discriminated record types, we must first determine the list of components that are selected by the (specific or default) discriminator values, then collect the intersection of the selected component names with their corresponding entries in the representation clause, and finally sort the surviving components names into (address/bit) representation clause order. As in the non-discriminated case, if there isn't a one-to-one mapping between the (surviving) component names and the (surviving) entries in the representation clause, then the type is flagged as "not-bitmap-able".

3.2 Arrays

An additional requirement is to handle arrays. Ada allows arrays to be components of a record type, as long as there are constraints upon the array component. (Granted, other pathological cases could be constructed, such as pointers to arrays, which we ignored for the first implementation.) For arrays, we must determine several properties:

1. the number of elements (derived from the constraints)
2. the type of the elements in the array.

If the component is an array of arrays, the tool continues to decompose the arrays until a base element type is discovered. Then, the dimensions of the array, as obtained during the array navigation, as well as the fundamental properties of the base element type, are reported. If the base element type is a record type, the tool creates a subsection and decomposes the record type. It should be understood that each time the tool encounters a record type, the subsection created has identical structure as when the record type is at the top-level.

Again, it's easy to construct pathological cases of non-homogeneous arrays that we haven't considered in this first implementation. Since the goal of the tool is to produce documentation for the Raytheon code base, our focus is to provide coverage of the constructs represented in that code, rather than develop a general solution.

3.3 Segmented Type Names

Types whose name consist of several segments (e.g. *somepackage.subpackage. typename*) offer a challenge. While it is possible to eventually navigate to the definition of a segmented type name, it is far easier to rely upon a navigation interface offered by the Ada Analyzer, **Ada_Program.Definition**, that cuts short the effort needed for navigation to the type declaration.

3.4 Record Handling

In all cases, we have a record declaration to start with. In Ada, a record declaration can contain both component and pragma entries. We ignore any possible pragma entries, as they are not represented in the Raytheon code base. For all practical purposes, we consider a record declaration to be composed of a number of component declarations. Each component declaration follows the format (with the initial value, optionally):

```
name : type_mark := initial_value ;
```

We begin by obtaining the list of the record components from the record declaration. The list is then operated upon by the Process_Component procedure, once per component (after resolution of derived types via **Asis.Type_Definitions.Type_Structure**, and resolution of private types by **Asis.Type_Definitions.Completed_Ground_Type**.)

The essence of Process_Component is a case statement, with a branch for each of the basic type kinds:

- A_Subtype_Definition
- A_Record_Type_Definition
- A_Derived_With_Record_Type_Definition
- An_Enumeration_Type_Definition
- A_Float_Type_Definition
- A_Decimal_Fixed_Type_Definition
- A_Fixed_Type_Definition
- An_Integer_Type_Definition
- A_Modular_Type_Definition
- An_Array_Type_Definition

Each component of the record is examined. We extract the component name, its dimensionality, the name of its base type, its range (derived from constraints upon the component subtype), size, accuracy, and any description, note or unit annotations.

Each type encountered during component decomposition may require special handling to extract this data. For example, the method used for gathering the size information from a (scalar) enumeration type differs from the method used for an array of enumeration types.

All this information about the component is then passed to the Add_Element_Table_Entry routine, which populates the in-memory intermediate representation.

3.5 Annotations

We mentioned previously the desire to take advantage of the many utilities provided by the Ada Analyzer. One such set of utilties is the annotation-gathering routines. It is quite easy to gather specifically formatted annotations "attached" to record components (in this case, represented by *An_Element*:

```
Annotation_Analysis.Collect (
        From_Decl_Or_Statement => An_Element,
        Config => Annotation_Configuration,
        Annots => Element_Annotations);
```

The Ada Analyzer code permits user configuration files to direct whether the annotations are expected to precede or follow the declaration. Rather than permit this potentially confusing configuration issue, the IDDET application has been hard-coded to expect annotations immediately before the declarations.

The project requires additional information to be provided for the creation of the IDD that can not be extracted by the ASIS interface. For these cases, we require the coders to insert annotations. The tool looks for the following annotations:

```
-- @ DESCRIPTION: This is an example description. These
--   annotations can span multiple lines.
-- @ NOTES: This is an example of a note.
-- @ UNITS: kilometers
-- @ ACCURACY: 1 meter
```

Record declarations (e.g. the top level record) can have a special annotation, **MSG_DESCRIPTION**, whose text populates the paragraph following the section heading.

3.6 Producing Output

Once the navigation and collection activity completes, the next step is to construct the element and structure tables, starting with the top-level record. Having created the intermediate representation, this step was straightforward. Records that are encountered during the decomposition of the top-level record follow are decomposed and represented in nested subsections, each with the appropriate header, description (from the **MSG_DESCRIPTION** annotation), element and structure tables.

An element table is a table that lists (in the order indicated by the representation clause) each component name, its base type (integer, modular, float, record, enum, array), its size, range, and any annotation-specified notes, description, and units.

A structure table is a pictorial representation of the memory layout of the record structure, with the bits along the horizontal axis, and word along the vertical axis.

The output format was chosen to be Rich Text Format, so that the tool-produced documentation would be editable by Microsoft Word. (We briefly explored HTML as an output mechanism, and found it to be expressive enough. However, the RTF was required by our customer.)

As an example of the input and output produced by the tool, consider the following record type *Message_Type* and its representation clause contained within the following package specification:

```
package Iddet_Test_Pkg is
  Word : constant := 4; -- storage unit is byte, 4 bytes per word
  type Mode_Type is (Fix, Dec, Exp);
  type Mode_Mask_Type is array (Mode_Type) of Boolean;
  type My_Float is new Float digits 5;
  subtype Sst is Integer range 1 .. 23;

  -- @MSG_DESCRIPTION: this is the Vrecord_Type annotation
  type Vrecord_Type (Mode : Mode_Type) is
    record
      -- @DESCRIPTION: This component is a non-variant
      --  Natural component.
      -- @UNITS: Kilograms
      -- @NOTES:  These are notes associated with Trange.
      Trange : Natural;
      case Mode is
        when Fix =>
          -- @DESCRIPTION: This component is a variant
          --  Boolean component.
          -- @UNITS: N/A
          -- @NOTES:  These are notes associated with Vboo.
          Vboo : Boolean;
        when Dec =>
          -- @DESCRIPTION: This component is a variant
          --  My_Float component.
          -- @UNITS: Kilograms
```

```
        -- @NOTES:  These are notes associated with Vflo.
        Vflo : My_Float;
      when Exp =>
        -- @DESCRIPTION: This component is a variant
        --  Sst component.
        -- @UNITS: Degrees Centigrade
        -- @NOTES:  These are notes associated with Sst.
        Vint : Sst;
    end case;
  end record;
for Vrecord_Type use
  record at mod 8;
    Mode at 0 * Word range 0 .. 7;
    Trange at 1 * Word range 0 .. 31;
    Vint at 2 * Word range 0 .. 31;
    Vflo at 2 * Word range 0 .. 31;
    Vboo at 2 * Word range 0 .. 1;
  end record;


subtype Mart is Integer range 1 .. 2;
type Fromt is array (Mart'First .. Mart'Last) of
    Vrecord_Type (Mode => Dec);

-- @MSG_DESCRIPTION: this is the Message_Type annotation
type Message_Type is
  record
    -- @DESCRIPTION: This component is an integer component.
    -- @UNITS: Meters
    -- @NOTES:  These are notes associated with X.
    X : Sst;
    -- @DESCRIPTION:This component is a Boolean component.
    -- @UNITS: N/A
    -- @NOTES:  These notes are associated with Y.
    Y : Boolean;
    -- @DESCRIPTION:This component is a nested
    --  variant component.
    -- @UNITS: N/A
    -- @NOTES:  These notes are associated with Z.
    Z : Fromt;
    -- @DESCRIPTION:This component is an array component.
    -- @UNITS: N/A
    -- @NOTES:  These notes are associated with Mode_Mask.
    Mode_Mask : Mode_Mask_Type;
  end record;
```

```
    for Message_Type use
      record at mod 8;
        X at 0 * Word range 0 .. 31;
        Y at 1 * Word range 0 .. 0;
        Z at 2 * Word range 0 .. 143;
        -- bits at 1..8 are not used
        Mode_Mask at 7 * Word range 9 .. 11;
      end record;
  end Iddet_Test_Pkg;
```

This example shows a top-level record **Message_Type** with both scalar (**X**, **Y**) and composite (**Z**, **Mode_Mask**) elements. Observe the **Z** component is an array of discriminated records.

The IDDET tool produces RTF-formatted tables as in Figures - .

1.1.1 IDDET_TEST_PKG.MESSAGE_TYPE

this is the Message_Type annotation

<table>
<tr><td>00</td><td>01</td><td>02</td><td>03</td><td>04</td><td>05</td><td>06</td><td>07</td><td>08</td><td>09</td><td>10</td><td>11</td><td>12</td><td>13</td><td>14</td><td>15</td><td>16</td><td>17</td><td>18</td><td>19</td><td>20</td><td>21</td><td>22</td><td>23</td><td>24</td><td>25</td><td>26</td><td>27</td><td>28</td><td>29</td><td>30</td><td>31</td><td></td></tr>
<tr><td colspan="32">X</td><td>Word 0</td></tr>
<tr><td>*</td><td colspan="31">Spare</td><td>Word 1</td></tr>
<tr><td colspan="32">[0.. 31] + Z (2 elements of Vrecord_Type)</td><td>Word 2</td></tr>
<tr><td colspan="32">[32.. 63] + Z (2 elements of Vrecord_Type)</td><td>Word 3</td></tr>
<tr><td colspan="32">[64.. 95] + Z (2 elements of Vrecord_Type)</td><td>Word 4</td></tr>
<tr><td colspan="32">[96.. 127] + Z (2 elements of Vrecord_Type)</td><td>Word 5</td></tr>
<tr><td colspan="16">[128.. 143] + Z (2 elements of Vrecord_Type)</td><td colspan="16">Spare</td><td>Word 6</td></tr>
<tr><td colspan="9">Spare</td><td colspan="3">Mode_Mask (3 elements of Enum)</td><td colspan="20">Spare</td><td>Word 7</td></tr>
</table>

Word	Bit	Name
1	0	Y

Fig. 1. This is the structure table for the top-level record type (Message_Type). The smaller sub-table following the structure table is an index into the structure table to describe elements whose typographic layout size prohibits in-table display

1.1.1.1 Iddet_Test_Pkg.Message_Type.Z (one element) (MODE => 1)

this is the Vrecord_Type annotation

<table>
<tr><td>00</td><td>01</td><td>02</td><td>03</td><td>04</td><td>05</td><td>06</td><td>07</td><td>08</td><td>09</td><td>10</td><td>11</td><td>12</td><td>13</td><td>14</td><td>15</td><td>16</td><td>17</td><td>18</td><td>19</td><td>20</td><td>21</td><td>22</td><td>23</td><td>24</td><td>25</td><td>26</td><td>27</td><td>28</td><td>29</td><td>30</td><td>31</td><td></td></tr>
<tr><td colspan="8">Mode</td><td colspan="24">Spare</td><td>Word 0</td></tr>
<tr><td colspan="32">Trange</td><td>Word 1</td></tr>
<tr><td colspan="32">Vflo</td><td>Word 2</td></tr>
</table>

Fig. 2. Structure table for the nested discriminated record. Note the heading indicates the discriminant value

1.1.2 IDDET_TEST_PKG.MESSAGE_TYPE

Name	Description	Type	Range	Acc	Units	Notes
X	This component is an integer component.	Integer	1.. 23		Meters	These are notes associated with X.
Y	This component is a Boolean component.	Enum	False=0 True=1		N/A	These notes are associated with Y.
+ Z	This component is a nested variant component.	Vrecord_Type			N/A	These notes are associated with Z.
+ Mode_Mask	This component is an array component.	Enum			N/A	These notes are associated with Mode_Mask.

Fig. 3. This is the element table for the top-level record. The + decoration on the component name indicates a composite structure

1.1.2.1 Iddet_Test_Pkg.Message_Type.Z (one element) (MODE => 1)

Name	Description	Type	Range	Acc	Units	Notes
Mode		Enum	Fix=0 Dec=1 Exp=2			
Trange	This component is a non-variant Natural component.	Integer	0.. 2147483647		Kilograms	These are notes associated with Trange.
Vflo	This component is a variant My_Float component.	Float	5		Kilograms	These are notes associated with Vflo.

Fig. 4. This is the element table (one element) in the array of discriminated records

In the element table (Figure), the range for the X component has been extracted via ASIS, as well as the enumeration values for the Y component. Since the type for X is a subtype, the ASIS code has extracted the base type of the component, and the ranges (e.g. constraints) appropriate to the subtype.

Note further that annotations associated with the records and their components are incorporated into the element table.

4 Transition

4.1 The Tool Has Helped

Hundreds of pages of interface description documents have been produced using this tool. When the source code changes now, instead of gathering an army of technical documentation specialists, the tool can be rerun across the new source code, and the most tedious and painstaking portion of the production of the interface documents automated.

Systems engineers who are analyzing and reviewing the design can now be sure that they are viewing the actual "as-built" interface design when they are looking at the IDD - something they couldn't be sure of in the past before IDDET. Some of the more software-proficient systems engineers would always be found muddling around in the code libraries just to make sure that the IDD reflected reality - often they found that it didn't. They can now focus on the problem at hand, knowing that the IDD does reflect the real software.

The use of IDDET also provides an unanticipated benefit. Before IDDET, changes to the interface design had to be governed by a change control mechanism which covered both the code and the document. If a designer wanted to change a 2-bit field to a 3-bit field, he had to go submit a change request against the code module, go through a formal change request board, get approval, and then go make the change. This process was repeated (or at best, on some programs, parallelized) for the interface documentation. With IDDET, only the code need be placed under formal change control, since the interface documentation is now only an artifact of the code. (Yes, IDDET itself and the IDD generation process need also be placed under formal change control, but changes to those items would be much less frequent than changes to the actual radar software.)

One other valuable aspect of this tool has yet to be realized when the development reaches the integration phase. (We are currently in the detailed design phase.) During the integration phase, it is common that the real data traffic conforming to interface messages defined by the IDD is analyzed by systems engineers and integrators to analyze the performance of the overall radar system. Past programs have had to deal with the issue of interface documentation (IDD) not matching the actual code. This results in integrators wasting a lot of time and making serious errors because they believe they are looking at the value of one field (perhaps in something as gruesome as a hex dump) when they're actually looking at some other field.

IDDET's benefits are being noticed; other programs within Raytheon are now also deploying the tool.

4.2 Looking Ahead

The tool functionality is currently frozen. However, looking ahead, several enhancements could be envisioned. One, the output routines could be rewritten to output XML, with hyperlinks between the components. This would allow a web-enabled document with easy traversal between the various record relationships.

Another enhancement that can easily be envisioned, is to convert the present ASIS code (based upon the Rational ASIS 1.1 implementation) to ASIS 2.0, and take advantage of Ada95's features.

An Ada95 Programming Style Checker Using the GNAT ASIS Implementation

Patrick Closhen* and Hans-Jürgen Hoffmann

Darmstadt University of Technology, Department of Computer Sciences,
Chair for Programming Languages and Compilers
Alexanderstr. 10, D-64283 Darmstadt, Germany
Tel.: 06151/16-3610, Fax: 06151/16-6648
{closhen,hoffmann}@pu.informatik.tu-darmstadt.de

Abstract. To enhance the quality of software, e.g. in safety-critical environments, we propose the introduction of a style checking phase into the software development cycle. Style checking in this case is to be understood as anything that normally goes beyond the capabilities of an ordinary compiler. An implementation of a style checking framework written in Ada95 and using the GNAT ASIS implementation is presented. This framework also allows to specify what is being checked.

Keywords: Software Quality, Style Checking, ASIS, GNAT, Framework

1 Motivation

The spreading impact of computers and information technology on modern society results in an ever-increasing demand for error-reduced software. This demand comes from the desire to use computers e.g. in safety-critical environments (processing units for hazardous materials, medicine, flight-control systems) or areas that involve large financial investments where failure of a software system might have catastrophic consequences either to involved persons or affected objects of value.

To ensure the production of error-reduced software, techniques like requirements analysis, specification, various design methods, testing and documenting have evolved to make up the software development cycle of software engineering. However, ensuring software to run without error once it has left development environments today depends mostly on the testing step mentioned above. Testing, to ensure that software really behaves according to the respective specifications is already the main focus of many research groups. A short overview of these efforts can be found in [ ].

Unfortunately, this step only achieves to find errors that are already "present in the software". If the number of these errors exceeds a certain limit, resulting costs either endanger the project or the required surplus of testing and redesign

* Contact person: Patrick Closhen

H. B. Keller and E. Plödereder (Eds.): Ada-Europe 2000, LNCS 1845, pp. 149– , 2000.

time breaks the development schedule, which may result in a too long time-to-market and consequently low sales. Apart from these facts, there is also the urge to "to do things right from the beginning", meaning that the desire to suppress errors is in itself a strong point of motivation.

Thus, researchers have come up with the idea to look into what makes some software designers produce code that contains less errors. Some of their findings are:

1. Using programming languages which are "less error-prone" than others
2. Coding according to certain "programming styles" which are the result of experience gained by working with programming languages

The first approach is often impossible to use since requirements defined by the customer may leave no choice. Furthermore, a proper judgement which programming language to choose is also hard to come by since all such decisions involve, to say the least, a strong subjective factor.

The second approach seems much more benefical because it inhibits designers from making errors and is mostly applicable in all given programming languages. This has lead to the development of style guides for all kinds of programming tasks [,]. Thus, the logical step to apply style guides in a software development cycle would be to make designers adhere to the given set of style guidelines the employing company issues. But how can this goal be achieved?

Problems connected to this question are:

1. What needs to be checked?
2. How to check for "style conformance"?
3. When to check?

These questions will be analysed in the following sections, the first hereafter, the second and third in section 3.

The goal of our work is to analyse the requirements and techniques for style checking in general. Secondly, we want to design and implement a framework which encapsulates all necessary functionality to produce a style checker, if possible for different programming languages and tasks. It will conclude in a prototypical implementation for a small set of languages. Furthermore, additional applications of these advanced code examination techniques will be considered, such as attributing code, supplying state information, etc. e.g. for auditing and documentation.

2 Quality and Style

There are many examples of what people consider "good style" in programming and this list can probably be augmented indefinitely. Some of the guidelines even hold true for different programming languages. Fields into which guidelines can be distinguished include rules for source code formatting and commenting, semantically error-prone constructs, issues of object-oriented programming, dynamically endangered constructs, improving performance and many more.

Generally speaking, style checking is an activity that goes beyond the functionality of a compiler since requirements are involved that are typically not necessary to accomplish the implementation of a given algorithm. So this brings up the question, what to look for in style checking? As can be seen, e.g. in [ ] there also exists a categorization of guidelines regarding whether something can be checked fully automated, or only partially autonomous, requiring interactive operator/programmer assistance, or not at all, thus excluding such guidelines from application in a style checking program.

Another necessary decision to make is the amount of checking that one will settle for. Too much checking may result in refusal or deadline problems, too little will not achieve any relevant change in software quality. Also, the amount of checking may vary during the development cycle, other areas of interest may arise during implementation. So, a sensible compromise has to be found which also needs to be able to adapt to the given cirumstances. Since these issues can and should be resolved separately from a style checking application to achieve the aforementioned adaptability, we will not go into detail here. Hopefully, a long term examination of the application of style checking will come up with results regarding the required compromise and techniques for scheduling and embedding a style checking phase in the software development cycle.

When trying to decide what to look for in code, one needs to keep in mind the complete life cycle of the emerging software. This involves going for increased maintainability to reduce the risk of "breaking" good code when implementing new versions on the foundation of existing software. Mostly all rules regarding readability and source code formatting as well as those for commenting code are an important issue here.

Finally, known sources of problems, like using goto statements, nesting constructs too deeply, making undocumented use of compiler defaults for certain constructs and omitting initializing statements for variables are good candidates for a style checker. It is common knowledge that more errors result from these simple "don'ts" than from using highly complex semantical relationships, which the programmer has to look up anyway, thereby further reducing the risk of making errors. Also, we need only a small first set for our prototypical implementation that lets us focus on adaptability. We expect to add rules here as needed.

With our goal of examining code coming from a lot of programming languages, our set of style guidelines may not look like a very sophisticated choice, but it will serve the purpose of testing whether software development will involve less errors when including a style checking phase than when omitting checking. An additional benefit is the improved acceptance of a checking phase which will be shorter if the base set of guidelines is kept to a minimum.

3 Requirements for a Style Checking Tool

As stated in the motivation this section will examine how and when checking will be accomplished, also adding some further requirements.

Style checking should be incorporated into the implementation cycle, before testing takes place. Otherwise, there would be less benefit, since it is more expensive to find errors by testing than by running a style check of the source code. Ideal would be a transparent integration into the designer's development environment which would initiate a check, e.g. whenever the designer saves his or her work, resulting in a log file that could add any found "style mistakes" to the designer's to-do list to be corrected in the next setting. Another approach would be to start the checking phase when the designer decides that he or she has reached a point, where an implemetation part could be considered finished. The checking tool could then analyse the code and result in checking logs that contribute to the milestone documentation, e.g. in distributed development environments. To place style checking at this point could also make it feasible to include requesting further information from the designer by way of an interactive user interface. This step is of course only necessary if the set of rules include those guidelines that can be tested only semi-automatically.

One further necessity is a means of analysing and also attributing code. Unfortunately, this includes as a first step having a grammar for the programming language in which the code is written. This can be a very restricting factor since these grammars make up the know-how of those software firms selling the used compilers and may therefore not be easily disclosed. Additionally, if a programming language is not described in a standard, there may be many dialects, to which a style checker would also have to be adapted, as well as differing implementations, which may result in problems if rules are to cover semantic or runtime issues.

Our prototypical approach is to implement a style checking tool as a stand-alone application which can be set up with regard to what is being checked, what kind of log messages will appear in the log file. The tool is run whenever deemed appropriate. This prototype will need to offer support for specifying what will be checked and to extend the given set of style checking rules. This stand-alone approach would need further integration, e.g. into version management, an interactive development environment and in the long run to a transparent use of its capabilities. The evolution of check log files could be included in the documentation of the project to emphasize the efforts to increase software quality.

4 A Prototype Implementation of the Style Checker

We will now present a prototypical implementation of a style checker for and written in Ada95, making use of the ASIS standard implementation for GNAT [, , ,].

The main design factors for this tool are:

1. Anything in the given programming language can be checked
2. Rules which express what is being checked can be added
3. The application can be parameterized at runtime
4. Fast checking phase

Thankfully, the ASIS implementation provides a good basis for the first requirement, as it offers complete access to all information of the code to be analysed. This also solves the problem to find a grammar for the given programming language. And last but not least Ada95 is covered by a well-developed standard that makes the style checker applicable to Ada95 code developed in any environment.

By initiating a call of the GNAT compiler, ASIS is provided with a completely attributed syntax tree of the code to be analysed. This tree is composed of nodes which represent the different language elements. The differentiation defined in the standard varies from abstract (e.g. different element kinds) to concrete (e.g. literal kinds). The syntax tree can then be traversed, running all necessary tests at each node a) when it is first being visited and b) when all its child nodes have been visited. This may include keeping state information stored for later analysis of nodes which have to be visited yet, e.g. for cross-checking of related lines of code that appear separated in the code.

The second requirement is met by a framework which enables the designer of a style checker to specify rule objects, implemented in separated rule packages. These rule objects are then contained in a collector which provides the interface for the style checking application. This application is derived from example applications in the ASIS standard.

In detail, the rules are implemented as concrete data types derived from an abstract type class defining the interface of all rule data types. A third kind of data type, the rule array, is used to return an initialized array which contains one rule object from each implemented rule type (see figure 1) .

4.1 Rule Data Types and Rule Implementation

To specify a new style checking rule, one needs to define a new rule type derived from the abstract version implementing the required interface. The signature of the two most important procedures is shown below:

```
procedure Pre_Procedure (
       R       : in out Rule_Obj;
       Element : in     Asis.Element;
       Control : in out Asis.Traverse_Control;
       State   : in out Info.Info_Node          );

procedure Post_Procedure (
       R       : in out Rule_Obj;
       Element : in     Asis.Element;
       Control : in out Asis.Traverse_Control;
       State   : in out Info.Info_Node          );
```

[1] All figures in UML notation

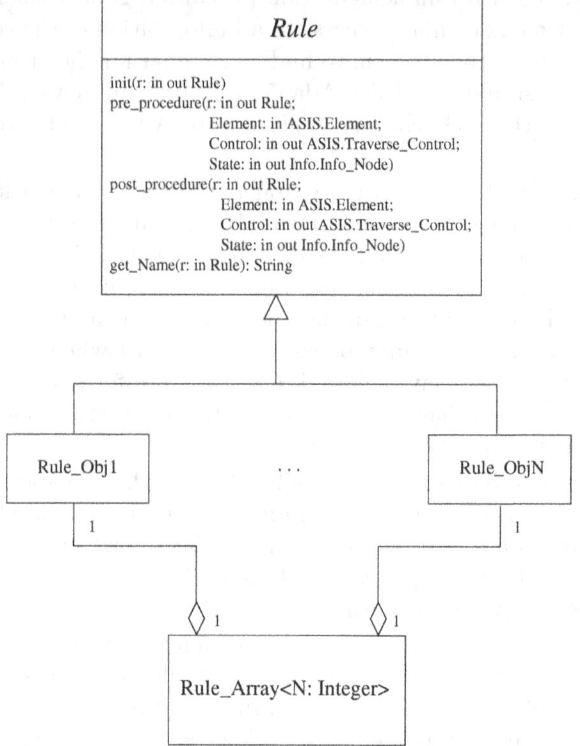

Fig. 1. Rule data types and inheritance relationships

These procedures are called when a node is newly visited and after all its child nodes are visited respectively. Their implementation usually conforms to the following pattern:

1. Testing whether the given `Element` is of the node type the rule object is looking for
2. If necessary, searching for other nodes that the rule object needs to find to accept that any given situation is really at hand
3. Performing any tests of the `Element`'s attributes
4. In both cases an error message is generated if the proper requirements are not met

To implement these two procedures properly the designer has to have knowledge of the way ASIS returns nodes and what node types are available. To simplify the design of rule objects we imagine an interactive tool that could help compose rules according to the mentioned pattern. By letting the designer choose from all available ASIS elements from a menu the conditional section of a rule object could be constructed as a logical combination of relevant node element types to look for, the range of attribute values that are allowed for these elements or other state information either stored in the rule object's attributes or globally (see below). The consequential section would then specify the error message to be logged in case of a style error or require appropriate interaction by the operator.

4.2 Structure of the Check_Style Application

Check_Style is implemented according to the examples accompanying the ASIS framework. The only difference lies in two points:

1. The actions taken when a specific construct of code appears that doesn't comply to style rules
2. The way new rule object packages can be included into the Check_Style framework, thus allowing for adaptation

Of course, the first point is obvious, since the ASIS example applications only show what ASIS may provide, namely source code analysis capability and don't dictate in what other designers will apply this capability.

To explain what makes up the second point we will describe the structure of the packages making up the Check_Style framework and their dependencies.

Packages specifying and implementing rule objects derived from the abstract rule object data type are included via the package `CS_Trav`. It serves as an interface to the main application, creating and supplying an instance of the `Rule_Array` containing initialized rule objects from each implemented rule object package. Also, it implements the necessary procedures `Pre_Procedure` and `Post_Procedure` that must be provided when an ASIS traversation is initiated. These two procedures simply contain loops that iterate through the provided rule array, calling the traverse procedures of each rule object that are shown above. They must not be mistaken as the procedures of the rule objects themselves.

By including `CS_Trav` the main application can instantiate a new ASIS iterator procedure making use of the two procedures that are included from `CS_Trav`. Figure 2 illustrates the dependencies as explained before:

All other procedures implemented in the body of the main application are straight forward, they comply to the ASIS application pattern. Their functions are:

1. Checking whether the filenames provided on the command line are present in the current directory
2. Displaying the synopsis of how to use Check_Style
3. Parsing an option string which defines what rules are to be activated in the traversation (by default all rules are activated)
4. Redirecting generated log output to a file whose name is given as a command line option
5. Printing a summary of style errors found

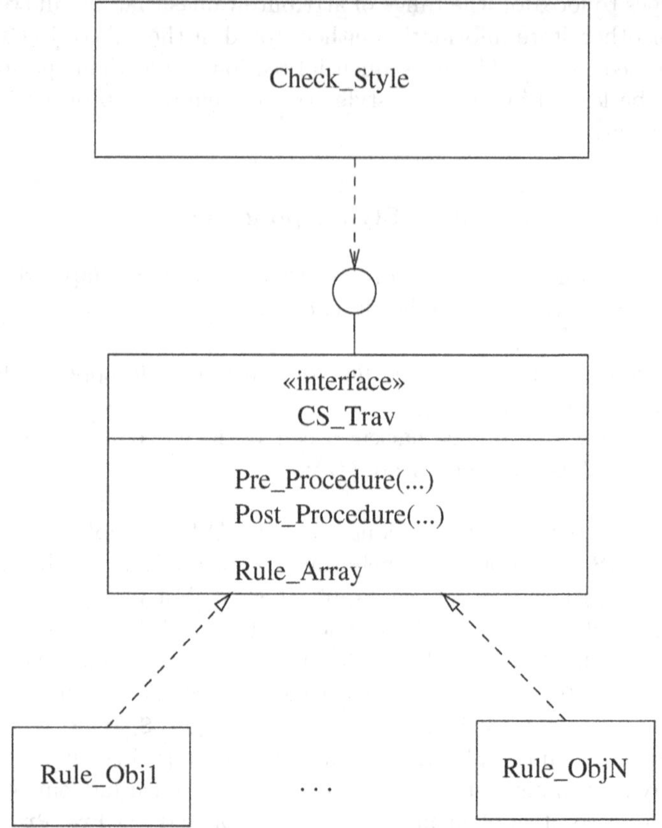

Fig. 2. The packages of Check_Style and their dependencies

The main application then activates the rule objects in the rule array according to the command line parameters, opens the provided unit files and initiates the ASIS environment in a loop running over the provided filename arguments. After traversation the ASIS environment is closed, an optional summary generated and the output file closed.

Since Ada95 is a compiled language, all additional rule object packages must be compiled, the package `CS_Trav` must be modified to take these new packages into account and then recompiled. This can be accomplished by a simple tool which analyses the directory containing all rule packages and creating a new version of `CS_Trav` according to a provided pattern file.

4.3 The Prototype of Check_Style

At the moment, the following rules are implemented (reference to the Ada95 Quality and Style Guide [ ] enclosed) and included in the prototype:

1. Each loop should be given a name (5.1.1)
2. Nesting of blocks beyond a certain depth is to be avoided (5.1.2)
3. Use loop names on all exit statements inside loop statements (5.1.3)
4. Use named parameter associations in calls of subprograms (5.2.2)
5. Show the mode indication of all procedure and entry parameters (5.2.4)
6. Use range constraints on subtypes (5.3.1)

This represents an initial set of rules that were easy to implement and originate on the one hand from the needs of our partner (see conclusion) and on the other hand from propositions of experts and evaluation of style guides. It doesn't imply that this set is ideal, nor complete. Further implementation of rules is projected which may include:

- Check for constructs and their restrictions with regard to runtime use of ressources to eliminate runtime errors (in the long run)
- Check for "completeness" of exception handling (might be problematic with regard to the distinction between user defined exceptions and system exceptions, so therefore the term completeness is subject to interpretation)
- Check for unnecessary declarations

Further issues can be found in Annex H of [,].

As was mentioned earlier, the execution of the style checker can be controlled by command-line parameters:

1. Specifying what rules are activated for the coming run
2. Specifying an output log file name
3. Display a list of all rules present
4. Display a short synopsis for using the tool

The first two points are most important, since they can be used to integrate the application into a development environment and control each check run according to the respective needs as far as the subset of rules is concerned.

The last initial design factor, the goal of achieving fast checking is accomplished by using the ASIS/GNAT combination, since it provides fast access to a syntax tree for analysis purposes in a single compilation run that omits the code generation phase. Nevertheless, research or development of tools for other programming languages might not be provided with such a profound advantage so this remains an important issue.

5 Conclusion

A motivation for style checking during software development, its requirements and a prototypical approach were presented. The work of analysing the effective impact of such an approach on software quality and the resulting decrease of time needed for testing still needs to be done. Also, new applications of the techniques described above will have to be discussed to make full use of their potential. These ideas include adapting the style checker so it can filter code for auditing purposes, pretty printing, etc. Additionally, an integration of the style checker into a distributed development environment is planned. Parts of such an environment might be:

- An object-oriented database that can store source code, results of check runs and additional formats of the code for documenting purposes
- An interactive tool to simplify the coding of new rule objects which might also be useful when developing ASIS applications in general
- Necessary additions to schedule and operate check runs automatically, possibly with regard to distributed development

This research project was in part initiated and substantially funded by the Deutsche Telekom AG, Forschungs- und Technologiezentrum Darmstadt, now T-Nova GmbH.

A Example of the Implementation of a Rule Object

This section gives a short overview of the `Pre_Procedure` and `Post_Procedure` of the rule object to check for the use of loop names if loops are nested.

The difficulty lies with the facts that the depths of the nested loops have to be taken into account and additionally if depth is greater than or equals 2 we have to look back at the nesting loop and find out whether it was named or not. This style guideline is a good example of how `Pre_Procedure` and `Post_Procedure` have to interact, since steps have to be taken when a loop statement is first visited (increasing account of nesting depth) and after all of its children statements have been visited (decreasing account of nesting depth).

```
procedure Pre_Procedure (
      R       : in out Rule_Obj;
      Element : in     Asis.Element;
      Control : in out Asis.Traverse_Control;
      State   : in out Info.Info_Node          ) is
  Line_Str  : Unbounded_String;
begin  -- Check for Rule:  5.1.1 Loop Names
       -- Associate names with loops when they are nested.

 case Asis.Elements.Element_Kind(Element) is
   when A_Statement =>
     case Asis.Elements.Statement_Kind(Element) is
  -- Search for a loop statement
       when A_Loop_Statement  =>
    -- Store depth of nested loops
         R.Depth := R.Depth + 1;
         if R.Depth >=2 then
        -- Does the outer loop have a name?
           if R.Last_Loop /= Null_Unbounded_String then
             Print_Error_Message(To_String(R.Last_Loop));
```

```
          -- Generate error message in summary
             Add_Error_To_Summary(R, R.Last_Loop);

             R.Last_Loop := Null_Unbounded_String;
           end if;

           -- Does this loop have a name?
           if Asis.Statements.Statement_Identifier(Element) = Nil_Element
               then -- no it does'nt
               Line_Str := To_Unbounded_String(
               Asis.Text.Line_Number'Image(
                 Asis.Text.First_Line_Number(Element)) & " -" &
               Asis.Text.Line_Number'Image(
                 Asis.Text.Last_Line_Number(Element)));

               Print_Error_Message(To_String(Line_Str));

            -- Generate error message in summary
               Add_Error_To_Summary(R, Line_Str);
           end if;
          else
       -- Store this loop's line numbers in case it has no name for
       -- there might be loops nested in it
          if Asis.Statements.Statement_Identifier(Element) = Nil_Element
               then -- again no name
             R.Last_Loop := To_Unbounded_String(
               Asis.Text.Line_Number'Image(
                 Asis.Text.First_Line_Number(Element)) & " -" &
               Asis.Text.Line_Number'Image(
                 Asis.Text.Last_Line_Number(Element)));
           end if;
         end if;

       when others =>
         null;
     end case;
   when others =>
     null;
 end case;

end Pre_Procedure;

procedure Post_Procedure (
      R       : in out Rule_Obj;
      Element : in     Asis.Element;
      Control : in out Asis.Traverse_Control;
      State   : in out Info.Info_Node          ) is
begin
  -- Find out whether we are looking at loop statement
  case Asis.Elements.Element_Kind(Element) is
```

```
    when A_Statement =>
      case Asis.Elements.Statement_Kind(Element) is
        when A_Loop_Statement  =>
          -- Decrease depth
          R.Depth := R.Depth - 1;

          -- is this the outermost loop?
          if R.Depth=0 then
            -- Reset attributes
            R.Last_Loop := Null_Unbounded_String;
          end if;
        when others =>
          null;
      end case;
    when others =>
      null;
  end case;
end Post_Procedure;
```

References

1. DoD AJPO: Ada 95 Quality and Style: Guidelines for Professional Programmers. SPC-94093-CMC, Version 01.00.10, Oct. 1995
2. Ada Reference Manual, Language and Standard Libraries, Version 6.0, Dec. 1994, International Standard ISO/IEC 8652 1995 (E)
3. Ada Semantic Interface Specification (ASIS), International Standard ISO/IEC 15291 1999 (E)
4. Sergey Rybin, Alfred Strohmeier, Eugene Zueff: ASIS for GNAT: Goals, Problems and Implementation Strategy, Proceedings of Ada-Europe'95, Toussaint (Ed.), LNCS (Lecture Notes in Computer Science) 1031, Springer, Frankfurt, Germany, October 2-6 1995, pp. 139-151
5. Sergey Rybin, Alfred Strohmeier, Alexei Kuchumov, Vasiliy Fofanov: ASIS for GNAT: From the Prototype to the Full Implementation, Ada-Europe'96: Proceedings, Alfred Strohmeier (Ed.), LNCS (Lecture Notes in Computer Science), vol. 1088, Springer, 1996, pp. 298-311
6. Osterweil, L., et al.: Strategic Directions in Software Quality. ACM Computing Surveys, Vol. 28, No. 4, Dec. 1996
7. Schonberg, E., Banner, B.: The GNAT-Project: A GNU-Ada9X Compiler. Proceedings of the 1994 Conference on TRI-Ada '94, ACM Press, 1994, pp. 48-57
8. Skublics, S., Klimas, E.J., Thomas, D.A.: Smalltalk with Style, Prentice Hall, 1996
9. Alfred Strohmeier, Vasiliy Fofanov, Sergey Rybin, Stéphane Barbey: Quality-for-ASIS: A Portable Testing Facility for ASIS, Ada-Europe'98, Springer-Verlag, 1998, pp. 163-175
10. S. Tucker Taft, Robert A. Duff (Eds.): Ada 95 Reference Manual: Language and Standard Libraries, International Standard ISO/IEC 8652:1995(E), Lecture Notes in Computer Science, vol 1246, Springer-Verlag, 1997, ISBN 3-540-63144-5

Enhancements in Software Project Risk Management

Peter Wieland*, Frode Høgberg, and Kristin Strømseng

Det Norske Veritas (DNV)
Veritasveien 1, N-1322 Høvik, Norway
{peter.wieland,frode.hogberg,kristin.stromseng}@dnv.com

Abstract. This paper presents the DNV approach to project risk management. It enhances most of the known approaches in two ways. First, it adds an initiation phase at the start of the process, before risk identification is started, in which the project objectives are defined. Knowing the project objectives it is much easier to identify risks and link them to the project objectives they have an impact on. The second aspect is the possibility of creating a risk model that includes all risks and their impact on various objectives, capturing their complex interaction. This way, the total risk picture of the project can be modelled and estimated, and uncertainties that affect more than one objective (often favourable against one objective, unfavourable against another) can be handled correctly. The presented (generic) ideas enhance and enrich currently available approaches for software project risk mangement.

Keywords: Project Risk Management, Risk Analysis, Software Quality, Software Engineering, Project management.

1 Introduction

Numerous surveys and articles (e.g. [ ], [ ], [ ]) show that software projects are often over budget and behind schedule, and sometimes the product quality suffers as well.

It is widely accepted that a combination of an optimised process, appropriate tools and educated and skilled people lead to success. This triangle is even more valid for IT projects. Since the term software crises was coined in the late sixties, many improvements have been made in different areas. The software process has been improved by methods like the waterfall model, the evolutionary model, the spiral model, the W-model, rapid prototyping, cleanroom software development, component based development etc. New tools like debuggers, CASE-tools, OO programming tools, code generators, test tools, requirement management tools etc. should increase productivity of the software developers. People have profitted from improved education and increased experience not only in computer science but also in project management. Especially during the last 10 years various types

* Contact: Peter Wieland, Phone: +47 / 67 57 87 08

H. B. Keller and E. Plödereder (Eds.): Ada-Europe 2000, LNCS 1845, pp. 161– , 2000.

of software process improvement programs have become more and more popular (e.g. Capability Maturity Model [ ]; Software Process Improvement and Capability Determination, SPICE - also known as ISO 15504 [ ]; Bootstrap [ ]; ISO 9000-3/TickIT [ ]). These programs serve as vehicles for improving software project management and the development process itself. They cover not only planning, but the whole life cycle of the software process, including support functions like configuration management, quality management, and subcontracting.

What is then the missing piece that enables us to deliver on time, within budget and with the promised quality? Already in 1991, Boehm claimed that [ ] "one pattern that emerged very strongly was that successful project managers were good risk managers." This is supported by the findings of the KPMG survey [ ]. They identified the following overrun reasons:

- Poor project planning (in particular, risks were not addressed or the project plan was weak).
- The business case for the project was weak in several areas or was missing several components.
- Lack of management involvement and support.

In the software community there is a strong and growing belief that the best way to rein in runaways is to practice adequate project risk management (e.g. [ ]). Gartner Group indicated in their 1999 symposium that "through 2001, organisations using ongoing risk assessment and abatement processes will reduce the incidence of 'failed' software projects by over 75 percent (0.7 probability)". Even though much literature has been published on software project risk management (e.g. [ ], [ ], [ ], [ ], [ ], [ ]), none of the software process improvement programs address risk management with the importance it deserves. It is then not surprising that the software project survey [ ] uncovered that only 38% of the failed projects did perform any risk management. More than half of those who did, did not use the results found during initial risk analysis.

As [ ] remarks organisations are unable to manage risks effectively for the following three reasons:

- A risk-averse culture (risks diminish the closer you get to top management). A risk-averse culture is often observed at the customers side.
- An inadequate management infrastructure to support risk management.
- A lack of a systematic and repeatable strategy to identify, analyse and follow up risks.

This paper introduces DNV PRM , a methodology for project risk management. Applied in software projects PRM enhances available methods as described in the comparison section below.

[1] Hereafter referred to as PRM

2 DNV Project Risk Management Process

After defining the used terminology, we will give an introduction in the presented DNV approach for project risk management (PRM).

2.1 Terminology

One of the most important aspects of PRM is that the central concept is uncertainty. Uncertainty is defined as:

> The difference between the information required for certain decision making and the information actually available . Uncertainty may be either negative (threats) or positive (opportunities).

The vocabulary reveals a symmetrical view on threats and opportunities. Uncertainties have potential consequences. The consequence may either be negative (risk) or positive (opportunity), corresponding to the threats and opportunities of uncertainties. The definition of risk is thus: Downside consequence of uncertainty. Note that the same uncertainty element may give rise to both risk and opportunity.

In the field of software project risk management, focus is often put mainly on negative consequences of uncertainties (risks) rather than positive ones. The reader should keep in mind that when the term risk is used in the paper, opportunity should also be considered.

2.2 DNV PRM

Project Risk Management (PRM) is a systematic approach to proactively predict and control risk in a project. Continuous monitoring of threats and opportunities provides the insight needed to provide early warnings and implement cost-effective countermeasures.

Interests and motives influence behaviour. Motives that are unknown, will lead to behaviour that may not be understood by the other party, resulting in misunderstandings and inefficient communication. Therefore, a mutual understanding of the project objectives is important.

Uncertainties are causes that may lead to either undesirable or desirable consequences. It is often more cost-effective to implement preventive risk-reducing measures than to intervene later. This is even more true for opportunities, because pro-active measures are often the only option for exploiting the upside risk potential.

This section provides a generic description of the PRM process. Risk management is a continuous activity. Some uncertainty elements varies from one project

[2] Even if the original PRM definition only covers lack of information, the concept can easily be extended to also cover lack of control and lack of time as sources of uncertainties as proposed by [ ]

phase to another, others stays on through all phases. The process is initiated for each project phase, and several iterations within a phase are recommended.

The generic PRM process can be described in five steps at the topmost level. The PRM process is illustrated in Fig. . The main steps in the PRM process are initiation, identification, analysis, action plan and follow-up, where the last four steps cover management of uncertainties. The information management activity documents the risk management process, covering documentation of PRM data and results.

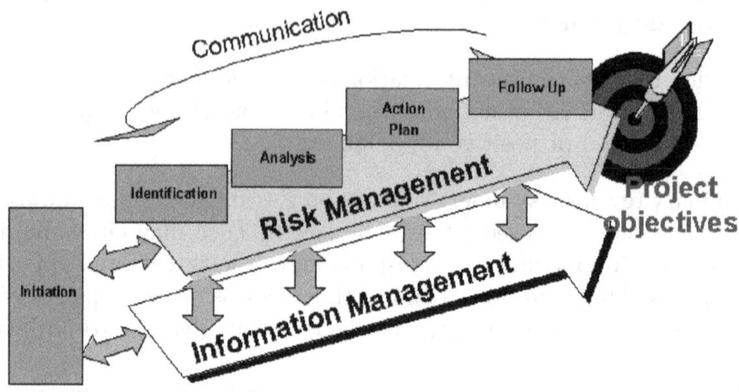

Fig. 1. PRM Process

Initiation. This initial step, initiation, focuses on definition and preparation of the PRM process for the project, i.e. the reason for executing the process, and establish a plan for execution of the process. In addition the project objectives are defined and all existing project information is reviewed.

It is essential to settle the objective with the PRM process, because this provides the basis for the preparation of scope of work for PRM. The scope of work is important input to preparation of the PRM plan. The objective of the PRM process must not be mixed up with the project objectives. The PRM plan is based on the defined PRM objective, and contains a plan for the PRM activities (each step in the PRM process), provides an overview of the personnel and resources intended to participate, identifies the participants' roles, and provides guidelines on which techniques and tools to be applied.

A precise definition and description of the project objectives forms the foundation for performing risk assessment. The PRM process identifies uncertainty elements preventing the project in achieving its objectives. The project objectives are then prioritised. For instance; is completion of the project within the planned schedule more important than avoiding cost overruns? The objectives can both have character as main objectives (e.g. planned finish date of project), or sub-objectives (e.g. project milestones). The project objectives represent the project's goals and targets, and it is of high importance that the project stakeholders agree on the priorities made.

Identification. A project may be influenced by uncertainties in many ways, caused by e.g. restricted budgets and tight schedules, project organisation and management, productivity, business, technology, relations between different actors in and outside the project, contracts, etc.

The first step is to prepare a list of all possible uncertainties that might influence the project. Different techniques can be applied to obtain this information, e.g. interviews with experts and project key personnel, brainstorming sessions, group meetings or checklists. These techniques are tools to reveal uncertainties in the project. It is important to consider unique aspects of the project. What is important to one person/actor may not be important to others. This because people have different experience, background, ability and will to look for project uncertainties, risk attitude, etc. Thus, the identification must be done in co-operation with principal actors in the project.

When the identification is accomplished, the list of uncertainties is normally rather extensive. The uncertainties identified must be systematised in a well-organised way before they are analysed further. Normally, uncertainties are systematised by their nature; i.e. discrete/continuous, internal/external, work package/subsystem etc.

Analysis. The purpose of this step is to analyse each uncertainty's influence on the project objectives. The results from the analysis shall reveal the most important uncertainties, and enable the project to give priorities. The analysis will visualise the total risk picture in the project.

There exists different techniques to perform risk analysis. Choice of technique depends on several factors; the nature of the uncertainty (continuous/discrete), complexity, availability of statistics and the required level of detail in the analysis. Three different techniques are distinguished; event analysis, estimate analysis and model analysis. These techniques are further discussed in section .

Action Plan. The purpose of this step is to prepare a plan of actions the project wants to initiate in order to exploit, reduce or transfer uncertainty. Adequate actions are the key to effective achievement of project success.

The ranked list of uncertainties, which was developed during the analysis step, is the starting point for identifying and assessing which actions to implement that exploit opportunities and reduce risks. Formally, all critical uncertainties require actions to be implemented, but normally focus is on the most important uncertainties. A systematic process, in addition to the project's experience and ability of new thinking, is the key to achieve this.

Controllability is an essential issue. Some uncertainties may be affected by implementing simple measures, others might not be possible to influence at all.

When identifying actions, it is important to focus on the side-effects, e.g. the cost of implementing the action, etc. When actions have been identified, the effect of the action may be analysed. The uncertainty is re-assessed, now with the effect of the actions included.

Follow-Up. The purpose of this step is to monitor the evolution of the identified uncertainties, follow-up and evaluate the action implementation, and if required, identify and initiate new actions.

The follow-up step consists of monitoring the development of identified significant uncertainties for which actions were not implemented, and critical uncertainties to verify that the implemented actions have the expected effect. Actions that have been implemented earlier must be re-assessed and followed-up. On the basis of the re-assessment of the effect of the actions, the decision to downgrade, maintain or upgrade the risks and opportunities is taken, and it is evaluated whether new actions are necessary.

After this process, all new actions must be included in the action plan for the project, they must be implemented and followed-up over time. This is a continuous process throughout the project. Risk surveillance and monitoring is accomplished through a continuous risk management activity in the project. It is important to document all evolvement and changes.

Communication. Management of uncertainty in a project is a continuous process, due to constant change inside and outside the project. Thus, communication is an important part of the PRM process. The purpose is a continuous communication of information between the actors in the project at all stages of the PRM-process. The objective is a common understanding of how uncertainty may influence the project, and the importance of implementation of actions planned. The intention is that the receiver of the information gets the total risk picture.

Risk management should be an integral part of the project management, thus the action implementation will interface with other actors in the project. It is important to establish a total understanding of the project uncertainties and actions, to obtain the priorities needed in the project.

The results from the uncertainty analysis describe uncertainties with major influence on project objectives and limits. This information must be communicated to the project management and superior, as well as the project members. It is of prime importance that everybody in the project gets a picture of how threats and opportunities may influence the project. Especially communication of external uncertainties is important, since these uncertainties are not or only partly controllable by the project.

If the receiver shall obtain knowledge and feel ownership to the project uncertainties, the information must be communicated in an understandable and comprehensible manner. Receivers at different levels have different needs for information. It is recommended to make use of simplified graphical presentations and to avoid complicated statistics.

Information Management. During the project execution, events will occur and important decisions are taken. This requires documentation on what really happened and on which basis.

Documentation on what happened during the process of risk management will contribute to assure the traceability during the project. Documentation is important to keep the project participants informed about assessments performed earlier in the project and what actions were implemented to reduce the total risk picture in the project.

3 How DNV PRM Enhances other Software Project Risk Management Methodologies

In this section we focus on two items that are essential for a mature software project risk management process. However, these items are not commonly found in other project risk management approaches.

First, the initialisation step is crucial to clarify and communicate the goals of the risk management process and the objectives of the project.

The second item concerns the way risk analysis is performed. Risks often have impact on different project objectives, and a risk model must be established to get the overall picture.

3.1 PRM Initiation

The PRM initiation step consists of two parts. The first part of PRM is to identify the objective and scope of the process, and making a Risk Management Plan that describes how the process will be performed. Similar concepts are introduced by e.g. [ ].

The second part in the PRM initiation process, the identification of project objectives, e.g. cost, schedule, and quality, was on the other hand not found in any other approach. It is important also to try to identify any 'hidden' objectives, either of the customer, the contractor, or of external origin. In most cases, only the objectives of the customer are identified. The contractor may, however, also have strong motives which are not communicated, but still exert a strong influence of the project behaviour and priorities of the contractor. Finally, external factors may be important to observe. The authorities may influence the possibilities of the project to achieve its objectives in a cost-efficient way when they demand e.g. offset arrangements, or when they enforce employment and district politics.

Defined project objectives should be realistic. If a detailed analysis including all risks concludes that the objectives cannot be reached, the project should be cancelled or the objectives should be changed.

3.2 Uncertainty Analysis

The DNV PRM methodology describes three ways in which uncertainty can be analysed, depending on the nature of the uncertainty. An uncertainty may either be a discrete event, of continous nature or a complex model combining several both discrete and continuous uncertainties.

Event Analysis. The event analysis manages uncertainties of a discrete nature, i.e. events that occur or do not occur. If an event occurs it has a consequence, and the uncertainty contribution is given by the likelihood of the event occurring and the associated consequence. Consequences may have positive or negative influence on the project objectives, positive consequence is named opportunities and negative consequences risks. After the quantification, likelihood and consequence, every uncertainty is assessed with respect to its effect on the project objectives. To get a total overview of the risk picture for a specific objective, one may consult the criticality matrix for that objective. This matrix provides the categorisation of the uncertainties into criticality classes, such as critical, significant and negligible. This is one way to prioritise the uncertainties. Uncertainties may now be ranked by the level of risk or opportunity they represent to the project. Most concepts of uncertainty analysis found in the literature (e.g. [ ], [ ], [ ], [ ], [ ]) cover event analysis.

Estimate Analysis. Estimate analysis handles uncertainties of a continuous nature. Estimate uncertainties are somehow "always" present, with consequences in an interval. Estimate uncertainties can in a simplified approach be described using a tree-point estimate (optimistic - expected - pessimistic) value for the affected objective. After the quantification, every uncertainty is assessed with respect to its effect on the plan items for an objective. To get a total overview of the risk picture for a specific objective, one may consult the tornado plot for that objective. The tornado plot shows the estimate uncertainties total contribution against the selected objective, and allows the categorisation of the uncertainties into criticality classes, such as critical, significant and negligible. This is one way to prioritise the uncertainties. Estimate uncertainties are ranked according to the total uncertainty they represent, as presented in the tornado diagram. In this way estimate uncertainties are ranked by criticality just like events.

Model Analysis. The two previous techniques are simplified methods for analysing the risk picture in a project. Both are based on assumptions not always representing the reality, but in many cases good enough to manage subjective assessments of uncertainties. However, in some cases it is neccessary to analyse the project uncertainties in more detail. Model analysis is a technique providing possibilities for modelling and more precise calculations of uncertainty. In the model analysis, one common model is prepared, representing the total risk picture in the project. This model covers all uncertainties, both of continuous and discrete nature. The model includes all uncertainties in the project, independent of their character. Additionally the model contains all objectives, in such a way that uncertainties influencing several objectives are considered correctly (favourable against one objective, unfavourable against another).

Influence diagrams are used in model analysis. They enable the computation of quantitative measures through Monte Carlo simulation, e.g. using the software tool Scenario. Before the simulation can proceed, all the variables (nodes) in the influence diagram (i.e. hazards, objectives, certain events, actions etc.) have to be assigned input values. This way, the total risk picture of the project can be modelled and estimated, and uncertainties that affects more than one objective can be handled correctly.

Advantages of model analysis:

- Total risk can be calculated
- Dependabilities between hazards can be considered
- Dependabilities between objectives can be considered (What is the cost of one month's delay?)
- Trade-off between objectives can be performed
- Uncertainties in the estimates (variance) are represented
- Expected cost and schedule can be estimated
- Cost-efficiency of actions can be considered
- The models represent familiar techniques from Project Management

Disadvantages of model analysis:

- Requires use of computer simulations
- Difficult to model the objective performance
- Requires more resources for data collection
- Can be difficult to explain and understand for non-expertise personnel

Reference to model based uncertainty analysis could not be found in the literature surveyed (e.g. [ ], [ ], [ ], [ ], [ ]).

4 Example

In this section we present a small example that will highlight some of the issues of the PRM methodology.

The company Forest Inc. has contracted Intelligentes Software GmbH to develop a new software product for managing the forests owned by the company. At the outset of the project it is decided that proper risk management is necessary for the success of the project, and a process is initiated in which both the customer and the supplier takes part. The project has three main objectives: to complete within 10 months (time) at a cost of no more than DM 3 mill, and with satisfactory quality. Quality is not easily measured, but one of the sub-goals is that training time to use basic functions should not exceed 4 hours.

During the uncertainty identification phase, three of the uncertainties identified were:

- Requirements are poorly understood,

[3] This is a fictitious example; any resemblance with real companies is purely coincidential.

- Dr. Arboretum, who has extensive domain knowledge, could potentially leave his job at Intelligentes Software,
- Software developers are unexperienced with the design tool just introduced.

The first uncertainty is likely to affect both time, cost and possibly also quality if understanding does not develop sufficiently during the early phases. The second uncertainty will probably affect time the most, since someone has to be found that can replace the person leaving. This is possibly one of the most serious uncertainties of the project. The third uncertainty is likely to affect both time and cost.

The second uncertainty is an event uncertainty, the two others are estimate uncertainties. We therefore choose to perform a model analysis. The resulting influence diagram for one of the objectives, time, is shown in figure . The project

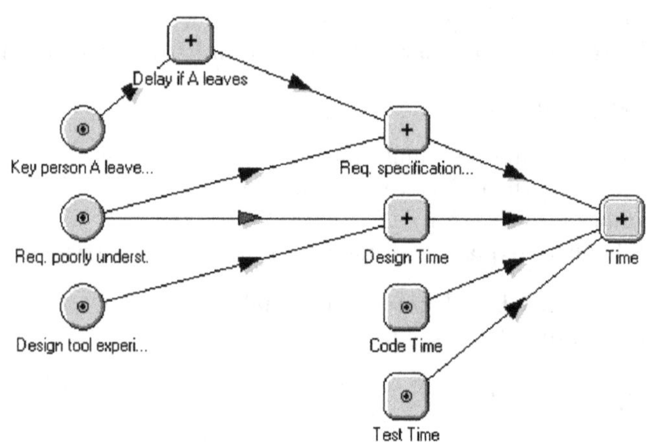

Fig. 2. Influence diagram for model analysis

duration is the sum of the duration of each of the phases (assuming a waterfall development model). The duration of each phase is given as a probability distribution. The effect of Dr. Arboretum leaving the company, is modelled as a node with a value of 0 (P(staying) = 0.7) or 1 (P(leaving) = 0.3) that is multiplied with the value of the node "Delay if A. leaves", which has a probability distribution. This delay is added to the time of the requirements phase. The other uncertainties are modeled as nodes with probability distributions of their own, affecting the duration of various project phases.

Performing a Monte Carlo simulation of this model we get a cumulative probability distribution (S-curve) of total project duration like the middle one in figure . Identifying Dr. Arboretum as key compentence to the project, we decide to see what happens if the probability for him leaving is changed. The

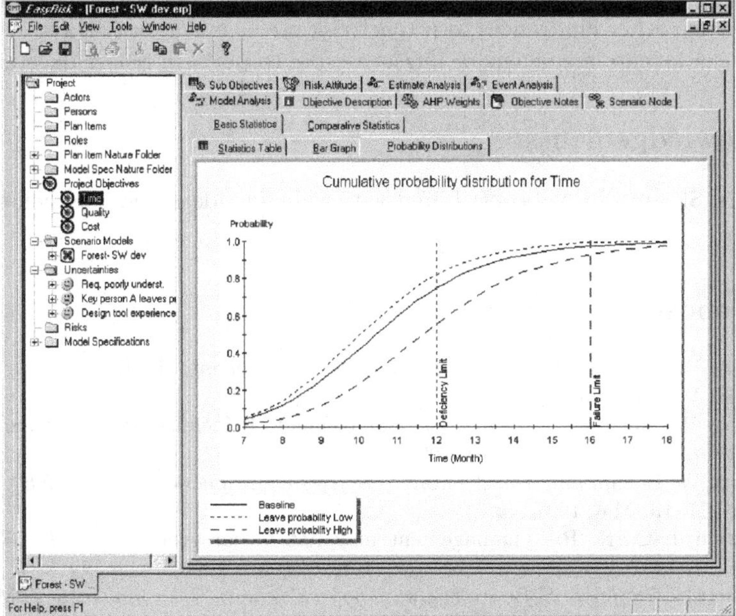

Fig. 3. Cumulative probability distribution for project duration with three different probabilities of Dr. Arboretum leaving the project. The pane to the left lists the objectives and uncertainties of the model

dotted and dashed curves of figure show the results of the simulations with P(leaving) = 0.1 and 0.9 respectively. The higher probability of Dr. Arboretum leaving increases the mean project time with 1.3 months. This is dangerously close to the deficiency limit beyond which the utility of the project is strongly decreasing. Maybe one should not, after all, postpone the introduction of the new consultancy model, which Dr. Arboretum had long been looking forward to?

5 Conclusion

As already mentioned, surveys indicate that lack of proper risk management is the most frequent cause of software project failure. [ ] mentioned that one of the reasons that risk management is not used, is the lack of a systematic method. However, several publications (e.g. [ ], [ ], [ ], [ ], [ ], [ ]) present risk management approaches that are applicable to software projects.

Most of these approaches seem to lack focus on project objectives. The DNV approach introduces the initiation phase to highlight the different objectives and priorities between them. The overall risk picture on how different uncertainties have impact on different objectives may be complex. The model analysis enables the analyst to include all risks, interdependencies, and the overall impact on objectives. Having a well structured methodology in place, organisations may focus on the other hindrances to project risk management: a risk averse culture and an inadequate management infrastructure to perform risk management.

Acknowledgements

Torbjørn Skramstad has contributed with valuable ideas and comments to the paper.

References

1. Barry W. Boehm. *Tutorial: Software risk management.* IEEE Computer Society Press, Washington, D.C., 1989. , , ,
2. Barry W. Boehm. Software risk management: Principles and practices. *IEEE Software*, 8(1):32–41, January 1991.
3. Barry W. Boehm and Tom DeMarco. Software risk management. *IEEE Software*, 14(3):17–19, May 1997. , , ,
4. Marvin J. Carr. Risk management may not be for everyone. *IEEE Software*, 3:21–24, 1997. ,
5. Robert N. Charette. *Software engineering risk analysis and management.* McGraw-Hill software engineering series. Intertext Publications / McGraw-Hill Book Co., New York, 1989. lc89083763 Robert N. Charette. , ,
6. A. Coletta. The SPICE project: An international standard for software process assessment, improvement and capability determination. *Lecture Notes in Computer Science*, 926, 1995.
7. Audrey J. Dorofee, Julie A. Walker, Christopher J. Alberts, Ronald P. Higuera, Richard L. Murphy, and Ray C. Williams. *Continuous Risk Management Guidebook.* Software Engineering Institute, Carnegie Mellom University, 1996. , , , ,
8. Robert L. Glass. *Software Runaways; Monumental Software Disasters.* Prentice Hall, 1997. ,
9. Elaine M. Hall. *Managing Risk: methods for software systems development.* SEI Series in Software Engineering. Addison Wesley Longman, Inc., Reading, Massachusetts, 1998. , , ,
10. International Organization for Standardization. *ISO 9000: Quality management and quality assurance standards; Part 3: Guidelines for the application of ISO 9001 to the development, supply and maintenance of software.* Geneva, Switzerland, 1991.
11. Capers Jones. *Patterns of Software Systems Failure and Success.* International Thomson Computer Press, 1996.
12. Dale Walter Karolak. *Software Engineering Risk Management.* IEEE Computer Society Press, 1996. , , ,
13. KPMG. What went wrong? unsuccessful information on technology projects., 1997. ,
14. P. Kuvaja. BOOTSTRAP: A software process assessment and improvement methodology. *Lecture Notes in Computer Science*, 926, 1995.
15. Mark C. Paulk. How ISO 9001 compares with the CMM. *IEEE Software*, 12(1):74–83, January 1995.

Constructing Reliable Embedded Systems Using the Results of System Safety Analysis

Giuseppe Mauri and Stefan Scheer

HISE group Computer Science Department The University of York
York YO DD U K telephone fax
Giuseppe.Mauri@cs.york.ac.uk

European Commission Joint Research Centre
Ispra VA Italy telephone fax
Stefan.Scheer@jrc.it

Abstract Thorough assessment of embedded systems in terms of reliability and safety requires the use of several analysis techniques Such an assessment accompanies system definition and construction from the beginning It is shown how standard analysis techniques can be combined along with traditional system decomposition With this type of integration it shall be possible to reach the level of software description and continue with appropriate analyses A sufficiently decomposed system will be reconstructed by continuously comparing the quantitative and qualitative results of fault tree analysis with user defined requirements satisfying reliability constraints

Introduction

Dependability analysis of complex system becomes more and more important as the number of embedded systems is growing rapidly and the use of such systems affects our everyday's life with more or less crucial consequences Sources of failure or wrong behaviour are manifold and due to system complexity rather difficult to locate In this context well established analysis methods have to be extended adapted to modern style systems and combined with each other

A methodology has been developed with which a system on one side can entirely be decomposed into layers each with a topology of components and on the other side be analysed in terms of safety and availability Within this approach several classical safety and reliability analysis techniques will be used in combination Thus a unique and consistent way of proceeding will be created Through this type of integration limitations and deficiencies of one technique will be complemented by the strengths of another more appropriate technique Where applicable the decomposition process will continue until the software level is reached thus identifying software components which might contribute to potential system failures

Following the classical V model in a second phase the system will be rebuilt in an opposite way To go back to a more abstract level is feasible only when certain conditions are fulfilled In the negative case some feedback to the decomposition and design phase takes place which means to restart the design process at this point Those

H B Keller and E Plödereder Eds Ada Europe LNCS pp

conditions usually are user defined and the methodology presented here proposes the application of a strongly deductive verification technique for each level of system description

The process as a whole is multiply iterative Once in the process the top level has been reached and there are no more precautions to look at it can be said that the system as it is in that moment meets the requirements concerning reliability issues

Combining System Analysis Techniques

In the phases of the lifecycle that are addressed here from the requirements specifications to the detailed hardware and software design phase it is common practice to perform the following safety and reliability analyses Functional Failure Analysis FFA Hazard and Operability Studies HAZOP Failure Mode and Effects Analysis FMEA and Fault Tree Analysis FTA The first three are exploratory methods used to drive the decomposition and design FTA on the other side is a deductive method which is used to investigate on causes of some hazards and estimate their likelihood

The selected and fragmented application of those methods implies difficulties in having a global overview of the quality of the system Often the results obtained are incompatible or even inconsistent In addition the relationship between hardware and software failures is not very well elaborated or known Nevertheless for the outcome of the overall assessment it is crucial to know how far functional failures of software components contribute to undesired hardware behaviour Thus a thorough in depth safety analysis of an embedded system should involve software parts as well

FFA [Papadopoulos McDermid] is an extension to Functional Hazard Analysis which aims at performing a *qualitative* analysis in the *early* stages of the design process to identify which functions of the system contribute to hazards The extension comprises to have for each function three mis behaviours analysed Function not provided Function provided when not required Function delivering wrong data malfunction

HAZOP [Kletz Villemeur] is currently performed after an outline equipment design is proposed showing the main design components and the flows between them HAZOP aims at achieving an imaginative anticipation of hazards At a mechanistic level it consists of completing a table according to some guide words e g *None More of Less of Part of More than Other* A guide word describes a hypothetical deviation from the normal expected value of a flow Driven by these guide words failure causes and their effects are listed The acceptability of the effects of the deviations is considered and measures proposed to decrease the likelihood of the failure cause or to mitigate the effects these are the derived safety requirements HAZOP has been extended to computer system and software analysis [Scheer et al] Guide words have been changed to *Early Late Omission Commission* and *Value* to reflect the properties of data flows as opposed to chemical flows

FMEA [Palady Villemeur] is an inductive analysis technique used to study the effects of component failure modes on a system FMEA starts from the knowledge of component failure modes and considers the effects of each failure It involves the study of all the components in a system and is often applied also to higher level assemblies and systems. It checks whether proposed components (with their known failure modes) fulfil system level safety requirements.

FTA [Vesely [illegible]] has widely been used in the aircraft and in the nuclear industry, then extended to software systems [Leveson et al. [illegible]]. The aim of FTA is to determine the possible combinations of causes that may give rise to some undesired events. A fault tree consists of several levels of events connected in such a way that each event at a given level is a consequence of events at the level just below, through various logical operators (gates). Events may be equipment failures, human errors, software defects, etc., likely to cause an undesired outcome. In a Fault Tree events must be independent of one another. Usually a fault tree is generated for each critical system state (referred to as "Top Event"). There may be a distinction between Top Events concerning unavailability issues and those concerning safety issues of a system. A fault tree analysis is made up of two phases: qualitative and quantitative analysis. The qualitative analysis aims at determining the minimum system failure modes, i.e. describing within Boolean formulae minimal combination of events that will hold for explaining a Top Event. A quantitative analysis will be done on those combinations for determining the probabilistic parameters of interest (unavailability, unreliability, expected number of failures, etc.) and the components' criticality measures useful to identify the relatively weak parts of the system where design improvements can be effective.

The integrated analysis of the decomposition and design phase and its relevant safety analysis process starts by analysing functions and their failures, proceeds by analysing systems and their flow deviations and finishes by identifying components and their failure modes with effects at system and functional levels. Each function is likely to involve several systems, each system is likely to be composed of several components and each component will have failure modes. Thus the amount of detail increases moving from functions towards components. In detail, the FFA should find out for each function what are the potential failure conditions, what are the underlying circumstances, and how severe are these failures. On a system level, when the architecture is defined, HAZOP are performed to identify those hazards that may be generated by deviations of flows among and inside systems. Deviations of flows can be identified on different levels of abstraction and for software modules as well, therefore, typically, HAZOP will be applied repeatedly in the whole analysis process. Finally, when components are known, effects of component failures (called failure modes) are investigated by FMEA. These analyses are performed in sequence while the design is progressing and provide feedback to the system development. To feed data to these analyses other techniques are needed; among these, we limit ourselves to the use of the FTA. FFA, HAZOP and FMEA have several things in common. They are performed on various design representations that reflect different levels of abstraction in the system design. It is, however, overly difficult to ensure the consistency of all design representations. One of the causes of inconsistency is that different design notations are used at different stages of the lifecycle; in addition, abstract system designs are not always kept updated and they do not reflect changes made in lower level designs. Inevitably the analyses performed on such designs yield inconsistent results. Moreover these techniques do not help in tracing the propagation of failure from low level failures to system malfunctions. Fault trees for hazardous functional failure modes are often built but they are usually so big that the results are incomprehensible and thus not very useful

The commonality among the four techniques is that they all record a causal relationship between failures and effects [Mauri et al] This property can be usefully employed to integrate the results of these safety analyses see Figure As basis for this we need a consistent hierarchical decomposition of the system In addition results of each technique can be used to drive the development and to feed the following analyses – this in both directions although the amount of information to deal with is continuously growing the farther away we get from the abstract levels of description

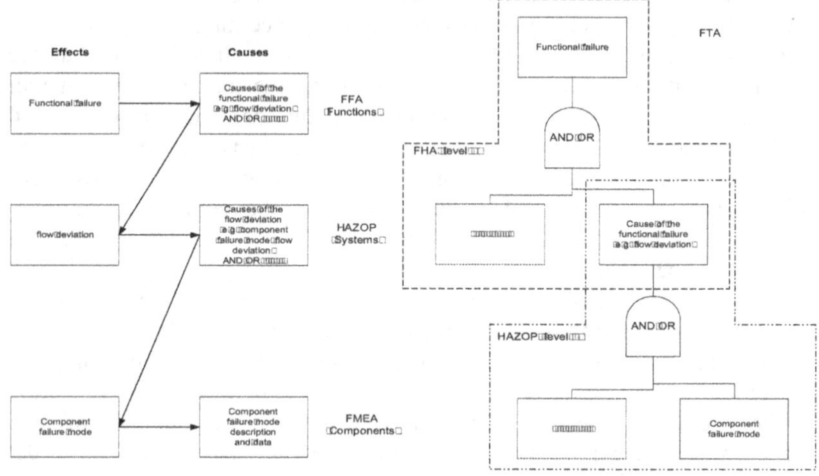

Figure Relationship among FFA HAZOP FMEA and FTA

The FTA technique is particularly used during the reconstruction phase On the basis of a highly structured hierarchy of topologies it will be possible to perform FTA locally Due to the fact that FTA is not dependent on the level of abstraction this can be done on every level The results of a FTA are both of quantitative and qualitative nature Quantitatively probability rates of event occurrence rates will be calculated With qualitative analysis it is clearly understood which are the sub events and which is their interrelation so that the event may occur It is obvious that when dealing with pure software functions a qualitative kind of calculation is the only applicable one

The acceptance of a subsystem's topology depends from the outcome of the FTA done on this topology If certain failure rates are within pre defined limits this subsystem as it is is acceptable For software modules the qualitative part of a FTA result has to be analysed if the analyst can "guarantee" that failures of the software components at this stage are excluded or at least widely by passed e g through introducing fault tolerance the software topology at this level of description is acceptable In the case that all subsystems of a certain system have been considered as acceptable the methodology goes back to the system level This is an iterative process which will be finished when the top level of a global system description has been re reached

Tables and Events

The methodology proposed requests a hierarchy of tables alongside the hierarchy of modules or components as these have been identified during the decomposition process see Figure Similarly to the propagation of flows in the hierarchy of modules the parallel hierarchy propagates events Events are unique entities inside this hierarchy and may represent both successes and failures They may represent mal functions module failure modes the intended flow to be delivered by the module its deviations from the correct value or tell whether data are delivered on time i e early or late not delivered at all or delivered when they were not supposed

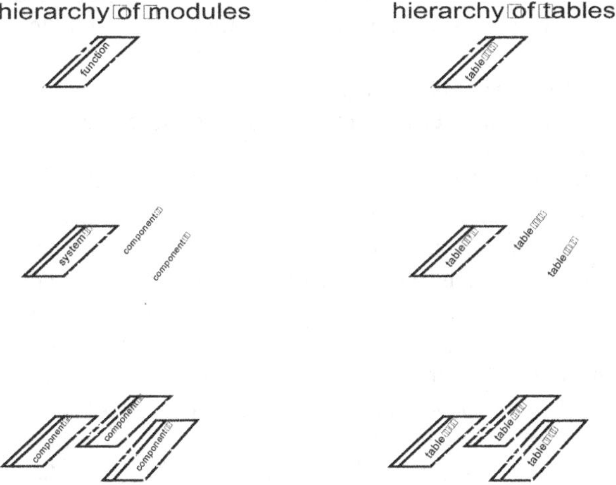

Figure Parallel development of component and table hierarchies

to be delivered For an extensive discussion on assessing potential software failures refer to [Scheer et al] Taking into account all possible basic kinds of topologies we get the following classification of events

- Outgoing events also called effects can either be propagated to tables of the hierarchically dependent level or to a higher level enclosing level
- Incoming events are either classified as input events or as secondary events to differentiate them from secondary events input events represent deviations of the variables e g flows data etc that are processed by the module On the other side secondary events represent deviations of flows supporting the function the module has to achieve They provide the module with what it needs to carry out its tasks e g the power supply For both types of incoming events a further sub classification whether they are directed to the same or to the enclosing level of description should be done
- Events generated inside a module are called Primary Events When the module represents a basic component which is not further decomposed the generated events are called Basic events For them it is generally possible to give reliability data i e failure and repair rates mean time to failure failure probability on demand etc However when the module represents a system that will be further

decomposed into more elementary modules, those primary events are called Primary Event Further Developed. Causes of primary events further developed have to be investigated with the analysis of the enclosed modules. In addition, it is important for basic events to have lifecycle information available as well; this is provided by the manufacturer and system designers. Lifecycle information lists defects or errors that may occur during the component lifecycle that are likely to cause the component to fail in one of its failure modes.

An event is directly connected with a component that has been identified during the decomposition process. Therefore an event expresses failure modes or deviations from normal component behaviour. During FFA, an event represents omission, commission and value failures. In the HAZOP, the event describes flow deviations, like high, low, less, etc. In FMEA, simple component failure modes will be addressed.

Example:

"O_brakingFunction" means the braking function's output does not appear.

"LE_outputPressure" means the component "outputPressure" is delivering a decreasing value.

In principle, for each component found during decomposition a table is created in which those effects are listed that have been identified as part of a cause in a previous step. Thus events fundamentally are used to link tables across the hierarchy. Typically, those tables contain much more information than what can be discussed in this paper. One of the key table entries is the "recommendations" column which should be filled up with maximal event occurrence rates or with other hints by the system developer. Values and comments deposited in that column will be compared in the verification and integration phase each time a local FTA is worked out.

The continuous creation of tables should finish when events have been encountered that cannot be split further and that can thus be considered as Basic Events. For events concerning hardware failures reliability data should be specified. Events that touch software behaviour should be developed further until a reasonably detailed level of understanding has been reached. For practical reasons it is not advisable to go down to code level but to stop decomposition at a higher level.

Verification and Integration

The aim of the verification and integration phase is to verify that each module and component of the hierarchy meets requirements, specifications, constraints and recommendations issued during the decomposition and design phase and written down in the "Recommendations" column. The process of verification starts from the basic components and proceeds towards higher levels of integration finishing at the top level. For each module the likelihood of each effect is evaluated using fault tree analysis. Top events of each FTA are considered as effects in this methodology. The tree structure is taken from the "Causes" columns and by parsing tables of included (i.e. lower level) modules. The likelihood of each top event is recorded in the column "FMEA results", as it is written down whether counter measures have been taken against detrimental software behaviour for the case that software modules had been inspected. It has to be borne out whether such recommendations are met after a local FTA has been accomplished. Otherwise a feedback mechanism towards the decomposition and design phase will be launched that will consequently lead to different preconditions possibly met in a subsequent iteration of the verification process Therefore the FTA must be re run to check the local top event occurrence rates It is obvious that for a specific level all components on this level have to be analysed properly and also for all effects identified for a specific component

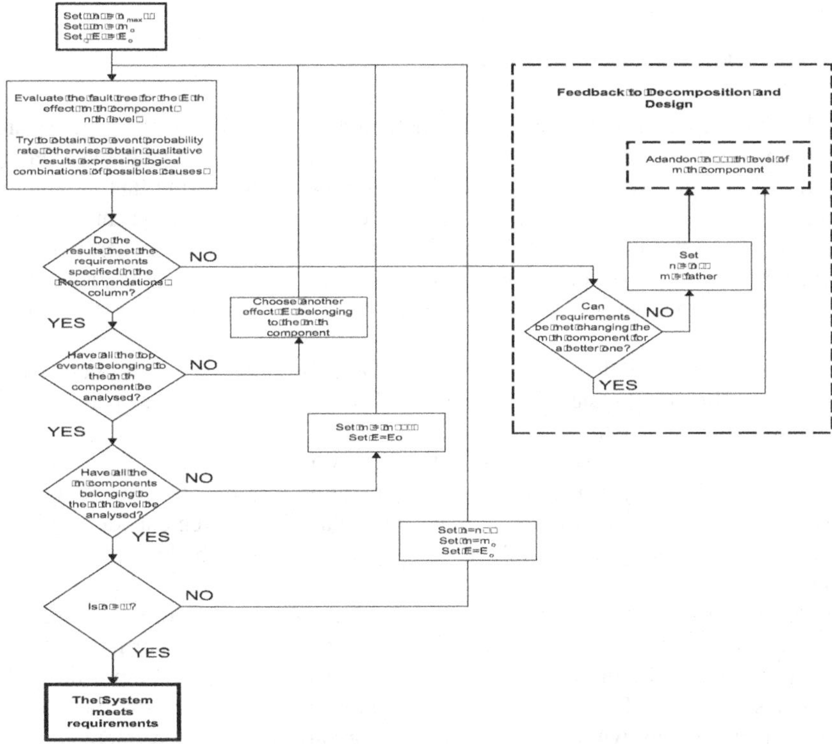

Figure Way of proceeding during the verification and integration phase

Figure shows how the overall process for the verification and integration phase works The feedback mechanism affects the change of components at the actual working level "can requirements be met changing the m th component ...?" or even at a lower level "set n=n m=father" Such a change may also have consequences on the topology For components that represent hardware they may be exchanged with components of better quality a change of the topology may be done when hardware redundancy is proposed In the case of software components we might have a look at them and "improve" them so that for example certain possibilities of malfunctioning are definitely excluded or that a specific service of data delivery is guaranteed The application of fault tolerance techniques is widely suggested to cope with these cases It is obvious that for whatever component in the system will try to find a better decomposition all previously elaborated decompositions for that m th component are not valid any more and thus have to be abandoned The methodology of feedback leads the developer back to the decomposition and design phase Figure shows also three concentric circuits the integration is based on first all events belonging to the m th component have to be analysed then all components belonging to the n th level must be looked after before the system is able to progress to the next higher level The process will terminate when the highest level of decomposition has been re reached

Implementation and Case Studies

A tool has been created implementing the methodology described so far see Figure The tool provides an interface and management facilities allowing the user to completely decompose a system as detailed as the user wants During the integration and verification process the necessary fault tree analyses are done through an interface to the Astra based FTA Astra [Contini et al] is an acronym for Advanced Software Tool Set for Reliability Analyses It is currently planned to introduce the methodology as an own tool thus becoming part of the Astra technology

Two case studies with satisfying results have been worked out one on a computer aided breaking system one on a fuel controller The examples below show parts of the analyses made in each case study

There are both quantitative and qualitative safety requirements for a Computer Aided Braking CAB system The qualitative requirements dictate that the system architecture should be fault tolerant The quantitative requirement defines the probability of a complete loss of braking i e the Top Event to be less than x per hour

The design decomposition is shown on the left side of Figure In this simplified case the CAB provides only one function braking which is proportional to the driver's demand The Figure also shows only parts of the whole decomposition and safety analysis process The segments on the right side demonstrate how the Causes column contains events which refer to the next architectural level Concretely the example shows how the functional failure mode "Complete_lack_of_braking" can be tracked down to its basic events This example shows a decomposition down to the operating system level In this special case a further decomposition is not feasible even reliability data cannot be given

Another case study in which the treatment of software modules is explained has been worked out on a fuel controller with which a constant flow should be managed through five valves [Papadopolous et al] These are controlled by an Electronic Controller EC The software basically is described by a state transition diagram which already proposes a fault tolerant architecture see Figure the system reaches the state BVB_CVB if either the event "cva_fails" or the event "bva_fails_closed" has occurred The event logic among others is the following

cva_fails ⇒ ESS_L ∧ CV _L ∨ ESS_H ∧ ¬CV _H ∧ sec_timeout
bva_fails_closed ⇒ ¬BVA ∧ sec_timeout

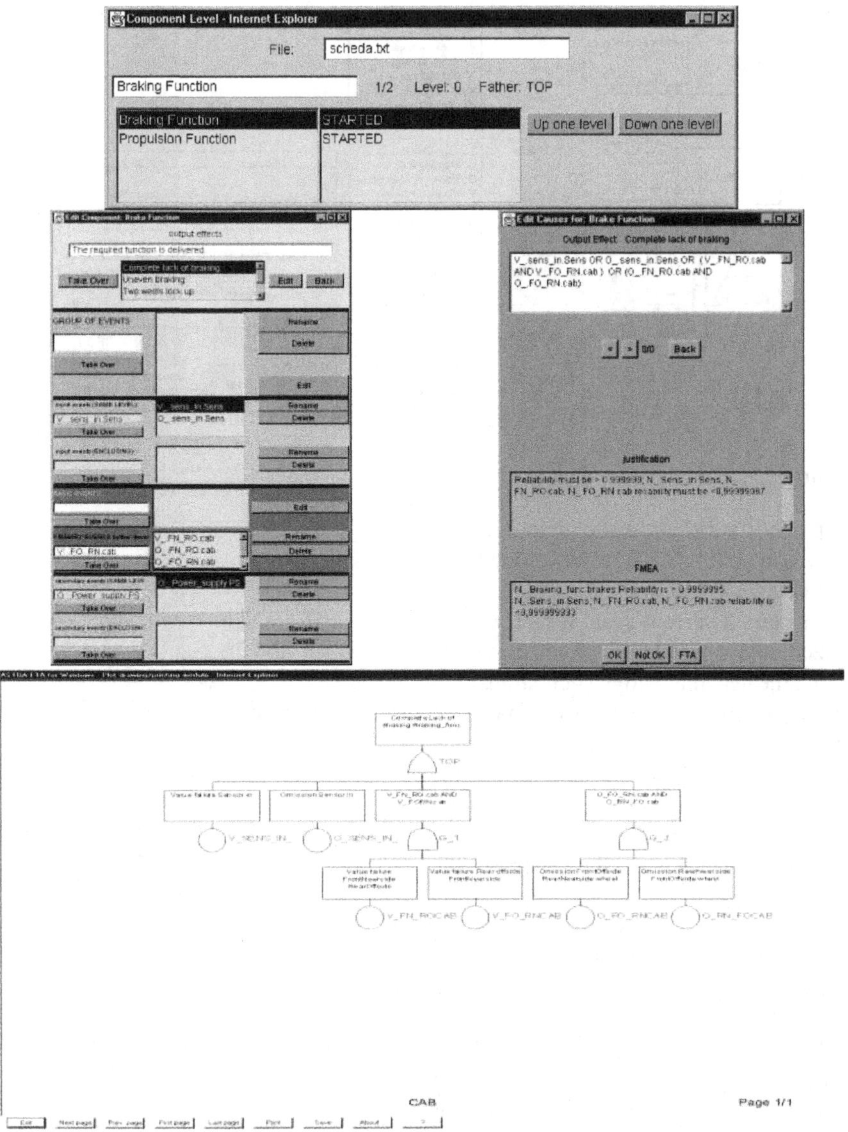

Figure Screenshots showing the components "Braking function" and "Propulsion Function" each with a decomposition started the editing of the effects belonging to "Braking function" the editing of the causes for the effect "Complete loss of braking" and the graphical representation of the fault tree belonging to "Complete loss of braking"

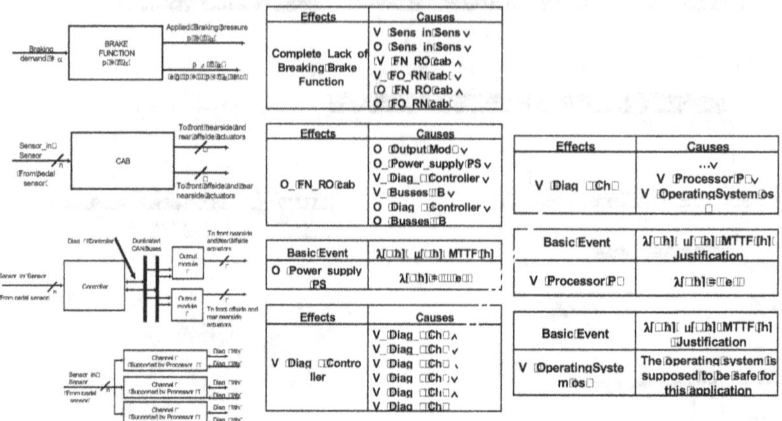

Figure Part of table hierarchy of the CAB case study

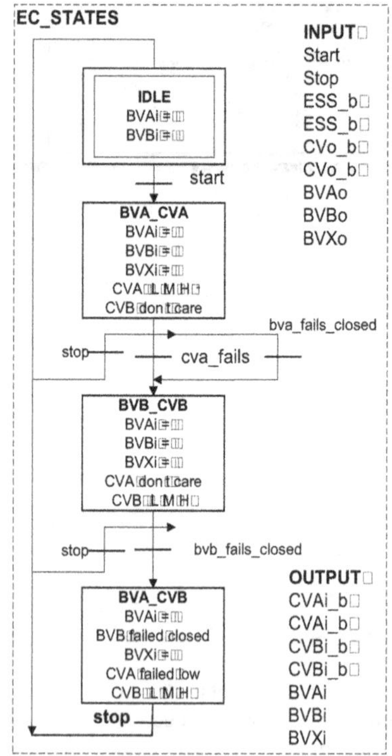

Figure State transition diagram of the Electronic Controller

"Stop" and "start" are simple signals The events concerning ESS are developed in a more detailed state transition diagram not shown here The real time aspect will be realized with the event " sec_timeout" which means that any such transition should take place within the specified time interval otherwise the "stop" signal will be sent in order to shut down the engine

Given the state transition diagram the methodology automatically generates the necessary tables for those effects i e values of state variables which appear in the diagram The relevant causes for the value "closed" of the variable "BVA" are displayed in Figure

The failure that valve BVA has been closed expressed as a commission failure appears at an higher level of system decomposition Usually the interface between hardware and software is more complex because one has to trace back potential failures through actuators circuits and registers before reaching the software level

An expression like C_BVA_CVB see Figure may represent a certain software procedure that if necessary may be further decomposed to seek for more explanations for failures

Explanations may differ according to the state the system is actually in Therefore the state has to be known for each cause The example in Figure shows how the automatism artificially introduces for each state a logical variable like "C_inStateBVA_CVA" and attaches it to the appropriate cause The example shows also how the search for causes within a state transition diagram can be seen from two sides In the case above

- the valve BVA may be closed because appropriate transitions have been done "commission" although they should not have been
- the valve BVA remains closed because appropriate transitions have not been done "omission" although they should have been done

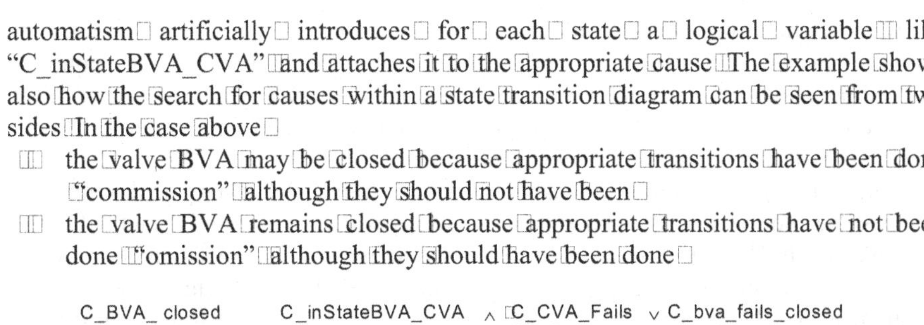

Figure Logical combination of causes for the effect "C_BVA_closed"

Conclusions

A methodology was presented that combines a variety of classical safety and reliability analysis techniques in a way that ensures the consistency of the result and leads to a better understanding and verification of the reliability and safety properties of the system The methodology works closely with what is proposed within the classical V Lifecycle The verification part is mainly done by successively applying Fault Tree Analysis on sub system topologies Results that locally do not satisfy minimal conditions on reliability or safety lead to have a component or the layer it belongs to redesigned with all the relevant verification part been done again

It has been shown that adhering to a specific formalism the subsequent application of various safety analysis techniques is possible Thus it is easy to apply different analysis techniques to different stages of decomposition

The non quantitative part of results from FTA has been demonstrated to be applicable to software failures so that an integrative analysis of an embedded system will be possible Software components are managed as state transition diagrams This formalism makes it easy to automate input for the logical parts of fault tree analysis It is obvious that repairs concerning software parts will have effects in terms of developer specific inspections on the software specifications

We experienced that when the methodology applies to real life complex real systems it leads to the production of a large quantity of tables that can hardly be managed manually Hence the automation of that task is a visible asset The tool that has been created incorporates powerful administration procedures handling all effects and tables generated so far and controlling the creation of potential events The strong links to the hierarchy of topologies and the topologies themselves makes it possible to identify a superset of events and to propose and to control these events in an automatic way The tedious effort of filling up tables during the design and decomposition phase is paid back by the confidence we have on the results of the analysis whose consistency is checked by the method As a matter of fact if tables are not consistent fault trees for high level functional failures cannot be built The stepwise verification is done in a bottom up way within a highly formal approach Thus the overall confidence will be gained starting from the basic components proceeding along the hierarchical decomposition and finally ensuring top level conditions Repairs of the system can be done on a rather local basis under permanent supervision of the consistency checking mechanism

In two main case studies it has been demonstrated that safety and reliability analysis does not have to stop when the level of software description is reached In the same way as the decomposition process can be continued the analysis process even if with some limitations can be advanced as well The involvement of software components in the general assessment process is crucial as software components might behave such that hardware components are triggered in a wrong way

The promising results of applying that methodology to embedded systems persuaded us to implement and to install it as a separate tool within the Astra tool set which already – among others comprises standard tools like fault tree analysis sensitivity analysis and software behaviour analysis

References

[Papadopoulos McDermid [illegible]] Papadopoulos Y McDermid J A Hierarchically Performed Hazard Origin and Propagation Studies in Lecture Notes in Computer Science [illegible] pp [illegible] Proceedings of SAFECOMP' [illegible] the [illegible]th International Conference on Computer Safety Reliability and Security Toulouse France Springer Verlag [illegible]

[Kletz [illegible]] Kletz T HAZOP and HAZAN Identifying and Assessing Process Industry Standards [illegible]rd Edition Hemisphere Publishers ISBN [illegible]

[Scheer et al [illegible]] Scheer S Maier T Towards Dependable Software Requirement Specifications in Proceedings of SAFECOMP' [illegible] ed Peter Daniel York [illegible]

[Palady [illegible]] Palady P Failure Modes and Effects Analysis PT Publications ISBN [illegible]

[Villemeur [illegible]] Villemeur A Reliability Availability Maintainability and Safety Assessment John Wiley and Sons Ltd ISBN [illegible]

[Vesely [illegible]] Vesely W E Fault Tree Handbook US Nuclear Regulatory Committee Report NUREG [illegible] US NRC Washington D C USA [illegible]

[Leveson et al [illegible]] Leveson N G Harvey P R Software Fault Tree Analysis Journal of Systems and Software [illegible] pp [illegible]

[Mauri et al [illegible]] Mauri G McDermid J A Papadopoulos Y Extension of Hazard and Safety Analysis Techniques to Address Problems of Hierarchical Scale in Proceedings of IEE Colloquium on Systems Engineering of Aerospace Projects IEE Digest no [illegible] pages [illegible] London [illegible]

[Contini et al [illegible]] Contini S Scheer S Wilikens M de Cola G Cojazzi G ASTRA An Integrated Tool Set for Complex Systems Dependability Studies in Tool Support for System Specification Development and Verification R Berghammer Y Lakhnech eds pp [illegible] – [illegible] Advances in Computing Science Springer [illegible]

[Papadopoulos et al [illegible]] Papadopoulos Y Mauri G McDermid J A Systematic Anticipation and Validation of Scenarios of Failure Propagation and Mitigation in PLC Controlled Processes in Proceedings of the PLC Conference Cologne [illegible]

An Application of the Chains-of-Rare-Events Model to Software Development Failure Prediction*

Néstor R. Barraza, Jonas D. Pfefferman, Bruno Cernuschi-Frías, and Félix Cernuschi

Facultad de Ingeniería, Universidad de Buenos Aires, and CONICET
Casilla 8, Sucursal 12 (B), 1412 Buenos Aires, Argentina
bcernus@fi.uba.ar

Abstract. Some of the best known models for software reliability are based on non homogeneous Poisson processes. Here, we analyze the application of the Chains-of-Rare-Events model to model grouped failures production. As it has been previously shown, this model can be analyzed as a compound Poisson with a Poisson Truncated at Zero as the compounding distribution. We introduce the mode estimator for the parameter of the Poisson Truncated at Zero. This estimator has the important characteristic of quickly reaching stability around the true value. We apply this model to several data and compare it with a non homogenous Poisson process model, and the Poisson distribution compounded by a geometric model.

1 Introduction

Software reliability has been an issue of increasing study for the last three decades, [, , , , ,]. Several measurements of software failures production have been reported and probabilistic models for software failures prediction have been proposed. Some of the best known models are the Goel-Okumoto model, [ ], and the Musa-Okumoto model, also known as logarithmic, [ ]. Both of these models are based on non homogeneous Poisson processes. These models may be applied for times between failures data, as well as grouped failures in interval times data. However, to obtain the occurrences of grouped failures requires less effort. Several software failures production data are given as grouped failures, [, , ,].

In order to model grouped failures production, a Poisson process compounded by a geometric distribution, GD, was introduced in [ ]. Since the expectation for the compound Poisson process is proportional to the elapsed time, this prediction model can be reduced to the simple Poisson process depending on the estimation method. Here, we apply the Chain-of-Rare-Events model we developed previously, [, ,]. As it has been shown, see [ ], this model can be

* This work was partially supported by the *Universidad de Buenos Aires*, grant No. TI-09, and the *Consejo Nacional de Investigaciones Científicas y Técnicas*, grant No. PIP-4030, CONICET, Argentina.

H. B. Keller and E. Plödereder (Eds.): Ada-Europe 2000, LNCS 1845, pp. 185– , 2000.

seen as a Poisson process compounded by a Poisson Truncated at Zero. Several methods for the estimation of the parameter of the Poisson Truncated at Zero are well known, [, ,]. The fact that some software failures data present dispersion, suggests the idea of using an estimator less sensitive to that dispersion. Here, we propose to use the mode of the samples for the estimation of the parameter of the Poisson Truncated at Zero.

The sample data we will consider include concave, s-shaped and two stage curves. The results we obtain for software reliability growth models are important to understand the behavior of several models and estimation methods with different data sets. This is important in order to choose the adequate model and estimation method for each case.

2 Models for Software Reliability Analysis

2.1 Non Homogeneous Poisson Models

Models usually proposed for software reliability, predict the number of failures which will be produced in a given interval test time. These models are known as growth models. Some of the best known growth models are NHPP, where the Poisson parameter is a given function of time, [,]. For example, in the Goel-Okumoto model, [ ], the mean value function is given by:

$$\mu(t) = a(1 - \mathrm{e}^{-bt}) , \quad a \geq 0 , \quad b > 0 , \tag{1}$$

and for the Musa-Okumoto model, [ ]:

$$\mu(t) = \frac{1}{\theta} \log(\lambda\theta t + 1) . \tag{2}$$

One of the main differences between these models is the behavior of $\mu(t)$ for $t \to \infty$. The former belongs to the finite category models, and the last one, to the infinite category models, in the Musa and Okumoto classification, [ ].

Another extensively used model is the Musa basic execution time, [ ]. It has the same mean value function $\mu(t)$ as the Goel-Okumoto model, see ( ). However, it is based on the actual execution time, rather than the calendar time. Also, it is based on different assumptions.

The function $\mu(t)$ attempts to model the behavior of the system. It relates the faults detected, faults expected, faults corrected, faults removed, etc. Each model has its own motivations and assumptions.

The data usually collected are of two types: failures per time period, or time between failures. NHPP models are specially designed for the last type of data. However, they can also be applied to failures per time period, [ ]. Also, other NHPP models are described in the bibliography, [, ,].

2.2 Compound Poisson Models

The compound Poisson Process, CPP, was proposed as a software reliability model in [ ]. The CPP is a growth model and, as opposed to NHPP models, the mean value function is proportional to the elapsed time. This characteristic results in simple analytical calculations and estimation procedures. CPP models were introduced to model grouped failures production. Failures grouped in given interval times are easier to collect, rather than times between failures. Data specially fitted for this type of models are failures per time period. The arrivals of grouped failures follow a Poisson distribution, and the number of failures in each group follow a given distribution which compounds the Poisson.

A CPP is given by the sum of M r. v.'s X_i, $i = 1, 2, \ldots$, i.i.d., with probability function $p_X(x)$, where M is a r. v. which follows a Poisson distribution, [,]. The CPP is obtained as, [ ]:

$$F_Y(x) = \sum_{m=0}^{\infty} e^{-\lambda\, t} \frac{(\lambda\, t)^m}{m!} \, [G_X(x)]^{m*} . \tag{3}$$

$F_Y(x)$ is a CPP distribution with compounding distribution $G_X(x)$. A r. v. $N(t)$ following a CPP, may be expressed as:

$$p_N(N(t) = n) = \sum_{m=0}^{\infty} e^{-\lambda\, t} \frac{(\lambda\, t)^m}{m!} \, \Pr\{\sum_{i=1}^{M} X_i = n | M = m\} . \tag{4}$$

The p.g.f. for $N(t)$ is given by, [ ]:

$$f_N(z, t) = \mathrm{e}^{-\lambda t} \mathrm{e}^{\lambda t g(x)} , \tag{5}$$

where $g(x)$ is the p.g.f. of the compounding random variable.

If the compounding probability is truncated at zero, i.e. $p_X(x = 0) = 0$, the sum in ( ) extends up to m since $\Pr\{\sum_{i=1}^{M} X_i = n | M = m\} = 0$ for $m > n$.

The compounding distribution proposed in [ ], is the GD, given by:

$$P_X(x) = r \quad (1 - r)^{x-1}, \quad x = 1, 2, 3, \cdots . \tag{6}$$

It should be noted that this is a decreasing function.

A characteristic usually applied to compare software reliability models is their predictive validity, [,]. Suppose that n_{tot} failures have been produced in time t_{tot}. The failure data produced up to time $t_{past} \le t_{tot}$ are used to estimate the parameters of the mean value function so that $\mu(t_{past}) = n_{past}$. Then, replacing the estimated values of the parameters in $\mu(t)$, an estimate of the number of failures up to t_{tot} is obtained as $\hat{\mu}(t_{tot})$.

It should be noted that if the mean value function $\mu(t)$ is proportional to time t, as it happens in the compound Poisson models, the remaining failures may be estimated as:

$$n_{rem} = \hat{\mu}(t_{tot}) - n_{past} = \\ \hat{\mu}(t_{rem} + t_{past}) - \hat{\mu}(t_{past}) = \hat{\mu}(t_{rem}) \, . \tag{7}$$

A remark on the estimation methods for compound Poisson models should be pointed out. The parameter of the Poisson probability is estimated as the arrival rate. Each arrival corresponds to a group of failures. Each group may correspond to failures in a given quantum of CPU, or failures per a given interval time, like seconds, days, weeks, etc. Hence, if m_{past} is the number of arrivals up to time t_{past}, the Poisson parameter λ is given by:

$$\hat{\lambda} = \frac{m_{past}}{t_{past}} \, . \tag{8}$$

The first moment of the compound Poisson probability is obtained as, [ ]:

$$E(N(t)) = \lambda t E(X) \, , \tag{9}$$

where $E(X)$ is the first moment of the r. v. which compounds the Poisson.

If the moments method is used to estimate the parameter of the probability function of the random variable X, the first moment of the samples should be equal to the first moment of X. Hence:

$$\hat{E}(X) = \frac{n_{past}}{m_{ast}} \, . \tag{10}$$

Replacing ( ) and ( ) in ( ), and since the expectation ( ) is the mean value function $\mu(t)$, it results:

$$\hat{\mu}(t_{rem}) = \hat{E}(N(t_{rem})) = \frac{m_{past}}{t_{past}} t_{rem} \frac{n_{past}}{m_{past}} \, . \tag{11}$$

After simplification, ( ) reduces to:

$$\hat{\mu}(t_{rem}) = \frac{n_{past}}{t_{past}} t_{rem} \, . \tag{12}$$

Equation ( ) is the same as that obtained using the simple Poisson model, when its parameter is estimated as the failures production rate $\hat{\lambda} = \frac{n_{past}}{t_{past}}$. It should be clear that, if a different estimation method is used, a different result would be obtained. For some compounding probability models, the maximum likelihood method, coincides with the moment method.

The model proposed here is a CPP compounded by a Poisson Truncated at Zero distribution, PTZ, [ ].

Since failures are registered in the instant they occur, then, there are no intervals with zero failures. Hence, the compounding distribution should be a truncated at zero distribution. A similar situation motivated the introduction of the PTZ in modeling accidents in a factory, see [ ]. However, when fixed interval times are considered, truncated at zero distributions can not be used since there could be interval times with zero failures.

Several estimators for the PTZ have been proposed, [,]. The minimum variance unbiased estimator was obtained in [ ]. This estimator, is difficult to use for large failures numbers, because it involves the Stirling numbers of the second kind, [ ]. On the other hand, for the PTZ, the maximum likelihood method coincides with the moments method. Taking in account the comments made previously, this estimator is not a good one for a compounding distribution in a predictive model. In [ ], a very simple unbiased estimator was proposed. From these observations, we will only consider the estimator derived in [ ] and the estimator proposed in the next section.

3 A Mode Estimator for the Poisson Compounded by the Poisson Truncated at Zero Model

Define X as a r. v. following a PTZ, i.e.:

$$P_X(x) = \frac{a^x}{x!}\,\frac{1}{e^a - 1} \qquad x = 1, 2, 3, \cdots . \tag{13}$$

It should be noted that ( ) has a maximum, as opposed to the GD defined in ( ).

For the case when the compounding is the PTZ given by ( ), the CPP results as, [,]:

$$\begin{aligned} &P_{N(t)}(N(t) = 0) = \mathrm{e}^{-\lambda t} , \\ &\text{and for } n > 0 : \\ &P_{N(t)}(N(t) = n) = \mathrm{e}^{-\lambda t}\,\frac{a^n}{n!} \sum_{m=1}^{n} \left\{ {n \atop m} \right\} \left(\frac{\lambda t}{e^a - 1} \right)^m . \end{aligned} \tag{14}$$

A CPP has a first moment given by, [ ]:

$$E(N(t)) = \lambda t E(X) , \tag{15}$$

where λ is the Poisson parameter and $E(X)$ is the first moment of the compounding random variable.

For the probability given by ( ), recalling that the first moment is the mean value function $\mu(t)$, the mean value function results:

$$\mu(t) = \frac{\lambda t e^a}{e^a - 1} . \tag{16}$$

Equation ( ) will be used to predict the number of failures as a function of time.

As previously explained, the Poisson parameter λ is estimated as the group of failures arrival rate:

$$\lambda = \frac{m_{past}}{t_{past}} , \tag{17}$$

where m_{past} is the number of arrivals, and t_{past} the elapsed time.

Let's call x_i the number of failures arrived at the arrival i, $i = 1, 2, \cdots, m_{past}$. For the model proposed here, the x_i are i.i.d. Poisson Truncated at Zero random variables.

One of the estimators we consider is the Plackett estimator, [ ]:

$$\hat{a} = \frac{1}{m_{past}} \sum_{\substack{i=1 \\ x_i > 1}}^{m_{past}} x_i \ . \tag{18}$$

This estimator is unbiased and it is very simple to obtain.

The estimates obtained for the parameter a using the Plackett estimator are very similar to those obtained using the maximum likelihood estimator. Since the maximum likelihood estimator coincides with the moments estimator for the PTZ, these results are similar to those obtained in [ ]. The analysis of the results obtained using the Plackett estimator, show that the value $\hat{a}$ is too large, due to some dispersion in the values of x_i. Also, the estimated parameter changes slowly when the characteristics of the samples change. These last two problems suggest the use of a mode estimator, which should have less sensitivity to dispersion and should adapt faster to sample changes. The value of $\hat{a}$ is determined as the value of x_i corresponding to the maximum number of occurrences. Another possible estimator is the median, however, the results obtained are similar to those corresponding to the Plackett estimator.

Next, the estimation method is described. For a given r. v. X following a PTZ, it follows that:

$$\frac{P_X(X = x)}{P_X(X = x + 1)} = \frac{x + 1}{a} \ . \tag{19}$$

Let's call x_{max} the mode. Then: $P_X(X = x_{max}) \geq P_X(X = x_{max} + 1)$, and, from ( ), $a \leq x_{max} + 1$. Also, $P_X(X = x_{max}) \geq P_X(X = x_{max} - 1)$, so that, $a \geq x_{max}$. If a is integer, then $P_X(X = a - 1) = P_X(X = a)$, and then x_{max} may be either taken as a or $a - 1$.

The criterion used in order to estimate the parameter a is simply to obtain the value having the maximum probability, i.e., the value of a corresponding to the x_i with the maximum number of occurrences.

Define k_i as the number of occurrences of the value x_i. The estimator is given by:

$$\begin{aligned} i^* &= arg \max_i (k_i) \ , \\ \hat{a} &= x_{i^*} \ . \end{aligned} \tag{20}$$

A simple study of this estimator can be made by means of computer simulations. We show in the following table the mean value and the relative efficiency respect to the Cramer-Rao minimum variance. Sample sizes of 100 were used for each value of the Poisson Truncated at Zero parameter a.

Table 1. Characteristics of the mode estimator

a	Mean Value	Efficiency
1	1.02	6.00
2	1.56	9.24
3	2.52	12.19
4	3.62	17.66
5	4.37	15.09
10	9.4	18.17
15	14.26	18.53
20	18.84	17.45
30	29.14	17.85
40	38.44	20.12

As it can be seen from Table , the estimator for the mode has an appreciable bias and poor efficiency, worsening for higher values of a. However, in predictive models, it is important to follow data variations. Particularly, the number of software failures produced in given interval times x_i gets smaller as time goes on. Hence, the x_{i^*} having the maximum number of repetitions, will take lower values in time. While other estimators are affected by previous values, this estimator is such that the current x_{i^*} is the only value used to determine the mode estimator. This characteristic seems important to follow data variations as it is discussed in the next section.

4 Applications to Software Failures Data

We compare the results obtained using a NHPP model, the compound Poisson geometric model, CPGEO, and the proposed compound Poisson-Poisson Truncated at Zero model, CPPTZ, to the following data: T5 from [ ] grouped by day; DS1, from [ ]; J5, data 8, SS1, from [ ]; and failures data for product B from [ ]. For the NHPP model, we use the Musa-Okumoto model, M-O, or the Goel-Okumoto model, G-O, as indicated in the figure captions. The results obtained using both models are very similar. We used the maximum likelihood method, ML, for the NHPP model when it was possible, and the least squares method, LS, otherwise. Conditions for the convergence of ML in NHPP models were given in [ ].

We evaluate the predictive validity for the models. Failures predictions are made in the same units of time as they were taken, except for the SS1 data for which they were not available.

Software failures data can be classified in accordance to the shape of the cumulative number of failures curve. Generally, it is a concave curve, showing a decreasing failures production rate. In other cases, it presents an increasing failures production rate at the beginning, followed by a decreasing rate after an inflection point. This last type of curve is called s-shaped.

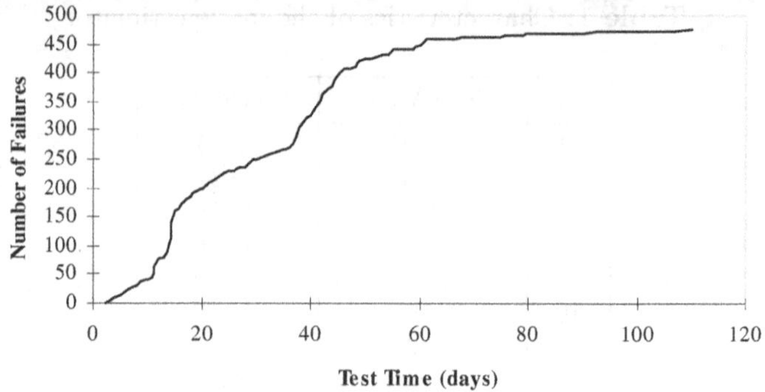

Fig. 1. Cumulative number of failures, data 8

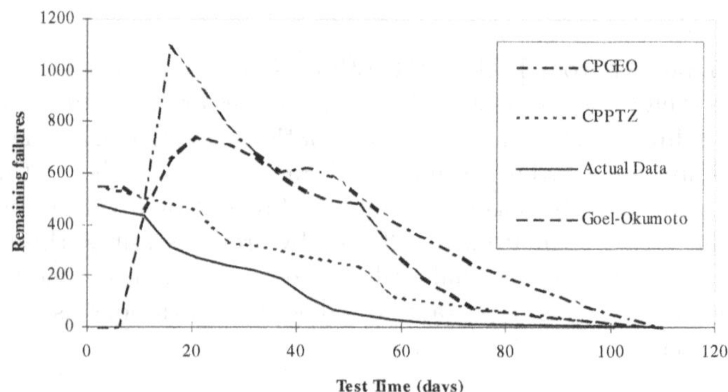

Fig. 2. Actual and predicted remaining failures, data 8. The ML method has been used, except for the G-O model for which the LS method was applied up to day 50

The data 8 set has the three characteristics mentioned before. It is an S-shaped system with an inflection point around the 18th day, joined with a second simple stage beginning around the 40th day, see Figure . As it can be seen in Figure , the model proposed has the better fit up to the 70th day. Besides that, it is the only one which follows the variations in the actual data. From the 70th day, the results obtained are similar to as those using G-O.

To see how the estimator we propose adjusts to the variations in the data, we show in Figure the estimates for the parameter of the PTZ using the mode, and the Plackett estimator. Also, the median is shown in the same figure. As it can be seen, the jumps in the mode estimated values indicate fast adaptation to changes in the system. This is not the case for the Plackett estimator, since the average given by ( ) implies slow changes in the estimated values.

Cumulative number of failures from data J5 are shown in Figure . The curve shows an almost constant failure rate. The prediction curves displayed in Figure show that the closest fit corresponds to the CPGEO and M-O models.

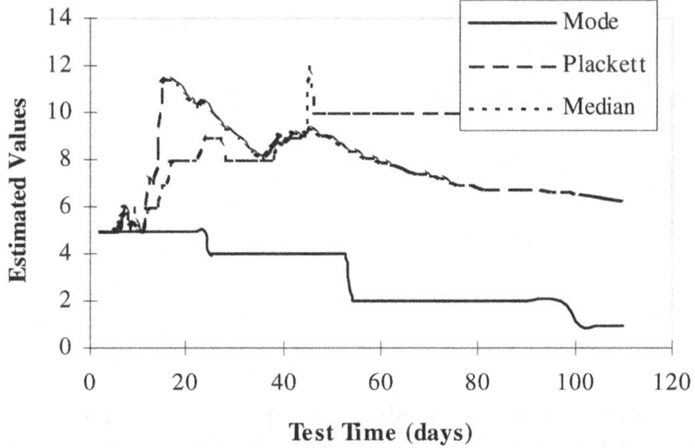

Fig. 3. Estimated values for the Poisson Truncated at Zero parameter, data 8

They give similar results from day 48. Results obtained using our model are lower than the actual data after a stable prediction in the day 30 is reached. This is opposite to predictions using the other models which give values greater

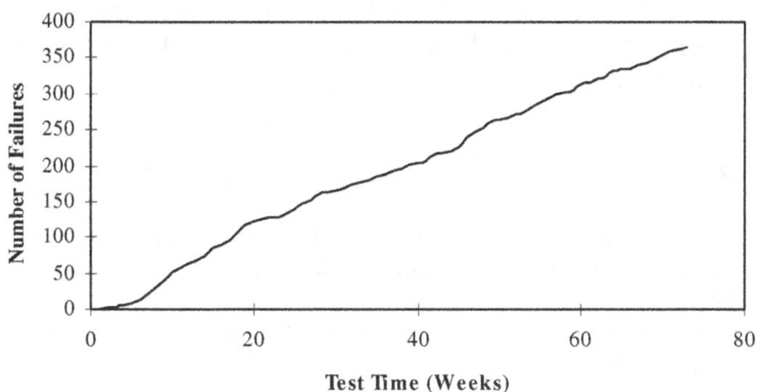

Fig. 4. Cumulative number of failures, data J5

5 Conclusions

The data analyzed shows that the proposed model performs better than the others, including the NHPP models, when the number of failures per time interval having the maximum number of occurrences, changes from high values at the beginning to low values at the end, and when there are significant number of

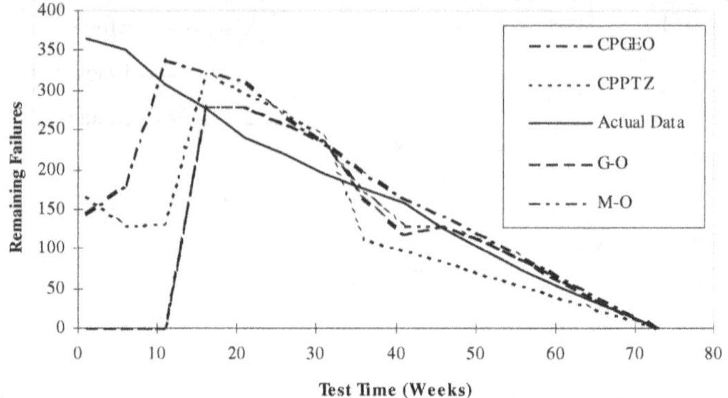

Fig. 5. Actual and predicted remaining failures, data J5. The ML method has been used, except for the G-O model for which the LS method was applied up to week 31

failures per time interval located far away from that maximum. If these data are ignored, better predictions are made, since the rate of failures is decreasing. The two characteristics mentioned above are present in data 8 and DS1. They show the advantages of the proposed model: it adapts to changes faster than the others, and it avoids excessively dispersed data.

For the other cases analyzed, the NHPP models give the best results, however, the proposed model gives values near these models, and it has the advantage of the simple calculation of the estimates of the parameters and acceptable prediction of failures.

References

1. Goel, A. L., Okumoto, K.: Time-Dependent Error-Detection Rate Model for Software Reliability and Other Performance Measures. IEEE Trans. Reliability **28** (1979) 206–211
2. Miller, A. M. B.: A Study of the Musa Reliability Mode. M. Sc. Thesis, University of Maryland (1980)
3. Sukert, A. N.: A Software Reliability Modeling Study. Technical report RADC-TR-76-247. Rome Air Development Center, USA (1976)
4. Sukert, A. N.: Empirical Validation of Three Error Prediction Models. IEEE Trans. Reliability **28** (1979) 199–205
5. Musa, J. D., Iannino, A. and Okumoto, K.: Software Reliability: Measurement, Prediction, Application. McGraw-Hill, New York (1987)
6. Pfefferman, J. D. and Cernuschi-Frías, B.: A Non-Stationary Model for Time-Dependent Software Reliability Analysis. Proceedings of the 1999 IASTED International Conference on Modeling and Simulation, MS' 99, Philadelphia, Pennsylvania (1999) 427–431
7. Derriennic, H., Le Gall, G.: Use of Failure-Intensity Models in the Software-Validation Phase for Telecommunications. IEEE Trans. Reliability **44** (1995) 658–665

8. Lyu, M. R. (Ed.): Handbook of Software Reliability Engineering. McGraw Hill, New York (1996)
9. Wood, A.: Software Reliability Growth Models. Tandem Tech. Report 96.1 (1996)
10. Sahinoglu, M.: Compound-Poisson Software Reliability Model. IEEE Trans. on Software Engineering **18** (1992) 624–630
11. Cernuschi, F., Castagnetto, L.: Chains of Rare Events. Annals of Mathematical Statistics **XVII** (1946) 53–61
12. Barraza, N. R., Cernuschi-Frías B., and Cernuschi, F.: A Probabilistic Model for Grouped Events Analysis. Proceedings of the 1995 IEEE Int. Conf. on Systems, Man and Cybernetics, Vancouver, Canada (1995) **4** 3386–3390
13. Barraza, N. R., Cernuschi-Frías, B. and Cernuschi, F.: Applications & Extensions of the Chains-of-Rare-Events Model. IEEE Trans. Reliability **45** (1996) 417–421
14. Plackett, R. L.: The Truncated Poisson Distribution. Biometrics **9** (1953) 485–488
15. Tate, R. F. and Goen, R. L.: Minimum Variance Unbiased Estimation for the Truncated Poisson Distribution. Annals of Mathematical Statistics **29** (1958) 755–765
16. Feller, W.: An Introduction to Probability Theory and its Applications, Vols. 1 and 2. Wiley, New York (1967)
17. Wood, A.: Predicting Software Reliability. IEEE Computer **29** (1996) 69–77
18. Haight, F. A.: Handbook of the Poisson Distribution. Wiley, New York (1966)
19. Knuth, D. E.: The Art of Computer Programming, Vol. 1. Addison Wesley, Reading MA (1969)
20. Musa, J. D.: Software Reliability Data. Bell Telephone Laboratories, Whippany NJ (1980)
21. Hossain, S. A. and Dahiya, R. C.: Estimating the Parameters of a Non-homogeneous Poisson-Process Model for Software Reliability. IEEE Transactions on Reliability **42** (1993) 604–612

Analysis, Design and Implementation of an Object-Oriented Framework in Ada95

Detlef Schmitt

[1] Sema Group GmbH
Kurt-Schumacher-Strasse 241,D-26389 Wilhelmshaven, Germany
Phone: +49-4421-802-224, Fax: +49-4421-802-555
Detlef.Schmitt@so.sema.de
[2] Open University,
Milton Keynes, MK7 6AA, United Kingdom

Abstract. This paper describes the analysis, design and implementation of an object-oriented framework for discrete event simulation in the programming language Ada95. The framework was constructed in an industrial setting so that conclusions are drawn from first-hand, practical experience with this approach. After defining the term 'Object-Oriented Framework', discrete event simulation is analyzed as the domain of concern in the given context, producing a class diagram for that domain in the Unified Modelling Language (UML). Following the analysis activities, the framework is designed and described, again using diagrams of the UML. In further sections the mapping from design artifacts to code in Ada95 and the usage of the framework are shown. The article finishes with a summary of the experience gained and the lessons learned.

Keywords: Frameworks, Object-Oriented Technologies, Experience Reports from Projects using Ada95, Case Studies and Experiments

1 Introduction

Object-oriented frameworks have become more and more common and widespread in use during the last few years. They are available for domains like graphical user interfaces (GUI), financial applications, manufacturing, banking, and others. Frameworks are exploited commercially by several software vendors or can be obtained from the public domain. For detailed descriptions of many diverse frameworks see [ ].

One of the most important advantages of framework application is the chance to enact reusability in a more economic form than was possible before the introduction of this technology. After having implemented many slightly differing applications in the area of discrete event simulation, the author's company looked for a way to develop such applications more economically. The efficient resue of domain expertise and experience gathered in many similar projects was another goal to be reached. Discrete event simulation is an area of application which is

H. B. Keller and E. Plödereder (Eds.): Ada-Europe 2000, LNCS 1845, pp. 196– , 2000.

used in many industrial projects and is based on very simple and few fundamental concepts. These concepts lend themselves to the use of an object-oriented framework as the nucleus of many different implementations in that domain.

The purpose of this paper is to show how the concept of object-oriented frameworks was applied to a domain like discrete event simulation in an industrial approach to software construction. The article will also describe how the resulting model was transformed to a framework in Ada95 and sheds some light on the experience gained during this project.

It also describes:

- what object-oriented frameworks are and which elements they comprise,
- explains how a domain analysis for the construction of an object-oriented framework in the area of discrete event simulation was performed,
- illustrates the translation of the domain model to the design of the framework,
- shows the mapping of UML notation and especially the resulting design model to code constructs in Ada95, and
- documents the experience gained and lessons learned during the project.

The paper finally draws the conclusions from the method used and identifies areas of further research.

Although the process from domain analysis through design and construction of the framework is described sequentially in this paper, it was not necessarily performed in this way. Based on already existing expertise, knowledge, and experience in the domain, analysis, design, and construction of the object-oriented framework were actually done iteratively and incrementally by abstracting from existing applications and generalizing across different implementations. Since it is not possible to show all steps of this process in a short paper, a sequential step-by-step explanation is used.

2 Object-Oriented Frameworks and Their Elements

Historically, frameworks were predated by class libraries which are simple collections of mostly unrelated abstract and concrete classes that can be instantiated and utilised by a user of the library. Class libraries are in the object-oriented paradigm what the function and subroutine libraries are in the structured world. They are entirely focused on the reuse of code and nearly no provisions are made to reapply the design and possible interactions or mechanisms between the classes. The inheritance hierarchy of the components is the main structural property of a class library. Dynamic aspects are either non-existent or neglected in total. Flow of control between the elements is not expressed, at least not explicitly.

When class libraries are used to model the reality and the circumstances of their domain better and in an extended comprehensiveness, they get bigger and more complex. It is inevitable that the classes in the library can not be independent from each other any more. As in the reality of a given domain, the classes representing the real-world entities are no longer autonomous; they are getting closely intertwined and logically coupled. At this stage, the need for structuring and ordering the static and especially the dynamic relationships between the individual classes arises. This demands a new concept for arranging the design of the classes, their logical connections and interactive behavior. Here the framework concept comes into play [ ].

The concept of object-oriented frameworks not only provides for the reuse of code as class libraries do, but also for recycling the architecture and design of a whole class assembly. This includes the mechanisms of their interactions. In this way, the framework reflects the conditions of collaboration and the logical links of the items in a given domain. It models and mirrors the real-world entities together with their relationships, mutual dependencies, and interactions.

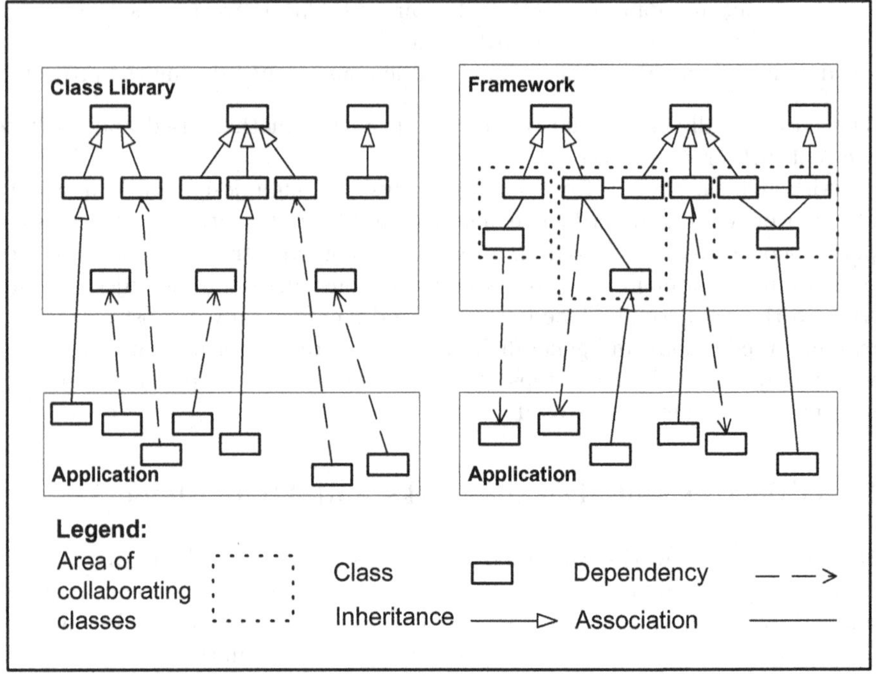

Fig. 1. Class Library versus Framework

Figure 1 shows the archetypical differences between class libraries and frameworks in a simple sketch. In both aggregates of classes the inheritance relationships represent the static (inheritance) connections between abstract and concrete classes in the library as well as in the application. The application calls operations or methods from the library and inherits from the library classes. No explicit interactions between the classes in the library take place.

In contrast to this relationship model for class libraries, the model for object-oriented frameworks incorporates the interactions of the classes and the dynamic interrelationships between the objects during run-time in addition to inheritance and other static relationships.

In reality, the archetypical exemplars of class library and object-oriented framework explained above are the end points of a wide spectrum of possibilities. A conglomerate of classes can appear mostly as a class library, as a pure framework, or as a mixture of both [ ]. The cooperating classes of a framework provide a skeleton which encapsulates and predetermines the overall structure or architecture of an application. The specific functionality is added to the framework through specialisation of abstract into concrete classes (white-box framework) or through configuration and parameterisation of concrete classes (black-box framework).

A framework is a prefabricated, semi-finished structure solving a good deal of the typical problems of an application domain. In this way, the framework encapsulates a lot of experience and knowledge from domain analysis, prior experience, and earlier implementations in the area of concern. A framework enables not only the reuse of code but also that of design, expertise, and domain-specific knowledge on a higher level of abstraction [ ].

In summary, object-oriented frameworks are collections or sets of abstract and/or concrete classes together with the interactions between them. In this way they provide a blueprint of the structure and behavior of the participating elements. Frameworks are always an abstraction of a real-world domain for which they provide standard solutions for standard problems. They build a foundation for the reuse of design as well as code and in this way provide a solid basis for the repeated utilisation of already existing assets on more than one level of abstraction.

3 Domain Analysis for Discrete Event Simulation

This section gives a brief description of the domain analysis process used and its results for the area of discrete event simulation. The outcome of this analysis is recorded as a model of the domain under consideration in the form of a UML class diagram (see [ ] and [ ]).

The purpose of domain analysis is the capturing and structuring of information in a given area of knowledge. It is a prerequisite to reusing the accumulated knowledge of the domain in order to solve the typical and recurring problems of that area in software. Put in the words of Prieto-Diaz and Arango, "Domain analysis deals with the identification, acquisition, representation of (potentially reusable) software-specifcation and software-implementation knowledge for classes of real-world problems" [ ].

Discrete event simulation is the imitation of real-world entities which change their behavior and state in time and/or through the influence of external events, also called triggers. This concept of simulation which forms the basis of the domain being analyzed knows only a few entities which have to be modelled.

The relevant classes in question were found by using the CRC (Class - Responsibility - Cooperation) cards approach described in Wirfs-Brock et al. [ ]. These classes represent the typical objects of the domain and their operations. They are:

- The simulation space which comprises all simulation objects to be simulated at a given simulation time,
- simulation objects that have a behavior depending on their current states as well as external events,
- a simulation manager which maintains the simulation space and time and also controls the scenario,
- the scenario which determines and administrates the events, and
- events which influence creation, deletion, and behavior of the simulation objects and each have an unfolding time, i.e. the time at which an event happens relatively to the beginning of the simulation run.

The result of this domain analysis is documented in the form of a high-level UML class diagram which is shown in figure 2 without further details.

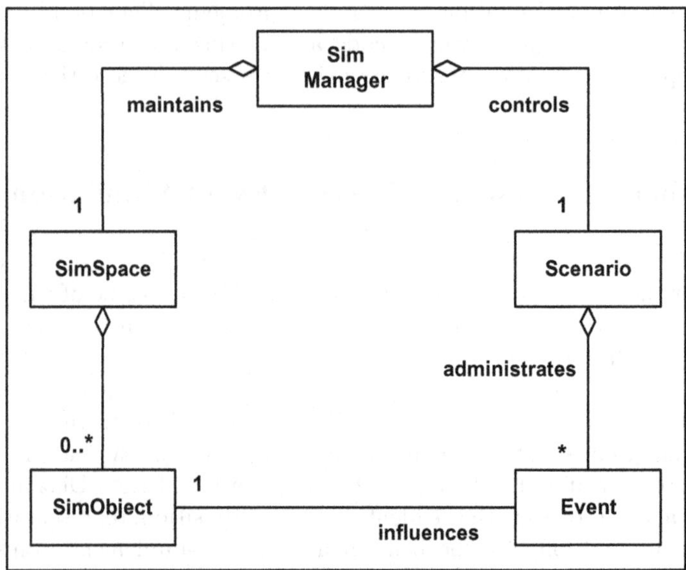

Fig. 2. Class Diagram of Discrete Event Simulation Domain

4 Design of the Simulation Framework

Having constructed a domain model for discrete event simulation and documented this model in an appropriate UML diagram, the next step in the process was the design of an object-oriented framework.

Starting with the class diagram as the main artifact developed during the domain analysis, the design of the framework for discrete event simulation was refined iteratively. All classes needed and their mutual relationships were documented so that all important aspects of the domain were covered.

In this section, the design process as well as its rationale and its resulting products are described and discussed in more detail.

4.1 Hot-Spots vs. Frozen Spots

Early during the design of the simulation framework, it became obvious that it is essential for its success to separate the parts which have to be adapted and therefore change often (i.e. the hot-spots) from the parts which need no adaptation because they are more stable (the frozen spots). This process is called hot-spot analysis and is based mainly on the domain experts knowledge of the aspects which differ from application to application. The flexibility of the behavior desired as well as the time when it is needed have to be taken into account at this stage. The hot-spot driven approach is described in [ ] with more detail.

4.2 Frozen Spots

Conducting a hot-spot analysis, the following classes were soon identified as frozen spots (i.e. classes which do not change very often):

- Simulation manager (class `SimManager`),
- Scenario (class `Scenario`), and
- Simulation space (class `SimSpace`).

All three of these classes are concrete, i.e. they are used directly to instantiate the respective objects. The framework is constructed so that only one object of each class is instantiated.

Class SimManager. The class `SimManager` is responsible for the control of a simulation run through its methods `Run()`, `Pause()`, and `Stop()`.

It also internally maintains the simulation clock and updates other instances not being part of the framework after they have registered appropriate callback methods via the `Register()` method of class `SimManager`. This mechanism is for example used to connect external parts of the application to `SimManager` in order to display the simulation results on a display, store them on permanent storage, or interact with the end-user.

---

[1] Classes and their operations are set in a different font in the rest of the article.

The class is active, i.e. its singular object is able to run concurrently with objects of other classes and therefore can initiate control activities which dynamically influence other objects in the final application.

During a simulation, updating of the simulation space (see class `SimSpace`) is initiated by class `SimManager` at regular intervals. They can be adapted by an appropriate method invocation implemented in this class (`SetFrequency`).

Class Scenario. This concrete class defines the static as well as the dynamic behavior of a complete simulation run and administrates a series of events in time influencing the simulated objects.

Its important methods are `Add()` for adding events to the scenario and `Activate()` to activate all relevant events between the simulated time and the time of the last update. `Save()`, and `Load()` are additional methods for saving and loading scenarios to or from permanent storage respectively.

Class SimSpace. `SimSpace` describes the simulation space, i.e. the collection of all simulated objects and administrates them. Its most important method (`Update()`) has to update all simulation objects, i.e. the instantiations of class `SimObject`.

4.3 Hot Spots

In this section the hot-spot classes found during the design and their relationships to other classes are described in more detail.

Class SimObject. The abstract class `SimObject` comprises common structure and state changes of simulation objects. In this way it describes their general properties.

In order to instantiate the abstract class `SimObject`, a concrete subclass has to be defined by the framework user. This concrete class inherits all properties from its abstract superclass. It needs to implement at least an update method (`Update()`) which has the time for the update relative to the starting time of the simulation as its input parameter.

The framework user has to implement the `Update()` method and needs to realize the desired state changes in it. He also has to provide the concrete state changes of the individual simulation objects by adding appropriate attributes to the concrete class which inherits from `SimObject`.

Class Information. General state-invariant information about a simulation object or a scenario is defined in the abstract class `Information`. This class is linked to the abstract class `SimObject` or the concrete class `Scenario` through an aggregation relationship and adds attributes defining general information on the referenced simulation object or scenario which does not influence the state of the object or the scenario. A concrete subclass implementing its method

`Init()` inherits from this abstract class as a prerequisite for object creation. The framework user has to subclass from `Information` and add appropriate attributes which describe state-invariant properties of the relevant simulation object or the scenario.

Class Event. In order to describe a simulation run, the class `Event` was introduced during the domain analysis and has been refined while designing the framework. `Event` is an abstract class which describes the general properties of an event. It collects common structure and the similar behavior of events influencing existence and state changes of simulation objects modelled by the class `SimObject`.

Every event has an associated point in time at which it is activated and influences its environment or the behavior of simulation objects. The common properties of events are concentrated in the class `Event` which is responsible for the activation at a predefined time, called the activation time. This point in time is measured relatively to the simulation starting time and determines when an event will happen. Concrete events are created by subclassing the abstract superclass `Event` and implementing its method `Activate()`.

Class Event.SimObject. The abstract class `Event.SimObject` inherits from the abstract class `Event`. It takes over all properties of its superclass and also adds a binary association to the target object derived from the class `SimObject` on which the event has some effect. By design and convention a single event always influences exactly one simulation object. This is guaranteed by the qualifier Identity (abbreviated Id) added to the qualified class `Event.SimObject`.

Event Service Classes. After using a first version of the framework for a while, it showed to be advantageous to factor the operations of the abstract class `Event.SimObject`, i.e. its methods `Create()`, `Delete()`, and `Change_Info()`, into distinct concrete classes because these operations were general enough to be implemented as part of the framework.

Class `Event.SimObject.Create`, for example, can be used to instantiate the general event of simulation object creation which is universally applicable in every simulation. Likewise, instantiating class `Event.SimObject.Delete` gives the framework user the ability to delete a simulation object from the simulation simulation space and therefore from the entire simulation run.

In order to create a simulation object of class `SimObject`, the event service class `Event.SimObject.Create` with its method `Activate` is used. In this way a one-to-one composition between `Event.SimObject.Create` and `SimObject` is constructed logically.

The main method of all event service classes is `Activate()` which makes the event service (i.e. simulation object creation, simulation object deletion, or change of information) happen at the predetermined activation time.

4.4 Overall Design of the Framework

An UML class diagram representing the simulation framework's final design, its important classes, and their main operations and relationships are shown in figure 3.

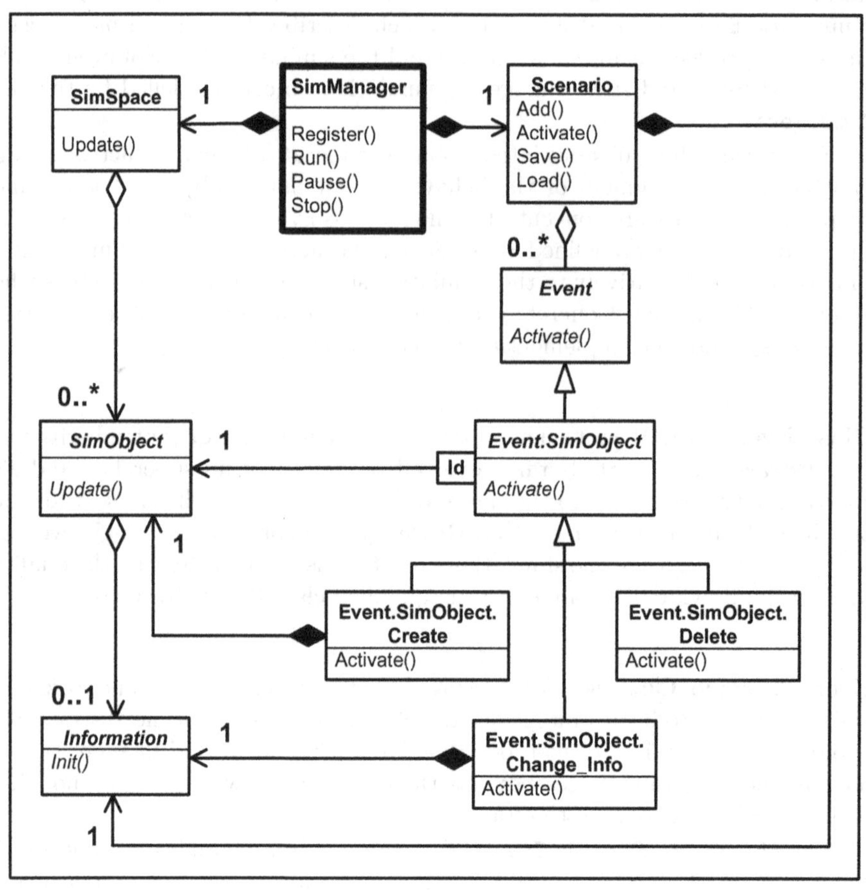

Fig. 3. Design of the Simulation Framework

5 Mapping of the Framework Design Description in UML to Ada95

After the design phase of the framework for discrete event simulation, the mapping of the classes found and their relationships documented in UML diagrams to the constructs of the programming language of choice, in this case Ada95 [ ], was the next step.

This section continues with a discussion of the mappings from UML constructs to Ada95 code idioms and examines the solutions found taking into consideration the requirements for this process found earlier.

The following general requirements for the mapping process have been identified:

- Uniformity and orthogonality of translation from design constructs to language idioms,
- simplicity of the overall approach,
- coverage of all relevant details in the UML constructs, and
- comprehensibility of the mapping.

The object-oriented concepts which are used in the design of the framework and had to be translated into Ada95 constructs are:

- Classes with their attributes and methods,
- inheritance,
- aggregations, and
- compositions.

Code Example for the Mapping. With the help of the following (incomplete) code fragment the mapping approach from object-oriented concepts to Ada95 idioms is explained in more detail.

Implementation of a class

```
package <ClassName> is
  type Public is abstract tagged
    record
       <public attributes>
    end record;
  type Object is [abstract] new Public with private;
  type Reference is access all Object'Class;
  type View is access constant Object'Class;
  <public methods>
  private
    type Object is [abstract] new Public with
      record
        <private attributes>
      end record;
    <private methods>
 end <ClassName>;
```

Classes. Single classes from the design model are implemented in single Ada packages. This is a coding convention which had to be followed by the framework implementer and satisfies the requirements for simplicity and comprehensibility.

All classes have the three types `Object`, `Reference`, and `View` (lines 6 to 8) in common.

The type `Object` is used in all class definitions to specify the class as a type. In case the class definition has private components, i.e. they are not visible from the outside, the type definition is implemented as a tagged record with a private extension (line 6). When the internal structure of type `Object` has to be visible from outside the scope of the package, it is defined as a abstract tagged record with public attributes (lines 2 to 5).

The main purpose of type `Reference` is to implement dynamic polymorphism using the Ada95 features for dynamic dispatching via class-wide types. In addition the internal structure of type `Object` can be accessed through establishing a pointer with type `Reference`. Its definition is shown in line 7.

Type `View` implements a restricted, read-only access type to `Object`. The definition of this type is given in line 8.

A main type defining the properties of the class is declared in the package. Additional types may be declared when there is a need to have references to and different views of the class.

Whenever inheritance relationships through subclassing have to be used, classes are implemented as tagged records.

Attributes. Attributes document the properties of a class. They have a type and one of the two access modes, public or private. The access mode determines whether a user of the class has direct access to the attribute or not.

The attributes of a class are implemented in Ada95 as record components. Depending on their visibility, attributes are declared as a type either in the public (lines 3 to 5) or the private part (lines 11 to 14).

Methods. Methods or operations realize the functionality of a class. Like attributes, they can either be public or private. Operations are implemented as procedures or functions and their declarations are allocated either in the public (line 9) or the private (line 15) part of the package depending on their visibility. Constant methods, i.e. methods which do only access internal values and not alter them, are implemented by using Ada's "in" parameters. To have a reference to the object in question, the input parameter "This" is used in every method invocation by convention.

Inheritance. Inheritance relationships are implemented with tagged records, similar to the realization of attributes. Only single inheritance is used in the case of the simulation framework, no provisions are made to implement multiple inheritance.

Aggregations and Compositions. The two remaining concepts of object-orientation which were used for the construction of the simulation framework, aggregations and compositions, are coded in the same way as attributes, so that the requirements for uniformity, orthogonality, and simplicity can be fulfilled.

Aggregations and compositions are seen as static associations which are defined at design time. Due to this fact, these relationships can be defined during object creation using the relevant classes taking part in the relationship. Furthermore, all associations, i.e. aggregations and compositions, are unidirectional by convention, no bidirectional relationships are allowed in design or implementation of the framework. The reason for this restriction is to keep the mapping of these concepts to Ada95 constructs simple and in accordance with attribute mapping described above. It also avoids circular relationships which introduce many complications both in designs and their implementation.

The unidirectional associations used in the design of the simulation framework can either be single (one-to-one) or multiple (one-to-many) relationships between two classes. According to [ ]and [ ], the aggregate or composite class is on the referencing side, the part class is on the referenced side of the relation.

In case of a single association, the part class is attached to the aggregate or the composite class via an attribute implemented in a record component within the aggregate or composite class which contains an exemplar of the part class' type `Reference`.

A single association is shown in the following, incomplete code example for the composite class `SimManager` and the part class `Scenario`.

Implementation of single associations

```
 with Scenario;
 package SimManager is
    type Object .....
    type Reference .....
    .....
 private
    type Object is record
       The_Scene : Scenario.Reference;
       .....
    end record;
    .....
end SimManager;
```

If a multiple association, the part classes are attached to the aggregate or composite class in a similar way as with the single association, except that the reference exemplars are kept in an appropriate data structure (e.g. list, set, map, etc.) controlled by the aggregate or composite class.

The following code fragment shows an example implementation of a multiple association for the aggregation class `Scenario` and the part class `Event`.

Implementation of multiple associations

```
with Event;
with SemaComp.Map;
package Scenario is
  .....
private
   package Event.Map is new
      SemaComp.Map(
         Key     => Duration,
         Element => Event.Reference);
   type Object is
      record
         .....
         Events : Event.Map.Object;
      end record;
      .....
  end Scenario;
```

6 Usage of the Framework

To give the reader an impression of how to apply the object-oriented framework for discrete event simulation described in this paper, this section summarizes its usage in a few sentences.

A programmer constructing a specific simulation application on the basis of the proposed framework firstly has to write a main program which instantiates objects from the concrete classes `SimManager`, `SimSpace`, and `Scenario`. This main program is also responsible for providing any interactions with an user and other entities like hardware appliances as input and output devices (e.g. displays, printers, and so on). The singular object simulation manager (instantiated from class `SimManager`) controls exactly one scenario and also has only one simulation space (objects instantiated from classes `Scenario` or `SimSpace`). The scenario object is linked to an object derived from class `Information` which comprises all necesarry information on the scenario.

In order to build a complete application, one or more concrete classes for simulation objects have to be derived from the abstract class `SimObject` by the application programmer using the framework. These concrete classes are then used to instantiate simulation objects as needed either during compile or run time. Similarily, the abstract class `Event.SimObject` is the basis for one or more concrete classes describing the events needed and providing the templates for event objects used in the simulation. For each event object an information object has to be instantiated from the concrete class `Information` and linked to it.

7 Lessons Learned and Open Issues

Drawing from the experience with analysis, design, construction, and usage of an object-oriented framework for discrete event simulation in Ada95, the following findings are noteworthy:

- The relevant entities and their relationships in the domain under consideration can be implemented in a framework once so that it was possible to reuse them efficiently in a number of different contexts.
- The development time for each new application was reduced significantly when applying the framework for a new simulation program.
- The design of the frameworks was revised several times to get to a solid and viable solution.
- It is possible to build a good object-oriented framework in Ada95.
- The completed framework gives guidance to the application programmer when putting together a new simulation program, but good documentation and examples are necessary for successful reuse.
- The framework lets an application programmer easily grasp the concepts of the domain and use them efficiently without being a domain expert, but again, good documentation is a must.
- A high degree of flexibility was gained through the use of an object-oriented framework in different solutions.
- The functionality of the framework grows incrementally when enhancing it iteratively.

Issues which could not be resolved during the project described in this paper are:

- The approach to the documentation of frameworks was insufficient and not clearly defined. It therefore needs more work.
- It is questionable if the approach to designing and implementing a relatively simple framework like the one described in this paper scales up to larger frameworks easily.
- The combination and cooperation of object-oriented frameworks is an area where more research has to be done.

Acknowledgements

The author wants to thank the anonymous reviewers, Leonor Barocca from Open University in the United Kingdom, and Michael Gonzalez Harbour from the University of Cantabria in Spain for their helpful comments and suggestions.

A special thank goes to his colleague Matthias Oltmanns for his support in this effort and the many discussions regarding design and implementation of the framework presented in this paper.

References

1. Booch, G., Rumbaugh, J., Jacobson, I.: The Unified Modeling Language User Guide, Addison-Wesley, Reading (1999)
2. Cotter, S., Patel, M.: Inside Taligent Technology, Addison-Wesley, Reading (1995)
3. Fayad, M., Johnson, R.: Domain-Specific Application Frameworks, Wiley, New York (1999)
4. Johnson, R., Foote, B.: Designing Reusable Classes, Journal of Object-Oriented Programming, Vol. 1 (1988), No. 2, (June) 22-35
5. Pree, W.: Design Patterns for Object-Oriented Software Development, Addison-Wesley, Wokingham (1994)
6. Prieto-Diaz, R., Arango, G.: Domain Analysis and Software System Modeling, IEEE Computer Society Press, Los Alamitos (1991)
7. Rumbaugh, J., Jacobson, I., Booch, G.: The Unified Modeling Language Reference Manual, Addison-Wesley, Reading (1999)
8. Taft, S.T., Duff, R. A.(Eds.): International Standard ISO/IEC 8652 Ada Reference Manual, Springer Verlag, Berlin, New York, Heidelberg (1997)
9. Taligent: The Power of Frameworks, Addison-Wesley, Reading (1995)
10. Wirfs-Brock, R., Wilkerson, B., Wiener, L.: Designing Object-Oriented Software, Prentice-Hall, Englewood Cliffs (1990)

MTS Integrating UML HOOD Ada in a Full Ada Operational Software Project

Thierry Lacomme, Séverine Carles, Agusti Canals, and François Normend

CS SI rue Villet Z I du Palays BP
TOULOUSE Cedex France
Phone Fax
thierry.lacomme@cisi.cnes.fr
severine.carles@cisi.cnes.fr
agusti.canals@cisi.fr

CNES Système pour l Observation de la Terre avenue Edouard Belin
TOULOUSE Cedex France
Phone Fax
francois.normend@cnes.fr

Abstract The development of the MTS simulator for the French space agency CNES proved to be a very enriching experience as regards the integration of UML HOOD and Ada in an operational project Developing a full Ada project using the UML formalism and the HOOD method for the analysis and design phases respectively was a challenge that we were successful in meeting Our results provide important guidelines for the future design of software appli cations of this type UML was used for the analysis phase HOOD for the de sign phase and generation of an Ada code skeleton Great intrinsic development security was achieved as a result of this technical integration

Introduction

This goal of this project was the development of the MTS Mémoire Tampon Statique = Static Buffer Memory simulator This paper begins with a brief overview of the project itself and of the present day status of the MTS software It then describes the specific features of the development of the application

This entails explaining the way in which the UML method was applied to project analysis the design was established using the HOOD method and the Ada language was used to develop code

A section detailing what we learned from this experience outlines the advantages and disadvantages of this technology as perceived by the development team over the

UML Unified Modelling Language http www rhein neckar de ~cetus oo_uml html

Hierarchical Object Oriented Design Version
http www rhein neckar de ~cetus oo_ooa_ood_methods html oo_methods_hood

H B Keller and E Plödereder Eds Ada Europe LNCS pp

course of the project. The conclusion offers suggestions for future improvements worth investigating and provides ideas on better applying our experience to other projects.

Management of the MTS Simulator

The MTS

The MTS is the memory of the SPOT and HELIOS satellites. It allows frame files[1] to be recorded. Recording is checked by mission instructions. This project was developed for CNES and is a small segment of a larger project called EGM (Ensemble Gestion Mission) which will manage the mission aspect of the satellite after it has been launched. We used the development of this MTS simulator to prepare method aspects using UML notation for analysis, the HOOD method for design and the Ada language. The lessons we learned from this experience will be applied to develop the complete EGM. In the text, use of the term "MTS" indicates the physical MTS equipment and the term "MTS simulator" refers to our computer program.

Current Status

The development of the MTS simulator has been completed and CNES is now using the resulting image files to find a better means of controlling the MTS. If MTS management can be improved, we will update our code.

MTS Description

The MTS allows:

- to record and to restore frame files;
- to write, read or write and read a frame file simultaneously;
- to activate only a part of the MTS if the storage of frame files requires little space, in order to minimise electrical consumption;
- to move frame files within the MTS to not activate a part of the MTS;
- to check itself if a problem occurs.

Input and output interfaces of the MTS simulator are described in the figure.

In a given context, the MTS simulator processes a plan of work with directives. If during processing errors occur, the logbook reports these errors.

It is thus possible to trace the error back to its source. If processing is correct, simulator results and final context are generated.

A logbook is generated in all cases. The MTS simulator is a good means of checking plans of work and directives files before sending the reports to the satellite.

[1] a frame file is a file which contains a satellite video frame

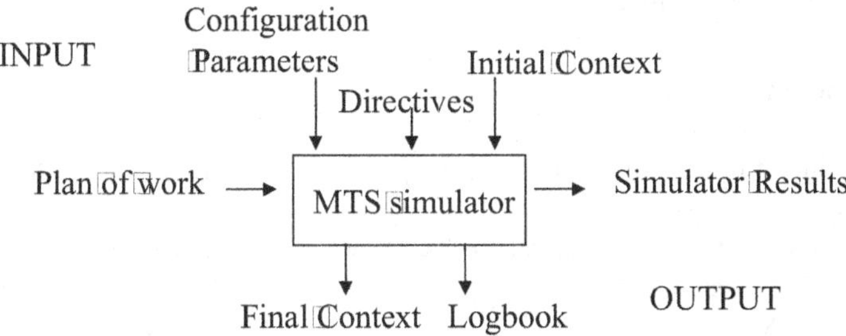

Fig [illegible] Diagram of Input and Output Interfaces of the MTS simulator

[illegible] Project Profile

[illegible] Team

The development team was composed of [illegible] people an experienced technical engineer and a novice technical engineer This team did not have extensive experience using the methods and language needed for the project We thus relied on a HOOD and Ada expert for support for the beginning and design phases of the project A quality engineer checked work and provided notes to describe the use of the new methods and the language thus defining a quality environment and at the same time preparing the quality environment for the future developments using the same technology and methodology The project was entirely developed within the Earth Observation Directorate of CS SI under the authority of a project manager

[illegible] Time Schedule

The development cycle of the MTS simulator spanned from June [illegible] to February [illegible] The development might have been finished by December [illegible] but our team chose to take the time necessary to learn the new methods and improve our use of these methods in order to establish a good environment for future projects

[illegible] Volume Code

The total volume of instructions that was produced about [illegible] instructions can be broken down as follows

- less than [illegible] of the instructions is reused code for the lists
- about [illegible] of the instructions is reused and adapted for the date management software and the logbook already employed by CNES
- the code skeleton was generated automatically
- the remainder was developed by our team

The Development Cycle

Introduction

The development cycle followed on the project was a classic V cycle adapted for this kind of project.

The development environment chosen is described below:

- a HP calculator,
- an OS HP UX,
- an Ada compiler version a followed by b from GNAT,
- STOOD from TNI (Techniques Nouvelles d'Information) to implement HOOD,
- ROSE from Rational to implement UML,
- SODA from Rational to have the Rose documentation with a Word format.

It is important to know that ROSE and STOOD can ensure the entire development cycle (from the preliminary design phase through coding and tests (an object's unit test procedures are included in the object itself) to integration and finally validation). With the client's input, we chose to develop the analysis phase with UML, and to continue with HOOD. Guarantee and maintenance modifications were ensured and will, in the future, may be handled by STOOD.

The Keeping Track of the Project

Author Reader Cycle for Analysis

The analysis phase included an author and reader specific cycle (see Figure) that was established by setting up two loops of this type.

The first loop was an internal CS SI loop and involved the CS SI expert assigned to the project, while the second external loop was for CNES and involved the CNES project technical leader.

Each cycle entailed cross reading an analysis output and discussing the reader's remarks to then take into account comments.

Follow Up after Analysis

At the end of the design and coding phases, "key point" meetings with CNES were set to track progress on the project (See Figure). At each key point, CNES remarks were studied by the CS SI team and were incorporated into the project. An author and reader cycle halfway through the design phase and the coding phase, was introduced to check proper advancement of the project and to ensure that HOOD and Ada rules were being respected (See Figure).

---

a STOOD evaluation kit is available: http://www.tni.fr

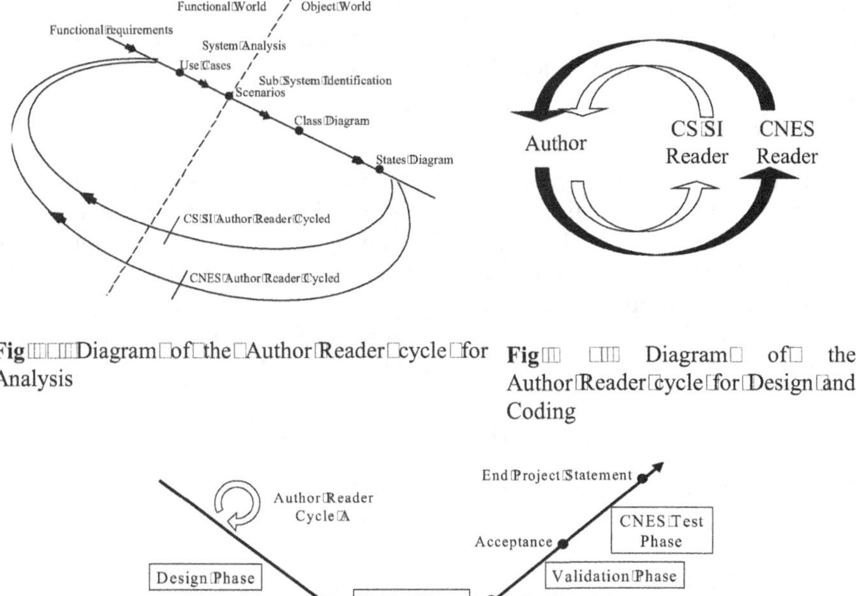

Fig Diagram of the Author Reader cycle for Analysis

Fig Diagram of the Author Reader cycle for Design and Coding

Fig Diagram of the V Cycle

These two author reader cycles had the same structure and were put into practice by setting up two loops the first was an internal CS SI loop which involved the CS SI HOOD Ada expert assigned to the project and the second dark arrow in conjunction with CNES involved both the CNES HOOD Ada expert and the CNES project technical leader

After the validation phase an acceptance meeting with CNES was held to review step by step all validation cases Upon completion of each phase the STOOD database was entered in the CS SI configuration base and was delivered to CNES After acceptance CNES took the time to check code with specific tests and at the end of this phase the entire project was delivered to CNES specifically the STOOD database the code validation tests and notes that define the project Additionally the numerous progress meetings between the technical team and the project manager allowed technical and scheduling advancement to be monitored

Analysis

An analysis method with UML did not already exist and therefore the CS SI team developed a process to obtain a complete development cycle with the UML object notation This method UML CS SI is described in the articles entitled Use of UML

CS SI development process [ ] and Use of Cisi UML development process [ ] CNES was very specific in its specifications for the MTS simulator and thus the class and actor for the system were identified from the outset

Use Cases Definition

After identification of the system actor the MTS activity must be described with use cases These use cases See figure allow system behaviour to be defined in order to prepare the validation tests This task was relatively simple thanks to the precise description of MTS management in the specifications The diagrams below illustrate a use case that was identified for the MTS system One user runs the Simulation use case as the use case diagram indicates and the sequence diagram defines a system behaviour scenario The chosen scenario has a nominal ending

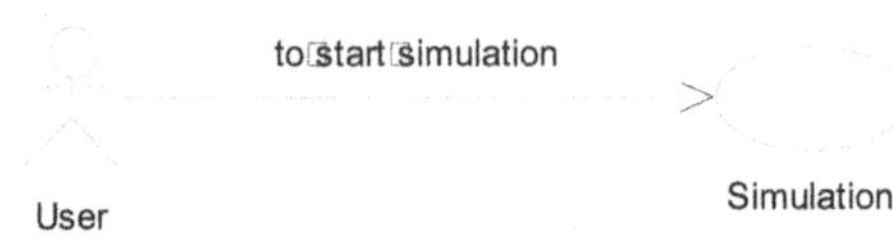

Fig Example of a use case

For this scenario See figure one actor who is the user and seven objects are identified the pilot the servitude directives the sequences Sequence and Sequence the MTS the logbook and the results There are two sequences Sequence and Sequence which are two instances of the same Sequence object A sequence is a group of requests In this scenario nominal simulation takes place with two sequences containing three requests

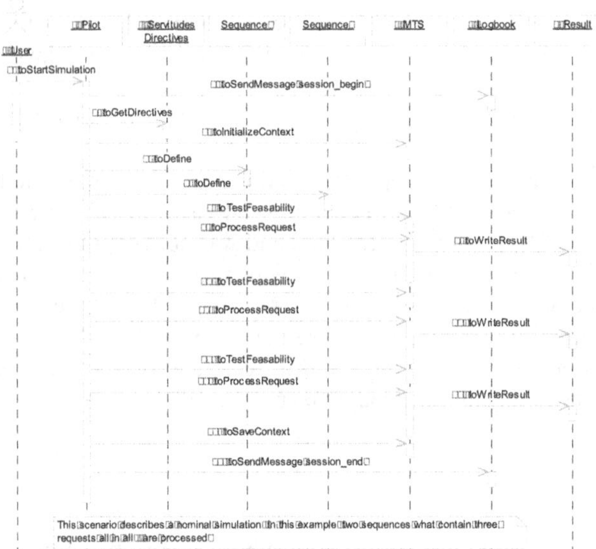

Fig Example of sequence diagram from the preceding use case

Class Diagram

After defining the use cases, we defined the class diagram to present the classes identified from the scenarios and from to MTS specifications (See figure) to present the relationships between these classes. Each link between two classes is closely studied to accurately define the system and to refine it. This activity is very difficult as the link name must be extremely explicit in order to correspond MTS specifications.
The classes had to be laid out and one class represented the conductor list, giving its name to the package. For example, in the diagram below, the MTS is the conductor. The pilot runs the simulation and the MTS asks the request class to process the request, the result class to generate results, and the memory class to manage memory.

Sub-system Definition

We then decided to group the classes into coherent sub-systems (See figure) with few relationships in order to prepare the HOOD design and the definition of the first HOOD architecture. In our application, we identified three sub-systems: Simulator, Logbook and MTS and they are packaged as follows.
The class diagram without the "Pilot" and the "Logbook" classes represents the MTS sub-system, the "Pilot" class and the "Logbook" class represent respectively the Simulator package and the Logbook package.

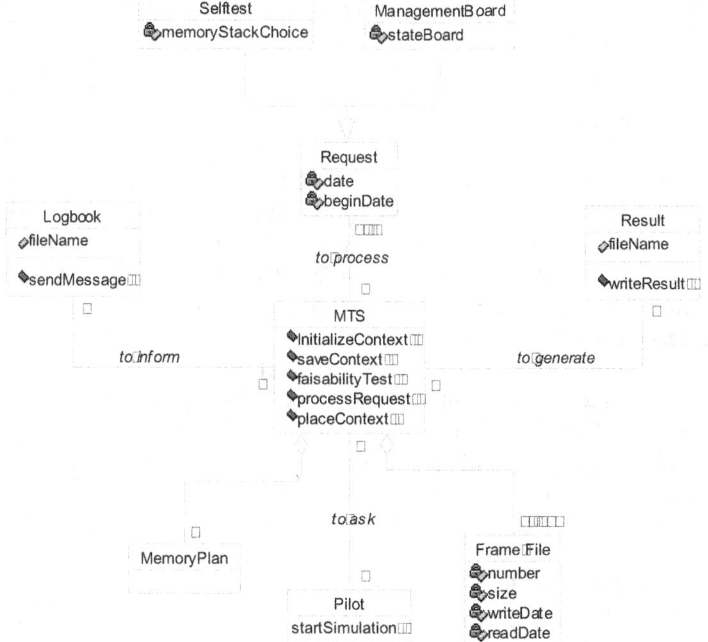

Fig. Example of class diagram

The project dimensions were relatively small and it was thus desirable to break the project down into classes about instead of into sub systems The identification and naming of the packages was rather simple but situating certain classes in a package proved a more difficult task The final development of our application would most likely be the same even if these classes were to be in the simulator package rather than the MTS package

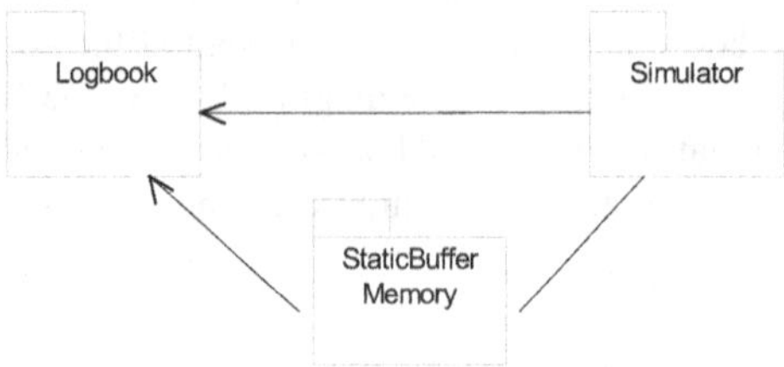

Fig Example of a dependency diagram

Re buckling Phase

The more a system is complex the more the development team must concentrate on the re buckling phase with the client As our project is not overly complex the analysis phase was short and only one re buckling phase was necessary The CNES re read and accepted our analysis notes

Design Phase

Once the analysis is done with the UML CS SI process we can choose either the HOOD or the UML notation for the design and the use in both cases UML CS SI In our case the customer proposes HOOD the target language is Ada the team experience was low but the HOOD support tool STOOD is very efficient The Stood tool is more efficient ten year use than the UML support tools and in particular for Ada code generation and for the model checking

HOOD is a design method that proposes a hierarchical decomposition of software into units based on identification of objects classes and operations reflecting problem domain entities The HOOD method includes textual and associated graphical representation allowing for formal refinement automated checking user customisable documentation generation and target language source code generation In this hierarchical decomposition the head is called root module and the stood tool uses the same notation

The use of UML made the beginning of the design phase simple The analysis phase allowed the important classes that would become the STOOD objects to be defined and the UML packages would become the STOOD roots The architecture of the MTS STOOD base began with seven roots See figure and other roots ap

a re buckling phase is an iteration phase with clients

peared to provide functional and type structural means The MTS UML package be came the management MTS gestion MTS root in the following environment
In this "parent functional diagram" of STOOD See figure the MANAGEMENT MTS root has the role of conductor list in the system configuration view This view allows the roots used by the MANAGEMENT MTS root to be displayed We rec ognise flows already identified in analysis as error flow between the MTS and the logbook
Usually each data flow has a name but we did not have enough place in the STOOD diagram to do this The "Simulator" root does not appear in this diagram as it uses the "MANAGEMENT MTS" root The "Request" root would normally be in the "MAN AGEMENT MTS" root but the design phase allowed us to move it elsewhere Also the "Configuration" root was added during the design phase Some roots such as "Time" were reused and adapted from other projects The root "Files SR " was created to interface with a reused archive in C for writing and reading of UNIX files At the end of the design phase analysis classes generally become the STOOD object and the inheritance s links are preserved

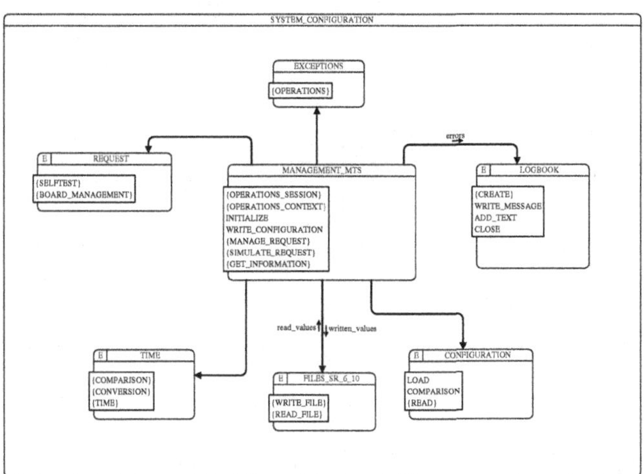

Fig Example of a stood parent functional diagram

The figures and that follow are the break down of the "Request" root
This root contains two modules a class named Abstract_Request that allows the abstract type A_Abstract_Request to be defined and a module Servi tudes_Requetes that contains two classes "Selftest" and "Management Board" de rived from the class "A_ Abstract_Request" A class appears in the Stood diagram as a box with square edges versus an object that appears as a box with rounded corners
The A_Selftest and A_Management_Board types are inherited from the A_Abstract_Request type The_Stack_Memory type is an attribute of the A_Selftest type

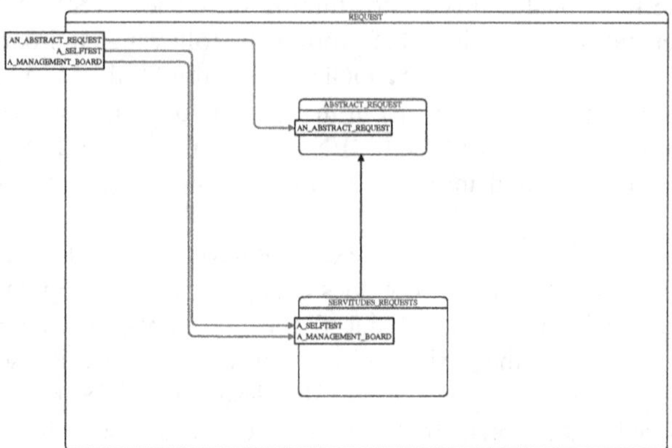

Fig Example of the parent structural diagram for Servitudes Request object

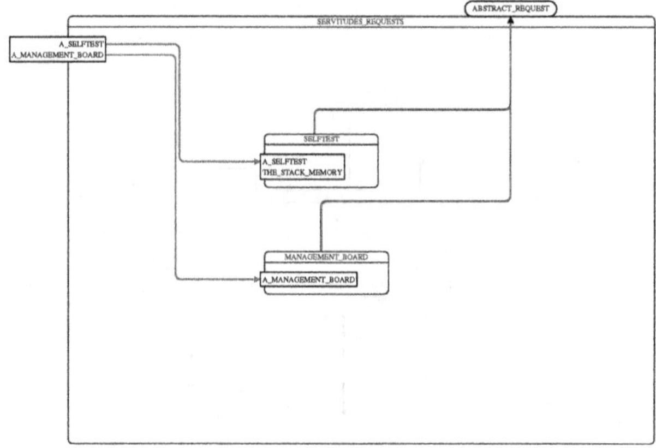

Fig Example of a stood structural diagram for SelfTest class

We decided to use Philippe Pichon s results [ ] and so did not use pseudo code As far as we are concurred the operation text description is sufficient for the operations list to be understood

The code was easily generated by STOOD At the end of this stage the application skeleton was completed and the development team had only to develop the operational body

At this point the project had been precisely defined and reports on hierarchical STOOD object cutting had been rapidly generated using STOOD and presented to CNES during a "key point" meeting This phase took more time than we had initially planned as the time necessary to precisely describe each function each procedure and the strategy chosen for objects and data exchange between objects was appreciable Our application contains objects for three hierarchical levels ten of which are classes

Coding

While design is established in a descending fashion coding is accomplished in an ascending fashion in order to optimise the integration phase Both developers wrote the MTS code It is possible to develop code in STOOD or without STOOD but using VI or EMACS editors
When functions or operations are being coded STOOD reversing allows code to be taken from the STOOD base In this way the project is continually updated STOOD reversing is very interesting as reversing is fast and very reliable
At the end of the project it was possible to generate the complete application from the STOOD base in five minutes and each structure of this code was inserted accompanied by a descriptive text
At the same time we were able to obtain a complete and updated documentation on the project in a few minutes To obtain such a result coding rules must be respected The STOOD keywords must never be destroyed during coding
For example an operation body must always be situated between the beginning and ending keywords of STOOD The cross reference a STOOD tool allows both design consistency and code to be checked
Most aspects of the Ada language were used including the interface between C and Ada as we reused a library written in C but excluding the package on memory allocation and signal management

Development Environment

Compilation with the Ada compiler GNAT a was practical because after a bad compilation a message appears describing the problem and the element required to solve it We used GNATMAKE which allows selective compilation to be performed
This tool is also practical to use as it performs compilation only after modifications to the code are made No “make file” procedure is required
However the use of a standard environment for debugging was not practical at all
Moreover the environment of the GNAT b with an easy to use MMI seems a better solution but this version came out after the coding period was already completed and so was not tested
To check memory PURIFY software was used We also used the GNATMEM tool but program execution was halted without reason
Finally we used GPROF for performance control but the compilation with the –pg addition found a segmentation error for of compilation units
After coding each object was checked with a unit test We began with self sufficient objects and finished with objects that require other objects in order to function The integration test was thus implicit

Testing and Validation

We used three unit test means
– a formalism which was developed at CS SI to test algorithmic objects

– the same formalism to test groups of objects as most of these objects define only structures and do not have associated coding,
– a main program asks for the operations of the object that writes the resulting files.

A classic validation plan followed to check the complete program. This validation phase was rapid, as most errors had previously been corrected during the unitary test phase.

Our Experience

UML

UML is a formalism and as such, must be adapted for each task. We used "UML-CS-SI" method that describes the analysis phase. Our usage was very well adapted.
With UML, the system description can easily be very detailed and the user must be particularly careful so as to produce an analysis document and not a detailed conception document. Fully aware of this problem, the "UML-CS-SI" method provides solutions in order to stay at an expected analysis or design level.

HOOD

The use of this method for our project did not pose any problem and the descending decomposition allowed us to ask the right questions at each stage. For this method, the object and functional approach can be employed and this is indeed very useful for the design phase.
The use of private types is recommended to obtain hidden structures from outside and therefore many operations and functions must be created to allow for data exchange between objects. As a result, we had a large number of functions and operations.
Because object decomposition is hierarchical, an object must sometimes use the functional list of its parent object to create consistency between objects in this hierarchical level. As far as we are concerned, this is not entirely natural but it is efficient. We did not use states diagrams and signal formalism (SYN, ASYN), so we will not address these parts of the method here.
We used classes but only to introduce aspects of inheritance into our project. Our classes were not dynamic, simple structures but they allowed us to simplify the design of the MTS simulator as more concept description may be used when object concepts are tolerated and the simplest structure is chosen from among the structures available.
The product information documents present the complete project but the volume can be too great if a descriptive approach is used to minimise the volume documents.
Generally, this HOOD method seems to be adapted to a multi-developer development for this type of project and it allows object design and functional design to be interchanged.
In HOOD, the notion of object is the basic structure of organisation: a object can be a module or a class. This particularity allows to obtain more solutions to find a design

for a problem. If we would have used UML for the design phase, we would have only obtained classes.
In C++, the notion of class is the basic structure of language organisation. In other hand, in Ada, it is the notion of package. A package can be a module or a class. Thus HOOD is well adapted to develop with Ada.

Ada

This language appears to be quite powerful even if certain of its functions were not used. We did not encounter any problems and the object formalism was satisfactory.
The automatic management of dynamic memory during the array definition (whose dimension is defined only upon execution) is an interesting characteristic of the language. The conversion from an enumerated structure to a character chain is useful and the type control is useful for compilation checking.
For C, the possibility to code and decode files was lacking, but using an adapted algorithm, we were able to obtain the desired result. The interface between Ada and the C language is possible and does not pose any problems.
We had already encountered roots developed with Ada 83 for other projects. We obtained a practical mix of classes and modules to define coding solutions. If we had chosen to use the C++ language, we would have only obtained a group of classes. On the whole, this language is very well suited to developing a HOOD design and the coding phase was quick and provided satisfactory results.

Tools

The ROSE tool is attractive and it implements many of the UML formalism concepts. But support materials could be better and are not very personalised. The training phase for Rose 98 is somewhat long. Moreover the use of SoDA tools is necessary for generating documents in a WORD format.
Documents for learning SODA tool are not of much interest but when the user knows macros, this tools allows all possible documents to be generated from ROSE. Unfortunately the generated WORD document is linked to its ROSE model by an absolute path and so it is not possible to open the generated WORD document in any directory. It is therefore necessary to eliminate links between SODA diagrams and the WORD document.
At first, the STOOD tool's graphical interface appeared somewhat outdated when compared to other, more current tools. For example, the data flows between objects were not displayed in our STOOD diagrams because we did not have enough space. In addition, the reference manual (at the time of development) was suitable for using the tools' different windows but was unsuitable for configuration purposes.
Some positive points are that:

- the hot line is highly reactive,
- the use of the tool is simple and access to information is rapid,
- the tool is easy to configure (to be adapted to the project or to add externals tools).

The structure of the information managed by STOOD one ASCII file per rubric is interesting as regards the use of external tools and for configuration management This structure allows the evolution of the database' different elements to be followed The reverse works very well and with a solid configuration it is possible to reverse new objects that were not in the first design
The STOOD tool includes very useful internal tools such as Cross Ref which en sure total consistency It is even possible to generate documents in several formats
It is very important to note that at the end of the project our code exactly mirrors the design and that the Ada code can be entirely generated using the STOOD tool
To conclude we preferred working with an open tool like STOOD that was able to be very readily adapted to the project rather than with other tools that may seem more attractive but which require many man hours for configuration

Traceability

Two traceability matrices were created for this project to show compliance between specifications and the analysis result document and specifications and the design result document The idea of creating two matrices for the same project may seem question able but this solution helped to finalise two development phases that did not share the same method Design traceability is useful in evaluating how specification changes affect code as objects that are improved are clearly identified

Conclusion

Our team was skilled in Ada and HOOD techniques but up to now had never inte grated object concepts into this type of project After developing the MTS simulator we realised that it is feasible to introduce class notions into a project with little trou ble We managed to install a UML notation for analysis and a HOOD notation for design both with UML CS SI method Design is always updated with code even after corrections and modifications and the project database is easily accessible by the CNES team In conclusion after a such project we now have the means and have been successful in developing a project using UML HOOD and Ada At this time another project with the same size is currently in development with this approach and we hope to start soon a third project very important in size MTS

References

Canals A *Use of "UML CS SI" development process* from Dasia'

Canals A and Bernard Y *Use of "Cisi UML development process" on GEDYS Project* from <<UML>>' International Workshop

Pichon P CCO MARS Integrating HOOD Ada and XinAda in a full Ada Operational Software Project from Reliable Software Technologies Ada Europe

Symbolic Data Flow Analysis for Detecting Deadlocks in Ada Tasking Programs

Johann Blieberger[1], Bernd Burgstaller[1], and Bernhard Scholz[2]

[1] Department of Computer-Aided Automation, Technical University of Vienna
Treitlstr. 1,A-1040 Vienna, Austria
{blieb,bburg}@auto.tuwien.ac.at

[2] Institute of Computer Languages, Technical University of Vienna
Argentinierstr. 8, A-1040 Vienna, Austria
scholz@complang.tuwien.ac.at

Abstract. It is well accepted that designing and analyzing concurrent software-components are tedious tasks. Assuring the quality of such software requires formal methods, which can statically detect deadlocks. This paper presents a symbolic data flow analysis framework for detecting deadlocks in Ada programs with tasks. The symbolic data flow framework is based on symbolic evaluation – an advanced technique to statically determine properties of programs.

The framework can guarantee the deadlock-freeness for an arbitrary hardware environment. Our approach differs from existing work in that tasks can be dynamically created and completed in the program. Examples are used to illustrate our approach.

1 Introduction

Modern software design includes concurrent programming, such as tasks, to enable the explicit expression of parallelism. Concurrent language constructs increase the expressiveness of a language in the description of concurrency. However, it is widely agreed that designing and programming a concurrent system are tedious tasks and can result in erroneous program behavior. Such anomalies are particular hard to detect as it is usually very difficult to reproduce them and to identify the source of the error. Clearly, it is of paramount importance to detect program anomalies in concurrent systems at compile time as compared to expensively testing programs at runtime. A static analysis tool that targets the detection of concurrent program anomalies supports the design and programming and improves the quality of the software.

In this paper we introduce a new static analysis framework to detect deadlocks and other tasking anomalies without executing the program. Our static analysis is based on symbolic evaluation – an advanced static analysis technique – in which symbolic expressions are used to denote the values of program variables and computations and a path condition describes the impact of the program's control flow onto the values of variables.

Our method goes beyond previous work in the following points:

H. B. Keller and E. Plödereder (Eds.): Ada-Europe 2000, LNCS 1845, pp. 225– , 2000.

1. The number of tasks in the program is not limited, it can grow dynamically during the execution of the tasking program. We can handle an arbitrary number of tasks, which can be dynamically created and completed in the program.
2. We analyze each task body only once, although several instances of the task can be created either statically (e.g. arrays of tasks) or dynamically by new statements.
3. Our framework correctly analyzes generic units.

To ease the analysis we assume that no global variable is read/written by different tasks (no shared variables). If such a variable is needed, a protected object has to be employed.

The remainder of the paper is organized as follows. In Section we give the notions of the symbolic data flow analysis for detecting deadlocks. In Section our approach is presented. Examples are used to illustrate our framework. In Section we survey related work. In Section we conclude this paper and describe future work.

2 Symbolic Evaluation

Symbolic evaluation is an advanced static program analysis in which symbolic expressions are used to denote the values of program variables and computations (cf. e.g. [ ]). A path condition describes the impact of the program's control flow onto the values of variables and the condition under which control flow reaches a given program point. In the past symbolic evaluation has been successfully applied to the reaching definitions problem [ ], to worst-case execution time analysis [ ], to cache hit prediction [ ], to alias analysis [ ], to optimization problems of High-Performance Fortran [ ], and to pointer analysis for detecting memory leaks [ ].

The underlying program representation for symbolic evaluation is the *control flow graph (CFG)*, a directed labelled graph. Its nodes are basic blocks containing the program statements, whereas its edges represent transfers of control between basic blocks. Each edge of the CFG is assigned a condition which must evaluate to true for the program's control flow to follow this edge. *Entry* and *Exit* are distinguished nodes used to denote start and terminal node.

In the center of our symbolic analysis is the *program context*, which includes *states* S_i and *state conditions* C_i. A program context completely describes the variable bindings at a specific program point together with the associated state conditions and is defined as $\bigcup_{i=1}^{k}[S_i, C_i]$, where k denotes the number of different program states. State S is represented by a set of pairs $\{(v_1, e_1), \ldots, (v_m, e_m)\}$ where v_i is a program variable, and e_i is a symbolic expression describing the value of v_i for $1 \leq i \leq m$. For each variable v_i there exists exactly one pair (v_i, e_i) in S. A state condition C_i specifies a condition that is valid for a given state S_i at a certain program point.

For all nodes in the CFG, a set of symbolic equations is used to compute program contexts. The equation system is solved by an elimination algorithm for data flow analysis [ ].

3 Symbolic Data Flow Equations for Tasking Programs

In previous work [, , ,] we have applied symbolic analysis for sequential programs. In order to analyze Ada programs with tasks we need a new form of analysis to cope with these notions of parallelism. To get a handle on the problem a new program representation, namely the *tasking control flow graph* (TCFG), is introduced which models the semantic behavior of concurrent Ada programs. In the following, semantics and the construction of TCFGs are discussed. Then, the symbolic equations for the program contexts are given and illustrated by two examples.

To symbolically analyze Ada programs with tasks, we are confronted with three major problems to model tasking correctly:

1. How do we handle dynamically allocated tasks?
2. If several entry calls are served by one accept statement, how can we ensure that control flow proceeds at the correct place?
3. According to the semantics of Ada tasks, a task is allowed to complete only if all its descendants have completed or are "waiting" at a select statement with a terminate alternative. How do we ensure this behavior?

Problem is solved by introducing symbolic *task identifiers* (task ids). Each task object is assigned a unique task id at creation time. Such a task id can in its simplest way be realized as a symbolic counter, that is incremented whenever a task is created. (In fact we propose a different counter for each task type, but this does not show up in the examples.) All local variables of a task object and other local objects such as even tasks or protected objects can be referenced uniquely with help of this task id. We denote such objects by $v[id]$, which are modelled as symbolic arrays [,].

Concerning problem we notice that entry calls are different from procedure calls because tasks have a *state*. A procedure call can be modelled by a suitable copy of the procedure with actual parameters supplied accordingly [ ]. In contrast, we solve Problem by introducing a symbolic variable $E_n[id]$ for accept statement n which is indexed by the task id of the calling task. The variable is assigned the value r if this is the rth entry call to n. We ensure that the control flow that enters n is propagated to the correct successor after the rendezvous by assigning condition $E_n[id] = r$ to the control flow from the end of the rendezvous to the correct successor.

In order to solve Problem , we introduce variable T_t if one or more instances of task t are created in statement d. The purpose of T_t is similar to that of $E_n[id]$ above in ensuring that if several tasks are created at different places in the program, their completion is awaited at the correct place. In addition, for each created task (with task identifier equal to id) we introduce a symbolic variable $C_{d,t}[id]$ which is initialized to 1. If the task completes or may complete because of a terminate alternative, this variable is set to 0 and the condition $C_{d,t}[id] = 0$ is checked at an appropriate program point to ensure that each created task ultimately completes.

3.1 Building the CFG Tasking Forest

To build the TCFG, for each task body and for the main program a CFG is constructed at first. The result is a *CFG tasking forest.*

1. In a task body each accept statement is a subgraph of the (task) CFG with one designated "header node".
2. There may be several (at least one) "end nodes" of a rendezvous according to the construction of a CFG.
3. A select statement of the callee is modelled like a case statement with the only difference that all conditions from the "header" to the "cases" are *true*. Select statements with a terminate alternative are described in Section .
4. Select statements of the caller are modelled like if-statements.

3.2 Building the Tasking CFG from the CFG Tasking Forest

Then, based on the CFG tasking forest we can construct the TCFG. Note that if ordinary control flow is indicated by a TCFG edge, we call this edge *control flow edge.* If the edge of the TCFG represents an entry call, an entry return, task creation or task completion, we call the edge *tasking edge.* Furthermore, we distinguish between kinds of TCFG nodes according to the following criteria:

1. If no tasking edge points to node n, we call n "control flow node".
2. One or more tasking edges point to node n which models an accept statement. Then n is called "header node" of a rendezvous.
3. One or more tasking edges point to the "start node" of a task, which is equal to the entry node of the CFG modelling the corresponding task body.
4. One or more tasking edges point from the end nodes of a rendezvous to the successor nodes of an entry call node ("entry successor node").
5. One or more tasking edges point from the original exit node of the task CFG to the exit node of the parent task. We call the latter exit node "synchronizing node" because all dependent tasks synchronize at this node before the parent task is allowed to complete.

The CFG tasking forest is now glued together to create the TCFG, which models the whole tasking program. This is done by inserting (dashed) tasking edges between certain nodes of the CFGs forming the forest and by removing certain (solid) control flow edges. The TCFG is build according to the following rules:

- For node n being the target of a tasking-related action:
  - Let id denote the task id of the calling task which in its simplest way can be realized by incrementing a symbolic counter each time a task is created statically or dynamically. Introduce variable $E_n[id]$ and initialize it to 0 when the called task is created. Set the value of $E_n[id]$ to r if this is the rth tasking edge pointing to n.
  - Insert a tasking edge (a dashed arrow) from the caller to the corresponding start node of the rendezvous.
  - Insert a tasking edge from all end nodes of the rendezvous to all entry successors nodes and assign the condition $(E_n[id] = r)$ to these edges.
  - Remove the control flow edges from the entry call node to its (control flow) successors.
- If one or more instances of task t are created in node d:
  - Introduce the variables T_t and for each created task $C_{d,t}[id]$ (T_t is initialized to 0, $C_{d,t}[id]$ to 1).
  - Create an intermediate node i_{dt} and insert tasking edges from d to i_{dt} and from i_{dt} to t. In addition, node i_{dt} is used to assign r to T_t if this is the rth tasking edge pointing to t.
  - Create an intermediate node between each exit node of task t and the synchronizing node of its parent. Similarly, create an intermediate node between all headers of a select statement with a terminate alternative and the synchronizing node of its parent.
  - Insert tasking edges to and from the intermediate node. In addition, the intermediate node is used to assign 0 to $C_{d,t}[id]$, the edge leading to the intermediate node is assigned the condition $(T_t = r)$ and the edge leaving the intermediate node is assigned the condition $(C_{d,t}[id] = 0)$.

3.3 Setting Up the Data Flow Equations

The symbolic equation system of concurrent Ada programs is given in this subsection. The equations are derived from the TCFG.

Let $C^c_{n' \to n}$ denote the symbolic condition of control flow edge $e^c = n' \to n$ and similarly $C^t_{n' \to n}$ the symbolic condition of tasking flow edge $e^t = n' \to n$. Furthermore, we denote the control flow predecessors of node n by $\text{Pred}^c(n)$ and the tasking flow predecessors by $\text{Pred}^t(n)$. We define the symbolic equations as follows:

1. If node n is a control flow node, we have

$$X_n = \left(\bigvee_{n' \in \text{Pred}^c(n)} (X_{n'} \wedge C^c_{n' \to n}) \right) \mid \{\ldots\}.$$

2. If node n is a header node, a start node, or an entry successor node, we define

$$X_n = \left(\bigvee_{n' \in \mathrm{Pred}^c(n)} (X_{n'} \wedge C^c_{n' \to n}) \right) \wedge$$
$$\left(\text{false} \vee \bigvee_{n' \in \mathrm{Pred}^t(n)} (X_{n'} \wedge C^t_{n' \to n} \wedge \mathrm{Guard}(n)) \right) \mid \{\ldots\},$$

where Guard(n) denotes a guard condition of an accept statement. Guard(n) is considered to be true if no guard condition is present or in case of start or entry successor nodes.
Note that if n is a header node and there is no entry call for this entry, then X_n = false.
3. If node n is a synchronizing node, we have

$$X_n = \left(\bigvee_{n' \in \mathrm{Pred}^c(n)} (X_{n'} \wedge C^c_{n' \to n}) \right) \wedge \left(\bigwedge_{n' \in \mathrm{Pred}^t(n)} (X_{n'} \wedge C^t_{n' \to n}) \right) \mid \{\ldots\},$$

The $\{\ldots\}$-part is supposed to contain the local changes to program variables in the same way as is described in [, ,].

Note that X_n means "non-blocking" at node n. If, after solving the equations and binding the – until now unbound – task identifiers of task t (id_t) by prepending $\bigwedge_t \bigwedge_{id_t}$ to all conditions, all X_n evaluate to true, then there is no deadlock in the tasking program. If some of the conditions do not evaluate to true, it has to be checked by hand whether

- there is a deadlock,
- there are some program paths with a false condition because the program is not supposed to terminate (this is typical for embedded systems), or
- there are some accept statements which are never called in the program.

3.4 A Simple Example

For sake of demonstration we have chosen a fairly simple Ada program with one task. Figure (a) lists the source code. The task consists of two accept statements. In the main program the two entry calls **Two** and **One** are invoked in subsequent order. In Figure (b) the TCFG of the Ada source is shown. Nodes 1, 2, 3, 4, and 5 correspond to statements of the Ada program. Nodes 6 and 7 are intermediate nodes introduced to model tasking correctly. Based on the semantic rules given in Subsection and artificial variables ($C_{e,4}[1]$, T_4, $E_4[1]$, and $E_5[1]$) are introduced and the TCFG of Figure (b) is amended by the following additional conditions and statements:

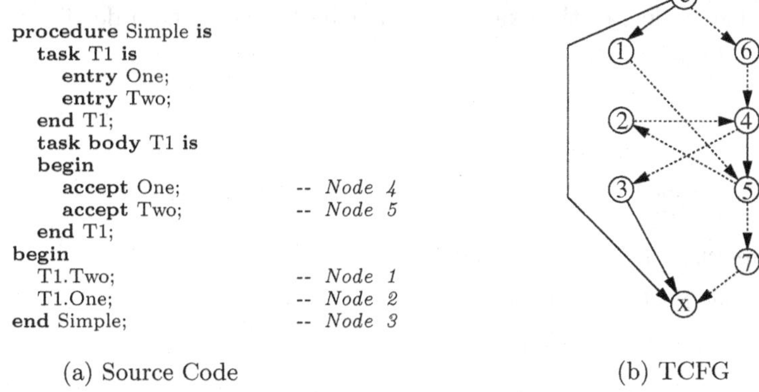

(a) Source Code

(b) TCFG

Fig. 1. Simple Deadlock Example

- $C_{\mathrm{e},4}[1] := 1$ in node e due to the fact that one task with task id 1 is created.
- $C_{\mathrm{e},4}[1] := 0$ in node 7 since the task is completed in this node.
- $E_5[1] := 1$ in node 1 and $E_4[1] := 1$ in node 2 represent call entries of node 1 and 2 respectively.
- Except task edge $4 \to 3$, $5 \to 2$, $5 \to 7$, and $7 \to \mathrm{x}$ the conditions of the task edges are set to true.
- Task edge $5 \to 2$ and task edge $4 \to 3$ get the condition $E_5[1] = 1$ and $E_4[1] = 1$, respectively.
- Task edge $5 \to 7$ gets assigned the condition $T_4 = 1$.
- Task edge $7 \to \mathrm{x}$ is conditioned by $C_{\mathrm{e},4}[1] = 0$ because task 1 is supposed to complete here.

The symbolic equations of the example are set up by the rules in Subsection as follows,

$$\begin{aligned}
X_{\mathrm{e}} &= \mathrm{true} \mid \{(T_4, 0), (C_{\mathrm{e},4}[1], 1)\}, \\
X_1 &= X_{\mathrm{e}} \mid \{(E_5[1], 1)\}, \\
X_2 &= (E_5[1] = 1) \wedge X_5 \mid \{(E_4[1], 1)\}, \\
X_3 &= (E_4[1] = 1) \wedge X_4, \\
X_4 &= X_2 \wedge X_6, \\
X_5 &= X_1 \wedge X_4, \\
X_6 &= X_{\mathrm{e}} \mid \{(T_4, 1), (E_4[1], 0), (E_5[1], 0)\}, \\
X_7 &= (T_4 = 1) \wedge X_5 \mid \{(C_{\mathrm{e},4}[1], 0)\}, \\
X_{\mathrm{x}} &= (C_{\mathrm{e},4}[1] = 0) \wedge X_7 \wedge ((\mathrm{false} \wedge X_{\mathrm{e}}) \vee X_3).
\end{aligned}$$

The equation system is solved step by step. First, we insert $2 \to 4$ and $6 \to 4$ and obtain

$$X_4 = ((E_5[1] = 1) \wedge X_5 \mid \{(E_4[1], 1)\}) \wedge X_{\mathrm{e}} \mid \{(T_4, 1), (E_4[1], 0), (E_5[1], 0)\},$$

which evaluates to false. Hence we also get $X_2 = X_3 = X_5 = X_7 =$ false. This proves that node 2 of the example cannot be reached, and a deadlock occurs in the given program.

```
generic
   type Num is mod <>;
procedure Dining;

procedure Dining is

   Current_Id : Num := Num'Last;

   function Next_One return Num is
   begin
      Current_Id := Current_Id + 1;
      return Current_Id;
   end Next_One;

   task type Philosopher(Id: Num := Next_One);

   protected type Fork is
      entry Seize;
      procedure Release;
   private
      Seized : boolean := false;
   end Fork;

   type Phil_Array is array (Num'Range) of
      Philosopher;
   type Fork_Array is array (Num'Range) of Fork;

   Phils: Phil_Array;                        -- Node 1
   Forks: Fork_Array;                        -- Node 1

   task body Philosopher is
      dur: duration;
   begin
      loop                                   -- Node 2
         Forks(Id).Seize;                    -- Node 3
         Forks(Id+1).Seize;                  -- Node 4
         Forks(Id).Release;                  -- Node 5
         Forks(Id+1).Release;                -- Node 6
      end loop;
   end Philosopher;

   protected body Fork is      -- loop -- Node 7, 8
      entry Seize when not Seized is         -- Node 9
      begin
         Seized := true;                     -- Node 9
      end Seize;
      procedure Release is                   -- Node 10
      begin
         Seized := False;                    -- Node 10
      end Release;
   end Fork;                                 -- end loop;

begin
   null;
end Dining;
```

(a) Source Code

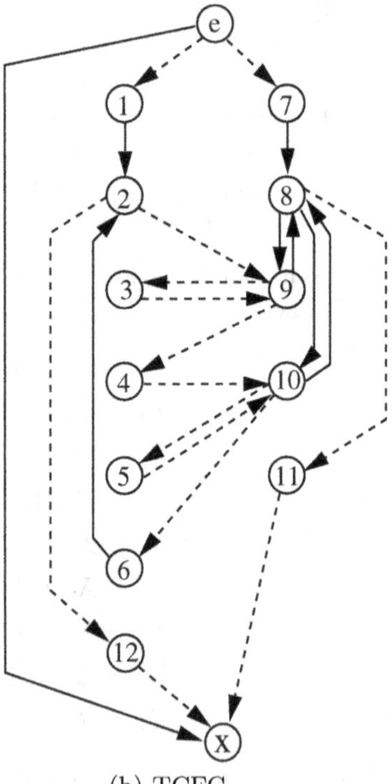

(b) TCFG

Fig. 2. Dining Philosophers Example

3.5 Modelling Protected Objects

Protected objects are semantically modelled as tasks. The corresponding task body consists of an endless loop containing a select statement with a terminate alternative. The select statement contains one accept statement for each protected operation. Guards are mapped from protected entries to task entries. Protected procedures and functions are mapped to task entries, whereby function return values are (conceptually) replaced with out parameters.

Entry families can easily be integrated in our approach. The same applies to task and entry attributes and to pragma Atomic.

3.6 Dining Philosophers Example

The second example is the well-known problem of the *Dining Philosophers.* The source code of an Ada specification and implementation are shown in Figure (a). The corresponding TCFG is depicted in Figure (b) where nodes 1 to 6 originally are part of the task *Philosopher* and nodes 7 to 10 are part of the protected type *Fork*. Control flow edges between nodes 2 and 3, nodes 3 and 4, nodes 4 and 5, and nodes 5 and 6 have been removed. Nodes 11 and 12 are intermediate nodes. To keep the example small, the intermediate nodes $i_{e,1}$ and $i_{e,7}$ have been omitted, since there is only one tasking edge to node 1 and to node 7, respectively. In addition, we do not model function `Next_One` which is used to obtain unique task identifiers (in the Ada program and not in its symbolically evaluated version). To ease the readability, arrays are denoted in an Ada-like notation instead of using the symbolic notation (compare [,]). The data flow equations have the following form:

$$
\begin{aligned}
X_e &= \text{true} \mid \{(C_{e,1}[0..N-1], 1), (C_{e,7}[0..N-1], 1), (\mathit{Seized}[0..N-1], \text{false})\} \\
X_1 &= X_e \\
X_2 &= X_1 \vee X_6 \mid \{(E_9[\mathit{id}], 1)\} \\
X_3 &= (E_9[\mathit{id}] = 1) \wedge X_9 \mid \{(E_9[\mathit{id}], 2)\} \\
X_4 &= (E_9[\mathit{id}] = 2) \wedge X_9 \mid \{(E_{10}[\mathit{id}], 1)\} \\
X_5 &= (E_{10}[\mathit{id}] = 1) \wedge X_{10} \mid \{(E_{10}[\mathit{id}], 2)\} \\
X_6 &= (E_{10}[\mathit{id}] = 2) \wedge X_{10} \\
X_7 &= X_e \mid \{(E_9[0..N-1], 0), (E_{10}[0..N-1], 0)\} \\
X_8 &= X_7 \vee X_9 \vee X_{10} \\
X_9 &= X_8 \wedge [(X_2 \wedge \neg \mathit{Seized}[\mathit{id}] \mid \{(\mathit{Seized}[\mathit{id}], \text{true})\}) \vee \\
&\qquad (X_3 \wedge \neg \mathit{Seized}[\mathit{id}-1] \mid \{(\mathit{Seized}[\mathit{id}-1], \text{true})\})] \\
X_{10} &= X_8 \wedge [(X_4 \mid \{(\mathit{Seized}[\mathit{id}], \text{false})\}) \vee (X_5 \mid \{(\mathit{Seized}[\mathit{id}-1], \text{false})\})] \\
X_{11} &= X_8 \mid \{(C_{e,7}[\mathit{id}], 0)\} \\
X_{12} &= \text{false} \wedge X_2 \mid \{(C_{e,1}[\mathit{id}], 0)\} \\
X_x &= (C_{e,1}[\mathit{id}] = 0) \wedge (C_{e,7}[\mathit{id}] = 0) \wedge X_e \wedge X_{11} \wedge X_{12}
\end{aligned}
$$

After performing the insertions $6 \to 2$, $2 \to 9$, $3 \to 9$, $4 \to 10$, $5 \to 10$, $7 \to 8$, $\mathrm{e} \to 7$, $\mathrm{e} \to 1$, $8 \to 9$, and $8 \to 10$, we obtain the two following recursive equations for X_9 and X_{10}

$$
\begin{aligned}
X_9 = {} & (X_\mathrm{e} \mid \{(E_9[id],0),(E_{10}[id],0)\} \vee X_9 \vee X_{10}) \wedge \\
& \{[(X_\mathrm{e} \vee ((E_{10}[id]=2) \wedge X_{10})) \wedge \neg \mathit{Seized}[id] \mid \{(E_9[id],1),(\mathit{Seized}[id],\mathrm{true})\}] \vee \\
& [((E_9[id]=1) \wedge X_9 \wedge \neg \mathit{Seized}[id-1]) \mid \{(E_9[id],2),(\mathit{Seized}[id-1],\mathrm{true})\}]\}
\end{aligned}
$$

and

$$
\begin{aligned}
X_{10} = {} & (X_\mathrm{e} \mid \{(E_9[id],0),(E_{10}[id],0)\} \vee X_9 \vee X_{10}) \wedge \\
& \{[(E_9[id]=2) \wedge X_9 \mid \{(E_{10}[id],1),(\mathit{Seized}[id],\mathrm{false})\}] \vee \\
& [(E_{10}[id]=1) \wedge X_{10} \mid \{(E_{10}[id],2),(\mathit{Seized}[id-1],\mathrm{false})\}]\}\,.
\end{aligned}
$$

Simplifying the involved boolean expressions and solving the recurrence relations we obtain

$$
X_8 = [X_\mathrm{e} \wedge \begin{cases}
(E_9[id]=1) \wedge \neg \mathit{Seized}[id-1] \,|\{(E_9[id],2),(\mathit{Seized}[id-1],\mathrm{true})\}] \vee \\
(E_9[id]=2) \mid \{(E_{10}[id],1),(\mathit{Seized}[id],\mathrm{false})\}] \vee \\
(E_{10}[id]=1) \mid \{(E_{10}[id],2),(\mathit{Seized}[id-1],\mathrm{false})\}] \vee \\
(E_{10}[id]=2) \wedge \neg \mathit{Seized}[id] \mid \{(E_9[id],1),(\mathit{Seized}[id],\mathrm{true})\}]
\end{cases}
$$

Inserting $\mathrm{e} \to 8$, $8 \to 11$, $11 \to \mathrm{x}$, $2 \to 12$, and $12 \to \mathrm{x}$ we see that $X_{12} = X_\mathrm{x} = \mathrm{false}$, which indicates that the program does not complete. On the other hand, this is clear because the philosopher tasks are supposed not to complete. It remains to check whether

$$
\begin{aligned}
X_8 = \bigwedge_{id} & [(E_9[id]=1) \wedge \neg \mathit{Seized}[id-1] \mid \{(E_9[id],2),(\mathit{Seized}[id-1],\mathrm{true})\}] \vee \\
& [(E_9[id]=2) \mid \{(E_{10}[id],1),(\mathit{Seized}[id],\mathrm{false})\}] \vee \\
& [(E_{10}[id]=1) \mid \{(E_{10}[id],2),(\mathit{Seized}[id-1],\mathrm{false})\}] \vee \\
& [(E_{10}[id]=2) \wedge \neg \mathit{Seized}[id] \mid \{(E_9[id],1),(\mathit{Seized}[id],\mathrm{true})\}] \qquad (1)
\end{aligned}
$$

is true. Since,

$$
\bigwedge_{id} [(E_{10}[id]=2) \wedge \neg \mathit{Seized}[id]] = \mathrm{true} \qquad (2)
$$

implies

$$
\bigwedge_{id} [(E_9[id]=1) \wedge \mathit{Seized}[id]] = \bigwedge_{id} [(E_9[id]=1) \wedge \mathit{Seized}[id-1]] = \mathrm{true},
$$

we find that ( ) evaluates to false if ( ) holds. Thus we get

$$
X_8 \Leftarrow \neg \bigwedge_{id} [(E_{10}[id]=2) \wedge \neg \mathit{Seized}[id]] = \bigvee_{id} [(E_{10}[id]=1) \vee \mathit{Seized}[id]]
$$

which means that the program deadlocks if each philosopher holds exactly one fork and tries to pick up the second one, which is held by its neighbor. Thus our framework obtains the correct answer to the problem.

4 Related Work

A large number of papers deals with detecting tasking anomalies in multi-tasking (Ada) programs, e.g. [, , , , , , , , ,]. SSA form for explicitly parallel programs is treated theoretically in [ ]. Explicitly parallel programs are restricted to a *(cobegin ... coend)*-like structure and are in strict contrast to the tasking in Ada. The semantic chosen for global variables is far too weak to model Ada programs with tasks. *Static Concurrency Analysis*, presented in [ ], is a method for determining concurrency errors in parallel programs. The class of detectable errors include infinite waits, deadlocks, and concurrent updates of shared variables. Infeasible Paths, however, represent a problem since they give rise to errors which actually cannot occur. In [ ] the authors propose symbolic execution to detect infeasible paths. Their approach is based on interleaving the execution of component processes. The interleaving approach, however, is poorly suited for formal verification. In [,] concurrency analysis of programs is studied. The approach allows recursive procedures and dynamically allocated tasks to be present. The presented approach can handle (recursive) procedures but cannot take into account the individual "instances" of the procedures and tasks, i.e., it is based on the source-code of the tasks and procedures and not on their runtime equivalent. In [, ,] static detection of infinite wait anomalies is studied. Classic data flow analysis is employed to solve this problem. This allows polynomial time analysis but cannot solve dead paths problems. In addition, Ada's generic units cannot be modelled adequately. In [ ] symbolic execution of Ada programs is presented. The analysis is restricted to a static task model where tasks can only be statically declared in the main program and the introduced framework cannot cope with dynamic task creation and completion. High-level Petri nets are employed in [ ] to perform some analysis for multitasking Ada programs. In [ ] Petri nets are used to reduce the state space of deadlock analysis for Ada programs. Petri nets can be used to perform a small class of deadlock detection, but they are not capable to analyze certain Ada features such as generic units. In [ ] three different approaches to deadlock analysis are surveyed, namely reachability search, symbolic model checking, and inequality necessary conditions. None of the methods cited above can handle the Dining Philosophers problem where the number of philosophers enters the problem domain as a parameter. Our approach is different: it correctly reflects the runtime properties of multitasking (Ada) programs, it correctly models statically and dynamically allocated tasks, and it correctly handles generic units.

5 Conclusion and Future Work

We have presented a symbolic data flow analysis framework for detecting deadlocks. Our framework can handle dynamic task creation and completion, which goes beyond existing work. As shown in the dining philosophers example our framework can cope with generic units as well. Note that the task body is only analyzed once although several instances of the task can be either created statically or dynamically. Moreover, we observed that if the conditions like those of the dining philosophers example, are very complicated, the program has good chances to deadlock. Deadlock-free tasking programs usually lead to simple conditions.

Our approach is also well-suited for other programming languages. In future we plan to build a similar analysis for object-oriented programming languages, in particular for Java.

References

1. J. Blieberger, *Data-flow frameworks for worst-case execution time analysis*, Real-Time Systems (2000), (to appear).
2. J. Blieberger and B. Burgstaller, *Symbolic reaching definitions analysis of Ada programs*, Proceedings of Ada-Europe'98 (Uppsala, Sweden), pp. 238–250.
3. J. Blieberger, B. Burgstaller, and B. Scholz, *Interprocedural Symbolic Evaluation of Ada Programs with Aliases*, Ada-Europe'99 International Conference on Reliable Software Technologies (Santander, Spain), pp. 136–145.
4. J. Blieberger, T. Fahringer, and B. Scholz, *Symbolic cache analysis for real-time systems*, Real-Time Systems, Special Issue on Worst-Case Execution Time Analysis (2000), (to appear).
5. E. Bruneton and J.-F. Pradat-Peyre, *Automatic verification of concurrent Ada programs*, Ada-Europe'99 International Conference on Reliable Software Technologies (Santander, Spain), pp. 146–157.
6. T. E. Cheatham, G. H. Holloway, and J. A. Townley, *Symbolic evaluation and the analysis of programs*, IEEE Trans. on Software Engineering **5** (1979), no. 4, 403–417.
7. J. C. Corbett, *Evaluating deadlock detection methods for concurrent software*, IEEE Transactions on Software Engineering **22** (1996), no. 3, 161–180.
8. L. K. Dillon, *Using symbolic execution for verification of Ada tasking programs*, ACM Transactions on Programming Languages and Systems **12** (1990), no. 4, 643–669.
9. E. Duesterwald, *Static concurrency analysis in the presence of procedures*, Tech. Report #91-6, Department of Computer Science, University of Pittsburgh, 1991.
10. E. Duesterwald and M. L. Soffa, *Concurrency analysis in the presence of procedures using a data-flow framework*, Proceedings of the 4th Symp. on Testing, Analysis and Verification (TAV4), pp. 36–48.
11. S. Duri, U. Buy, R. Devarapalli, and S. M. Shatz, *Application and experimental evaluation of state space reduction methods for deadlock analysis in Ada*, ACM Trans. on Software Engineering and Methodology **3** (1994), no. 4, 161–180.
12. T. Fahringer and B. Scholz, *Symbolic Evaluation for Parallelizing Compilers*, Proc. of the ACM International Conference on Supercomputing.
13. D. Long and L. A. Clarke, *Data flow analysis of concurrent systems that use the rendezvous model of synchronization*, Proceedings of the ACM Symp. on Testing, Analysis, and Verification, pp. 21–35.
14. S. P. Masticola, *Static detection of deadlocks in polynomial time*, Ph.D. thesis, Graduate School—New Brunswick, Rutgers, The State University of New Jersey, 1993.

15. S. P. Masticola and B. G. Ryder, *Static infinite wait anomaly detection in polynomial time*, Proceedings of the 1990 International Conference on Parallel Processing, pp. II78–II87.
16. B. G. Ryder and M. C. Paull, *Elimination algorithms for data flow analysis*, ACM Computing Surveys **18** (1986), no. 3, 277–315.
17. B. Scholz, J. Blieberger, and T. Fahringer, *Symbolic Pointer Analysis for Detecting Memory Leaks*, ACM SIGPLAN Workshop on "Partial Evaluation and Semantics-Based Program Manipulation" (PEPM'00) (Boston). ,
18. E. Stoltz, H. Srinivasan, J. Hook, and M. Wolfe, *Static single assignment form for explicitly parallel programs: Theory and practice*, Tech. report, Dept. of Computer Science and Engineering, Oregon Graduate Institute of Science and Technology, Portland, Oregon, 1994.
19. R. N. Taylor, *A general-purpose algorithm for analyzing concurrent programs*, Communications of the ACM **26** (1983), no. 5, 362–376.
20. M. Young and R. N. Taylor, *Combining static concurrency analysis with symbolic execution*, IEEE Trans. on Software Engineering **14** (1988), no. 10, 1499–1511.

Exceptions in OO Languages: Using Them and Reasoning about Them

Neelam Soundarajan* and Stephen Fridella

Computer and Information Science, Ohio State University
Columbus, OH 43210
{neelam,fridella}@cis.ohio-state.edu

Abstract. Exceptions are generally considered as *signals* with little or no internal structure to them. Using such exceptions, a method can signal to its caller that the operation could not be completed properly, and let the caller take appropriate corrective action. While this is sufficient to deal with simple situations, it severely limits the information that the method can provide to the caller when the exception is raised. In order to solve this problem, some OO languages treat exceptions as full-fledged objects. This adds to the power of the exception mechanism, but it also adds to the difficulty of the already complex task of understanding the behavior of programs that utilize exceptions. Hence, in order to effectively exploit the power of these mechanisms, we need appropriate techniques that can be used to reason precisely about the behavior of systems built using them. This paper develops such techniques and demonstrates their usefulness via some simple examples.

Keywords: Software quality; Software development methods.

1 Introduction

Exceptions are often [, ,] viewed as *signals* with no internal structure to them. A procedure or a method of a class will, when it is unable to complete its task, *raise* an exception *E*. When this happens, the system searches for, and transfers control to, a matching *exception handler* along the calling chain. While exceptions of this kind are undoubtedly useful, and are sufficient to deal with many simple situations, the amount of information that the signaling method can provide to the caller by means of such exceptions is severely limited since the exception is little more than its name. In order to solve this problem, some OO languages such as *C++* and *Java* treat exceptions as full-fledged objects. In *Ada 95* [ ], exceptions are not full-fledged objects but they are not just named signals either; instead, the Ada.Exceptions package defines the internal structure of, and a rich set of operations that may be performed on, exceptions. Allowing

* Contact author: N. Soundarajan

[1] In this paper, we will focus on class methods since we are primarily interested in Object-Oriented languages.

H. B. Keller and E. Plödereder (Eds.): Ada-Europe 2000, LNCS 1845, pp. 238– , 2000.

exceptions to have a rich internal structure, whether by treating them as full-fledged objects or via the somewhat more restricted *Ada 95* approach, adds considerably to the power of the exception mechanism. As we will see in the next section, even relatively simple classes can usefully exploit the ability to include information in the internal structure of exceptions. But enriching the structure of exceptions also adds to the difficulty of the already complex task of understanding the behavior of programs that utilize exceptions. Hence, in order to exploit the power of these mechanisms, it is essential to develop appropriate techniques that can be used to reason precisely about the behavior of systems built using them. In this paper we develop such techniques and demonstrate their usefulness via some simple examples.

A number of authors [, , , ,] have considered ways to reason about the behavior of systems that utilize exceptions. While these systems differ from each other in details, what is common to all of them is that they deal only with the simple type of exceptions, i.e., exceptions that are named signals with no internal structure. Our goal is to extend some of this earlier work to allow for exceptions that may have complex internal structure, and may indeed be full-fledged objects.

There are two distinct problems that we need to address in a reasoning technique that deals with the behavior of systems that utilize exceptions as objects. The first, and this is common with the case of simple exceptions, is the sudden jump in the flow-of-control from the method raising the exception to the exception handler (which may be several steps away in the calling chain). The second, and this is a result of allowing exceptions to be complete objects, is the coming into existence of a new object corresponding to the exception being raised, with this object becoming available to the exception handler. Systems such as those of [,] show us how to deal with the jump in the flow-of-control. The approach we develop builds on these earlier systems by providing appropriate notations to capture information about the exception object created when the exception is raised, and rules to reason about this object when analyzing the exception-handling code.

The key contributions of this paper may be summarized as follows:

- Argues for the importance of allowing exceptions to have a rich internal structure rather than just being named signals.
- Develops a reasoning technique for understanding the behavior of systems that utilize such exceptions.
- Applies the technique to analyze the behavior of a simple example.

The rest of the paper is organized as follows: In Section 2 we present a simple example to illustrate the advantages of considering exceptions as objects rather than merely as signals. In Section 3 we develop our reasoning technique for dealing with programs that raise and handle such exceptions; specifications in our approach are written in a simple extension of *OCL* [ ]. In Section 4 we apply the technique to the example of Section 2. In the final section we summarize our work, compare it with existing approaches to reasoning about exceptions, and identify some problems for future research.

2 Exceptions as Objects

Consider a banking application consisting of two classes, Bank and Account; we will focus our attention on the Account class. It consists of a member variable balance and operations getBal(), deposit(), and withdraw(), for getting the current balance in the account, and for depositing money into and withdrawing money from the account. In Figure we have provided a precise specification of the behavior of each operation of Account using standard pre- and post-conditions.

Account :: getBal() : real
pre : true
post : $(\text{result} = \text{balance}) \wedge !\{\text{balance}\}$

Account :: deposit(a:real) : void
pre : $a > 0.0$
post : $(\text{balance@pre} \geq 1000.00 \Rightarrow \text{balance} = \text{balance@pre} + a)$
$\wedge\ (\text{balance@pre} < 1000.00 \Rightarrow \text{balance} = \text{balance@pre} + a - 1.0)$

Account :: withdraw(a:real) : void
pre : $a > 0.0$
post : $(\text{balance@pre} \geq 1000.00 \Rightarrow \text{balance} = \text{balance@pre} - a)$
$\wedge\ (\text{balance@pre} < 1000.00 \Rightarrow \text{balance} = \text{balance@pre} - a - 1.0)$

Fig. 1. Specification of Account class

The format we have used is consistent with that of the *Object Constraint Language (OCL)* [ ] which is a part of the UML-standard[ ]. The notation x@pre which may appear (only) in post-conditions denotes the value of x at the pre-condition stage, i.e., when the operation was invoked. The specifications of deposit() and withdraw() tell us that there is a service charge (of 1.0) for these operations if the balance in the account at the start of the operation is below 1000.0. We also use (but this is not officially part of OCL) the notation !{x,y} in the post-condition to mean that the final values of x and y are the same as their corresponding initial values. Thus the specification of getBal() in the figure tells us that it returns a result of type real; the pre-condition tells us that this operation may be invoked at any point (since true is always satisfied); and the post-condition tells us that the result returned by getBal() is the same as the value of balance, and furthermore the clause !{balance} assures us that a call to getBal() will not change the value of balance.

The specification of withdraw() in Figure imposes no limits on the amount that may be withdrawn from an account. Real banks do not, of course, allow customers to withdraw arbitrary amounts. One possibility, to take account of

[2] For concreteness, we will use a *C++/Java*-like terminology and syntax but there is nothing language-specific about our work. Also, we ignore rounding errors caused by the use of floating point numbers in our examples.

this, would be to modify the pre-condition of withdraw() to include the clause:

$a \leq balance$

This would require the Bank class (or whichever class uses the Account class) to ensure, before invoking the operation b.withdraw(a), b being the account object from which to withdraw, that the balance in b is no less than a. An alternative approach, and the one we will consider, is to have the withdraw() operation raise an exception if the amount being attempted to be withdrawn from the account is greater than its current balance [3]. A signal-like exception, let us call it InsufficientFunds, would seem to be all that is needed to deal with this situation, but consider the following code outline that appears in a method of the Bank class:

```
try { ... BMC ... }
catch( InsufficientFunds ) { ... EHC ... }
```

Suppose during execution of the bank method code BMC, there is a call to withdraw() which results in an exception being raised, and control is transferred to the exception handling code, EHC. If there is only one call in BMC to withdraw(), then it is clearly that call that must have resulted in the exception being raised, so we would know, for example, which particular account was involved, and we could take appropriate action in EHC, such as freezing the offending account. What if there were several calls in BMC to withdraw() and these calls involved different accounts? How then do we identify the involved account?

There are two possible solutions. The first is to rewrite the code so that each call to withdraw() is in a separate try block; in this case if control transfers to the exception handling code attached to a given try block, there would be no question about which account must have been involved. While this approach works, it results in considerable code duplication and the overall code is broken up into numerous try blocks. A better approach is to include information concerning the identity of the offending account *within the exception.* If exceptions were not just signals but could have a rich internal structure, this is easily done. All we would need is for the InsufficientFunds exception to have a member variable that is initialized at the time the exception is created to be a reference to the involved account. Note that the exception is created in the withdraw() operation and that

[3] Using exceptions in this example may be something of an overkill; the caller could easily check, by using the getBal() operation prior to the call to withdraw(), that there is an adequate balance in the account, so strengthening the pre-condition is probably the simpler and hence better approach. As with any powerful mechanism, there is a danger with exceptions of their being misused. The question of which situations are suitable candidates for use of exceptions is outside the scope of this paper. Our use of exceptions in this example is just to help explain in a simple setting why exceptions are usefully considered as objects rather than as just signals, and to illustrate our reasoning technique, and not intended as a paradigmatic example of when and where exceptions are appropriate.

Also, as noted by a referee, all of the discussion in this paper assumes a sequential setting. Extending our approach to deal with concurrency, in other words dealing with two or more concurrent calls to operations such as withdraw(), would require substantial changes, including in particular such issues as *interference freedom* [ ].

operation, of course, knows the account that is involved. Indeed the operation must have been invoked on the offending account so a reference to this account would be contained in the *Java* variable this. In *Smalltalk* the self variable would contain this reference. The Ada.Exceptions package does not provide information concerning the identity of the object an operation on which resulted in the exception being raised; we believe it would be very useful to extend Ada.Exceptions to include this information; we will return to this in the final section.

The use of exceptions in this example, as noted earlier, is probably inappropriate. But where exceptions are used, the ability to include information, such as the identity of the involved object, can be of value to the exception handler. In the next section we turn to reasoning about operations that raise exceptions and code that handles them. Before concluding this section we should note that, for the most part, we ignore abstraction issues since abstraction and exception handling are generally orthogonal issues; but in the final section we will briefly consider an important potential difficulty involving abstraction and exceptions.

3 Reasoning about Exceptions

Suppose f is a method of a class C and that f may raise exceptions during its execution. The specification of f will consist of:

- The *pre-condition*, $f.pre$; this is an assertion over the values of the member variables of C at the time of the call to f and the values of the parameters to f; for convenience, we will assume that all parameters are passed by-value.
- The (normal- or) *n-post-condition*, $f.post$; this is an assertion over the values of the member variables of C at the time f finishes as well as their values at the time of the call (these being identified by the suffix @pre). If f returns a result, we use the symbol result in $f.post$ to refer to it.
- For each type of exception E_i that f may raise during its execution, the (exception- or) *e-post-condition*, $f.E_i.post$; this is an assertion over the parameter values of f, the initial values of the member variables of C at the time of the call, and their final values when f terminates by raising an exception of type E_i, *and* the values of the member variables of the (exception) class E_i. $f.E_i.post$ will not include information about result since if f terminates by raising an exception, it does not return a result.

This specification is valid if whenever execution of f begins with $f.pre$ being satisfied, one of the following occurs:

[4] Further, we also assume that there are no pointer variables, etc. Extending our approach to deal with value-result (i.e., in-out) parameters would be straightforward, but dealing with pointers would be substantially more complex since we would have to address such questions as aliasing. Aliasing is, of course, a general problem, not one introduced by exception handling.

1. f terminates normally with the parameter values received by f, the initial and final values of C's data members, and the value of the result (if any) returned by f satisfying the n-post-condition $f.post$;
2. Or f terminates by raising an exception of type E_i and at the time of f's termination, the parameter values of f, the initial and final values of the data members of C, and the values of the data members of E_i (in the exception object that f throws) together satisfy the e-post-condition, $f.E_i.post$;

Note that if f were capable of terminating by throwing either e_1 or e_2, both of which are of the same type E_i, the same e-post-condition, $f.E_i.post$, describes both situations. This is reasonable since the exception handling code in the caller will be specified by the type of the exception it can handle, so the code corresponding to the type E_i must be designed to deal with both e_1 and e_2.

It is worth noting that if $f.pre$ is not satisfied when f is invoked, the specification tells us nothing about what may happen. In some systems such as *Eiffel* [ ], if "assertion checking" has been turned on, the system would raise an exception in this case. We are not considering system generated exceptions of this kind in this paper. Rather, our focus is on exceptions programmed explicitly into the system (using the `throw` command that we will consider shortly). Thus we are also ignoring other system generated exceptions such as "out-of-memory" etc.

How do we show that f meets its specification? For this, we need *rules* corresponding to the various statements that may appear in f. For statements not concerned with exceptions, we can borrow standard rules [ ], with minor modifications to let us 'carry forward' information about exceptions. For example, our rule for sequential composition is:

R1. Sequential Composition

$$\frac{\begin{array}{l}\{p\}\, S_1\, \{q'\}\, \{E_1.post,\, E_2.post, \ldots, E_n.post\}\\ \{q'\}\, S_2\, \{q\}\, \{E_1.post,\, E_2.post, \ldots, E_n.post\}\end{array}}{\{p\}\, S_1;\ S_2\, \{q\}\, \{E_1.post,\, E_2.post, \ldots, E_n.post\}}$$

$\{E_1.post,\, E_2.post, \ldots, E_n.post\}$ are the e-post-conditions corresponding to exceptions that may be raised during execution of $S_1; S_2$. To execute $S_1; S_2$, we start with S_1. Now S_1 may terminate by raising an exception E_i, in which case $S_1; S_2$ also terminates with E_i; or S_1 may terminate normally, in which case we execute S_2 which may terminate normally or with an exception. The first antecedent of R1 requires us to show that S_1 will terminate normally with q' being satisfied, or by raising an exception E_i, with $E_i.post$ being satisfied. The second antecedent similarly requires us to consider S_2 but only if S_1 finishes normally, that is q' is satisfied when S_2 begins; i.e., if at some point S_1 terminates with an exception E_i, then $S_1; S_2$ also terminates at that point with the

[5] We do not consider the case of non-termination so f must necessarily terminate, either normally or by raising an exception. In other words, ours is a total correctness, rather than partial correctness, approach. But in this paper, we will ignore the details of establishing termination since these are fairly standard and the addition of exceptions does not change these details.

same exception. Given these antecedents, R1 allows us to conclude that $S_1; S_2$ will terminate normally with q being satisfied at termination, or will terminate with the exception E_i being raised with $E_i.post$ being satisfied.

Although sequential composition itself cannot raise an exception, S_1 or S_2 may do so. That is why R1 requires us to show that (if and) when this happens, the corresponding e-post-condition is satisfied. But R1 seems to require the exceptions that may be raised during the executions of S_1 and S_2 to be identical to each other. What if they are not? R2 will allow us to deal with such situations:

R2. Rule of Consequence

$$\frac{\begin{array}{l}\{p\}\,S\,\{q\}\,\{E_1.post,\,\ldots\,,E_k.post\}\\ p' \Rightarrow p,\; q \Rightarrow q',\; E_1.post \Rightarrow E_1.post',\;\ldots,\;E_k.post \Rightarrow E_k.post'\end{array}}{\{p'\}\,S\,\{q'\}\,\{E_1.post',\,\ldots\,,E_k.post',E_{k+1}.post'\}}$$

This is a natural generalization of the usual rule of consequence that allows us to strengthen the pre-condition (from p to p'), weaken the n-post-condition (from q to q'); the rule also allows us to weaken e-post-conditions; and to *add* an e-post-condition corresponding to a new exception; this is reasonable because if we have already shown that S must terminate normally or by raising one of $E_1, \ldots, E_k$, we can also say that S must terminate normally or by raising one of $E_1, \ldots, E_k, E_{k+1}$. It is important to be able to add exceptions in this manner; this allows us to meet the requirement of R1 that the exceptions included in the results concerning S_1 and S_2 to be identical to each other. Using R2 we can meet this requirement by adding to the result about each of S_1, S_2, the exceptions that are missing from it. This is similar to what happens in the standard rule for if-then-else where we are required to weaken the post-conditions of the two branches of the if-then-else to make them identical to each other.

The analogy with if-then-else may lead one to ask the question, as an anonymous referee did, why have distinct post-conditions corresponding to the different exceptions instead of combining them into a common one; the answer is that there will different exception handlers in the calling chain corresponding to the different exceptions. In rule R5 for handlers, we will see that only the exceptions that the handler in question is designed to handle will be caught by the handler, the rest will be passed on up the calling chain. Hence individual statements (such as the S of rule R2) must provide distinct post-conditions corresponding to the individual exceptions they may raise, so that a given handler clause need worry only about dealing with the assertion corresponding to the particular exception it will catch.

Let us now consider statements that raise exceptions. The first of these is the throw statement. Consider what happens when

throw $E_i(\bar{x})$

is executed. This constructs a new (exception) object of type E_i by calling the constructor function of the class E_i ($\bar{x}$ is passed as arguments to this function), and 'throws' it. We will use the symbol ε to denote this newly created exception object. Since at most one exception object will be in existence at any time, no confusion should arise by our use of a single symbol to denote this object. Note that the claim that at most one exception object will be in existence at any time holds even if an exception is raised inside an exception handler. This is because, before the exception handler can raise a (new) exception (using, the throw statement since that is the only way to raise an exception), it must have "caught the current exception"; as soon as an exception is caught, as we will see in rule R5, the object is no longer an exception object; instead it becomes a normal object (referred to by a symbol such as e_j as determined by the handler, rather than by ϵ). Thus if the exception handler were to throw an exception, that will be the only exception in existence at that point.

The following rule captures the effect of the throw:

R3. Throw Statement

$$\frac{(p \wedge E_i.ppost^{\bar{u},\,\bar{d}}_{\bar{x},\,\varepsilon.\bar{d}}) \Rightarrow E_i.post}{\{p\}\ \mathsf{throw}\ E_i(\bar{x})\ \{false\}\ \{E_i.post\}}$$

$E_i.ppost$ is the post-condition of the constructor function of the class E_i obtained from the specification of that class . This post-condition will be an assertion over $\bar{u}$, its formal parameters, and $\bar{d}$, the member variables of the class E_i. Since the actual arguments being passed to the constructor function are $\bar{x}$ and since the exception object is named ε, we need to perform the indicated substitutions; note that the class E_i may have a member variable whose name, say y, is identical to that of a member of the class C and $E_i.post$ may refer to both, but this will not cause any problems because the former would be denoted by ε.y in this assertion. The rule for throw then requires us to show, given the pre-condition of the throw statement and the post-condition of the constructor of the E_i class (with the specified substitutions), that the appropriate e-post-condition, $E_i.post$ will be satisfied. And since control will leave this point, we may assert *false* as the n-post-condition of the throw statement.

There is another statement that may also result in an exception being raised, this being a call to another method, with the called method raising an exception during its execution. This is handled by the following rule:

R4. Method Call

$$\frac{\begin{array}{l} p \Rightarrow g.pre^{\bar{u},\,\bar{d}}_{\bar{y},\,\mathsf{x}.\bar{d}} \\ \exists \bar{d}'.\,[p^{\mathsf{x}.\bar{d}}_{\bar{d}'} \wedge g.post^{\bar{u},\,\#\bar{d},\,\bar{d}}_{\bar{y},\,\bar{d}',\,\mathsf{x}.\bar{d}}] \Rightarrow q \\ \exists \bar{d}', \bar{y}'.\,[p^{\bar{y},\mathsf{x}.\bar{d}}_{\bar{y}',\bar{d}'} \wedge g.E_j.post^{\bar{u},\,\#\bar{d},\,\bar{d}}_{\bar{y},\,\bar{d}',\,\mathsf{x}.\bar{d}}] \Rightarrow \\ \qquad\qquad E_j.post,\ for\ all\ E_j\ that\ g\ may\ raise \end{array}}{\{p\}\ \mathsf{x}.g(\bar{y})\ \{q\}\ \{E_1.post,\ E_2.post, \ldots\ E_n.post\}}$$

Note that x is the object that g is being applied to, the other arguments being $\bar{y}$. So references to member variables and formal parameters $\bar{u}$ of g, in the pre-

[6] Some languages allow a class to have more than one constructor; we ignore this possibility. More to the point, we also ignore the possibility that the constructor itself raises an exception. In general it may be a good idea to not allow constructor functions to raise exceptions, else we have to deal with 'partially constructed' objects.

and post-conditions of g have to be replaced by the corresponding components of x and $\bar{y}$. The first antecedent of the rule requires us to show that the pre-condition of g is satisfied immediately before the call. The second considers the case when g terminates normally; in this case we are required to show, given the n-post-condition of g (applied to the actual arguments passed to it and to x's members), and whatever information we have (concerning the other variables of the caller) from the pre-condition p of the call, that the n-post-condition q will be satisfied; note that whatever p says about the members of x (or the other arguments to g) apply to their values *before* the call, not their current values; this is taken care of by the quantifier. The last antecedent does the same with respect to the e-post-conditions for all exceptions that g may raise. This rule again is a natural generalization of the standard rule for procedure call; the key addition that R4 makes is to take account of the possibility of g terminating by raising an exception rather than normally.

Let us now consider the statement that allows us to *handle* the exceptions. Consider the following segment of code:

try{ S }
catch($E_1\ e_1$) { S_1 }
...
catch($E_k\ e_k$) { S_1 }

If S terminates normally, the catch clauses have no effect; if it terminates with an exception of type E that is not one of $\{E_1, \ldots, E_k\}$, the catch clauses have no effect, and the execution of the entire command terminates with the exception of type E being thrown (to be handled, presumably, by a catch attached to the try block of the calling method). If S terminates with an exception of type E_i, control transfers to the corresponding catch clause, e_i is bound to the exception object (ε) and S_i begins execution; at this point, the exception is considered handled, and e_i is just another object. The execution of S_i may terminate normally in which case the execution of the entire try block finishes normally (and e_i goes out of scope); or S_i might raise an exception! In the interest of keeping the presentation simple, we ignore this possibility in the rule below (but we will briefly indicate how the rule could be modified to account for this). The following rule captures this behavior of the try block. In the conclusion of the rule we use C_i to denote the ith catch clause catch ($E_i\ e_i$) S_i.

R5. try block

$$\frac{\begin{array}{l}\{p\}\, S\, \{q\}\, \{E_1.post, \ldots, E_i.post, E_{i+1}.post, \ldots, E_k.post\} \\ E_j.post \Rightarrow p_j{}^{e_j}_{\varepsilon}\,,\ j = 1, \ldots, i \\ \{p_j\}\, S_j\, \{q\}\,,\ j = 1, \ldots, i\end{array}}{\{p\}\ \text{try}\ S\, C_1\ \ldots\ C_i\, \{q\}\, \{E_{i+1}.post, \ldots, E_k.post\}}$$

We are first required to establish the appropriate result about S, the main body of the try block. There are k e-post-conditions here, the first i of which will be handled by the $C_1, \ldots, C_i$. Next we must ensure that if an exception of type E_j is raised, the pre-condition p_j of the corresponding catch clause, with ε being substituted for e_j, is satisfied. The third antecedent ensures that the body of each catch clause does what it is supposed to do – establish the post-condition q. The conclusion of the rule lists only the e-post-conditions $E_{i+1}.post, \ldots, E_k.post$ since the exceptions of type $E_1, \ldots, E_i$ will be handled by the catch clauses. Note that the post-condition q applies to the case when S executes and finishes normally, as well as the case when during the execution of S an exception $E_j (j = 1, \ldots, i)$ is raised (perhaps in some call that S makes), the clause C_j catches it, and the body S_j is executed. In both cases the assertion q will be satisfied; as far as what follows the try block is concerned, there is no difference between these two cases. If, on the other hand, an exception E_{i+1} is raised, the assertion that holds at this point will be q_{i+1} but control will not continue with the statement that follows the try block but will rather go up to the most recent exception handler that can catch E_{i+1}.

Let us now consider the possibility of S_j raising an exception. If S_j were to raise an exception of type E, the entire block would terminate with this exception – even if E were one of $\{E_1, \ldots, E_i\}$; so the catch clauses only apply to exceptions raised during execution of the main body S. How do we modify R5 to allow for this possibility? Two changes would have to be made: add, to the result which is the third antecedent of the rule, e-post-conditions corresponding to the exceptions that S_j might raise; and add each of these (corresponding to each of $S_1, \ldots, S_i$) to the conclusion of the rule.

We conclude this section with an observation. In practice, formal specification of program behavior is somewhat more important than formal verification using our rules. The point is that the rules give us an extra tool that be can be used to ensure that the programs behave as per their specifications, but we should not blindly rely on them since it is quite possible to make mistakes in applying them. Hence they should be used to complement our operational understanding, not replace them. But specifications serve as the *basis* for any kind of understanding since they tell us how the program is intended to behave. In our discussion of the example in the next section, we will be careful in writing down the specification of the Account class precisely but will be a bit informal in the rest of our reasoning.

4 Example

Let us consider how our technique applies to the Account example of Section 2. As we noted in Section 2, the withdraw() function, when it raises an InsufficientFunds exception, could include a reference to the particular Account object. Further, information about the amount of money the client attempted to withdraw (this information is not in the state of the Account) may be useful. Consider the following exception class in a *Java* style syntax:

```
public class InsufficientFunds {
  public real amtOver; public Account act;
  public InsufficientFunds( real amt, Account a ) { amtOver = amt; act = a; }
}
```

Next we need to revise our original specification (see Figure) of withdraw() to include information about the InsufficientFunds exception it may raise:

$$\begin{array}{l}
\underline{\mathsf{Account :: withdraw(a:real) : void}} \\
\mathsf{pre} : \mathsf{a} > 0.0 \\
\mathsf{n\text{-}post} : (\mathsf{balance@pre} \geq \mathsf{a}) \wedge !\{\mathsf{a}\} \wedge \\
\qquad (\mathsf{balance@pre} \geq 1000.00 \Rightarrow \mathsf{balance} = \mathsf{balance@pre} - \mathsf{a}) \wedge \\
\qquad (\mathsf{balance@pre} < 1000.00 \Rightarrow \mathsf{balance} = \mathsf{balance@pre} - \mathsf{a} - 1.0) \\
\mathsf{InsufficientFunds\text{-}post} : (\mathsf{balance@pre} < \mathsf{a}) \wedge !\{\mathsf{a,balance}\} \wedge \\
\qquad (\varepsilon.\mathsf{act} = \mathsf{this}) \wedge (\varepsilon.\mathsf{amtOver} = \mathsf{a})
\end{array}$$

The e-post-condition states that when an InsufficientFunds exception is raised, the balance and a are unchanged, the original balance was less than a, and the newly created exception object (ε) will contain a reference to the account (in act) and a copy of a (in amtOver). This post-condition by itself does not guarantee that if balance@pre is less than a the exception will be raised. This follows, however, from the first clause of our (slightly modified) n-post-condition, which states that upon normal termination, the original value of balance must be greater than or equal to a. So this specification tells us that if balance@pre is less than a, the operation would terminate with an InsufficientFunds exception, else it will terminate normally .

Consider the following piece of client code (perhaps part of the Bank class):

```
Account ac1, ac2; ...
try { ac1.withdraw(50.0); ... ac2.withdraw(50.0); ... }
catch InsufficientFunds (e) {
  print( e.act.getName(), e.act.getBal(), e.amtOver ); }
```

This code invokes withdraw() on two different accounts, ac1, ac2. If an exception is raised, the catch clause prints the name of the account holder , the account's current balance, and the amount of the withdrawal that caused the overdraft. What if we wanted to do something more elaborate, such as 'rolling back' the withdrawal from ac1 if the withdrawal from ac2 raised an exception? There is no simple way in which the exception object raised during an operation an on ac2 can give us a reference to some other account such as ac1. So in this case, we would need to write a much more complex piece of code that keeps track of which operation has been completed etc. Exceptions by themselves do not simplify the handling of such situations.

What kind of reasoning can we do about this code? Suppose we know at the start of the try block that the balance in ac1 is more than 50.0; can we

[7] But a weaker specification may not be quite as explicit. For example, suppose we had omitted the first clause of InsufficientFunds-post. Then we could not conclude that the exception would be raised *only if* the starting balance in the account was less that a. In this example, this would probably be inappropriate but in other situations it may correspond to the fact that the specifier is allowing some leeway to the implementer on whether or not to raise exceptions under certian circumstances.

[8] We are assuming that the Account class provides an operation getName() which can be invoked for this purpose.

show (assuming there are no further withdraw()'s in the elided code) that the name that is printed out by the catch clause is not that of ac1's holder? Yes, indeed. What we would need to do is to have, as pre-condition for this clause, an assertion that says ε.act is ac2. Given this pre-condition, it is straightforward to use the rule for the catch clause to show that the name it will print will be that of ac2's holder. But the try block rule will require us to ensure that the code within the try block is consistent with this pre-condition, that is any statement in that block that may raise an InsufficientFunds exception will make sure that this assertion is satisfied. It would seem this would be difficult to ensure with respect to the first invocation of withdraw() because the method is applied to ac1; but this is not really a problem; recall that the e-post-condition of withdraw() tells us that the balance@pre in the account must be less than 50.0, the amount being withdrawn, but the pre-condition of try, we assumed, told us this was not the case. So combining these two we can conclude that ac1 could not be the cause of the exception. (More formally, we would use R2, the rule of consequence, to show that the e-post-condition of the first call to withdraw() does imply the required pre-condition of the catch clause.)

5 Discussion

Exception handling mechanisms provide a powerful tool for structuring complex programs. They allow the main code to be separated cleanly from the code for dealing with exceptional situations. The simplest kind of exceptions are just named signals; while such exceptions are useful, the amount of information that the signaling method can provide to the handler by means of such exceptions is very limited. Our analysis showed that even simple examples can benefit greatly from having exceptions that have internal structure.

Ada 95 provides for a limited amount of information to be included in exceptions. Specifically, the operation that raises the exception may provide an arbitrary string to be stored in the exception, and the handler may retrieve this using the Exception_Information operation provided by the Ada.Exceptions package. In our example the withdraw() operation could have used this to store the name of the holder of the account in the InsufficientFunds exception. While this would allow the handler to, for example, print out this name, it would not allow us to do anything more complex, such as *freezing* the account . We believe this is a common pattern – often the handler will need to know which object was responsible for the exception being thrown; hence it would be very useful for the Ada.Exceptions package to be extended to provide an access variable that would allow the handler code to refer to this object. Even this may be a bit limited; it would not allow, for example, the withdraw() operation to include information about *how much* was attempted to be withdrawn when the exception was raised. To include such information, it would seem exceptions would have to be treated as full-fledged objects.

[9] Freezing the account would of course require the Account class to provide a suitable operation; the point here is the handler also needs to know *which* account to freeze.

Exception handling, like most powerful mechanisms, is fairly complex mechanism and warrants careful treatment in the form of formal specifications of program behavior. We introduced a notation, a direct generalization of the standard pre- and post-condition notation, to precisely express the behavior of operations of classes that may raise exceptions. The key was to include, in addition to the normal post-condition, a set of e-post-conditions, corresponding to the various exceptions that an operation may raise; and include information in the e-post-conditions about not only the state of the object raising the exception but also about the exception object. Given such a specification, we can reason about the behavior of the exception handling code that has to deal with the exceptions that may be raised. And we presented rules that may be used for this task. Previous work, for example [, ,], in the area has considered ways of dealing with simple types of exceptions with no internal structure to them. The specification and reasoning system we have presented is an important extension of these earlier systems to account for exceptions with rich, internal structure. Using our approach, designers will be able to specify and reason about the behavior of systems that take advantage of exceptions as full-fledged objects.

Throughout the paper, we ignored abstraction issues because exception handling is an orthogonal issue as we noted earlier. But, as pointed out by an anonymous referee, there is one potential problem that can cause a conflict between the two. Suppose an exception is not caught in the operation $X.f()$ in which it is raised, and it is passed several levels up the calling chain. Suppose the exception object contains a reference to the object X. Isn't this a violation of abstraction? The client code several levels up is, or should be, unaware of the existence of X since X very likely corresponds to a particular representation that the designer chose to use at the low level and there is no reason for the client code to be concerned about these details. But by passing the exception up to the client code level and by including in the exception object a reference to X, are we not violating this abstraction? This is indeed a difficult question; the answer would seem to be one of programming methodology: Even if code at a given level L does not know how to deal with an exception E that may be raised by an operation that it invokes, L should pass E up to the next higher level only if E contains no information that would be inappropriate to pass to that higher level; else, the code at level L should 'handle' E and in the handler raise E', a 'sanitized' version of E, that contains only information appropriate to the higher level; E' would typically contain an abstraction of the information contained in E.

We conclude with a couple of problems for future work. In the kind of exception mechanism we have considered, once an exception is raised, the method that raises exception terminates. If the caller handles the exception, then control continues with whatever statement follows the try-catch block of the caller. An alternative that has been suggested is to allow control to *resume* in the method that raised the exception. This may be more appropriate in certain circumstances, and we plan to investigate how to change our formalism to apply to this type of exception mechanism. A second problem that is worth investigating is the relation between inheritance and exceptions. This is important because in languages such as *Java*, an exception handler will catch not only exceptions of the specified type but also any subtype. Changing our formalism to deal with this should be relatively easier; for example, we would have to revise the rule for the try, so that we consider a given catch clause not only if the type of the exception matches but also if it is a subtype.

Acknowledgments

The authors would like to thank the anonymous referees for numerous comments that improved the presentation considerably.

References

1. J. Barnes. *Programming in Ada 95.* Addison-Wesley, 1998.
2. G. Booch, J. Rumbaugh, and I. Jacobson. *The Unified Modeling Language User Guide.* Addison-Wesley, 1999.
3. N. Cocco and S. Dulli. A mechanism for exception handling and its verification rules. *Comput. Lang.*, 7:89–102, 1982.
4. F. Cristian. Correct and robust programs. *IEEE Trans. on Software Eng.*, 10:163–174, 1984.
5. J.B. Goodenough. Exception handling: issues and a proposed notation. *Comm. ACM*, 18:436–449, 1975.
6. D. Gries. *Science of Programming.* Springer-Verlag, 1981.
7. D.C. Luckham and W. Polak. Ada exception handling: An axiomatic approach. *ACM TOPLAS*, 2:225–233, 1980.
8. B. Meyer. *Object-Oriented Software Construction.* Prentice Hall, 1997.
9. S. Owicki and D. Gries. An axiomatic proof technique for parallel programs. *Acta Informatica*, 6(1):319–340, 1976.
10. J. Warmer and A. Kleppe. *The Object Constraint Langauge.* Addison-Wesley, 1999.
11. S. Yemini and D. Berry. A modular verifiable exception handling mechanism. *ACM TOPLAS*, 7:214–243, 1985.

(True) Polymorphism in SPARK2000

Tse-Min Lin and John A. McDermid

Department of Computer Science, University of York
York YO10 5DD, England
ltm@poboxes.com
jam@cs.york.ac.uk

Abstract. The SPARK programming language and associated tools are specifically intended for the implementation of high integrity systems. SPARK2000 is an extension to the SPARK95 language to support object-oriented programming.
This paper presents how polymorphism can take place in SPARK2000 through restrictions on the use of access types. Those restrictions ensure that neither aliasing nor definition of recursive types can occur in SPARK2000. Due to the last restriction, the storage requirement of any program can be statically determined.

Keywords: SPARK, Ada, Object-Oriented Programming, Polymorphism

1 Introduction

The SPARK [ ] programming language is a subset of Ada that is suitable for the development of high integrity software. This is achieved by removing some features of Ada that can bring difficulties in proving that a program is correct (e.g. generics, exception, access types, etc.), and introducing features known as annotations that are used to support flow analysis, visibility control and formal proof.

We have designed SPARK2000 [ ] to support object-oriented programming while allowing modular reasoning. This is made possible due to the use of a notion of behavioural subtype$_{oo}$ [, ,].

Ada95 allows for dynamic/late binding without the necessity of using access types, but polymorphism can only be achieved through the use of class-wide types. Our first proposal of SPARK2000 does not allow the use of access types,

[1] The subscript "$_{oo}$" is used to indicate that the meaning of a particular word comes from the object-oriented paradigm and not from the Ada terminology. In the object-oriented paradigm a class$_{oo}$ specifies an abstract data type and from the type viewpoint it defines a type. The operations of the type are called methods$_{oo}$. Inheritance can be interpreted as specialization, therefore an ancestor (or superclass$_{oo}$) introduces a supertype$_{oo}$ and a descendent (or subclass$_{oo}$) defines a subtype$_{oo}$. The equivalent of class$_{oo}$ in Ada95 is a tagged type together with its primitive operations. Non-primitive operations are not considered because they do not dispatch.

H. B. Keller and E. Plödereder (Eds.): Ada-Europe 2000, LNCS 1845, pp. 252– , 2000.

therefore no variables declared through class-wide types can be truly polymorphic — once initializated a variable of class-wide type cannot have its type modified. Since it cannot take more than one form (type) during its life-time (scope), it cannot be considered polymorphic.

This restriction upon class-wide types is too strong and it hinders the benefits of the object-oriented paradigm provided by SPARK2000. For example, one cannot declare a list (or array) of points in which each element could be either a 2D or 3D point.

This work presents how access types can be allowed in SPARK2000 without compromising the approach. To reach such goal, two main problems must be addressed — aliasing/sharing of objects shall be forbidden and memory requirements shall be predictable.

The first problem is that aliasing of objects must not be allowed, to avoid side-effects. The second problem is that memory requirements of any program in SPARK2000 must be predictable, because error can occur if not enough memory is available during execution.

Due to the second problem the definition of recursive types must not be allowed. The use of pointers implies dynamic allocation and deallocation of memory. In the absence of a (proved correct) garbage collection system [ ], an explicit mechanism for memory management must be provided.

The main goal behind the definition of SPARK2000 is its use as the implementation/code language in a rigorous approach for the refinement of MooZ specifications [, , ,].

This paper is organized as follows: the next section presents a brief introduction to SPARK2000, section describes how access types can be introduced in SPARK2000, and the last section presents the conclusions and directions for further research.

2 SPARK2000

SPARK2000 is an object-oriented extension to SPARK95. The introduction of object-oriented programming in the SPARK approach was made possible due to the use of a notion of behavioural subtype$_{oo}$ that supports modular reasoning.

The behavioural subtype$_{oo}$ relation guarantees that each extended type behaves like its ancestor types. Moreover, an extended type is allowed to have a different behaviour from its ancestors if and only if this behaviour cannot be observed by a user of an ancestor type. Therefore, if a set of well-defined rules are satisfied, a tagged type can be extended on derivation without the need to re-verify previous (correct) programs/proofs.

A stronger notion of behavioural subtype$_{oo}$ is used in SPARK2000 due to some restrictions imposed by Ada95 — an extended type cannot modify the type (or name) of the components inherited, and the modifications allowed on

[2] MooZ stands for Modular Object-Oriented Z and it is an object-oriented extension to the Z notation [, ,].

the signature of any primitive operation inherited are restricted because all controlling arguments must have the same type.

Therefore, an extended type cannot choose a suitable name for the components that are inherited, nor can it modify their types to allow for a more efficient implementation of the abstraction. Moreover, the flexibility of covariance/contravariance of arguments/results are restricted to the ones that ensure that all inherited subprograms are primitive operations. Overloading and the definition of a subprogram that is not a primitive operation are not allowed in SPARK2000.

Because Ada95 does not support a message sending abstraction and the dispatch mechanism does not assign a special status to any arguments of an operation , in SPARK2000 the *first argument* of any method introduced by a class has a special meaning — it represents the object that receives the message.

SPARK2000 introduces six new annotations:

(1) **class_invariant**	(3) **type_conversion**	(5) **private**
(2) **initialstate**	(4) **public**	(6) **wraps**

Annotation (1) can only be used in tagged records. It specifies the invariant that must be maintained by the components of an object before and after each primitive operation execution. The invariant can be considered as part of the pre and postconditions of all primitive operations of a tagged type, except in the precondition of subprograms with annotation (2).

Annotation (2) can only be introduced in procedures. It indicates that the procedure is an initial state operation, and as such it must be the first subprogram to be executed for any object, except formal parameters. If there is more than one initial state procedure, it does not matter which one is used first.

In SPARK2000, type conversion of objects in a hierarchy cannot be freely used, only subprograms with annotation (3) are allowed to have statements for type conversion and record aggregate.

Either annotation (4) or annotation (5) must be introduced in each primitive operation to indicate whether a subprogram is public or private. A private subprogram is a procedure or function that can only be used by other subprograms of its type.

Annotation (6) is used to indicate to the examiner/proof tool (to be developed) for SPARK2000 that the primitive operation is actually a wrap subprogram — its sole existence is to convert the arguments into the correct types and views before applying them to the wrapped operation. This annotation is important for the refinement of MooZ specifications into SPARK2000 code.

[3] One argument used to support this approach is that for some operations, such as `Is_equal (x,y)`, it would be natural to assume that there is no object responsible to accomplish the comparison. However, this affirmation is not true in SPARK2000 and the reason can be found in section .

[4] Any argument in the signature of a subprogram could be used. However, to simplify traceability of a MooZ's method$_{oo}$ into an Ada95's primitive operation, it was decided that it would be the first argument. The statement `obj method (arg`$_1$`, ... ,arg`$_n$`)` in an object-oriented language is expressed as `method (obj,arg`$_1$`, ... ,arg`$_n$`)` in SPARK2000.

The behavioural subtype$_{oo}$ relation in SPARK2000 is composed of syntactic and semantic rules. Syntactic rules are used to guarantee signature compatibility and ensure that only primitive operations can be defined by the programmer. Moreover, except for the first argument of a primitive operation all other formal arguments whose type is a tagged type must allow for polymorphism (through class-wide types).

Semantic rules are used to guarantee that an extended type behaves like all its ancestors. However, a primitive operation in the extended type can operate outside the domain of applicability of its ancestors' subprogram, and return a result that would be unacceptable for an ancestor's object. This is only possible because aliasing is not allowed in SPARK2000 — such behaviour cannot be observed by a user of any ancestor type.

SPARK2000 is a conservative extension to SPARK95 — all rules defined for SPARK2000 only apply to packages that introduce tagged types.

3 Polymorphism in SPARK2000

This section presents how access types can be introduced in SPARK2000 to support true polymorphism. Section introduces some syntactical rules for definition of tagged types and signatures of primitive operations. Section presents the concept of primitive class$_{oo}$. Section explains how storage can be explicitly managed to support allocation and deallocation of objects. Section introduces the primitive operations that must be used to copy and compare objects. Section describes the operations that can be used for type enquiry and type conversion. Finally, section presents an example of application of the new syntactical rules and (re)definition of the operations introduced by a primitive class$_{oo}$.

3.1 Rules for Type Definition and Variable Declaration

To support a coherent naming of all type definitions and declaration of variables, the following convention rules are proposed:

1. In the definition of a tagged type its name shall end with `_class`;
2. For each tagged type there is exactly one globally declared access to class-wide type. This access type is named after the name of the tagged type with `_class` substituted by `_object`;
3. The first formal argument of a primitive operation must be an access parameter and the type used is as defined in the first rule;
4. Except for the first argument, if any other formal argument has its type defined by a tagged type then it must be declared as an access parameter whose type is a class-wide type of a named type as defined in the first rule;
5. Except for formal arguments, any variable declared by a user of a tagged type shall be declared using the named type defined in the second rule.

The first and second rules ensure that all tagged types are distinguished from the other types. The third rule is a consequence of the requirement upon the first formal argument of any primitive operation. The fourth rule guarantees that if a formal argument has its type defined by a tagged type, then it allows the use of an object of an extended type as actual argument in a call. The last rule ensures that a user of a tagged type can only declare variables that are truly polymorphic.

The type requirement on the formal arguments of all primitive operations implies that an actual argument cannot be null (nil/void value), and it cannot be modified because access parameters are of mode **in**.

This means that a tagged type does not provide any primitive operation able to deal with null pointers. All declarations of variables, using the named type described in the second rule above, must explicitly allocate an object of the nominal type during declaration.

The mode of an access parameter only states that the pointer itself cannot be modified to point to another object, nothing is said about what can happen to the object pointed to. Therefore, side-effect can occur in functions that have access parameter as formal argument.

A solution for this problem is the introduction of an annotation that states how an access parameter can be manipulated inside a subprogram: **access_mode**. Hence `--#` **access_mode** `(obj:` **in out**`; arg:` **in**`);` states that the object pointed to by the first argument can be read and modified whereas the object pointed to by the second argument can only be read.

To ensure that access parameters of mode **in** do not have their objects modified, they cannot be used as actual arguments to a subprogram if the associated mode annotation allows modification. To enforce encapsulation SPARK2000 does not allow dereference even when the components of a tagged type are not hidden/private.

3.2 Primitive Class$_{oo}$

Pure object-oriented programming languages, such as Smalltalk and Eiffel, and some object-oriented specification notations, such as MooZ, have the notion of *Primitive Class*$_{oo}$. In general a primitive class$_{oo}$ is used to introduce methods$_{oo}$ that are common to all classes$_{oo}$ in the language (copy, equality, type enquiry, etc.), and types and facilities that are directly related to language concepts (integer, array, string, etc.), properties of the compiler and environment (file management, exceptions, memory, arguments, etc.).

---

[5] Except for the names introduced by the first and second rules, no other name can end with `_class` and `_object`. Other than the access type defined in the second rule, no other access type definition can be introduced by the user.

[6] Although valid in Ada95, an initialization of a variable with a pointer to an object of a derived type is not allowed in SPARK2000. This ensures that the correct initialization operation is always applied. An assignment, using `Copy_to`, after initialization can be used to achieve the same effect.

[7] This rule does not apply to the code of any primitive operation of the type.

Some languages that provide object-oriented programming facilities, such as C^{++} and Ada95, do not have primitive class$_{oo}$ because its facilities are already provided by the non-object-oriented portion of the language, or there is no common functionality among classes$_{oo}$ defined in different hierarchies. SPARK2000, as defined in this work, has mechanisms that are common to all tagged types whatever their derivation class — the copy, comparison and type conversion operations, together with the explicit storage management mechanism.

In SPARK2000 almost all operations defined in a primitive class$_{oo}$ must be generated automatically by a tool. This is an important requirement because the proposal of SPARK2000 is not to extend Ada95 but to provide a mechanism that is as much as possible similar to the one provided by a pure object-oriented language. If this was not the case, the implementation of a specific compiler for SPARK2000 would be necessary.

The main disadvantage of this approach is that after (pre-)processing a user will end up with types that have more primitive operations than the ones introduced explicitly by the user. However, this does not represent a problem because the operations introduced by the user are not modified as the result of (pre-)processing — only new subprograms are introduced to redefine the ones defined in a primitive class$_{oo}$.

The conceptual flexibility provided by the notion of primitive class$_{oo}$ together with the elimination of possible errors introduced by the user in the definition of such operations for all tagged types, are enough to justify the inclusion of this notion in SPARK2000.

A new type, named `Spark2000_class`, is introduced as part of SPARK2000 own definition. Although it would be possible to assume that it is implicitly inherited by all tagged types (just like primitive class$_{oo}$ in true object-oriented languages) it was decided that this would not be the case for SPARK2000.

One reason is because Ada95 does not support multiple inheritance, the other reason is that while without tool support we would still like to be able to type-check a SPARK2000 program using any validated Ada95 compiler .

The specification for the type `Spark2000_class` and its primitive operations are presented below:

```
with Ada.Finalization;
with Ada.Unchecked_Deallocation;
package Spark2000 is
   type Spark2000_class is new
        Ada.Finalization.Controlled with private;
   type Spark2000_object is access all
        Spark2000_class'Class;
   procedure Create (
         obj: access Spark2000_class);
   procedure Free (obj: access Spark2000_class);
   procedure Copy_to (
         src: access Spark2000_class;
         dst: in out Spark2000_object);
   function Is_equal (
         obj1: access Spark2000_class;
         obj2: access Spark2000_class'Class)
      return boolean;
   function Is_same_type (
         obj1: access Spark2000_class;
         obj2: access Spark2000_class'Class)
      return boolean;
   function Is_ancestor (
```

[8] Although a SPARK2000 program on its own (without the automatically generated operations) is a syntactically valid Ada95 program, it certainly is semantically incorrect. For the operations introduced in a primitive class$_{oo}$ do not take into account the new component(s) of any extended type.

[9] Clearly this type-checking would be incomplete. For an Ada95 compiler does not verify/enforce the extra rules required by SPARK2000.

```
      obj1: access Spark2000_class;
      obj2: access Spark2000_class'Class)
    return boolean;
  function Is_descendant (
      obj1: access Spark2000_class;
      obj2: access Spark2000_class'Class)
    return boolean;
  function Is_in_same_hierarchy (
      obj1: access Spark2000_class;
      obj2: access Spark2000_class'Class)
    return boolean;
  procedure Convert_to_parent (
      src: access Spark2000_class;
      dst: access Spark2000_class'Class);
  procedure Convert_from_ancestor (
      dst: access Spark2000_class;
      src: access Spark2000_class'Class);
private
  type Spark2000_class is new
      Ada.Finalization.Controlled with
      record null; end record;
  procedure Initialize (
      obj: in out Spark2000_class);
  procedure Finalize (
      obj: in out Spark2000_class);
end Spark2000;
```

Three operations introduced by Spark2000_class do not need to be redefined by any tagged record — Is_descendant, Convert_from_descendant and Convert_-from_hierarchy — because they are defined in terms of the other operations.

```
package body Spark2000 is
  ...
  --# function Is_descendantPF (
  --#            obj1: Spark2000_class;
  --#            obj2: Spark2000_class'Class)
  --#         return boolean;
  function Is_descendant (
       obj1: access Spark2000_class;
       obj2: access
             Spark2000.Spark2000_class'Class)
       return boolean
    --# public;
    --# return Is_descendantPF (obj1, obj2);
    is begin
      return Is_ancestor (obj2, obj1);
    end Is_descendant;
  --# function Convert_from_descendantPF (
  --#            dst: Spark2000_class;
  --#            src: Spark2000_class'Class)
  --#         return Spark2000_class'Class;
  procedure Convert_from_descendant (
      dst: access Spark2000_class;
      src: access
           Spark2000.Spark2000_class'Class)
    --# public;
    --# type_conversion;
    --# access_mode (dst: in out; src: in);
    --# derives dst from src;
    --# post dst = Convert_from_descendantPF (
    --#              dst~, src);
    is
      temp: Spark2000.Spark2000_object := new
            Spark2000.Spark2000_class;
    begin
      Create (temp);
      if Is_descendant (src, dst) then
        Convert_to_parent (src, temp);
        Convert_from_descendant (dst, temp);
      else
        Copy_to (src,
             Spark2000.Spark2000_object (dst));
      end if;
      Free (temp);
    end Convert_from_descendant;
  --# function Convert_from_hierarchyPF (
  --#             dst: Spark2000_class;
  --#             src: Spark2000_class'Class)
  --#         return Spark2000_class;
  procedure Convert_from_hierarchy (
      dst: access Spark2000_class;
      src: access
           Spark2000.Spark2000_class'Class)
    --# public;
    --# access_mode (dst: in out; src: in);
    --# derives dst from src,dst;
    --# post dst = Convert_from_hierarchyPF (
    --#              dst~, src);
    is begin
      if Is_ancestor (src, dst) then
        Convert_from_ancestor (dst, src);
      elsif Is_descendant (src, dst) then
        Convert_from_descendant (dst, src);
      elsif Is_same_type (src, dst) then
        Copy_to (dst,
             Spark2000.Spark2000_object (src));
      end if;
    end Convert_from_hierarchy;
end Spark2000;
```

Section presents how the other primitive operations can be (re)defined in an example Points Hierarchy.

Initialize, Free and Finalize are described in the next section. The importance of the methods Copy_to and Is_equal is explained in section .

Is_same_type, Is_ancestor, Is_descendant, Is_in_same_hierarchy, Convert_to_-parent, Convert_from_ancestor, Convert_from_descendant and Convert_from_hierarchy are presented in section .

The operation Adjust, inherited from Ada.Finalization.Controlled, does not need to be redefined because it will never be called during execution. Except for

Is_equal, Convert_to_parent and Convert_from_ancestor, all other primitive operations cannot be redefined by the user — their names are regarded as reserved words in SPARK2000.

3.3 Explicit Storage Management

The explicit storage management mechanism of SPARK2000 makes use of the facilities provided by Ada95 to manage memory using controlled types [, §7.4].

By making Spark2000_class a derived type of Ada.Finalization.Controlled, it is possible to have "recursive" allocation and deallocation of memory done automatically by the run-time mechanism of the language.

No explicit values can be assigned by the Initialize operation. Only initial states primitive operations can be used to assign initial values to the components of a tagged type. To ensure that all memory allocated is eventually made available, it is a requirement that in every operation (except Copy_to) all local pointers must be explicitly deallocated just before return of control — flow analysis can be used to verify compliance to these rules.

To support explicit storage management, SPARK2000 must not allow a function to return a result that contains a pointer to an object. The reason is to avoid the creation of an object whose address is not assigned to any variable.

The actual code in a Points Hierarchy for the primitive operations Initialize, Finalize and Free is presented in section . A keen SPARK programmer will notice the use of **aliased** in the body of Free. Its use is required because the formal type of the argument for the instance of Ada.Unchecked_Deallocation is a pointer to an object of a tagged type. The annotation **hide** is used to indicate that the body of Free must not be verified for the purpose of flow analysis.

The presence of recursively defined types can be statically verified, therefore a tool can be used to point out all types that are recursive. However, polymorphism makes it impossible to calculate the exact memory requirement of a SPARK2000 program. But it is possible to calculate the *maximum* memory required for safe execution, because the derivation class of any tagged type is statically known.

For each variable declared as an access type, the maximum memory required to store it is the space necessary for a pointer type plus the size of the largest derived type (due to polymorphism). The space necessary to store an object of a tagged type is the sum of the (maximum) space requirements of all its components. If a tagged type contains only basic types (excluding access types), like the types defined in the Points Hierarchy, then this value is fixed. If a type contains pointers to objects of other types then the maximum memory required

[10] Notice that there is no inconsistency due to the use of the this annotation in the definition of SPARK2000 — SPARK also hides the body of some packages used in its own definition (e.g. Spark_IO).

[11] One must also take in consideration the problem that can occur due to fragmentation of memory space and the extra bits/bytes necessary for alignment of objects in valid addresses in memory.

is calculated assuming the worst case, when the pointers refer to the largest derived type. The attribute `size` can be used as a base for a program that calculates this value.

3.4 Assignment and Comparison Methods

To avoid aliasing, variables declared as an access type cannot be used in assignments. Each tagged type must introduce a primitive operation which is used to allocate a new slot in memory and realize a "deep" copy of an object. This operation, called `Copy_to`, must be used instead of an assignment.

This restriction alone ensures that aliasing cannot occur in SPARK2000 because the only operation available to make assignment is the one that makes a deep copy of an object.

The repeated use of an actual argument in an operation is allowed if and only if all corresponding formal arguments are not exported (they are of mode **in** only) — multiple readings of an actual parameter does not cause aliasing. This rule is already enforced in the SPARK approach [, §6.7].

Unfortunately, the signature and use of `Copy_to` is quite awkward because the second argument cannot be declared as an access parameter — a new object is created and the old object is deallocated, therefore its mode must be **in out**. However, calls to this primitive operation are always done in the same way: `Copy_to (src, Spark2000.Spark2000_object (dst));`.

In the operation `Copy_to`, the source (first argument) must be in the derivation class of the destination (second argument). This condition can be statically verified using the nominal type of each variable involved.

Because aliasing does not occur in SPARK2000, the equality operator = is useless when comparing variables declared as access type — except for the repeated use as an actual argument, no two variables can point to the same object.

Therefore, each tagged type must introduce a primitive operation used to compare objects. This function is analogous to the `Copy_to` operation in that it must realize a "deep" comparison if the object itself is composed of pointer(s) to another object(s).

This operation, called `Is_equal`, can be defined automatically, however the particular semantics associated to equality for each type means that the user might be required to (re)define this function.

3.5 Type Enquiry and Conversion Operations

In Ada95 it is necessary to manipulate some attributes (`tag` and `class`) explicitly to gather information about the actual/dynamic type of a variable declared as

---

[12] In the case of the Points Hierarchy, the largest type is `Point_3D_class`.

[13] This is the only case where type conversion can be used without the necessity of the annotation **type_conversion**. However, the type used is restricted to `Spark2000_object`, no other type can be used and a tool for SPARK2000 must enforce this requirement upon all calls to `Copy_to`.

a class-wide type. To simplify this task, SPARK2000 provides four primitive operations for type enquiry — `Is_same_type`, `Is_ancestor`, `Is_descendant` and `Is_in_same_hierarchy` — and four primitive operations for type conversion — `Convert_to_parent`, `Convert_from_ancestor`, `Convert_from_descendant` and `Convert_from_hierarchy`.

All operations take two arguments and, due to the use of a notion of primitive class_{oo}, the type enquiry operations can be called with a second argument of any derivation class.

`Is_same_type` returns true if and only if both arguments have the same (dynamic) type. `Is_ancestor` returns true if and only if the (dynamic) type of the first argument is an ancestor of the (dynamic) type of the second argument. `Is_descendant` does exactly the opposite of `Is_ancestor`. The last type enquiry operation returns true if and only if the (dynamic) type of one argument is in the class rooted at the (dynamic) type of the other argument. Notice that a type is not regarded as ancestor or descendant of itself.

The operation `Convert_to_parent` converts the first argument into its view as a parent's object and `Convert_from_ancestor` converts the second argument into its view as an object of the first argument's type. The user is required to define these two operations because they are used to relate extended and parent type's objects.

`Convert_from_descendant` converts the second argument into its view as an object of the type of the first argument. The syntactical requirement is that the nominal type of the second argument must be in the derivation class rooted at the nominal type of the first argument.

In the operation `Convert_from_hierarchy`, if the dynamic type of one argument is in the derivation class rooted at the type of the other argument, then it converts the second argument into its view as an object of the type of the first argument. If the condition is not satisfied then the first argument is left unchanged.

3.6 Example

This section presents the code for the type `Point_3D_class` of the Points Hierarchy. It is not necessary to redefine the primitive operations `Initialize` and `Finalize`, inherited from `Spark2000_class`, because only basic types are used as components of `Point_2D_class` and `Point_3D_class`.

---

[14] Both methods require that the nominal type of the second argument is an ancestor type of the first argument and this requirement can be statically verified by a tool for SPARK2000. In `Convert_from_ancestor`, if the dynamic type of an actual second argument is of the same type, or is an extended type, of the first argument then a copy of the second argument is assigned to the first argument.

[15] This restriction ensures that it is not possible to call `Convert_from_descendant` with an object as second argument whose dynamic type is an ancestor of the first argument.

[16] The tagged type `Point_2D_class` is not presented. From `Point_3D_class` one can easily find out how the actual code for `Point_2D_class` can be defined.

```
with Ada.Finalization;
with Ada.Unchecked_Deallocation;
with Spark2000;
package Points is
  type Point_2D_class is new
       Spark2000.Spark2000_Class with private;
  type Point_2D_object is
       access all Point_2D_class'Class;
  ...
  type Point_3D_class is new
       Point_2D_Class with private;
  type Point_3D_object is
       access all Point_3D_class'Class;
  procedure Create (
       obj: access Point_3D_class);
  procedure Free (obj: access Point_3D_class);
  procedure Copy_to (
       src: access Point_3D_class;
       dst: in out
            Spark2000.Spark2000_object);
  function Is_equal (
       obj1: access Point_3D_class;
       obj2: access
             Spark2000.Spark2000_class'Class)
       return boolean;
  function Is_same_type (
       obj1: access Point_3D_class;
       obj2: access
             Spark2000.Spark2000_class'Class)
       return boolean;
  function Is_ancestor (
       obj1: access Point_3D_class;
       obj2: access
             Spark2000.Spark2000_class'Class)
       return boolean;
  function Is_in_same_hierarchy (
       obj1: access Point_3D_class;
       obj2: access
             Spark2000.Spark2000_class'Class)
       return boolean;
  procedure Convert_to_parent (
       src: access Point_3D_class;
       dst: access
            Spark2000.Spark2000_class'Class);
  procedure Convert_from_ancestor (
       dst: access Point_3D_class;
       src: access
            Spark2000.Spark2000_class'Class);
  ...
  procedure Add (
       obj1: access Point_3_class;
       obj2: access Point_2D_class'Class);
  procedure Set_Coord3 (
       obj: access Point_3_class;
       val: integer);
  function Get_Coord3 (
       obj: access Point_3D_class)
       return integer
private
  type Point_2D_class is new
       Spark2000.Spark2000_Class with
       record x, y: integer; end record;
  type Point_3D_class is new
       Point_2D_Class with
       record z: integer; end record;
end Points;
```

Some primitive operations of Point_2D_class that where not presented above are inherited by Point_3D_class without modifications.

```
package body Points is
  ...
  procedure Create (p: access Point_3D_class)
    --# public;
    --# initialstate;
    --# access_mode (p: out);
    --# derives p from;
    --# post p.x=0 and p.y=0 and p.z=0;
    is begin
      p.x := 0; p.y := 0; p.z := 0;
    end Create;
  procedure Free (obj: access Point_3D_class)
    --# public;
    --# access_mode (obj: in out);
    --# derives obj from ;
    is
      --# hide Free;
      type Point_3D_ptr is access all
                           Point_3D_class;
      procedure Free_object is new
               Ada.Unchecked_Deallocation (
               Point_3D_class, Point_3D_ptr);
      temp : aliased Point_3D_object;
    begin
      temp := Point_3D_ptr (obj);
      Free_object (temp);
    end Free;
  --# function Is_equalPF ( ... )
  --#          return boolean;
  procedure Copy_to (src: access Point_3D_class;
       dst: in out Spark2000.Spark2000_object)
    --# public;
    --# type_conversion;
    --# access_mode (src: in);
    --# derives dst from src;
    --# post Is_equalPF (src, dst);
    is
      temp: Point_3D_object := new
                               Point_3D_class;
    begin
      Create (temp);
      temp := (x => src.x, y => src.y,
               z => src.z);
      Free (dst); dst := temp;
    end Copy_to;
  function Is_equal (
       obj1: access Point_3D_class;
       obj2: access
             Spark2000.Spark2000_class'Class)
       return boolean
    --# public;
    --# return Is_equalPF (obj1, obj2);
    is
      temp: Point_3D_object := new
                               Point_3D_class;
      result: boolean;
    begin
      Create (temp);
```

---

[17] For example: Set_coord1, Get_coord1, Set_coord2 and Get_coord2.

```
    if Is_in_same_hierarchy (obj1, obj2) then
      Convert_from_ancestor (temp, obj2);
      result := (obj1.x=temp.x and
                 obj1.y=temp.y and
                 obj1.z=temp.z);
    else
      result := false;
    end if;
    Free (temp); return result;
  end Is_equal;
--# function Convert_to_parentPF ( ... )
--#          return Spark2000_class'Class;
procedure Convert_to_parent (
    src: access Point_3D_class;
    dst: access
         Spark2000.Spark2000_class'Class)
  --# public;
  --# type_conversion;
  --# access_mode (src: in; dst: in out);
  --# derives dst from src;
  --# post dst = Convert_to_parentPF (
  --#            src, dst~);
  is
    temp: Point_2D_object := new
                             Point_2D_class;
  begin
    Create (temp);
    temp := (x => src.x, y => src.y);
    Copy_to (temp,
        Spark2000.Spark2000_object (dst));
    Free (temp);
  end Convert_to_parent;
--# function Convert_from_ancestorPF ( ... )
--#          return Point_3D_class;
procedure Convert_from_ancestor (
    dst: access Point_3D_class;
    src: access
         Spark2000.Spark2000_class'Class)
  --# public;
  --# type_conversion;
  --# access_mode (dst: in out; src: in);
  --# derives dst from src;
  --# post dst = Convert_from_ancestorPF (
  --#            dst~, src);
  is
    tmp1: Point_2D_object := new
                             Point_2D_class;
    tmp2: Point_3D_object := new
                             Point_3D_class;
  begin
    Create (tmp1); Create (tmp2);
    if Is_ancestor (src, dst) then
      Convert_from_ancestor (src, tmp1);
      tmp2 := (x => tmp1.x, y => tmp1.y,
               z => 0);
    else
      Copy_to (src,
        Spark2000.Spark2000_object (tmp2));
    end if;
    Copy_to (tmp2,
        Spark2000.Spark2000_object (dst));
    Free (tmp1); Free (tmp2);
  end Convert_from_ancestor;
  ...
--# function AddPF ( ... )
--#          return Point_3D_class;
procedure Add (
    obj1: access Point_3D_class;
    obj2: access Point_2D_class'Class)
  --# public;
  --# access_mode (obj1: in out; obj2: in);
  --# derives obj1 from obj1, obj2;
  --# post obj1 = AddPF (obj1~, obj2);
  is
    temp: Point_3D_object := new
                             Point_3D_class;
  begin
    Create (temp);
    Convert_from_ancestor (temp, obj2);
    obj1.x := obj1.x + temp.x;
    obj1.y := obj1.y + temp.y;
    obj1.z := obj1.z + temp.z;
    Free (temp);
  end Add;
end Points;
```

The actual codes for the subprograms `Is_same_type`, `Is_ancestor`, `Is_descendant`, `Is_in_same_hierarchy`, `Set_coord3` and `Get_coord3` have not been described — an interested reader should not have problem in finding out how they could be defined.

4 Conclusion and Future Work

This paper presented a proposal to support polymorphism in SPARK2000 through restrictions on the use of access types. In particular, aliasing and the definition of recursive types are not allowed. Due to the second restriction, and the use of an explicit memory management approach, it is possible to determine the maximum memory required for a safe execution of any SPARK2000 program.

To deal with access parameters another annotation was introduced — **access_mode** — to make explicit the mode under which the object pointed to by an access parameter can be manipulated. SPARK2000 supports the SPARK approach by requiring:

1. Behavioural subtype$_{oo}$ relation — allows proofs to be discharged using only nominal types;
2. Definition of a deep copy operation — means that aliasing cannot occur;
3. No recursive types — guarantees that the amount of storage space used is predictable;
4. Only primitive operations can be defined — ensures that all operations can dispatch and overloading is not possible, which avoids the possiblity of ambiguous calls;
5. Variables defined using tagged types shall support polymorphism — allows a uniform approach to deal with object-oriented programming in SPARK2000;
6. Formal arguments defined through tagged types shall use class-wide type — means that an actual argument can be an object of any extended type.

Operations that are usually assumed to be symmetrical (e.g. `Is_equal(x,y) = Is_equal(y,x)`) might be asymmetrical in SPARK2000. This happens due to the fact that two different definitions for the same operation might be used. The operation `Is_equal` might not be strictly symmetrical, however one can prove that if the dynamic types of both arguments are the same, then `Is_equal` behaves like a symmetrical operation.

This is ongoing work and as such it leaves a broad scope of topics for further research:

1. Tool support — for the adoption of SPARK2000 in practice, tool support is of vital importance and this represents the biggest disadvantage of SPARK2000 in relation to other approaches, like SPARK itself;
2. Case study — the small example presented is clearly insufficient to illustrate the full potential of the language. Case studies presenting examples of simple and complex systems are required;
3. Generic units — SPARK95 excluded generics on the grounds that it can present difficulties in proving that a program is correct. However, the ability to define generic types represents a powerful abstraction mechanism. MooZ allows the definition of generic class$_{oo}$ and supports multiple inheritance. Ada95 requires the use of generic units not only to support the definition of generic types, but also to provide a mechanism similar to multiple inheritance [, §4.6];
4. Behavioural subtype$_{oo}$ definition — while a proper support for contra/covariance of arguments/results would require changes in Ada95's dispatch mechanism, it is possible to have a mechanism that simulates the ability to redefine the components inherited by an extended type. Although this mechanism would not be efficient/elegant we believe that it might be useful in practice.

[18] If `x` and `y` are of type $\mathcal{X}$ and $\mathcal{Y}$ respectively, then the statement `Is_equal(x,y)` will call the primitive operation defined for $\mathcal{X}$ and `Is_equal(y,x)` will execute the primitive operation defined for $\mathcal{Y}$. If `Is_equal(x,y)` is true, this means that `y` can be used in place of `x`, and under $\mathcal{X}$ viewpoint it is not possible to distinguish `y` from `x`. On the other hand, if `Is_equal(y,x)` is true, this means that `x` has a view as a $\mathcal{Y}$'s object that is equal do `y`.

Acknowledgements

We would like to thank the (anonymous) referees for their valuable comments and Ian Toyn for his suggestions and corrections on previous versions of this paper. Lin is financially supported by CNPq/Brazil, grant 200938-92/4.

References

1. J. G. P. Barnes, editor. *Ada 95 Rationale: The Language, The Standard Libraries*, volume 1247 of *Lecture Notes in Computer Science*. Springer-Verlag, 1997.
2. J. G. P. Barnes. *High Integrity Ada: The* SPARK *Approach*. Addison-Wesley, 1997.
3. S. M. Brien and J. E. Nicholls, editors. *Z Base Standard (Version 1.0)*. ZIP Project, Programming Research Group, Oxford University, 1992.
4. K. K. Dhara and G. T. Leavens. Forcing behavioral subtyping through specification inheritance. Technical Report 95-20c, Dept. of Computer Science, Iowa State University, 1995.
5. R. Jones and R. D. Lins. *Garbage Collection: Algorithms for Automatic Dynamic Memory Management*. John Wiley & Sons, 1996.
6. K. C. Lano and H. P. Haughton, editors. *Object-Oriented Specification Case Studies*. Prentice Hall Object-Oriented Series. Prentice Hall, 1994.
7. T-M Lin. A formal semantics for MooZ (in portuguese). Master's thesis, Dept. of Informatics, Federal University of Pernambuco (UFPE), 1993. Available from `ftp.di.ufpe.br:/pub/projects/mooz/` or e-mail `ltm@poboxes.com` for a copy.
8. T-M Lin. SPARK2000 - an object-oriented extension to SPARK95 (draft). 1999. E-mail `ltm@poboxes.com` for a copy.
9. B. H. Liskov and J. M. Wing. A behavioral notion of subtyping. *ACM Transactions on Programming Languages and Systems*, 16(6):1811–1841, 1994.
10. S. R. L. Meira and A. L. C. Cavalcanti. The MooZ specification language (version 0.4). Technical Report ES/1.92, ProTeM/CC/NE - Dept. of Informatics, Federal University of Pernambuco (UFPE), 1992. Available from `ftp.di.ufpe.br:/pub/projects/mooz/` or e-mail `srlm@di.ufpe.br` for a copy.
11. J. M. Spivey. *The Z Notation: A Reference Manual*. Prentice Hall International Series in Computer Science. Prentice Hall, second edition, 1992.
12. S. Stepney, R. Barden, and D. Cooper, editors. *Object Orientation in Z*. Worshops in Computing. Springer-Verlag, 1992.
13. M. Utting. *An Object-Oriented Refinement Calculus with Modular Reasoning*. PhD thesis, Dept. of Computer Science, University of New South Wales, 1992.
14. J. C. P. Woodcock and J. Davis. *Using Z – Specification, Refinement, and Proof*. Prentice Hall International Series in Computer Science. Prentice Hall, 1996.

Improving the Reliability of Object-Oriented Software through Object-Level Behavioral Simulation*

Mahesh Deshpande, Frank Coyle, and Jeff Tian

Dept. of Computer Science and Engineering, Southern Methodist University
Dallas, Texas 75275, USA
{mahesh,coyle,tian}@seas.smu.edu

Abstract. In this paper we propose an Object-level Behavior Simulation Model (OBSM) that simulates the behavior of each object according to the message pattern exhibited by behavioral design pattern to verify it for its correctness. The model evaluates the existing reliability of the object-oriented software and allows developer to improve it during early phases of the development.

Keywords: object-oriented software, design patterns, reliability and quality, behavior simulation.

1 Introduction

The development of an object-oriented system involves identifying objects, defining and implementing classes, inheritance and association relations among objects during the analysis, design and coding phases of the software life cycle [ ]. The recent development has resulted in Design Patterns — elements of reusable object oriented software [ ]. The main advantages of using design patterns are reusability and maintainability during and after the software development. The reusability allows existing design or code functionality to be re-applied to solve new and different software problems. The maintainability allows for easy modification and enhancement to the previously developed software.

The object-oriented paradigm allows mapping of real world entities into their software counter-parts during development and hence such software is usually easy to understand and maintain. The use of this paradigm also affects the reliability of the resulting object-oriented software systems. The reliability of a software systems is the probability of its failure free operations for a given time duration or a given set of input under a specific environment [ ]. These failures are observable deviations to the expected behavior triggered by certain system operations when the software components used to implement these operations contain faults injected into the software systems during development. For example, failing to implement a requirement, failing to implement a design decision

* This work is supported in part by NSF/CAREER award CCR-9733588 and Nortel Networks.

H. B. Keller and E. Plödereder (Eds.): Ada-Europe 2000, LNCS 1845, pp. 266– , 2000.

during the design phase or failing to implement a programming feature correctly during the programming phase, results in incorrect and undesirable functionality that affects the reliability of the software. Injected faults may also produce cascading effects during development due to reuse, and reduce the reliability of the software even further. Our recent research has focused on early measurement of software reliability and identification of problematic areas, so that timely remedial actions can be taken to effectively ensure and improve software reliability [ ]. If the reliability is evaluated during each phase and also during the transition from one phase to another, it will allow developer to take necessary measures and improve the reliability during the development itself. Such an approach to the reliability improvement may result in more reliable object-oriented software.

In object-oriented software systems, the messages that an object sends and receives through its interface defines its behavior. If the design and programming decisions do not conform to the specification or to the constraints imposed by the application, it may result in software which is less reliable. In case of object-oriented software development using behavioral design patterns, the resultant software often becomes less reliable when the message pattern exhibited by a particular behavioral design pattern is not implemented correctly due to incorrect design and/or programming decisions.

In this paper we focus our attention to improving reliability of object-oriented software that involves use of behavioral design patterns during development. We propose a model that verifies correctness in the use of design patterns by simulating the object-level behavior during design prototyping and early implementation phases of the development cycle. The model identifies failures and allows for their correction and thus aims at improving reliability during early stages of the development [ ].

The organization of this paper is as follows. In the next section we discuss the Observer design pattern and describe, with examples, how various design and programming decisions can affect the reliability of the resultant object-oriented software. In Section 3, we describe the Object-level Behavioral Simulation Model (OBSM) and how it verifies the correctness of design and implementation through object-level behavioral simulation. In Section 4, we briefly discuss the related work on object-oriented software reliability and testing, and in Section 5, we present our conclusions and future work.

2 Need for Evaluating the Reliability of OO Software

The essential elements of developing any object-oriented software are identifying, designing and implementing classes, objects and inheritance relations to solve the problem. The logically related classes are grouped together in hierarchies. Each object represents an instance of some class. The class hierarchies and the types of relations between different objects represent the application knowledge. The objects pass messages to each other during the program execution to implement the application knowledge.

Design patterns provide generalized and elegant solutions to commonly occurring object-oriented problems and are often directly used during design prototyping and initial implementation phases. The messages that an object can receive and send through its public interface defines its behavior. A behavioral design pattern defines the behavior of a group of objects in the form of specific message patterns that address the problem. A behavioral design pattern is thus characterized by its message pattern. However, such a direct use of a message pattern may result in object-oriented software which may not reflect the desired functionality or may implement undesired functionality, if applied incorrectly. In either case, the resultant object-oriented software's behavior deviates from user expectations, and the software becomes less reliable.

We next describe a behavioral design pattern called Observer, which is used as an example pattern in this paper. We illustrate how incorrect design and programming decisions in the use of the Observer pattern results in undesired functionality that may reduce the software reliability.

2.1 Observer Design Pattern

The intent of the Observer pattern is to define a one to many dependency between objects so that when one object changes state, all its dependents are notified and updated automatically [5]. The key objects in this pattern are 'subject' and 'observer'. A subject may have any number of dependent observers. All observers are notified whenever the subject's state is changed. In turn each observer queries the subject to synchronize its own state with that of the subject.

The interaction diagram in Fig. shows the collaborations between a subject, two observers and a user object and captures the basic message pattern of the Observer. The user object refers to an application object other than the subject or observer objects. The user object causes change in subject's state by invoking 'setState' operation on the subject. The subject then notifies all its observers by invoking 'update' operation on each observer. Each observer in turn invokes 'getState' operation on the subject to synchronize its own state with that of the subject.

The major constraints as enforced by the Observer pattern over the subject and its observers are,

1. When the subject's state is changed by the user object to a state which is different than its observers' state, the subject must notify all of its observers of the change in its state.
2. When the subject's state is changed by one of its observers, the subject must notify all of its observers of this change in its state.
3. The observers, upon receiving notification from the subject, must update themselves with the subject's state.
4. The subject's state and all of its observers' state must be consistent with each other just before and after the interaction.

In order to understand what different design and programming decisions can violate the above constraints, several variations of the Observer pattern were

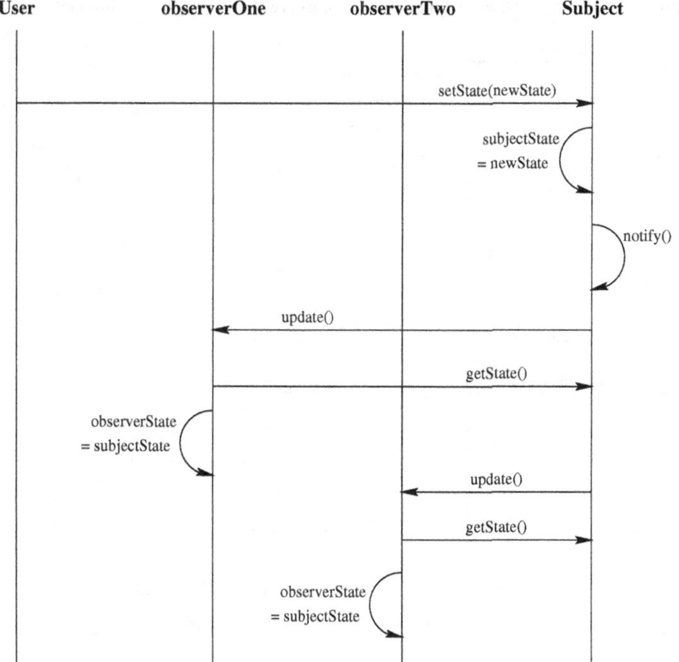

Fig. 1. Observer message pattern

implemented in C++. It was observed that subject and its observer objects result in inconsistent states due to the design and programming decisions that violate the above constraints. This study helped us in identification of major design and programming decisions affecting the reliability of the object-oriented software [ ].

2.2 Design Decisions Affecting Reliability

In case of Observer pattern the designer's decisions that may affect the reliability include:

- incorrect implementation of dependencies between subject and its observers
- failing to assign object responsibilities
- incorrect implementation of inheritance
- incorrect associations or part of relationships between objects
- incorrect decision about whether to handle or ignore a notification
- unexpected updates
- inappropriate decision over public, private, protected interface of a class
- incorrect assumption about the references among subject and observer objects

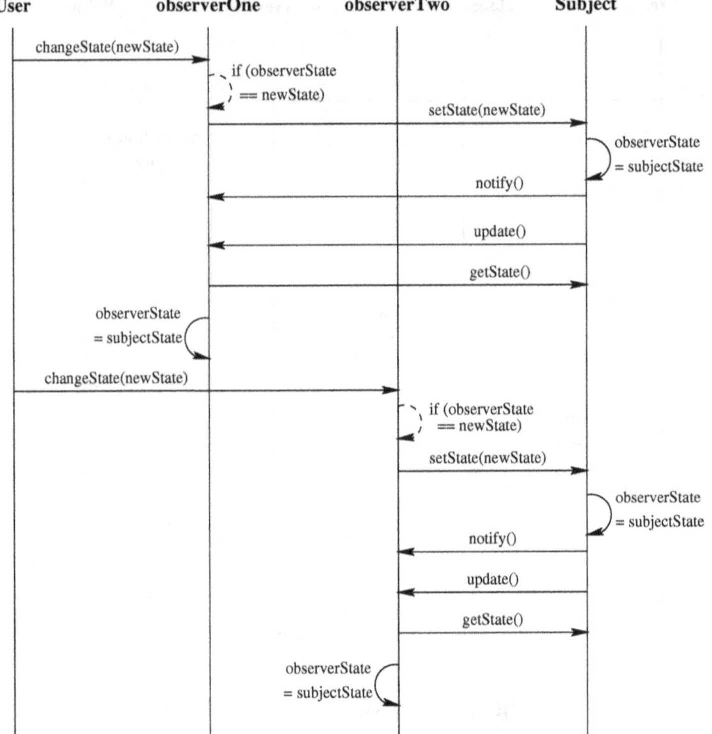

Fig. 2. When a subject doesn't maintain reference to its observers

As an example, the event trace diagram in Fig. illustrates a scenario when a subject doesn't maintain reference to its observers. Since the subject fails to keep reference to all of its observers, only the observer who invokes the 'setState' operation on the subject gets notified by the subject and updates its own state with that of the subject but other observers' state remains unchanged. The final state of the subject and its observers become inconsistent due to this design decision. It violates one of the major constraints specified by the Observer pattern and therefore results in software which is less reliable.

2.3 Programming Decisions Affecting Reliability

In case of Observer pattern the programming decisions that may affect the reliability include:

- forgetting to call an operation
- passing incorrect parameters
- incorrect sequence of operations
- failing to register newly created observer

- failing to remove deleted observer from the subject's list
- failing to initialize observer or subject states when they are created or updated
- failing to check subject state for its self-consistency before notification
- failing to inform observers of the deleted subject

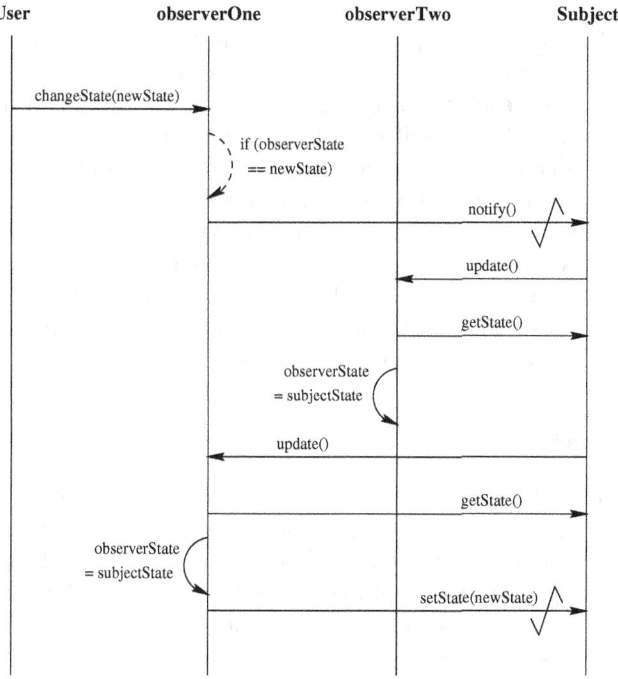

Fig. 3. Incorrect order of operations

As an example the event trace diagram in Fig. illustrates the scenario when programmer implements an incorrect sequence of operations by calling 'notify' before 'setState'. In this scenario the observers are notified by the subject before its own state is set to newState, resulting in observers updating their own state with the old subject state. The final state of the subject and observer objects become inconsistent and therefore results in less reliable software.

In case of Observer pattern there exists a one to many dependency between subject and its observer objects. Thus the subject and its observer objects exhibit a specific message pattern. Each observer's state depends upon its subject's state. When there is a change in the subject's state, it is responsibility of the subject to notify all its observers of change in its state. The observers then synchronize their own state with that of the subject. The subject and observers' state must be consistent just before and after any interaction. These interactions thus define a protocol between subject and its observers. Every major object in itself also exhibits a specific message pattern when it interacts with other objects. With these observations we formalize the message pattern exhibited by an individual object and group of objects when they collaborate, which together forms our formal model.

3 Object-Level Behavior Simulation Model (OBSM)

The main idea behind the proposed model is to simulate the corresponding formal model over every major object to verify it for its correctness. To be more specific, it simulates each and every message captured by the formal model over the input object and checks if it satisfies the model. If the model is satisfied for each and every individual object and also by the group of objects then we can conclude that design and programming decisions conform to the constraints enforced by the design pattern and hence the resultant software is reliable in the given context. On the other hand even if single object does not confirm to the formal model we can conclude that some design or programming decision does not conform to the constraints enforced by the design pattern and hence the resultant software is less reliable in the given context.

3.1 Basic Idea

The objective of the proposed model is to evaluate and improve the reliability of the software by verifying it for its correctness. In case of behavioral design patterns, major objects exhibit a specific message pattern when they collaborate. The message pattern is captured in the formal model. The proposed model then verifies this formal model over the input objects for its correctness. The verification process involves,

1. Verification of the specific message pattern specified by the formal model over the input.
2. Verification of the data values passed through these messages.
3. Verification of the order of messages passed between input objects.
4. Verification of the initial and final values of subject and observer states for their consistency.

The proposed Object-level Behavior Simulation Model (OBSM) consists of three major components: input (I), simulator (S) and formal model (F), as shown in conceptual block diagram in Fig. . The simulator simulates the formal model over input for the verification of its correctness.

I = {subject, observers, User}
S = {subject, observers}
F = {g1, g2, g3, ... , cg1, cg2, cg3, ... , fm}
O = {yes, no} if O = 'no' then output is a 'list of failures'.

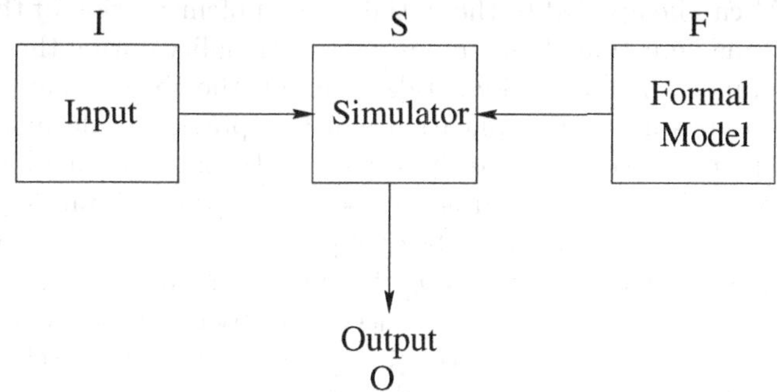

Fig. 4. Object-level Behavior Simulation Model (OBSM)

Following is the description of the member components,

- subject and observers are class objects. User represents an application object.
- subject and observers in simulator S, are the copies of the subject and observer objects.
- g1, g2, g3, ... are formal graphs of the formal model. Each graph g(i) represents only one responsibility of an object. The g(i) graph only depicts an 'invoking message' as received and the 'response message' as sent out by an object for particular responsibility.
- cg1, cg2, cg3, ... are also formal graphs of the formal model and each cg(i) component depicts the responsibility represented by the corresponding g(i) component, in its completeness. For example, cg1 graph represents complete scenario of the responsibility depicted by the corresponding g1 graph. cg(i) graph consists of object that sends an 'invoking message' and also involves object or objects that receive 'response message'. It also takes into account any other messages sent out or operations performed by these objects.
- fm is also the formal graph of the formal model and depicts an intent of the Observer pattern in one complete graph and captures only those collaborations among the subject and its observers that *must* be essentially present to enforce the basic intent of the Observer pattern. The fm graph captures the message *sequence* among these objects.
- Each formal graph consists of set of nodes and set of edges. Nodes represent objects and edges represent messages and/or data received by objects.
- When the input satisfies the formal model, output of the verification process is objective in nature and is represented by 'success' otherwise output is a file containing list of failures.

3.2 Input

The major advantage of using the OBSM is that it can be applied both during and after the development equally effectively. During development, it can take as an input the objects that are instances of the class prototypes being developed.

Thus, OBSM can be applied to the initial code implementation of the class prototypes allowing detection of any undesired functionality during the early phases of the development. The OBSM can take as input, the objects that are instances of class prototypes from an application which is previously developed and has failures which are not yet detected. It may also take as input, an application that has failed to implement constraints imposed by the behavioral design pattern, Observer in our case [ ]. Since the Observer pattern imposes its constraints based on message passing dependency among the subject and observers, only those application objects that represent the subject and observer objects are considered as input. The message identifiers used in input object must match the message identifiers captured in the formal model in order to avoid manual mapping of identifiers. The model then verifies the message-passing pattern between the input objects for its correctness by simulating the formal model over input objects for detecting failures.

3.3 Formal Model

In object-oriented systems, an object can be assumed to exhibit three types of services during its interaction with other objects [ ].

- set of services that it offers to other objects when it receives an invoking message
- set of services it performs on other objects when it sends an invoking message to other objects and,
- set of services it performs for itself when it sends an invoking message to itself

The formal model formalizes for each object, the set of services *offered* by an object to other objects when it receives an invoking message and a set of services it *performs* for itself [ ]. By formalizing the services offered by the object, formal model eliminates the need to formalize services performed by that object because the services performed by the object are the services offered by the other object and are formalized as a part of formalizing the services offered by the other object. The formal model of the Observer pattern formalizes each responsibility and hence each service offered by the subject and observer objects. In case of formal model of the Observer pattern, each g(i) graph formalizes only one responsibility of the subject or observer object. It consists of, an incoming edge representing the invoking message, a node representing the subject or observer object and an outgoing edge representing the response message.

- an incoming edge shows invoking message name
- an outgoing edge shows response message name for a particular responsibility of the subject or observer object
- an edge may also show any data carried by that message
- node representing the subject or observer object contains placeholder for subject state or observer state.

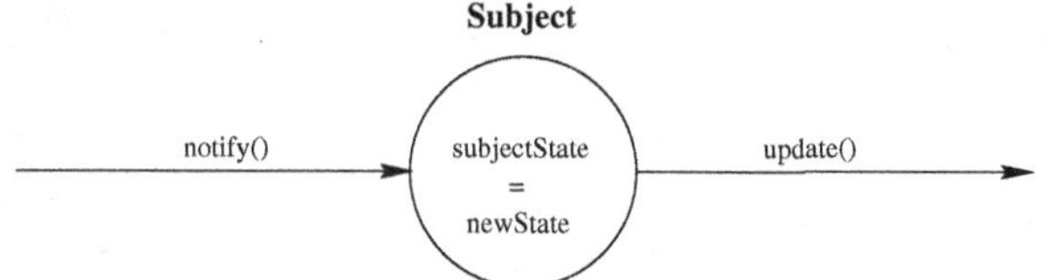

Title: Notify responsibility graph g(i).

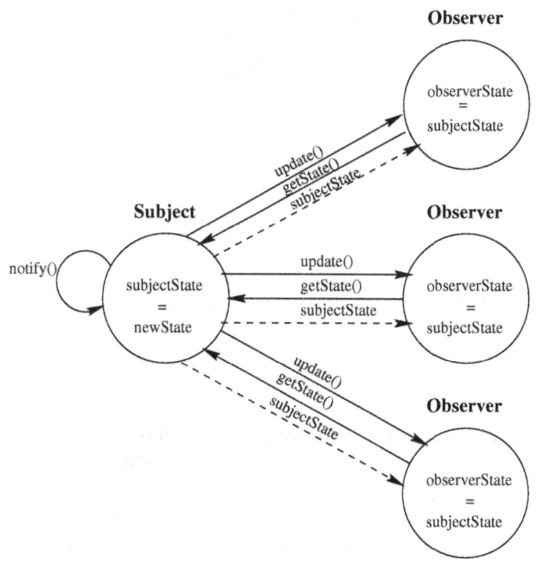

Title: Notify responsibility scenario cg(i).

Fig. 5. Formal model: Notify responsibility graphs

The g(i) graph only formalizes how subject and observer objects respond to an invoking message. The cg(i) graph on the other hand formalizes the responsibility indicated by corresponding g(i) graph in its completeness. The cg(i) graph formalizes all the objects and messages involved in carrying out that particular responsibility. As an example, Fig. illustrates g(i) and corresponding cg(i) formal graphs for the 'notify' responsibility. Fig. illustrates the 'fm' formal graph that captures the complete message pattern exhibited by the Observer pattern. The fm graph thus formalizes the *sequence* of message pattern. The formal graphs are developed and implemented for each responsibility of each object. At the implementation level the formal graphs can be constructed and stored in the form of linked list where each node can store the object name, object state, incoming message name, outgoing message name and the placeholder for the date that a message may carry. These graphs together constitute the formal model (F) component of the OBSM.

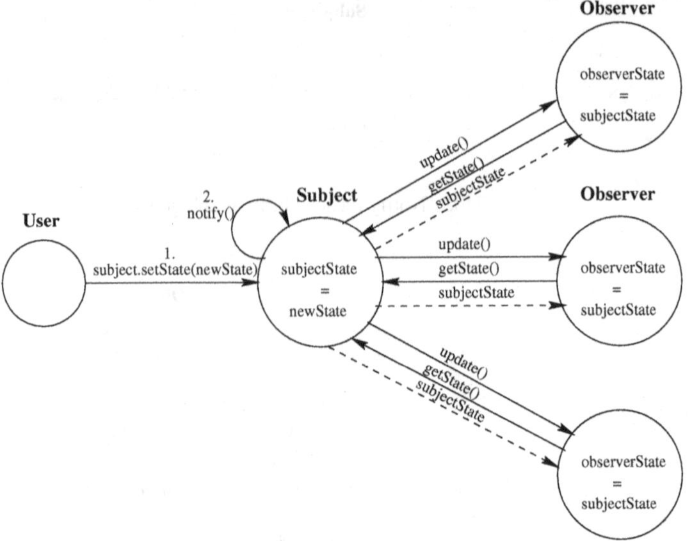

Fig. 6. Formal model: Observer pattern scenario

3.4 Simulator

The simulator is used to simulate the formal model over input objects and specify the result of the simulation process as an output. The main functionality of the simulator is to check whether the input objects satisfy all of the following,

1. implement the specific message pattern as specified by the formal model.
2. pass messages with data values of specific data types as specified by the formal model.
3. pass messages in specific order as specified by the formal model.
4. have their initial and final states consistent just before and after the interaction.

In order to accomplish the above tasks, simulator first checks whether the subject and observer objects carry out their responsibilities as specified by g(i) and cg(i) graphs of the formal model. The simulator then simulates the fm graph over the input objects for verification of its correctness. The g(i) and cg(i) graphs are useful for verifying the object-level responsibilities however fm graph is useful for verifying the *sequence* of message passing between these objects because fm graph captures the basic message pattern exhibited by the behavioral design pattern.

To verify g(i) and cg(i) graphs, simulator for each type of input object, and for each of its responsibility performs following steps in sequence.

1. reads the formal model specification for that particular responsibility. The specification of a responsibility is in the form of g(i) and cg(i) graphs as shown in Fig. .

2. simulates each of these graphs over a copy of the input object. First, it simulates g(i) graph by sending the invoking message as specified by the g(i) and verifying whether object sends out the response message as specified by the g(i) graph. The corresponding cg(i) graph depicts the responsibility in its entirety. The simulator then simulates cg(i) graph over the input object in a similar fashion by sending a message to object and verifying message or messages sent out or operations performed, as in cg(i) graph.
3. checks for a specific order of messages and data values carried out by these messages while simulating formal graph. It also checks for the pre-state and post-state values of the objects involved, for their consistency.
4. maintains a status report of the above simulation process over the input object for each of its responsibility, by storing the result of each simulation into a text file.

Using the above four steps, the simulator confirms that each input object carries out its responsibilities as specified by g(i) and cg(i) graphs of the formal model. The simulator then checks whether all input objects together follow 'complete formal model' as specified by the fm graph shown in Fig. and satisfies the intent of the Observer pattern when they collaborate.

When the object performs an operation in response to an invoking message instead of sending out some message, it is necessary to verify the result of the operation to ensure the correctness of the implementation. This is not an easy task to achieve, even with the help of advanced debugging or testing tools. Also, if the developer has failed to write a piece of code that will inform him of the status of the operation after its execution, using any kind of test data is insufficient, that would give him confirmation of the correct execution of the operation. To handle such a situations simulator instruments copies of input objects with piece of code that allows simulator to verify correctness of the implementation. Since simulator works on the *copies* of input objects in its own environment, actual input is *not* changed for the purpose of verification. An object instrumentation is a part of implementation of the OBSM and is not discussed in this paper.

3.5 Output, Analysis and Followup

The output of the OBSM is the result of the simulation process. The simulator simulates g(i), cg(i) and fm graphs of the formal model over copies of the input objects and logs the result of each simulation into a text file. The result of the simulation can be either 'success' or 'failure'. During the simulation, if each object sends out same message or performs same operation in response to an invoking message with correct pre-states and post-states as specified by the corresponding g(i), cg(i) and fm graphs, the result of the simulation is 'success' otherwise 'fail'. In case of 'fail', the log gives detail information about object type, message name, data type, data value, sequence of messages sent/received, sequence of operations performed, list of other objects invoked etc. for each failure.

If the output is 'success' for each message of the object and if this is also true for all the objects then we can conclude that class prototypes and the implementation of their objects is correct with respect to the formal model and hence the class prototype and its implementation under evaluation is reliable in the given context. If the output is 'fail' even for a single message of an object the class prototype and its implementation is incorrect with respect to the formal model and hence it is less reliable or unreliable.

The use of OBSM model gives us a precise log information about the failure as mentioned above. Such information can then be fed into various software reliability growth models (SRGMs) [ ] for reliability assessment and prediction, or fed into our tree-based reliability models (TBRMs) [ ] to identify problematic areas for focused defect removal which promises effective reliability improvement. It thus allows developer to remove those failures and improve the reliability of the software during the early phases of the development.

4 Related Work

Chow proposed a method called 'automata theoretic' for testing the control structures that can be modeled by a finite state machine [ ]. The test results derived from the design are evaluated against the specification but no executable prototype is required. The method consists of three major steps,

1. estimate the maximum number of states in the correct design;
2. generate test sequences based on design that may have errors;
3. verify the responses to the test sequences

The specification is stated in the form of set of axioms against which the design is tested. The correctness of the program is based on the specification. It describes the methodology for testing the control flow of the program against its specification. Thus the automata theoretic method can be applied for testing the software that can be evaluated against the specification however the usefulness of this method is limited due to the difference in representation of specification and the design or program.

Binder extended above approach for testing objects in object-oriented systems [ ]. In his view, classes are often designed to accept certain message sequences and reject others and respond differently for a particular set of encapsulated values. He proposed a state-based testing that could be used to verify behavior with few test cases. The states of a class are the subsets of the set of all possible combinations of attribute values. The method uses Chow's procedure to derive state transition test sequences. Although this method focuses to verify behavior with few test cases it may suffer from state explosion problem as the states of a class are subsets of the set of all possible combinations of attribute values.

Robson describes a black-box testing method for testing the interactions between the features of an object and the object's state [ ]. The object's features refer to the object's methods. The methods are invoked in several different ways.

The input and output states for each features are identified from the specification and then test cases are used to validate each state transition. The effectiveness of this method is dependent upon the degree of control information that exists as a part of data representation of the class.

5 Conclusions and Perspectives

By carefully studying the behavior of an object-oriented system that uses behavioral design patterns, we can understand how design and programming decisions that are critical to the correctness of the system can affect reliability. In this paper we proposed an Object-level Behavior Simulation Model (OBSM) that first evaluates the existing reliability by verifying the correctness of design prototypes and their initial implementation against the formal model. It simulates the behavior of each object and verifies it for its correctness. The simulation process detects the failures and provides a detailed log of each failure. This information can be used in our tree-based reliability models [ ] to assess the current reliability as well as to identify problematic areas for focused reliability improvement. The developer can then remove individual failures and can recursively apply the model until the desired reliability target is achieved. The OBSM can be extended to verify other behavioral design patterns by replacing the formal model of the Observer pattern by the formal model of the corresponding pattern. The Object-level Behavior Simulation Model (OBSM) thus evaluates the reliability of the object oriented software and also creates a scope for the developer to improve it during the early phases of the development cycle.

References

1. R. Binder. State-based testing. *Object Magazine*, pages 75–78, Aug. 1995.
2. G. Booch. *Object-Oriented Analysis and Design with Applications.* Addison-Wesley, 1994.
3. T. S. Chow. Testing software design modeled by finite-state machines. *IEEE Trans. on Software Engineering*, 4(3):178–187, May 1978.
4. M. Deshpande. Detecting design violations in the use of design patterns, *Masters Thesis*, CSE Department, Southern Methodist University, Dallas, Texas, Dec. 1998.
5. E. Gamma, R. Helm, R. Johnson, and J. Vlissides. *Design Patterns: Elements of Reusable Object-Oriented Software.* Addison-Wesley, 1995.
6. M. R. Lyu, editor. *Handbook of Software Reliability Engineering.* McGraw-Hill, New York, 1995.
7. D. J. Robson and C. D. Turner. The state based testing of object-oriented programs. In *Proc. Int. Conf. Software Maintenance*, pages 302–311, 1993.
8. J. Tian. Integrating time domain and input domain analyses of software reliability using tree-based models. *IEEE Trans. on Software Engineering*, 21(12):945–958, Dec. 1995.

Results of an Investigation into Software Integration Testing Automation

Simon Kiteley and Jonathan Draper

BAE SYSTEMS□
Airport Works□Rochester□Kent□ME□□XX□UK
Tel□□□□□□□□□□□□□□□□□□□□□Fax□□□□□□□□□□□□□□□□□□
simon□kiteley@gecm□com□
jonathan□draper@gecm□com

Abstract□ 'Faster□Cheaper□Better' is a phrase commonly used□ With unit and integration testing□ typically being □□□ of the cost of development□ significant improvements can be made by either reducing the required effort or increasing the effectiveness of testing□ Tools such as □TestMate and StateMate can be used to further increase the level of automation used in unit and integration testing□ even to the point of producing inputs and expected results□ This paper presents the procedures developed by the SITAR project and the results of the evaluation showing a cost saving□

□□ Introduction

This paper describes the background□ objectives□ plans and results for the Software Integration Testing Automation Review □SITAR□ project□

SITAR focused on the improvement of software integration testing by automating the generation□ application and analysis of test cases using the tools TestMate and StateMate□ It also investigated how these tests can be used to replace some of the unit testing□

This paper first describes the objectives of SITAR□ It then puts the experiment into the context of the overall software development lifecycle by describing the processes of software unit testing and software integration testing□ The plan for the experiment is described and a comparison drawn between the conventional and SITAR methods of testing□ Finally□ the paper reports on the experiment and the results□

□□ Background

SITAR □Ref□□□ was a □□ month project□ which was funded by the CEC as a European Systems and Software Initiative □ESSI□ Process Improvement Experiment □PIE No□ □□□□□□ The sole participant in SITAR is BAE SYSTEMS Avionics Limited□

H□B□ Keller and E□ Plödereder □Eds□□ Ada Europe □□□□□ LNCS □□□□□ pp□□□□□□□□□□□□□

BAE SYSTEMS Avionics Limited formally trading as Marconi Avionics is one of Europe's largest producers of aviation electronic and ground support equipment for the world's civil and military aircraft Avionic Systems an operating division within BAE SYSTEMS Avionics is involved in the development of hardware and software for safety related applications

Objectives of SITAR

The main business objective of SITAR is to reduce the cost of software testing This is achieved by increasing the automation of the integration process allowing more test cases to be developed in less time This objective can be refined to the following technical tasks

- Evaluate the use of TestMate for Unit Testing
- Evaluate the feasibility of removing Unit Testing with enhanced Integration Testing
- Evaluate Automated Integration Testing using TestMate and StateMate

Software Testing

Testing Ref covers a range of verification activities performed on software after the design and implementation phases There may be other verification activities such as code inspection or static code analysis before or between the different testing activities There are three main levels of software test activities

Software Unit Tests these test each code unit in isolation against its design
Software Integration Tests these test the software against the software requirements usually within the host environment
Systems Integration Tests these test the complete software running on the target hardware against the system requirements

Software unit tests are designed to meet functional coverage such as design parameter boundary analysis and structural coverage such as statement coverage Unit tests usually use stub routines to simplify testing

Software integration tests are performed on the host testing the complete or progressively larger builds of the software with models of the hardware interfaces Tests are designed to meet different levels of coverage both functional such as requirement boundary analysis and structural such as every procedure or function called at least once

Systems integration tests are created directly from the requirements of the system and are used to test the complete hardware and software

There are seven tasks within the overall unit or software integration testing activity

- Construction of Test Harness
- Construction of stubs

- Application of the test cases to the software under test
- Comparison of the expected test results with the actual test results
- Calculation of structural test coverage
- Selection of test case inputs
- Calculation of expected results

The first five tasks are generally automated by existing commercially available tools TestMate not only supports the currently automated tasks but also provides some functionality for test case input generation

Automated generation of expected outputs were calculated by using a StateMate model of the software requirements

Tools Used during Experiment

Two main tools were used during this experiment TestMate and StateMate TestMate is developed by Rational as part of its Apex development environment It is fully integrated into the development environment and takes advantage of its configuration management environment

TestMate uses a table to specify the inputs and expected outputs It also allows the user to stub routines and call supporting routines The series of expected inputs and outputs can be specified for when the stub routines are called

TestMate takes a copy of the original code to allow it to be instrumented TestMate uses the table to create the required harness and stub routines TestMate then builds and runs the tests On completion of the run the results of the test are presented in another table and a textual script output is produced which can be examined to identify why any tests failed

Coverage can also be analysed during the runs The coverage results can be accessed via the Results Table

Three different levels of coverage were measured statement decision and MCDC Statement coverage measures the percentage of statements that have been executed Decision coverage also considers both the true and false decisions and all cases within a case statement MCDC also checks that each condition within a decision behaves correctly independently from the other conditions Ref

StateMate is developed by I logix StateMate provides support for modeling using State Charts including editing checking and graphical animation and generation of C code

A segment of the baseline projects requirements have been modeled within StateMate The modeling is in the form of state transition diagrams This is suited to the nature of the baseline project that is largely a control program

Additional functionality can be embedded into the model by using standards C code C code was used to implement the parser that read the test list file and generated the outputs to be placed into the test list

The model is used to generate C code which can then be built and run either from within the tool or as a standalone executable

To allow the model to be used as more of a prototype graphical interfaces can be created that allow input and output

Structure of the Experiment

The experiment tested configured builds of software from the baseline project and constructed a StateMate model of the software requirements to calculate expected results

The testing evaluation was performed in three stages Unit testing manual software integration testing and automated software integration testing

The performance of unit testing provided metrics on applying testing and re testing at the normal point in the life cycle The unit tests were written to achieve the different levels of coverage statement decision and Modified Condition Decision Coverage MCDC

To determine the different metrics the testing was performed to statement coverage then improved to decision and finally to MCDC

Two sets of Software Integration Tests were created The first were manual tests on a subset of a Stores Management System SMS using manually created inputs and expected outputs The second set of tests simulated the use of automatically generated inputs and expected outputs with the aid of StateMate

The results for the different types of integration tests and unit tests were compared with each other and those of the conventional test processes used on the baseline project

Baseline Project

SITAR investigated the effectiveness of these new testing techniques on an avionics baseline project The baseline project is part of an upgrade to an aircraft SMS with the upgrade being the addition of new store types

The baseline project is a real time embedded system that is typical of the software developed by Avionic Systems The stores management system keeps an inventory of the stores loaded and their current status It also controls the arming and release of the stores

The baseline product is written in Ada It is a control based system so it is suitable for modelling in StateMate The part that was used in SITAR is approximately lines of Ada which is about of the total software

For unit testing the baseline project used one in house tool THUG to automatically generate test harnesses and test stubs apply test cases and compare the results The tests themselves are created as script files which are interpreted by THUG The test case inputs were selected manually and the expected results calculated manually A separate tool LOGISCOPE was used to measure the test coverage

A third VAX based tool LIFESPAN is used to configure the testing descriptions harnesses and results along with all other configurable parts of the development

Software and Hardware integration was performed as a single operation Integration testing was a manual activity with the help of a Test Rig to provide inputs and display outputs The inputs and expected results were derived from the requirement No integration structural coverage was measured

A second project was used to evaluate the TestMate tool for Ada This project uses Apex for its environment so unlike the main baseline project did not require importing into the environment and is more typical of the type of system to be developed within the environment This project develops component for re use within other projects with the aim of improving re use

Results

There are three areas of results

- Evaluation of TestMate for Unit Testing
- Evaluation of TestMate for Enhanced Integration Testing
- Evaluation of TestMate for Automated Integration Testing

Evaluation of TestMate for Unit Testing

Unit testing has been performed on units of these units have been re tested after being updated

The graph below compares the time taken for a test to be performed on the baseline project compared to the time taken on the parallel project to create new tests update existing tests and update tests that are affected by side affects to different levels of coverage This baseline project column is the time taken for new updated and side affected tests averaged over the number of new and updated tests

The results **Fig** show of the effort required on the baseline project was needed on the parallel project to achieve decision coverage Statement coverage was of the cost of performing decision coverage An extra of effort was required to achieve MCDC from decision testing

Statement coverage requiring as much as of the effort to perform decision coverage was unexpected While testing to statement level it was not intended to try to test to decision coverage but by going through the routine testing the true branches and then adding tests to assert other true branches already tested branches were ignored which resulted in the false branch often being executed

Updating a test to re establish decision coverage takes of the time to create a new test This seems higher than is expected but is due to the time taken to familiarise yourself with the test and determine why existing tests now fail the time taken to run the test and type changes A type changing that is used for a global variable or parameter definition within the Test List requires that the related columns need to be deleted and replaced by columns using the new type definition Keeping global stores to a reasonable size could improve this figure

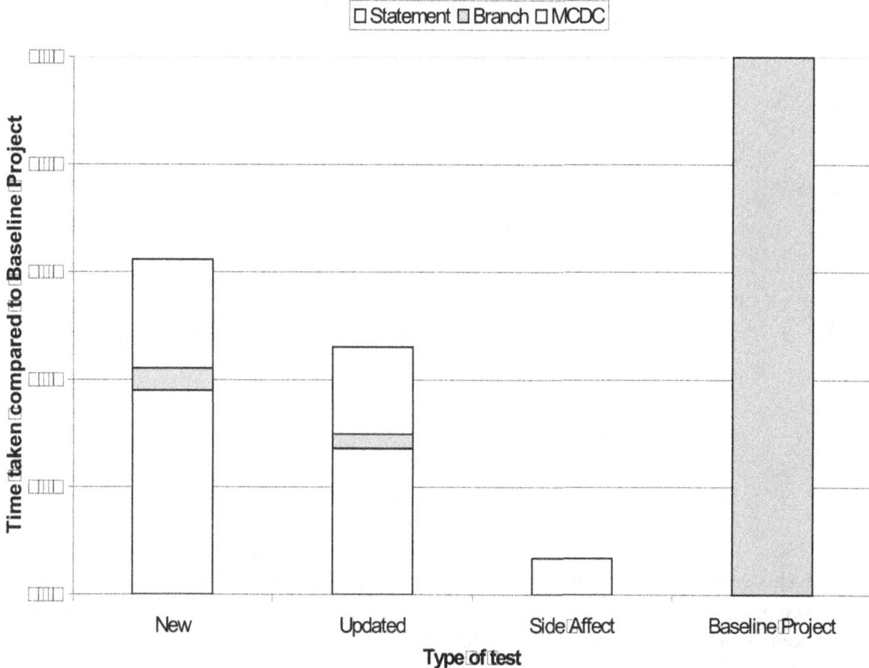

Fig Compares the effort required to generate a new unit update an existing test and side affected test compared to the average time taken to perform a new or updated test on the baseline project

A consideration must be made when looking at these figures in that the parallel project had a team size of compared to the baselines This means an overhead should be added appropriate to the overheads expected for a given team size Though project leading was not included into the baseline projects metrics some time would have been spent by the testers assisting the testing team leader by providing progress

Fig shows how the time to test a unit is affected by the size of the unit The size is measured in the number of source code lines The point at which the Time Compared to Average is represents that average time taken to complete a new unit test in **Fig** The graph is flatter than expected

of the time spent testing was waiting for the tests to complete TestMate creates a harness which contains the inputs and required outputs This means that the harness is compiled and linked with the rest of the closure and can take a considerable amount of time especially on the first run when the testing tower is created This should not be a problem for systems developed from the start using the SubSystem facility unlike the baseline project which was imported into a single subsystem within Apex

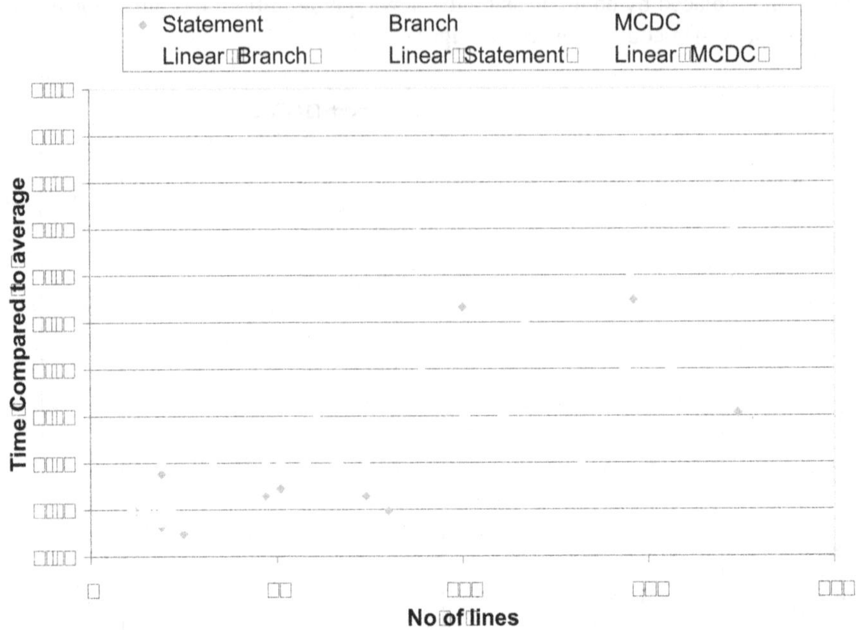

Fig This graph shows how the effort required to create a new test is affected by the number of source lines within the unit being tested on the time compared to average scale is the time taken by the average unit tested within the experiment

If a system is to be imported into Apex purely for testing then build times should be considered Some limitations of the TestMate tool were found in particular the use of separates TestMate does not support separates meaning that separates need to be moved into the body of the package A tool is provided within Apex to perform this move but it creates configuration problems due to the development build being different to the testing build If separates are avoided then this is not a problem

The effectiveness of the testing is hard to determine due the late base lining of the code and the Unit and Integration testing being performed concurrently All the Integration and Unit test problems found were due to design errors reflected within the code As such could not be detected by Unit Testing alone

The reduction in the cost of unit testing due to the use of TestMate has been attributed to the better integration of TestMate on the baseline project the coverage analysis is performed by a separate tool and the use of a tabular input format The functionality performed by TestMate and Apex integrate the functionality of performed by THUG LOGISCOPE and LIFESPAN

The tabular input format is an easy to understand format which allow the inputs and outputs to be seen easily and encourages reuse of tests using the cut and paste operations

Evaluation of TestMate to Enhance Integration Testing

This section contains the results of the evaluation of the use of TestMate as an integration test tool and how integration can be enhanced to allow the possible removal of Unit Testing from the development lifecycle.

Originally a complete build of the system was to be tested. One day of effort was spent converting the baseline project so that the complete closure could be built. This was not a considerable amount of time. Initial testing of the System build identified this approach as not feasible as the executive within the software would not allow the inputs of temporal data as the parameters and global data, it also made it impossible to stop execution at a given point. For this approach to work harnesses would need to be written to stimulate the system and observe its behavior at given times. The Test List could then be used to communicate with the harness and check result given back by it.

Though this is a possible solution it is likely that a test rig already exists for formal qualification, which may be fully automated. Unless rig time is restricted, it would be a weigh up of the cost of building the harness that represents the already existing hardware rig against the time needed to test the system on the rig.

Apex favours component based development with the idea of SubSystems to split the development into more manageable chunks. This allows TestMate to be used to test the system in a top down approach adding a component at a time.

For this experiment it was decided to test a section of the main baseline projects system. All the code tested was called by a tree starting from a single routine. This exercise identified that global data can play an important role when testing to requirements. Only a single parameter is returned from the called routine. This situation is helped by good design, which would abstract data away from the interface routines.

From the tests performed it was found that decision coverage was achieved. This was assessed by creating tests for all the requirements associated with a particular routine, and the routines calling it. This may not be the case in all situations but it does show that high coverage should be expected from simply testing to the requirement.

The general testing strategy is the given that SubSystem A is imported into B. SubSystem A would be completely tested to prove that it performs to the requirements. Then SubSystem B would be tested with the emphasis of testing to the coverage requirement of B and the parts A that support B.

On completion of testing the coverage reports can be combined to give an overall coverage result for the complete system.

The second baseline project with the aims of achieving very high re-use figures has adopted a component approach to system development. Each component, usually a single SubSystem, has its own requirements.

To make this process feasible it requires that TestMate is considered early in the project. This will allow the early development of stubs to be created. These will be in the form of SubSystems, which need to be planned, developed and configured along with the normal development of the system.

This will allow the SubSystems containing stubs to be linked into the system being integrated. These SubSystems could be developed to behave differently by setting global data from the Test List.

For the first test integration a given unit was found to cost about [illegible] more that to unit tests. This increased cost is down to the need to find the original source of the data needed to test the unit. Data that needs to be set to allow the system to get to the part of the code that implements the requirements that you are trying to test also needs to be determined. Units tested within the same subsystem tend towards the time taken to unit test the code due to the extra work to determine the actual inputs and outputs have already been performed. The actual figures may differ greatly depending on the nature of the system.

After the completion of the integration test of two routines [illegible] of decision coverage was achieved for the units within the closure. From inspection of the code, the integration testing of [illegible] of the [illegible] units would cover nearly all of the units within the closure.

The level of Integration Testing performed within the experiment makes it difficult to estimate any savings over the processes used on the main baseline project. However if Unit Testing is required to exist as a separate phase in development, using this approach could result in a saving of up to [illegible] on the cost of Unit Testing.

It is possible to fully test the requirements without achieving the required level of coverage. In this situation the tester must assess the best way to test the remaining code. For some code it may be better to revert to normal Unit Testing and then combining the coverage statistics together.

[illegible] Evaluation of TestMate for Automated Integration Testing

This section evaluates the use of TestMate and StateMate. It details the time needed to create a model and identifies problems that have been encountered during the experiment.

The StateMate model covers around [illegible] Ada units. The cost of building the model (including the interface to TestMate but without including any time to use the model for testing) is about the same as the cost of [illegible] unit tests with the baseline processes and tools (or [illegible] units with TestMate). The cost of extending an existing model to enable it to be used for testing (by adding the interface to TestMate) is about the same as the cost of [illegible] unit tests (or [illegible] with TestMate).

Careful consideration needs to be made for the interface between the model and the development code. It is important that the data used to manipulate the model and code are similar enough so that they can be used by both. This must include global data that will appear within the design. The building of the model depends on this information otherwise a great deal of modification will be required.

This was demonstrated by the difficulties encountered on SITAR where the model was built without consideration of the actual architecture of the baseline project.

The structure of the parameters used within the model were created using the assumption that the software would be similar However the information pertinent to the model are part of a larger structure not relevant to the model

It has not been possible to fully automate the process because of the above problem Another problem that prevented full automation was that the instruction required to update the test list does not function correctly This problem has been raised with Rational

Optimisations introduced into the design can cause problems An example of this is when a continuous setting of an output depending on the state of inputs is optimised to when it is only set when the input states change

This requires that either that this type of optimisation is not used within the code or you proceed through the state changes in a realistic fashion occasionally starting from the beginning again

These problems would be minor within a normal integration tasks but because this process is derived from picking combinations of all inputs it is not likely that the state changes within the automated tests will follow a possible route through the software

One solution is to not implement these types of optimisation without reflecting them into the requirement analysis or introduce these optimisations into the requirements analysis This will not only ensure that the requirements are better reflected by the design but that these optimisations are within the scope of the requirements

The cost of modelling the software requirements in StateMate was found to be relatively expensive The initial development of the model needs to be looked at A more formal approach to creating requirements and requirements analysis using a case tool with a code auto generation process may make the approach more cost effective

For projects that do not require unit testing but do require code coverage TestMate can be used a gain coverage during Software Integration Testing

The elimination or reduction of unit testing could make the development of an appropriate requirement model feasible with the added advantage of having a better integration phase

Conclusions

TestMate is a capable tool for Unit Testing The tool gives improved efficiency over the baseline projects processes and Tools The improvement is due to the user friendly interface and the integration of Testing and Coverage into one application

If a component by component process is to be used for integration testing stopping short of the executive then this tool is fully capable and efficient

The ability to stub out hardware routines and the integration of the coverage analysis and Configuration Management functions make it possible to bring some of the advantages to Software Integration Testing usually found in Unit Testing With projects such as VERA Ref supporting the use of Static Code Analysis and FAGAN Inspection as a very effective way of detecting faults combined with the ability to check coverage to ensure full execution of the system Unit Testing could feasible be dropped altogether

In practice automated integration testing using TestMate and StateMate will work However it is probably only practicable with the integration of the model development into the life cycle of the project

A model only used for integration testing is not going to improve productivity by a large amount Because of the confidence that can be gained from using this process it might be used to model a subsection to test a high risk sections of the system

Overall TestMate is a fully capable tool for both Unit and Software Integration Testing The use of the tool in itself should bring improvements to these processes due to the integration of the testing activities and close links to the Rational Apex tool

References

Draper J Kiteley S SITAR Investigation into Software Integration Testing Automation Proceedings of DASIA Conference ESA SP

Myers M The Art of Software Testing ISBN

Rational Software Rational TestMate User s Manual Part Number Rev A

Rees C Hemeury B Hollom J VERA Verification Evaluation Review and Analysis FINAL REPORT ESSI Project Number

On the Minimal Essential Subsets and Minimal Representative Sets*

T. Y. Chen** and M. F. Lau***,†

Department of Computer Science and Software Engineering
The University of Melbourne, VIC. 3010, AUSTRALIA
{tyc,mfl}@cs.mu.oz.au

Abstract. Test suite reduction aims at generating representative sets defined as subsets of a test suite that satisfy the same test objective. There are various types of representative sets. Those representative sets without redundancy are referred to as the minimal representative sets. A subset of the test suite is referred to as essential if the remaining test cases cannot collectively satisfy the same test objective when the subset is removed from the test suite. This paper studies the relationships between the set of minimal representative sets and the set of essential subsets.

Keywords: minimal essential set, minimal representative set, test suite reduction, set covering, software testing

1 Introduction

Establishment of a test objective or criterion is the first fundamental task when testing a program. Satisfying the test objective is equivalent to satisfying a set of test requirements, which hereafter will be referred as a set of *requirements*. For example, if the test objective requires all branches of the program to be executed at least once, then each branch is considered as a test requirement. Test cases are designed so that they can collectively satisfy all requirements. A set of test cases that can satisfy all requirements is known as a *test suite*. Subsets of a test suite that are able to satisfy all requirements are known as its *representative sets* [ ].

Two types of test cases can be identified in a test suite; namely *essential test cases* and *redundant test cases*. A test case is said to be *essential*, if its removal renders some requirements unsatisfied. Otherwise, the test case is said

* This research is supported in part by a grant of the Hong Kong Research Grants Council.

** Present Affiliation : Department of Computing and Mathematics, The Hong Kong Institute of Vocational Education (Chai Wan), Vocational Training Council, Hong Kong.

*** Corresponding author.

† Present Affiliation: Department of Information and Applied Technology, The Hong Kong Institute of Education, Hong Kong.

H. B. Keller and E. Plödereder (Eds.): Ada-Europe 2000, LNCS 1845, pp. 291– , 2000.

to be *redundant.* In other words, a test case is redundant if and only if it is not essential.

If all test cases in a test suite are essential, the only representative set is the test suite itself. On the contrary, if some test cases in a test suite are redundant, some proper subsets of the test suite can be representative sets. In this case, we say that the test suite contains redundancy because test cases can be removed without affecting the complete satisfaction of all requirements.

Intuitively speaking, as many redundant test cases should be removed as possible. However, when two or more redundant test cases are removed together, some requirements may not be satisfied by the remaining test cases. The concepts of essential subsets are based on this observation. A subset of a test suite is said to be *essential*, if its removal renders some requirements unsatisfied. Obviously, a subset consisting of only essential test cases is essential. However, as mentioned above, a subset containing two redundant test cases may be essential. Thus, test cases in an essential subset may be essential or redundant. Since any set containing an essential subset is essential, we are interested in the minimal elements of the set of essential subsets.

As the costs of executing test cases and managing the test suite may often be quite significant, software testers would aim to reduce the size of the test suite. This is the well known test suite reduction problem [,] which is commonly encountered in regression testing [, ,]. In the previous studies [, ,], the emphasis is on the representative sets with the smallest cardinality, known as the *optimal representative sets.* The problem of finding the optimal representative sets is NP-complete because it is equivalent to the optimization of the set covering problem which is NP-complete [,]. The optimal representative sets are the best solutions only when the costs for test cases are uniform. In this paper, we provide solutions to the more general situation where the costs of test cases are different. Our emphasis is on the representative sets without redundancy such that all proper subsets of them are not representative sets. In fact, representative sets without redundancy are the minimal elements of the set of representative sets with respect to set inclusion, and they include the optimal representative sets.

A popular approach towards test suite reduction is the use of the divide-and-conquer methodology [ ]. This approach basically involves three steps, namely (1) to decompose the original problem into smaller sub-problems, (2) to find solutions for the decomposed sub-problems, and (3) to construct solutions for the original problem from those of the decomposed sub-problems. This approach has been very successful in many areas of computer science [ ]. However, a main drawback of this approach is that not every decomposition strategy can guarantee to yield minimal representative sets.

Although it is sufficient to find one solution for most problems, there are situations, in software testing, where knowing all minimal representative sets may help in selecting a better testing set. For example, test cases are constructed to satisfy a certain testing objective when a program is tested. If the testing overhead of the constructed test case are uniform, it is sufficient to know *only one* optimal representative set. Since test cases may have different testing overheads, it may happen that any of the optimal representative sets may not be the most "cost effective" solution. Nevertheless, the most "cost effective" solution must be a minimal representative set. For example, suppose that $T_1 = \{t_1, t_2, t_4\}$, $T_2 = \{t_2, t_3, t_5, t_6\}$ and $T_3 = \{t_3, t_7, t_9, t_{10}\}$ are all the minimal representative sets. If the testing overheads of T_1, T_2 and T_3 are in the order $T_2 < T_3 < T_1$, T_2 is the most "cost effective" solution although it is not optimal.

Besides the testing overheads, the fault detecting capabilities of the constructed test cases may not be uniform. Hence, it is necessary to know all minimal representative sets in order to select the one with the highest fault-detecting capability. In software testing, there may be more than one testing objective to be satisfied [ ]. Usually, a test suite is constructed based on the primary testing objective. If all minimal representative sets are known, the one which satisfies the secondary testing objective "most" can then be selected. For example, if a certain program component contains many errors (as recorded by previous testing), it would be better to select a minimal representative set that can "visit" this component as often as possible.

Since test cases and requirements can be modelled by a table whose rows and columns correspond to the test cases and requirements respectively, decomposition strategies then correspond to methods of decomposing or reducing the table. There are two simple ways to reduce the size of a table, namely removal of rows (test cases) and removal of columns (requirements). For the removal of test cases, a test case can be removed from the table if all requirements satisfied by it are also satisfied by another test case. This is a special type of redundancy (known as *1-to-1 redundancy* for test cases). For a discussion of this type of redundancy, interested reader can refer to [ ]. In this paper, we are studying redundancy in a general context without any restriction. For the removal of requirements, a simple way is to remove a requirement from the table if there is another requirement such that any test case satisfying the latter requirement can also satisfy the former requirement. The study in this paper can provide further insights into better strategies for removing requirements as a by-product.

This paper investigates the properties of various types of representative sets, in particular, those representative sets without redundancy, namely, the minimal representative sets. We establish relationships between the set of representative sets and the set of essential subsets.

The rest of this paper is organised as follows. Section introduces some basic concepts and notation. In Section , we present the concepts and the properties of the essential subsets. Section discusses the relationships of the set of minimal representative sets and the set of minimal essential subsets.

2 Preliminaries

In this section, we present some definitions and notation. For any set A, we use $|A|$ and $\mathcal{P}(A)$ to denote the cardinality and the power set of A respectively.

Definition 1. *A* partial ordering $\sqsubseteq$ *on a set* A *is a binary relation on* A *such that*

1. $a \sqsubseteq a$ *for every* $a \in A$
2. $a \sqsubseteq b$ *and* $b \sqsubseteq a$ *imply* $a = b$
3. $a \sqsubseteq b$ *and* $b \sqsubseteq c$ *imply* $a \sqsubseteq c$

Definition 2. $(A, \sqsubseteq)$ *is a* partially ordered set *if* $\sqsubseteq$ *is a partial ordering on the set* A.

Definition 3. *Let* $(A, \sqsubseteq)$ *be a partially ordered set,* $a \in A$ *and* $B \subseteq A$.

1. a *is a* minimal *(*maximal*) element of* A *if for each* $b \in A$, $b \sqsubseteq a$ $(a \sqsubseteq b)$ *implies* $a = b$.
2. a *is a* least *(*greatest*) element of* A *if* $a \sqsubseteq b$ $(b \sqsubseteq a)$ *for all* $b \in A$
3. a *is a* lower *(*upper*)* bound *of* B *if* $a \sqsubseteq b$ $(b \sqsubseteq a)$ *for all* $b \in B$.
4. a *is a* greatest lower *(*least upper*)* bound *of* B *if* a *is the greatest (least) element of the set of all lower (upper) bounds of* B.

Obviously, once a least element, a greatest element, a least upper bound or a greatest lower bound exists, it is unique. For any partially ordered set A, the least upper bound of A is denoted by $\mathbf{lub}A$.

When testing a program P with input domain D, the set R of all test requirements has to be defined first. For example, in statement, branch or path coverage testing, test requirements correspond to the statements, branches or paths of the program respectively. In this study, we assume that R is finite and for each $r \in R$, there exists $t \in D$ such that t satisfies r.

A *test suite* is defined as a set of test cases that can collectively satisfy the set R of all test requirements. For finite R, obviously a finite test suite $T \subseteq D$ always exists. As a result, all sets studied in this paper are finite. In this study, we further assume that for any $t \in T$, there exists $r \in R$ such that t satisfies r. It is straightforward to show that $(\mathcal{P}(T), \subseteq)$ is a partially ordered set. For any non-empty $Q \subseteq \mathcal{P}(T)$, $\mathbf{lub}Q$ always exist. In fact, $\mathbf{lub}Q = \bigcup_{Q_i \in Q} Q_i$.

In this paper, T and R are used to denote the test suite and the set of all requirements respectively, unless otherwise specified. For non-empty T and R, test case $t \in T$ satisfying requirement $r \in R$ can be represented as a binary relation $S(T, R)$ from T to R, known as the *satisfiability* relation.

Definition 4. *The* satisfiability *relation* $S(T, R)$ *from* T *to* R *is defined as the set* $\{(t, r) \in T \times R : t \text{ satisfies } r\}$.

We will use S instead of $S(T, R)$ whenever there is no ambiguity. As a reminder, $S(T, R)$ is defined for non-empty T and R in this paper.

Definition 5. *Let* $S(T, R)$ *be the satisfiability relation from* T *to* R.

1. *The set of all requirements satisfied by* $t \in T$ *is defined as*

$$Req(t) = \{r \in R : (t, r) \in S(T, R)\}$$

2. *The set of all requirements satisfied by* $T_1 \subseteq T$ *is defined as*

$$Req(T_1) = \begin{cases} \emptyset & \text{if } T_1 = \emptyset \\ \bigcup_{t \in T_1} Req(t) & \text{otherwise} \end{cases}$$

The following lemma gives some properties of *Req*.

Lemma 1. *Let* S *be the satisfiability relation from* T *to* R *and* $T_1, T_2 \subseteq T$.

1. *If* $T_1 \subseteq T_2$, *then* $Req(T_1) \subseteq Req(T_2)$.
2. $Req(T_1 \cup T_2) = Req(T_1) \cup Req(T_2)$.
3. $Req(T_1 \cap T_2) \subseteq Req(T_1) \cap Req(T_2)$.
4. $Req(T_1) \setminus Req(T_2) \subseteq Req(T_1 \setminus T_2)$.

Proof. Immediate from definition.

Definition 6. *Let* $S(T, R)$ *be the satisfiability relation from* T *to* R.

1. *The set of all test cases in* T *satisfying* $r \in R$ *is defined as*

$$Test(r) = \{t \in T : (t, r) \in S(T, R)\}$$

2. *The set of all test cases in* T *satisfying* $R_1 \subseteq R$ *is defined as*

$$Test(R_1) = \begin{cases} \emptyset & \text{if } R_1 = \emptyset \\ \bigcup_{r \in R_1} Test(r) & \text{otherwise} \end{cases}$$

Similar to the characterizations of *Req* in Lemma , *Test* has the following properties.

Lemma 2. *Let* S *be the satisfiability relation from* T *to* R *and* $R_1, R_2 \subseteq R$

1. *If* $R_1 \subseteq R_2$, *then* $Test(R_1) \subseteq Test(R_2)$.
2. $Test(R_1 \cup R_2) = Test(R_1) \cup Test(R_2)$.
3. $Test(R_1 \cap R_2) \subseteq Test(R_1) \cap Test(R_2)$.
4. $Test(R_1) \setminus Test(R_2) \subseteq Test(R_1 \setminus R_2)$.

Proof. Immediate from definition.

The problem of test suite reduction involves the determination of subsets of the test suite that can still satisfy all requirements. Such a subset is known as a *representative set* [ ] and is defined as follows.

Definition 7. *Let* S *be the satisfiability relation from* T *to* R *and* $T_1 \subseteq T$. T_1 *is said to be a* representative set *of* S *if* $Req(T_1) = R$.

Let $REP(S)$ denote the set of all representative sets of S. Since $T \in REP(S)$, $REP(S) \neq \emptyset$. In the previous studies [, ,], the elements of $REP(S)$ are ordered by their cardinalities. This leads to the search of the representative sets with the smallest cardinality, namely the *optimal representative sets*. However, this approach may not be an appropriate one when the costs of executing test cases are not uniform.

In this paper, our approach is to relate the elements in $REP(S)$ by set inclusion. Obviously, $(REP(S), \subseteq)$ is a partially ordered set. Then, the minimal elements of $(REP(S), \subseteq)$ are exactly the representative sets without redundancy since their proper subsets are not representative sets. In other words, despite of the non-uniform costs of executing a test case in most cases, the best representative sets, in the sense of least cost, are still amongst the minimal representative sets. Thus, it is of paramount importance to be able to identify all minimal representative sets.

Obviously, $REP(S)$ is closed under set union but not set intersection. Therefore, $REP(S)$ has $\mathbf{lub}REP(S) = \bigcup_{T_1 \in REP(S)} T_1 = T$ as its greatest element, but its least element may not exist.

Let $MIN\_REP(S)$ denote the set of all minimal representative sets of S. Since $REP(S)$ is non-empty, $MIN\_REP(S)$ is obviously non-empty. It should be noted that $MIN\_REP(S)$ is not necessarily a singleton set and its elements may be of different cardinalities.

Example 1. Suppose $T = \{t_1, \ldots, t_5\}$ and $R = \{r_1, \ldots, r_5\}$ with the satisfiability relation as given in Table . If $(t, r) \in S$, the corresponding entry is marked with a 'X'.

Table 1. The satisfiability relation S

	r_1	r_2	r_3	r_4	r_5
t_1	X	X	X		
t_2		X		X	
t_3	X		X		X
t_4				X	
t_5			X		X

It is easy to see that $\{\{t_2, t_3\}, \{t_1, t_2, t_5\}, \{t_1, t_3, t_4\}, \{t_1, t_4, t_5\}\}$ is the set of all minimal representative sets.

3 Essential Subsets

In this section, the concepts of essential subsets are introduced and their properties are investigated. Intuitively speaking, a test case is said to be essential if it must appear in every representative set. In other words, any subset of the test suite missing an essential test case will never satisfy all the requirements. Similarly, we can extend the notion of essential test case to the notion of essential subset. A subset of test cases are said to be *essential* if, when this subset of test cases is removed from the test suite, the set of all requirements cannot be collectively satisfied by the remaining test cases. The formal definition is given below.

Definition 8. *Let S be the satisfiability relation from T to R and $T_1 \subseteq T$. T_1 is said to be an* essential subset *with respect to S if $R \neq Req(T \setminus T_1)$.*

The set of all essential subsets with respect to S is denoted by $ES(S)$. Obviously, $ES(S) \neq \emptyset$ because $T \in ES(S)$. It is straightforward to show that $ES(S)$ is closed under set union but not set intersection. Thus, $ES(S)$ has $\mathbf{lub}ES(S) = \bigcup_{U \in ES(S)} U = T$ as its greatest element. However, the least element of $ES(S)$ may not exist. From the definition, it is obvious that T_1 is an essential subset if and only if T_2 is an essential subset for every T_2 such that $T_1 \subseteq T_2 \subseteq T$. Furthermore, an essential subset can never be empty.

A necessary and sufficient condition for a subset of test cases to be essential is presented as follows.

Lemma 3. *Let S be the satisfiability relation from T to R and $T_1 \subseteq T$. T_1 is an essential subset with respect to S if and only if there exists a requirement $r \in R$ such that $Test(r) \subseteq T_1$.*

Proof. **(if part)** Suppose there exists $r \in R$ such that $Test(r) \subseteq T_1$. Now, for every $t_1 \in (T \setminus T_1)$, $t_1 \notin Test(r)$. Thus, $r \notin Req(T \setminus T_1)$. Therefore, $R \neq Req(T \setminus T_1)$. The result follows.
(only-if part) Since T_1 is an essential subset, $R \neq Req(T \setminus T_1)$. Thus, there exists $r \in R$ and $r \notin Req(T \setminus T_1)$. Therefore, for every $t \in T$ such that $t \in Test(r)$, $t \notin (T \setminus T_1)$. Since $Test(r) \subseteq T$, $t \in T_1$. Therefore, $Test(r) \subseteq T_1$.

Let $\mathcal{T}(S(T,R)) = \{T_1 \subseteq T : \exists r \in R \text{ such that } T_1 = Test(r)\}$. Similarly, $\mathcal{T}(S)$ will be used instead of $\mathcal{T}(S(T,R))$ whenever there is no ambiguity. An interesting relationship between $\mathcal{T}(S)$ and $ES(S)$ is as follows.

Lemma 4. *Let S be the satisfiability relation from T to R. Then, $\mathcal{T}(S) \subseteq ES(S)$.*

Proof. Immediate from Lemma . □

In other words, $Test(r)$ is an essential subset of T for every $r \in R$. However, not every element of $ES(S)$ is of the form $Test(r)$ as shown in Example that $T = \{t_1, t_2, t_3, t_4, t_5\} \in ES(S)$, but $T \notin \mathcal{T}(S) = \{\{t_1, t_3\}, \{t_1, t_2\}, \{t_1, t_3, t_5\}, \{t_2, t_4\}, \{t_3, t_5\}\}$.

Since the least element of $ES(S)$ may not exist and sets containing an essential subset are essential, we are thus most interested in the minimal essential subsets. Let $MIN\_ES(S)$ denote the set of all minimal elements of $(ES(S), \subseteq)$. Since $ES(S)$ is non-empty, $MIN\_ES(S)$ is obviously non-empty. Although $ES(S)$ is closed under set union but not set intersection, $MIN\_ES(S)$ is neither closed under set union nor set intersection. An interesting relationship between $MIN\_ES(S)$ and $\mathcal{T}(S)$ is described as follows.

Lemma 5. *Let S be the satisfiability relation from T to R. Then, $MIN\_ES(S) \subseteq \mathcal{T}(S)$.*

Proof. Let $T_1 \in MIN\_ES(S)$. Since $T_1 \in ES(S)$, by Lemma , there exists a requirement $r \in R$ such that $Test(r) \subseteq T_1$. By Lemma , $Test(r) \in ES(S)$. Since T_1 is minimal, we have $T_1 = Test(r)$. Thus, $T_1 \in \mathcal{T}(S)$. The result follows. □

However, the converse is not true (that is, not every $Test(r)$ is a minimal essential subset) as illustrated in the Example .

Example 2. Suppose $R = \{r_1, \ldots, r_7\}$ and $T = \{t_1, \ldots, t_5\}$. The satisfiability relation S from T to R is given in Table .

Table 2. The satisfiability relation S

	r_1	r_2	r_3	r_4	r_5	r_6	r_7
t_1	X			X		X	
t_2	X		X		X		
t_3		X		X		X	
t_4		X			X		
t_5			X		X		X

It is easy to see that $Test(r_1) = \{t_1, t_2\}$, $Test(r_2) = \{t_3, t_4\}$, $Test(r_3) = \{t_2, t_5\}$, $Test(r_4) = \{t_1, t_3\}$, $Test(r_5) = \{t_2, t_4, t_5\}$, $Test(r_6) = \{t_1, t_3\}$, $Test(r_7) = \{t_5\}$. However, $MIN\_ES(S) = \{\{t_1, t_2\}, \{t_1, t_3\}, \{t_3, t_4\}, \{t_5\}\}$. Thus, $Test(r_5) \notin MIN\_ES(S)$. Note also that $\{t_1, t_2, t_3\} \in ES(S)$. Hence, $MIN\_ES(S) \subsetneqq \mathcal{T}(S) \subsetneqq ES(S)$.

From Lemmas and , we have $MIN\_ES(S) \subseteq \mathcal{T}(S) \subseteq ES(S)$. Furthermore, Example shows that these subset relationships are proper ones.

Let $MIN\_\mathcal{T}(S)$ denote the set of all minimal elements of $(\mathcal{T}(S), \subseteq)$. In fact, $MIN\_ES(S) = MIN\_\mathcal{T}(S)$. We need the following lemma to prove this property.

Lemma 6. *Let S be the satisfiability relation from T to R. For any $Test(r) \in \mathcal{T}(S)$, there exists $T_1 \in MIN\_ES(S)$ such that $T_1 \subseteq Test(r)$.*

Proof. For any $Test(r) \in \mathcal{T}(S)$, two cases arises.

1. Suppose $Test(r) \in MIN\_ES(S)$. Simply let $T_1 = Test(r)$.
2. Suppose $Test(r) \notin MIN\_ES(S)$. By Lemma , $Test(r) \in ES(S)$. Hence, there exists $T_1 \in MIN\_ES(S)$ such that $T_1 \subseteq Test(r)$.

Thus, the result follows. □

Proposition 1. *Let S be the satisfiability relation from T to R. Then, $MIN\_ES(S) = MIN\_\mathcal{T}(S)$.*

Proof. (**$\subseteq$ part**) For any $T_1 \in MIN\_ES(S)$, $T_1 = Test(r)$ for some $r \in R$ by Lemma . Suppose $T_1 \notin MIN\_\mathcal{T}(S)$. Then, there exists $r'(\neq r) \in R$ such that $Test(r') \subseteq Test(r)$ and $Test(r') \neq Test(r)$. Since $Test(r') \in ES(S)$ by Lemma , this contradicts the minimality of T_1. Thus, $MIN\_ES(S) \subseteq MIN\_\mathcal{T}(S)$.
(**$\supseteq$ part**) For any $T_1 \in MIN\_\mathcal{T}(S)$, $T_1 = Test(r)$ for some $r \in R$. By Lemma , there exists $T_2 \in MIN\_ES(S)$ such that $T_2 \subseteq Test(r)$. Suppose $T_2 \neq Test(r)$. Then, by Lemma , there exists $r' \in R$ such that $T_2 = Test(r')$. Thus, we have $Test(r') \subseteq Test(r)$ and $Test(r') \neq Test(r)$ which contradicts $Test(r) \in MIN\_\mathcal{T}(S)$. Therefore, $T_2 = Test(r)$. Thus, $MIN\_\mathcal{T}(S) \subseteq MIN\_ES(S)$. □

In summary, the relationships between $ES(S)$ and $\mathcal{T}(S)$ are illustrated by the schematic diagram in Fig. .

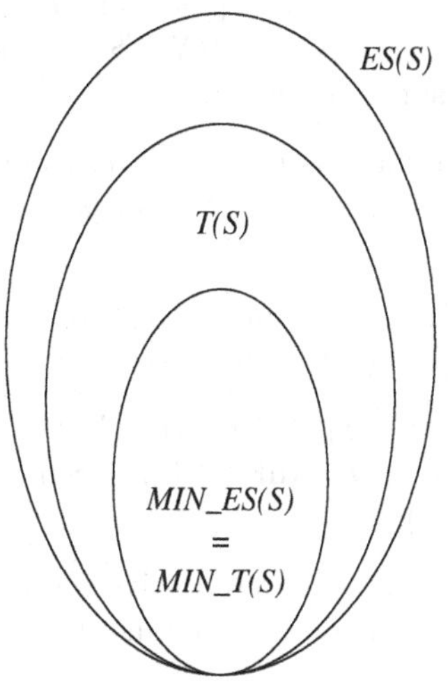

Fig. 1. $MIN\_ES(S) = MIN\_\mathcal{T}(S) \subseteq \mathcal{T}(S) \subseteq ES(S)$

4 Minimal Representative Sets and Minimal Essential Sets

In this section, we investigate the relationship between the set of all minimal essential subsets and the set of minimal representative sets. Obviously, a minimal essential subset is not necessarily a representative set, and a minimal representative set may not be an essential subset. However, **lub**$MIN\_ES(S)$ is a representative set of S.

Lemma 7. *Let S be the satisfiability relation from T to R. Then,* $\mathbf{lub}MIN\_ES(S) \in REP(S)$.

Proof. For every $r \in R$, by Lemma , there exists $T_1 \in MIN\_ES(S)$ such that $T_1 \subseteq Test(r)$. Thus, $r \in Req(T_1)$ for some $T_1 \in MIN\_ES(S)$. Therefore, $r \in Req(\mathbf{lub}MIN\_ES(S))$. The result follows. □

Interestingly, the intersection between $\mathbf{lub}MIN\_ES(S)$ and any representative set is still a representative set.

Lemma 8. *Let S be the satisfiability relation from T to R. Then, for any $T_1 \in REP(S)$, $T_1 \cap (\mathbf{lub}MIN\_ES(S)) \in REP(S)$.*

Proof. For any $r \in R$, let t be a test case in T_1 such that it satisfies r. If $t \in \mathbf{lub}MIN\_ES(S)$, we are done. If $t \notin \mathbf{lub}MIN\_ES(S)$, $Test(r)$ is an essential subset but not a minimal essential subset after Lemma and . Hence, there exists a minimal essential subset in the form of $Test(r_1)$ such that $Test(r_1)$ is a proper subset of $Test(r)$ and $r_1 \neq r$. Since T_1 is a representative set, there exists $t_1 \in T_1$ such that t_1 satisfies r_1, that is, $t_1 \in Test(r_1)$. Therefore, $t_1 \in \mathbf{lub}MIN\_ES(S)$ because $Test(r_1) \in MIN\_ES(S)$. Since $Test(r_1) \subseteq Test(r)$, t_1 satisfies r. Hence, the result follows. □

An implication of Lemma is that, for any representative set T_1 of S, if T_1 contains elements in $T \setminus (\mathbf{lub}MIN\_ES(S))$, T_1 is not minimal as stated in Corollary .

Corollary 1. *Let S be the satisfiability relation from T to R. For any $T_1 \in REP(S)$, if T_1 contains elements in $T \setminus (\mathbf{lub}MIN\_ES(S))$, $T_1 \notin MIN\_REP(S)$*

Proof. Since $T_1 \in REP(S)$, $T_1 \cap (\mathbf{lub}MIN\_ES(S)) \in REP(S)$ by Lemma . Since T_1 contains elements in $T \setminus (\mathbf{lub}MIN\_ES(S))$, $T_1 \cap (\mathbf{lub}MIN\_ES(S)) \neq T_1$. Hence, $T_1 \notin MIN\_REP(S)$. □

Corollary means that any representative set $T_1 \in REP(S)$ containing elements in $T \setminus \mathbf{lub}MIN\_ES(S)$ contains redundancy.

Proposition 2. *Let S be the satisfiability relation from T to R. Then,* $\mathbf{lub}MIN\_REP(S) \subseteq \mathbf{lub}MIN\_ES(S)$.

Proof. For any $T_1 \in MIN\_REP(S)$, it follows from Corollary that T_1 does not contain elements in $T \setminus (\mathbf{lub}MIN\_ES(S))$. Thus, $T_1 \subseteq \mathbf{lub}MIN\_ES(S)$. In other words, $\mathbf{lub}MIN\_ES(S)$ is an upper bound of $MIN\_REP(S)$. Therefore, $\mathbf{lub}MIN\_REP(S) \subseteq \mathbf{lub}MIN\_ES(S)$. □

Proposition means that test cases in a minimal representative set appear in some of the minimal essential subsets as $\mathbf{lub}MIN\_REP(S) = \bigcup_{U \in MIN\_REP(S)} U$ and $\mathbf{lub}MIN\_ES(S) = \bigcup_{V \in MIN\_ES(S)} V$. Therefore, test cases which do not belong to any minimal essential subset would never appear in any minimal representative sets. In other words, we can then further reduce the test suite T to the set $\mathbf{lub}MIN\_ES(S)$ ($= \mathbf{lub}MIN\_T(S)$ by Proposition) for finding minimal representative sets.

5 Conclusions

For the partially ordered set $(REP(S), \subseteq)$, we observe that its greatest element always exists but its least element need not. However, the set of its minimal elements is always non-empty. We are particularly interested in the minimal representative sets because they do not contain redundancy. Therefore, irrespective of whether the costs for test cases are uniform or not, the most cost effective representative sets are still amongst the minimal representative sets even though they need not be the optimal representative sets.

In this paper, we have investigate the relationship between the set of all minimal representative sets and the set of all minimal essential subsets. We have extended the concepts of essential test cases to the concepts of essential subsets. Since any set which contains an essential subset is essential, we are interested in the minimal elements of the set of essential subsets. The relationship $\mathbf{lub}\mathit{MIN\_REP}(S) \subseteq \mathbf{lub}\mathit{MIN\_ES}(S)$ suggests that we can further reduce a test suite T to $\mathbf{lub}\mathit{MIN\_ES}(S)$ without rendering the set of all minimal representative sets. Further investigation on the relationship among $\mathit{MIN\_REP}(S)$ and $\mathit{MIN\_ES}(S)$ may lead to further strategy for test suite reduction.

References

1. A. V. Aho, J. E. Hopcroft, and J. D. Ullman, *The Design and Analysis of Computer Algorithms*, Addison-Wesley Publishing Company, Reading, MA, USA, 1974.
2. T. Y. Chen and M. F. Lau, "Dividing strategies for the optimization of a test suite", *Information Processing Letters*, vol. 60, no. 3, pp. 135-141, Nov. 1996.
3. T. H. Cormen, C. E. Leiserson, and R. L. Rivest, *Introduction to Algorithms*, MIT Press, Cambridge, MA, 1990.
4. M. J. Harrold, R. Gupta, and M. L. Soffa, "A methodology for controlling the size of a test suite", *ACM Transactions on Software Engineering and Methodology*, vol. 2, no. 3, pp. 270–285, July 1993.
5. J. Hartmann and D. J. Robson, "Approaches to regression testing", in *Proceedings of Conference on Software Maintenance.* 1988, pp. 368–372.
6. J. Hartmann and D. J. Robson, "Techniques for selective revalidation", *IEEE Software*, pp. 31–36, January 1990.
7. H. K. N. Leung and L. White, "Insights into regression testing", in *Proceedings of Conference on Software Maintenance.* 1989, pp. 60–69.
8. E. Kit, *Software testing in the real world: improving the process.* ACM Press, Reading, MA, 1995.

Author Index